WRITTEN COMMUNICATIONS RESOURCE DIGEST

A Customized Edition of

Technically—Write!: Communicating in a Technological Era, Fourth Edition
Ron S. Blicq

The Career Tool Kit: Skills for Success
Carter • Kravits • Vaughan

Technical Writing: Process and Product
Gerson • Gerson

Writing in the Disciplines: A Reader for Writers, Second Edition
Kennedy • Kennedy • Smith

Technical Writing: A Practical Approach, Second Edition
William S. Pfeiffer

Learning Workplace Writing
Judith R. Rice

Communication for Technicians: Reading, Writing, and Speaking on the Job
Tench • Thompson

Professional and Technical Writing Strategies: Communicating in Technology and Science
VanAlstyne • Maddison

Compiled by
Pamela J. Gurman

SIMON & SCHUSTER
CUSTOM PUBLISHING

Cover design by Linda Blier.

Pages 159–164 are taken from *Technically—Write!: Communicating in a Technological Era,* Fourth Edition, Ron S. Blicq
Copyright © 1993, 1986, 1981, 1972 by Prentice-Hall, Inc.
A Simon & Schuster Company
Englewood Cliffs, New Jersey 07632

Pages 398–401 are taken from *The Career Tool Kit: Skills for Success,* Carol Carter, Sarah Lyman Kravits, and Patricia Spencer Vaughan
Copyright © 1995 by Prentice-Hall, Inc.

Pages 3–59, 72–89, 105–127, 145–159, 162–176, 177–209, 251–263, 349–366 are taken from *Technical Writing: Process and Product,* Sharon J. Gerson, Steven M. Gerson
Copyright © 1992 by Prentice-Hall, Inc.

Pages 264–346 are taken from *Writing in the Disciplines: A Reader for Writers,* Second Edition, Mary Lynch Kennedy, William J. Kennedy and Hadley M. Smith
Copyright © 1990, 1987 by Prentice-Hall, Inc.

Pages 67–71, 90–93, 210–247 are taken from *Technical Writing: A Practical Approach,* Second Edition, William S. Pfeiffer
Copyright © 1994 by Macmillan Publishing Company
A Simon & Schuster Company
Englewood Cliffs, New Jersey 07632

Pages 128–142 are taken from *Learning Workplace Writing,* Judith R. Rice
Copyright © 1994 by Prentice-Hall Career & Technology, Prentice-Hall, Inc.

Pages 61–67 are taken from *Communication for Technicians: Reading, Writing, and Speaking on the Job,* Ann Gregson Tench and Isabelle Kramer Thompson
Copyright © 1988 by Ann Gregson Tench and Isabelle Kramer Thompson

Pages 93–104 are taken from *Professional and Technical Writing Strategies: Communicating in Technology and Science,* Judith S. VanAlstyne and Gordon R. Maddison
Copyright © 1994, 1990, 1986 by Prentice-Hall, Inc.

This special edition is published in cooperation with Simon & Schuster Custom Publishing.

10 9 8 7 6 5 4 3

ISBN 0–536–58882–1
BA 96447

SIMON & SCHUSTER CUSTOM PUBLISHING
160 Gould Street/Needham Heights, MA 02194
Simon & Schuster Education Group

CONTENTS

Introduction

Students have been required to write all during their elementary and secondary educational careers. This process starts with forming the letters, writing simple sentences and paragraphs and filling out workbooks. Usually, no later than the third or fourth grade, the student begins writing stories and reports. By the seventh or eight grade the student is assigned a research paper. All this is completed prior to secondary school where the process is often repeated. In most states, students spend approximately ten and one-half years of their first twelve years of formal education studying writing. One might assume that with all this emphasis on writing the colleges would find students who have a firm grasp of how to write clearly and correctly. Employers could expect someone who had gone through twelve years of formal education could write a letter or even a brief analysis of a situation.

Unfortunately, both professors and employers have been disappointed and have become critical crying out "HIGH SCHOOL GRADUATES CANNOT WRITE!" Colleges blame high schools, high schools blame elementary schools, and elementary schools blame the early childhood home development.

Students have often taken the attitude that writing is something that only a select few can effectively master. They are not interested in taking just another writing course or reviewing grammar. The students who are enrolled in the technical and scientific courses are often those who have identified themselves as non-writers. They often are the ones who resist writing courses and will do what it takes to get out of the class rather than "get anything" out of the course. Since they do not plan to be "writers," they see no reason to spend any more time in a classroom trying, once again, to form sentences and write paragraphs or meaningless essays. This is the dilemma faced by curriculum designers and adult educators. They have tried to respond with new methods and approaches or have tried to go back to the basics.

It is the author's belief that writing skills are similar to most other skills and are learned when there is a need or desire. Individuals write for a reason and will strive to master the skills when they are confronted with that reason. Time must be spent marketing the mastery of writing. Students need to see how these skills must be generalized and applied as a tool. Adult students must take responsibility for improving their writing skills as a long term commitment. The commitment must not end with freshman composition class but rather continue as a lifelong learning process.

This Written Communications Resource Digest has been compiled for the students who are seeking to achieve a degree and be employed in a technical field. It is a composite of instructions and samples of writing that is required by employers of technical staff. It is designed to accompany a basic writers' handbook and to be used in a college freshman process writing class. The student will use a standard writer's handbook, dictionary, thesaurus and this resource digest as tools for improving written communication. The student will learn process writing skills and how to effectively use standard English to communicate for a specific purpose. In this endeavor the student will develop the knowledge and skills to produce the documents covered in the resource digest.

The digest includes a variety of works by different authors and teachers of writing, compiled so that the writer can refer to it as a "how-to" resource. Although the selections included in this text are from the technical arena, the writing process is the focus. The instructor's guide will provide collaborative writing and process writing activities.

Acknowledgments

The writer wishes to thank Andrea Worrell who gave many hours and ideas to each step of the project and without whose basic philosophy, "There must be a better way to help each student take responsibility for his/her own learning," we would not have tried a new approach to the difficult task of designing a course that will meet the needs of students and benefit their future employers.

The writer also wishes to thank Mr. Frank S. Burrows, Jr., Managing Editor for this project. His belief in the concept and his patience and support made this project possible. Additionally, Karen Moreau gave the author the idea that the project could be accomplished and demonstrated continued support and encouragement. Finally the writer wishes to thank her daughters, Whitney and Rachael, for the love and encouragement they continue to provide.

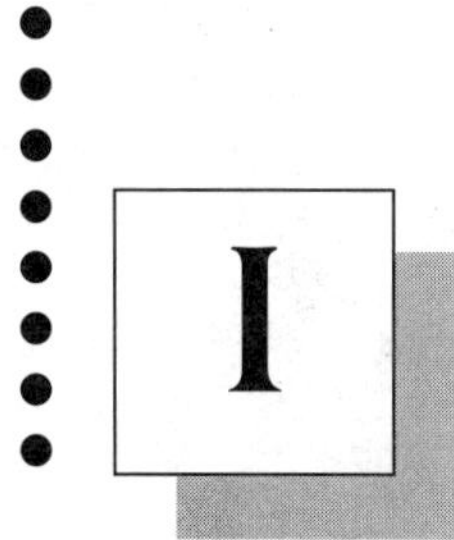

Correspondence

The two basic types of correspondence used in business and industry today are letters and memos. Both time and money have been lost due to unclear correspondence. This section provides detailed instruction on the components and the techniques of letters and memos.

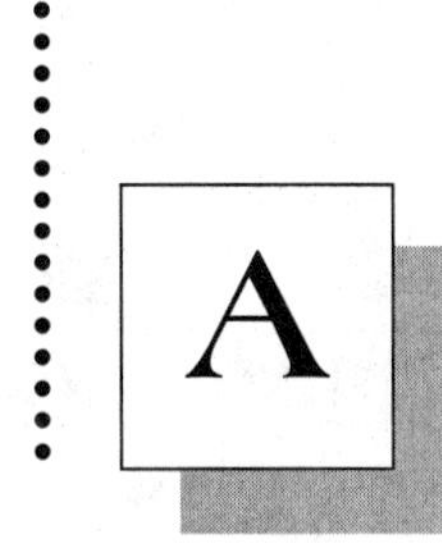

Letters

OBJECTIVES

Letters are external correspondence that you send from your company to a colleague working at another company, to a vendor, to a prospective client, to an agency, or to a friend who lives around the corner or across the continent. Letters leave your work site (as opposed to memos, which stay within the company).

Because letters are sent off site to readers in other locations, you must write them effectively. Your letters not only reflect your communication abilities, but also are a reflection of your company. If your letter is sloppy, marred with grammatical errors, or creates a negative tone, you will look bad and so will your company. Even worse, if your letter communicates incorrect information regarding prices, guarantees, due-date promises, or equipment and labor commitments, your company will be held legally responsible. When you write on your company's letterhead stationery and sign it, your letter constitutes a legally binding contract. Therefore, no matter what type of letter you're writing, you must take care to follow accepted letter formats, maintain the proper tone, and avoid errors.

This chapter helps you write the following kinds of letters: (a) inquiry, (b) cover (transmittal), (c) good news, (d) bad news, and (e) sales. To write these letters effectively, we provide you with letter components and formats, criteria for writing different types of letters, process (and a process log) to follow for writing letters, and examples.

LETTER COMPONENTS

☐ Essential Components

Your letter should by typed on 8½" × 11" unlined paper or printed on 8½" × 11" word processing paper. Leave 1" to 1½" margins at the top and on both sides.

Your letter must contain the following components (see Figure 1.1).

1. Writer's Address

This section contains either your personal address or your company's address. (You may be writing on printed, letterhead stationery.)

If the heading consists of your address, you will include (a) your street address (do not abbreviate the words *street, avenue, road, drive,* etc.), and (b) the city, state, and zip code. Do not include your name. The state may be abbreviated with the appropriate two-letter abbreviation.

If the heading consists of your company's address, you will include (a) the company's name; (b) the street address; and (c) the city, state, and zip code.

2. Date

You must document the month, day, and year in which you have written your letter. You can set up your date in one of two ways: May 31, 1991, or 31 May 1991.

Place the date two spaces below the writer's address (if the letter is long) or three to eight spaces below the writer's address (for shorter letters). For a short letter, leave more space so the spacing on the letter is balanced.

3. Inside Address

This is the address of the person or people to whom you are writing. The inside address contains, in the following order,

- ☐ Your reader's name (If you do not know the name of this person, begin the reader's address with a job title or the name of the department.)
- ☐ Your reader's title (optional if you include the name)
- ☐ The company name
- ☐ The company street address
- ☐ The company city, state, and zip code

Place this information two lines below the date.

① *Writer's address* — UNITED SPECTOGRAPH
19015 Lakeview Avenue
Columbus, OH 43212

② *Date* — June 10, 1991

③ *Inside address* — Jennifer Miller
Corporate Communications, Inc.
1245 Grant
Chicago, IL 60611

④ *Salutation* — Dear Ms. Miller:

⑤ *Letter body* —

Attached is the schedule for your presentations during our Basic Information Training for Supervisors (BITS) seminar. You will hold your sessions in our Training Center at 19015 Lakeview Avenue.

Your two, eight-hour seminars will meet as follows:

GROUP 1

Day	*Date*	*Time*
Monday	July 6, 1991	8:00 A.M.-5:00 P.M.

GROUP 2

Day	*Date*	*Time*
Wednesday	July 8, 1991	8:00 A.M.-5:00 P.M.

As you requested, the training room will have an overhead projector, screen, flip chart, and pad. Thank you for being one of our presenters. We are looking forward to working with you again.

⑥ *Complimentary close* — Sincerely,

⑦ *Signed name* — Ashley Hirschorn

⑧ *Typed name* — Ashley Hirschorn

FIGURE 1.1 Essential Letter Components

4. Salutation

The traditional salutation, placed two spaces beneath the inside address, is your reader's last name, preceded by *Dear* and followed by a colon.

Dear Mr. Smith:

You can also address your reader by his or her first name if you are on a first name basis with this person.

Dear John:

If you are writing to a woman and are unfamiliar with her marital status, address the letter as follows:

Dear Ms. Jones:

However, if you know the woman's marital status, you can address the letter accordingly:

Dear Miss Jones:
or
Dear Mrs. Jones:

Occasionally, you will write to someone whom you do not know and who has a non-gender-specific first name, such as Pat, Kim, Kelly, Stacy, or Chris. In this case, avoid either Mr., Miss, Mrs. or Ms., and write as follows:

Dear Chris Evans:

Often, when writing to another company, you will not know your reader's name. In this instance, you have limited options. You could address the reader by his or her title (Dear Vice President of Operations:) or address the letter to the reader's department (Accounting Department:). If you address the letter to the department, *Dear* would be inappropriate and should be omitted.

Each of the aforementioned salutations is acceptable. However, several common salutations are no longer valid. For example, as discussed in Chapter 2A, sexist salutations such as *Dear Sir* and *Gentlemen* cannot be used (unless you know beyond all doubt that each of your readers is a man; however, we suggest that you eliminate the problem by avoiding the sexist salutation).

Other awkward salutations include *Good morning* (since mail is delivered twice daily at many corporations), *To whom it may concern* (which is trite, insensitive, and imprecise), and *Greetings* (which either has a seasonal ring to it or a military connotation). *Dear Sir/Madam* is also ineffective and should be avoided.

To avoid these pitfalls in salutations, you might want to call the company to which you're writing and ask them for the name of your intended reader (and the correct spelling of the name).

5. Letter Body

Begin the body of the letter two spaces below the salutation. The body includes your introductory paragraph, discussion paragraph(s) and concluding paragraph. The body should be single spaced with double spacings between paragraphs. Whether you indent the beginnings of each paragraph or leave them flush with the left margin is determined by the letter format you employ. We discuss this issue later in this chapter.

6. Complimentary Close

Place the complimentary close, followed by a comma, two spaces below the concluding paragraph. Although several different complimentary closes are acceptable, such as *Yours truly* and *Sincerely yours*, we suggest that you limit your close to *Sincerely*.

7. Signed Name

Sign your name legibly beneath the complimentary close.

8. Typed Name

Type your name four spaces below the complimentary close. If you wish, you may type your title one space beneath your typed name.

Sincerely,

Henry Marshall

Henry Marshall
Comptroller

□ Optional Letter Components

In addition to the aforementioned letter essentials, you can include the following options.

Subject Line

A subject line, which is mandatory in memos (see Chapter 1B), is applicable in letters. You can type the subject line two spaces below the inside address and two spaces above the salutation.

Dr. Ron Schaefer
Linguistics Department
Southern Illinois University
Edwardsville, IL 66205

Subject: Linguistics Conference Registration Payment

Dear Dr. Schaefer:

You also could use a subject line instead of a salutation.

Linguistics Department
Southern Illinois University
Edwardsville, IL 66205

Subject: Linguistics Conference Registration Payment

A subject line not only helps readers understand the letter's intent, but also (if you are uncertain of your reader's name) helps you avoid such flawed salutations as *To whom it may concern, Dear Sirs,* and *Ladies and Gentlemen.*

In the simplified letter, both the salutation and the complimentary close are omitted, and a subject line is included.

New-page Notations

If your letter is longer than one page, you'll need to cite your name, the page number, and the date on all pages after page one. Place this notation either flush with the left margin at the top of subsequent pages or across the top of subsequent pages.

MARGIN LEFT SUBSEQUENT PAGE NOTATION

Mabel Tinjaca
Page 2
May 31, 1991

SECOND PAGE NOTATION ACROSS THE TOP

Mabel Tinjaca	2	May 31, 1991

Writer and Typist Initials

If the letter has been typed by someone other than the writer, include both the writer's and the typist's initials two spaces below the typed signature. The writer's initials are capitalized, the typist's initials are typed in lowercase, and the two sets of initials are separated by a colon. If both the typist and the writer are the same person, this notation is not necessary.

Sincerely,

W. T. Winnery

W. T. Winnery
WTW: mm

Enclosure Notation

If your letter prefaces enclosed information, such as an invoice, a report, or graphics, mention this enclosure in the letter and then type an enclosure notation two spaces below the typed signature (or two spaces below the writer and typist initials). The enclosure notation can be abbreviated *Enc.*; written out—*Enclosure*; show the number of enclosures, such as *Enclosures (2);* or specify what has been enclosed—*Enclosure: January Invoice.*

Copy Notation

If you have made a carbon copy or a photocopy of your letter, show this in a copy notation. A carbon copy is designated by a double lowercase *c* (cc); a photocopy is designated by lowercase *pc*. Type the copy notation two spaces below the typed signature or two spaces below either the writer and typist initials or the enclosure notation.

Sincerely,

Brian Altman

Brian Altman

Enclosure: August Status Report

pc

If you are sending copies of the letter to other readers, list these readers' names following the copy notation.

Sincerely,

Brian Altman

Brian Altman

Enclosure: August Status Report

pc: Andrew Dubrov
    Erica Nochlin

LETTER FORMATS

Type your letter using any of the formats shown in Figures 1.2-1.5.

CRITERIA FOR DIFFERENT TYPES OF LETTERS

☐ Letters of Inquiry

If you want information about degree requirements, equipment costs, performance records, turnaround time, employee credentials, or any subject matter of interest to you, you write a letter requesting that data. Letters of inquiry require that you be specific and precise. For example, if you write, "Please send me any information you have on the XYZ transformer," you're in trouble. You'll either receive any information the reader chooses to dispose of or none at all. Look at the following letter of request.

> Dear Mr. Jernigan:
>
> Please send us information about the following filter pools:
>
> 1. East Lime Pool
> 2. West Sulphate Pool
> 3. East Aggregate Pool
>
> Thank you.

The disgruntled worker replied as follows:

> Dear Mr. Scholl:
>
> I would be happy to provide you with any information you would like. However, you need to tell me ***what*** information you require about the pools.
>
> I look forward to your response.

To receive the information you need, you must write an effective letter of inquiry. Successful letters of inquiry contain all the letter essentials, maintain an effective technical writing style, achieve audience involvement through pronoun usage, and avoid grammatical and mechanical errors.

In addition, you must accomplish the following:

Introduction

1. Clarify your intent in the introduction. Until you tell your readers why you are writing, they do not know. It's your responsibility to clarify your intent and explain your rationale for writing. You must also tell your reader immediately what you are writing about (the subject matter of your inquiry). You can state your intent and subject matter in one to three sentences, as follows:

> My company is planning to purchase thirty new tractors by the end of the year. Your 1991 tractor with the on-board computer might be the answer to our problems. In addition to sending us a picture brochure of the CP95 tractor, could you also answer the following questions about your vehicle?

In this example, the first two sentences explain why you are writing. The last sentence explains what you want.

Discussion

2. Specify your needs in the discussion. To ensure that you get the response you want and need, you must ask precise questions or list specific

1119 South Bend
Chico, CA 95926

November 1, 1991

Dr. Robert Cottrell
7806 Northway
Austin, TX 78752

Dear Dr. Cottrell:

Introduction

Discussion

Conclusion

Sincerely,

Sue Timmons

Sue Timmons

ST:sg

cc: Jeremy Isaacs

FIGURE 1.2 Full Block Format

7501 Carriage
Coconut Grove, FL 33133

September 7, 1991

Mr. Robin Massin
7926 Candle Lane
Pittsburgh, PA 15237

Subject: Marketing of Robotics Applications

Dear Mr. Massin:

Introduction

Discussion

Conclusion

Sincerely,

Ruth Schneider

Ruth Schneider

RS:sl

FIGURE 1.3 Full Block Format with Subject Line

3628 East Vista Road
Chamblee, GA 30341

August 13, 1991

Mr. Kenny Frankel
7810 Warrensburg
Hackensack, NJ 07649

Dear Mr. Frankel:

Introduction

Discussion

Conclusion

Sincerely,

Katie Roche

Katie Roche

FIGURE 1.4 Modified Block Format

935 West Hermosa
Oakland, CA 94610

September 5, 1991

Edie Kreisler
1126 Ranleigh Way
San Antonio, TX 78213

Subject: Purchase of Beachfront Property

Introduction

Discussion

Conclusion

Walt McDonald

Walt McDonald

Enclosures (3)

FIGURE 1.5 Simplified Format

topics of inquiry. You must quantify. For example, rather than vaguely asking about machinery specifications, you should ask more precisely about "specifications for the 12R403B Copier." Rather than asking, "Will the roofing material cover a large surface?" you need to quantify—"Will the roofing material cover 150' x 180'?"

Conclusion

3. Conclude precisely. First, explain when you need a response (because until you tell the reader, he or she does not know). Don't write, "Please respond as soon as possible." Provide dated action—tell the reader exactly when you need your answers. Dated action doesn't mean you'll get the answers when you want them, but your chances are better. Second, to sell your readers on the importance of this date, explain why you need answers by the date given.

> Please send the above information by August 15. This will allow my shop supervisor to study the manuals and arrange for a test drive prior to our Board of Director's meeting on September 1.

Figure 1.6 will help you understand the requirements for effective letters of inquiry.

□ Cover Letters

In business, you are often required to send information to a client, vendor, or colleague. You might send multipaged copies of reports, invoices, drawings, maps, letters, memos, specifications, instructions, questionnaires, or proposals. The reader may have requested this information. Maybe you're sending the data on your own accord. Whatever the situation, if you merely submit the multipaged data without a cover letter, your readers will be overwhelmed with information that they must wade through.

A cover letter accomplishes two goals. First, it lets you tell readers up front what they are receiving. Second, it helps you focus your readers' attention on key points within the enclosures. Thus, the cover letter is a reader-friendly gesture geared toward assisting your audience.

As with the previously discussed letters, successful cover letters include the letter essentials, maintain an effective technical writing style, avoid grammatical and mechanical errors, and achieve audience recognition and involvement. In addition, a well-written cover letter contains an introduction, discussion, and conclusion.

Introduction

In the introductory paragraph, tell your reader *why* you are writing and *what* you are writing about. An appropriate introduction providing your reader a rationale for your writing might read as follows: "To help you prepare for next week's audit, we have enclosed the following necessary forms."

What if the reader has asked you to send the documentation? Do you still need to explain why you're writing? The answer is yes. Although the reader requested the data, time has passed, other correspondence has been

TOLLIE FREIGHTWAYS, INC.
1020 Sunshine Road
Jamaica Plain, MA 02130

July 23, 1991

Mr. Jack Halligan
Director of Marketing
White Motor Company
4718 West 91st Street
Tacoma, WA 81492

Dear Mr. Halligan:

My company plans to purchase thirty new tractors by the end of the year. Your 1991 Model CP95 tractor with fuel-saving features may be the answer.

Along with a picture brochure of the CP95, please send the following:

1. Cost per tractor
2. Financing options offered by White Motor Company
3. Operation manual for the on-board computer
4. Operation manual for the eight-gear system
5. Comfort features in the cab
6. Delivery date for thirty tractors

Please send this information by August 15 so my shop supervisor can study the manuals and arrange for a test drive. Then I will present my proposal for the purchase to our Board of Directors on September 1. I look forward to a successful agreement.

Sincerely,

Sue Woods

Sue Woods
Vice President, Operations

SW:jh

FIGURE 1.6 Letter of Inquiry

written, and your reader might have forgotten the initial request. Your job is to remind him or her. Write something like, "In response to your request, enclosed are the completed questionnaires from our engineers." These introductory sentences provide the reader information about why you are writing and what you are sending. Note that neither exceeds one sentence. Clarity of intent can be provided *concisely*.

Discussion

In the body of the letter, you want to accomplish two things. First, you either want to tell your reader *exactly what you've enclosed* or *exactly what of value is within the enclosures.* In both instances, you should provide an itemized list. For example, you can itemize enclosures as follows:

```
To help you prepare for next week's audit, we have enclosed
the following necessary forms:
☐ Year-to-date sales figures
☐ Fiscal year sales figures
☐ Year-to-date expenditures
☐ Fiscal year expenditures
```

Similarly, you can itemize the important facts within the enclosures as follows:

```
In response to your request, enclosed are the completed
questionnaires from our engineers.
Of special interest to you within the questionnaires are
their answers to questions regarding the following:
   ☐ Easement dimensions  . . . . . . . . . . .page 1
   ☐ Sewer construction materials . . . . . . .page 3
   ☐ Residential/commercial ratios  . . . . . .page 5
```

This example shows where important information can be found within the enclosure. Page numbers are a friendly gesture toward your audience. Instead of just dumping the data on your reader and saying, "best of luck—hope you find what you want," you're helping the reader locate the important information. In so doing, you're achieving audience recognition and involvement.

However, including page numbers has a greater benefit than audience involvement. These page numbers also allow you to focus your reader's attention on what you want him or her to see. In other words, if you merely provide the enclosure without a cover letter, then you leave it up to readers to sift through the information and decide on their own what's important. In contrast, by providing an itemized list with page numbers, you direct the reader's attention. You can emphasize, for your benefit, the points in the enclosure which you consider to be important.

Conclusion

Your conclusion should tell your readers *what* you want to happen next, *when* you want this to happen, and *why* this data is important. Without such a conclusion, your reader will review the documentation and say, "OK, so what? What do you want me to do with the data?" or "OK, but what are your future plans?"

The *what* clarifies your intentions. The *when* specifies the date. The *why* either sells the importance of this date, possibly hinting at the urgency, or suggests your conscientiousness.

Here are examples of cover letters, complete with conclusions.

> To help you prepare for next week's audit, we have enclosed the following necessary forms:
>
> - ☐ Year-to-date sales figures
> - ☐ Fiscal year sales figures
> - ☐ Year-to-date expenditures
> - ☐ Fiscal year expenditures
>
> Please fill out these forms before our Wednesday arrival. Doing so will facilitate the audit, thereby allowing you and your colleagues to return to your regular work activities more rapidly.

> In response to your request, enclosed are the completed questionnaires from our engineers.
>
> Of special interest to you within the questionnaires are their answers to questions regarding the following:
>
> - ☐ Easement dimensions . . . . .page 1
> - ☐ Sewer construction materials . . . . .page 3
> - ☐ Residential/commercial ratios . . . .page 5
>
> We would be happy to meet with you at your convenience to discuss this issue in greater detail. After you have had a chance to review these enclosures, please call my office at 469-8500 to set up a meeting. We want to answer your questions regarding our construction planning.

The cover letter seen in Figure 1.7 contains letter essentials.

MID-AMERICA HEALTH CARE
1400 Laurel Drive
Denton, TX 76201

November 11, 1991

Stacey Simon
Director of Outpatient Care
St. Michael's Hospital
Westlake Village, CA 91362

Dear Ms. Simon:

Thank you for your recent request for information on our line of specialized outpatient care equipment. Mid-America Health Care has manufactured stairway lifts, bathlifts, and vertical wheelchair lifts for over forty years.

To give you a better idea of how we can serve you and your patients, we've enclosed the following for your review:

1. A Mid-America brochure outlining our products, programs, and services
2. A credit application form
3. Price lists for all our products

Please look over the enclosed material. Early next month, I'll call you to set up an appointment. At that time, I will be happy to answer your questions. I'm looking forward to sharing with you the ways Mid-America can provide exceptional outpatient health care in your community.

Sincerely,

Arthur Chaiken

Arthur Chaiken
Sales Representative

Enclosures (3)

FIGURE 1.7 Cover Letter

☐ Good News Letters

You'll often have the opportunity to write good news letters. For example, you might write a letter promoting an employee or offering an individual a job at your corporation. You might write to commend a colleague for a job well done. Maybe you'll write to tell a customer that his or her request for a refund was justified.

Introduction

As in other letters discussed in this chapter, the introduction should explain immediately *why* you're writing and tell *what* you're writing about. The point of these letters is good news.

Furthermore, since your goal is to convey good news, you should begin with positive word usage, as in the following examples:

Example 1
Commending a colleague (Introduction)
Judy, you've proven to be indispensable again. Your work for the textbook committee has made all of our jobs easier.

Example 2
Promoting an employee (Introduction)
Congratulations! We're proud to offer you early promotion, Jan.

Discussion

Once you've explained why you're writing and what you're writing about, the next step is to provide the detail—to show *exactly what* has justified the commendation or the promotion.

Example 1
Commending a colleague
(Introduction and discussion)
Judy, you've proven to be indispensable again. Your work for the textbook committee has made all of our jobs easier.

Thank you for performing the following services:

- ☐ Meeting with all the sales reps to convey our departmental requirements
- ☐ Reviewing those texts with computer aided design components
- ☐ Screening the textbook options and selecting the three most suited to our needs

Example 2
Promoting an employee
(Introduction and discussion)
Congratulations! We're proud to offer you early promotion, Jan.
You've earned a grade raise to E30 for the following reasons:

1. *Productivity:* Your line personnel produced 2,000 units per month throughout this quarter.
2. *Efficiency:* You maintained a 95% manufacturing efficiency rating.
3. *Supervisory Skills:* You received only four grievances; your annual performance appraisals showed that your subordinates appreciated your motivational management techniques.

SFA
1101 21st Street
Galveston, TX 77071
800-55S-1212

May 31, 1991

Mr. Cargos De La Torre
1234 18th Street
Galveston, TX 77070

Dear Mr. De La Torre:

You were right; we were wrong. After reviewing your records, we discovered that you had been overcharged when you recently visited our service center.

Your automobile has an extended warranty which covers all parts and labor for three years or 50,000 miles. This includes the water pump you had replaced. We incorrectly charged you for parts even though your car is still under warranty. We're sorry for the annoyance we've caused you.

You will receive a refund for the full amount of the overcharge early next month (we mail our invoices and service payments the first of each month). To compensate for our mistake, we are also enclosing a VIP service card. This provides you with free oil changes for the life of your car. Thank you, Mr. De La Torre, for bringing this oversight to our attention. We look forward to servicing your car in the future.

Sincerely,

Holbert Lang

Holbert Lang
Service Manager

Enclosure: VIP service card

FIGURE 1.8 Good News Letter Responding to Customer Complaint

Conclusion

Once you've clarified exactly what has resulted in the good news, your last paragraph should state *what* you plan next (or expect from your reader next), *when* this action will occur, and *why* the data is important. The following good news letters are complete with introductions, discussions, and conclusions.

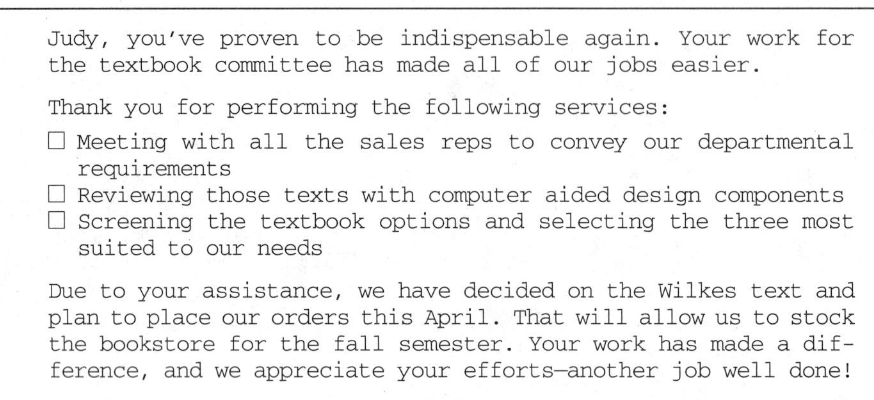

Judy, you've proven to be indispensable again. Your work for the textbook committee has made all of our jobs easier.

Thank you for performing the following services:

- ☐ Meeting with all the sales reps to convey our departmental requirements
- ☐ Reviewing those texts with computer aided design components
- ☐ Screening the textbook options and selecting the three most suited to our needs

Due to your assistance, we have decided on the Wilkes text and plan to place our orders this April. That will allow us to stock the bookstore for the fall semester. Your work has made a difference, and we appreciate your efforts—another job well done!

Congratulations! We're proud to offer you early promotion, Jan.

You've earned a grade raise to E30 for the following reasons:

1. ***Productivity*** Your line personnel produced 2,000 units per month throughout this quarter.
2. ***Efficiency*** You maintained a 95% manufacturing efficiency rating.
3. ***Supervisory Skills*** You received only four grievances; your annual performance appraisals showed that your subordinates appreciated your motivational management techniques.

Due to your excellent work, you will receive your pay increase the first of next month. Good work, Jan. You deserve it.

The good news letter in Figure 1.8, complete with all the letter essentials, was written to a customer in response to his request for a refund.

☐ Bad News Letters

Unfortunately, you occasionally will be required to write bad news letters. These letters might reject a job applicant, deny an employee a raise, tell a vendor that his or her company's proposal has not been accepted, or reject a customer's request for a refund. Maybe you'll have to write to a corporation to tell them that their manufacturing is not meeting your company's specifications. Maybe you'll need to write a letter to a union documenting a grievance. You might even have to write a bad news letter to fire employees.

AAA Electronics
11031 Bellbrook Drive
Stamford, CT 23091
(213) 333-8989

September 7, 1991

Dear Friends:

For some time now, forces influencing our industry have caused us to alter the way we have conducted business. You have recognized these influences for several years. Reorganization, customer participation, repetitious rate case activity, competition, deregulation, and technical innovations are just a few of the changes affecting us.

These influences, coupled with the current recession, have created an oversupply in our work force. We have tried to limit employee levels through attrition, hiring freezes, early retirements, and reassignments. However, our staffing is still too high, and we can no longer delay the inevitable. Therefore, your job is being terminated as of the end of this month.

We have taken great pride in the stability of our work force. I personally consider each of you a family member. Thus, to help you in this difficult time, we are providing you options for future employment. Our company has set up training seminars, resumé and application workshops, interviewing sessions, and new job networking hotlines We haven't given up on you. When the economy eases up and our company releases the new-hire freezes, we'll call you immediately. Until then, we want to help you in any way we can. Thank you for your patience and your understanding.

Sincerely,

Darryl Kennedy

Darryl Kennedy

FIGURE 1.9 Bad News Letter

In any of these instances, tact is required. You can't berate a customer or client. You shouldn't reject a job applicant offensively. Even your grievance must be worded carefully to avoid future problems.

Since the point of a bad news letter is bad news, you'll need to structure your correspondence carefully to avoid offending your reader.

Introduction

We've suggested throughout this chapter that your introduction should explain why you're writing and what you're writing about. However, such conciseness and clarity in a bad news letter would be harsh and abrupt. Therefore, to avoid these lapses in diplomacy, begin your bad news letter with a buffer. Start your letter with information that your reader can accept as valid but that will sway your reader to accept the bad news to come.

Example 1
Rejecting a job applicant (Introduction)

Thank you for your recent letter of application. As you can imagine, we received many letters from highly qualified applicants and appreciate your interest in Acme.

Example 2
Terminating a client/vendor relationship (Introduction)

John, as you know, our business demands exact tolerances and precise workmanship. Due to these requirements and the reputation your company has for quality production, we were happy to pursue a long-term contract with you.

Discussion

Once you've provided the buffer, swaying your audience to your point of view, you can no longer delay the inevitable. The discussion paragraph must provide the bad news. However, to ensure that the reader accepts the bad news, preface your assertions with quantifiable proof.

Example 1
Rejecting a job applicant (Introduction and discussion)

Thank you for your recent letter of application. As you can imagine, we received many letters from highly qualified applicants and appreciate your interest in Acme.

The advertisement specifically required that all applicants have an MS in computer science and at least five years' experience in telecommunications. We also suggested that a knowledge of fiber optics would be preferred. Your degree met our criteria successfully. However, your years of experience fell below our requirements, and your resumé did not mention fiber optics expertise. Therefore, we must reject your application.

Example 2
Terminating a client/ vendor relationship
(Introduction and discussion)

John, as you know, our business demands exact tolerances and precise workmanship. Due to these requirements and the reputation your company has for quality production, we were happy to pursue a long-term contract with you.

However, your last two shipments contained flawed goods. In fact, we found these problems:

☐ 37% of your shipped components were off tolerance by .025 mm.
☐ Your O-rings suffered stress fractures when under 2,000 lbs. of pressure.

Due to these failures, we are returning the products.

Conclusion

If you end your bad news letter with the bad news, then you leave your reader feeling defeated and without hope. In contrast, you want to maintain a good customer-client, supervisor-subordinate, or employer-employee relationship. Therefore, you need to conclude your letter by giving your readers an opportunity for future success. Provide your readers options which will allow them to get back in your good graces, seek employment in the future, or reapply for the refund you've denied. Then, to leave your readers feeling as happy as possible, given the circumstances, end upbeat and positively.

The following examples are complete with introductions, discussions, and conclusions.

Thank you for your recent letter of application. As you can imagine, we received many letters from highly qualified applicants and appreciate your interest in Acme.

The advertisement specifically required that all applicants have an MS in computer science and at least five years' experience in telecommunications. We also suggested that a knowledge of fiber optics would be preferred. Your degree met our criteria successfully. However, your years of experience fell below our requirements, and your resumé did not mention fiber optics expertise. Therefore, we must reject your application.

If you have fiber optics knowledge or have acquired additional work experiences which pertain to our work requirements, we would be happy to reconsider your application. In any case, we will keep your letter on file. When new positions open up, your letter will be reassessed. Good luck in your job search.

John, as you know, our business demands exact tolerances and precise workmanship. Due to these requirements and the reputation your company has for quality production, we were happy to pursue a long-term contract with you.

However, your last two shipments contained flawed goods. In fact, we found these problems:

☐ 37% of your shipped components were off tolerance by .025 mm.
☐ Your O-rings suffered stress fractures when under 2,000 lbs. of pressure.

Due to these failures, we are returning the products.

If you can correct these problems and document to our satisfaction that the errors have been eliminated, we would be willing to reconsider our stance. We have enjoyed working with you, John, and look forward to the possibility of future contracts.

Although the preceding two letters convey bad news, they couch the negatives in positive terms. For example, although the first letter rejects a job applicant, the writer uses words and phrases such as *thank you, appreciate, successfully, happy,* and *good luck.* The second letter does the same: *quality, happy, enjoyed,* and *look forward to.* As the writer of the bad news letter, you're in charge of the tone. Why not make it positive?

The example in Figure 1.9, which is from a CEO informing employees that they will be laid off, clarifies how a bad news letter should be constructed. The letter is complete with all the letter essentials, except an inside address. If a letter is mass mailed to a large group, no inside address is needed.

□ Sales Letters

You've just manufactured a new product (an electronic testing device, a fuel injection mechanism, a fiber optic cable, or a high-tech, state-of-the-art computer). Perhaps you've just created a new service (computer maintenance, automotive diagnosis, home repair, or telecommunications networking). Congratulations!

However, if your product just sits in your basement gathering dust or your service exists only in your imagination, what have you accomplished? To benefit from your labors, you must market your invention. You must connect with your end-users. You must let the public know that you exist. The question is, how? If you have unlimited time, money, and personnel, you can try telemarketing or door-to-door cold calls. However, a more time-efficient and cost-effective way to market your product or service is to write a sales letter. You write a sales letter once (which saves money) and mass mail it (which saves time).

To write your sales letter, you'll have to include the letter essentials discussed earlier in this chapter, maintain an effective technical writing style with a low fog index, and avoid grammatical and mechanical errors. You will also have to accomplish the following:

Arouse Reader Interest

The introductory paragraph of your sales letter must tell your readers *why* you are writing (you want to increase their happiness or reduce their anxieties). You also must tell your readers *what* you are writing about (the product or service you are marketing). However, studies tell us that you have only about thirty seconds to grab your readers' attention, after which they will lose interest and toss out your letter. To lure readers into your correspondence, you must arouse their interest imaginatively in the first few sentences. Try any of the following lead-ins:

- □ An anecdote—a brief, dramatic story.

  It's late at night, the service stations are closed, and you've just had a blowout on Highway 35. Don't worry. Our new Tire-Right will solve your problems!

- ☐ A question—to make your readers read on for an answer.

"Where will I get the money for my kid's college education?" "How am I going to afford to retire?" "Will my insurance cover all the medical bills?" You've asked yourself these questions. Our estate planning video has the answers.

- ☐ A quotation—to give your letter the credibility of authority.

"Omit needless words," technical writers say. If you can't, let us help you. *Write Now,* our new office communications service, can help you write your in-house newsletters—clearly and concisely.

- ☐ Data—researched information, again ensuring your credibility.

You're not alone. In fact, if you're at least 25 years old, you're in the majority. Today, 51 % of our students are older than 25. So why not enroll now? Our college offers the nontraditional student many benefits.

Develop Your Assertions

In the discussion paragraph(s), specify exactly what you offer to benefit your audience or how you'll solve your readers' problems. You can do this in a traditional paragraph. In contrast, you might want to itemize your suggestions in a numerical or bulletized list. Whichever option you choose, the discussion should accomplish any of the following:

- ☐ Provide data to document your assertions.

  Eighty-five percent of the homeowners contend that . . .

  or

  Seven out of 10 buyers said they would . . .

  or

  Ten thousand retired metalworkers can't be wrong!

- ☐ Give testimony from satisfied customers.

  The Job Corps of Blue Valley, Titan Co., Amex Inc., and the Southwestern Parish swear by our product.

- ☐ Document your credentials—years in business, certification of employees, number of items sold, and/or satisfied customers. (This last point overlaps with our suggestions regarding data.)

  In business since 1889.

  or

  Each of our mechanics is ASA certified.

  or

  We've sold over two billion widgets.

  or

  Over 3,000 corporate managers and supervisors have benefited from our training services.

Make Your Readers Act

If your conclusion says, "We hope to hear from you soon," you've made a mistake. Such a weak conclusion forces you to stare at the phone, twiddle your thumbs, and hope for a customer response. The concluding paragraph of a sales letter can't let the reader off the hook. You must do something to make the reader act. Here are some suggestions:

- ☐ Give directions (with a map) to your business location.
- ☐ Provide a tear-out to send back for further information.
- ☐ Supply a self-addressed, stamped envelope for customer response.
- ☐ Offer a discount if the customer responds within a given period of time.
- ☐ Give your name or a customer-contact name and a phone number (toll free if possible).

Style

Your sales letter should not only convey the necessary information, but also it should present an appealing style. Consider the following requirements:

- ☐ Use verbs: Verb usage, or power writing, will give your letter punch.
- ☐ Format for reader-friendly ease of access: Highlight through white space, underlining, boldface, bullets, numbers, etc.
- ☐ Achieve audience recognition and involvement through *You* orientation.
- ☐ Show ease of use: Sprinkle the words *easy* and/or *simple* throughout your correspondence.
- ☐ Imply urgency: Use the words *now, today, soon,* or *don't delay* to force the reader to immediate action.

Figure 1.10 is an example of a successful sales letter.

PROCESS

Now that you know what letters of inquiry, cover letters, good news letters, bad news letters, and sales letters entail, the next question is, "How do I write these letters?" If you merely get out a blank piece of paper, or turn on your computer screen, and then fill it with words, assuming that they'll be good enough, you're making a mistake. No one can write a successful letter the first time through. In contrast, you need to approach writing more sys-

September 8, 1991

Mr. & Mrs. Hyde Park
1122 Gillham Road
Kansas City, Missouri 64010

Dear Mr. & Mrs. Park:

Is your family starting to feel CRAMPED in your home? Have you got a room or basement that you would like to RE-DO? Would you like a NEW house feel without moving-or starting a NEW MORTGAGE ?

ARCHITECTURAL DISTINCTIONS wants to help you turn your old house into your dream house! We are

Members of the Association of Interior Architects and The Builder's Association.

The FIRST PLACE WINNER of the 1988 International Design Award for Renovation and Remodeling.

Specialists in bathroom and kitchen remodeling for over 25 years.

Creative people who take pleasure in turning your dreams into reality.

We can do ANY job to fit ANY budget. For a FREE, NO OBLIGATION estimate from one of our experienced designers, please send us the self-addressed stamped postcard. We look forward to hearing from you!

Sincerely,

Joe Metcalf

Joe Metcalf

enclosure

1211 Broadway Kansas City, Missouri 64100 555-4211

FIGURE 1.10 Sales Letter

tematically. To construct effective correspondence, you must approach writing as a step-by-step, sequential process.

You should do the following:

- ☐ Prewrite (to gather your data and to determine your objectives).
- ☐ Write a draft (to organize and format your text).
- ☐ Rewrite (to revise your correspondence, making it as perfect as it can be).

☐ Prewriting

To overcome the blank-page syndrome or writer's block, you must spend some time, *prior* to writing your letter, gathering as much information as you can about your subject matter. After all, how can you expect to write an effective letter if you aren't sure what you want to say? In addition, you must determine your objectives. Ask yourself why you're writing the letter and what you want to achieve.

No single way of prewriting is more effective than another. In fact, a primary focus of this text is to introduce you to numerous prewriting techniques. Our goal is to teach you various ways to gather data and determine objectives so you'll have options to choose from.

One prewriting technique that lends itself to letters is reporters' questions. By providing answers to *who, what, when, why, where,* and *how,* you can help yourself write more effective letters. Answers to these questions provide you content for your correspondence as well as focus in your writing objectives.

Following is a *reporters' questions checklist* for a letter of inquiry.

LETTER OF INQUIRY—REPORTERS' QUESTIONS CHECKLIST

1. ☐ Who is your audience?
   —High-tech peer
   —Low-tech peer
   —Lay reader
   —Management
   —Subordinate
   —Multiple audiences
2. ☐ *Why* are you writing?
3. ☐ *What* is the general topic of your request?
4. ☐ *What* exactly do you want to know (the specifics itemized in the discussion paragraph of your letter)?
5. ☐ *What* do you want the reader to do next?
6. ☐ *When* do you want the reader to act (dated action)?
7. ☐ *Why* is this date important?

☐ Writing

Once you've gathered your data and determined your objectives, the next step in the process is to begin your rough draft. Doing so requires the following:

1. Study the letter criteria. By studying the specific criteria for the type of letter you'll write, you can remind yourself of what information should be included in each paragraph.

2. Review your prewriting. Now that you have reminded yourself of what each paragraph should include, reviewing the prewriting will help you determine if, in fact, you have provided the correct details. Have you omitted any significant information? If so, now's the time to add missing content. Have you included unnecessary information? If so, now's the time to delete these irrelevancies.

3. Organize the data for your discussion paragraph. One organizational pattern especially effective for most letters is *importance.* When you organize by importance, you place the most important information first and less important ideas later. To do so, you can use the inverted journalist's pyramid shown in Figure 1.11.

This method works well for itemizing the discussion paragraph in your sales letters, letters of inquiry, and cover letters. You also can use importance to organize the body paragraph in your good news letter.

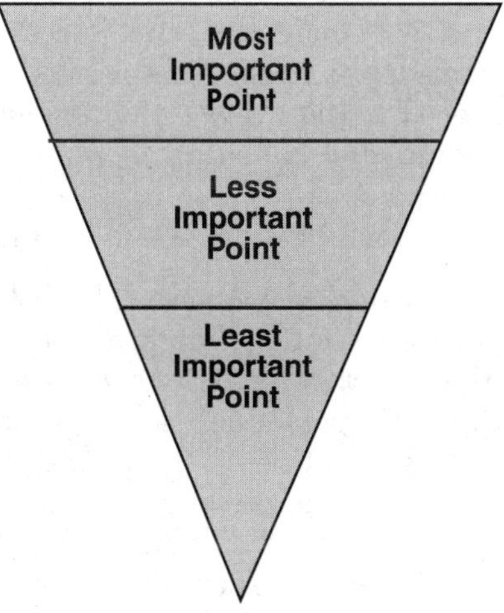

FIGURE 1.11 Inverted Journalist's Pyramid

However, since a bad news letter leads up to the bad news rather than begins with it, importance would not be an effective organizational pattern. Instead, you'll want to organize your ideas inductively (indirectly)—specifics to general result. For instance, in a bad news letter, you'll begin with the specific causes leading to bad news (recession, depression, changes in the market, unfavorable work habits, etc.). Then, after setting the stage with these specifics, you'll relate the general conclusion reached—the bad news (layoffs, refunds denied, promotions rejected, etc.). The bad news letter examples in this chapter reveal this inductive organizational pattern.

4. Draft your correspondence. Finally, after you've organized your information, the last step is to write your rough draft. Throughout this text, we suggest that you write a rough draft using a technique called *sufficing.* Once you know what you want to say, you should just say it—and let it suffice for the moment. Write a rapid rough draft, focusing on content and organization, not on grammar, mechanics, or style. Your primary goal in a rough draft is to get words on the paper or screen. The time for fine tuning comes later in rewriting. During rewriting, you'll be able to check your spelling, consider your punctuation, and perfect your tone. Drafting, in contrast, should be a stage in the writing process still free of those fears caused by grammar anxiety. After all, if you're worrying about the correctness of every word while you write it, you'll never complete a sentence.

☐ Rewriting

After you've drafted your correspondence, the final step in the writing process and, in many people's opinion, the most important step, is to revise your rough copy. Rewriting is the step that most mediocre writers omit. Poor writers merely let the rough draft suffice as their finished version. They assume that their draft is sufficient. It isn't. Successful writers, in contrast, realize that an effective letter must be as perfect as it can be. To achieve this level of expertise, good writers revise their rough drafts—fine tuning, honing, sculpting, molding, and polishing so what leaves their hands is something they can be proud of.

To revise your letters, consider the following revision criteria:

1. Add for clarity and correctness. Look back over your rough draft. In doing so, ask yourself what you might need to add for clarity. This might entail reviewing the reporters' questions. For example, has your letter clarified *who* will do the work (personnel), act as a contact person (liaison), manage the system (management), etc.? If not, then you need to provide further information by answering the reporters' question *who.* Have you correctly stated *when* you'll follow up, when you need the information, or when the bad news will occur? If not, add these dates. The same applies for all the reporters' questions. Add any missing information regarding *what, why, where,* or *how.*

In addition to adding answers to the reporters' questions, review your draft and add any missing letter essentials: letterhead address, date, inside address, salutation, complimentary close, typed and/or signed signature, and optional inclusions such as enclosure or copy notations.

2. Delete for conciseness. Deleting relates to style and content. Review your rough draft to delete any dead words and phrases. Delete irrelevant content. This might include background sentences in the introductory paragraph which delay your main point. Writers often feel compelled to lead in to their thesis. This is a mistaken notion in technical writing. All the reader really wants to know is why you are writing and what you are writing about. Get to your point immediately; delete the unneeded background data.

3. Simplify to aid easy understanding. You should avoid old-fashioned words and phrases, such as *pursuant, accede, supersede,* and *in lieu of.* Rather than using such pompous words, simplify. Just write naturally. Why not say *after, accept, replace,* and *instead of?* This simplified style not only affects your fog index positively but also helps your readers understand your content, and that's the goal of good writing.

4. Move information for emphasis. This involves cutting and pasting—moving information within your letter. For example, let's say you've read your rough draft and realized that the itemized discussion paragraph is not organized according to importance. In fact, you have buried a key point deep in the body where readers might miss it. To focus your reader's attention on this idea, you should move it from the bottom of the list to the top. Doing so makes the idea more emphatic.

5. Reformat for reader-friendly ease of access. Review your letter's format. How does the letter look on the page? The letter's appearance affects your readers before they read one word. If the letter is open and appealing, then you're off to a good start. If the letter is blocky and inaccessible, then you've already done yourself a disservice.

Before you type your final copy, answer the following questions.

- ☐ Have you used enough (or too much) white space?
- ☐ Should you underline a key word or phrase?
- ☐ Are bullets appropriate in your discussion paragraph, or should you use numbers instead?
- ☐ Could you use a colored highlighter to emphasize a sentence?
- ☐ Would boldfacing help you draw attention to a key concern?

6. Enhance the letter's tone. Letters aren't the inanimate objects they appear to be. They don't just dump data. Your letter is a reflection of your interpersonal communication skills and your company's attitudes. Reread your rough draft; is it revealing the personality or attitude that you want it to reveal? If the letter is stuffy, impersonal, high-handed, abrupt, offensive, or mean-spirited, then you must alter the tone.

To do so, add more pronouns, especially *you*-oriented ones; add verbs for punch; use contractions for a conversational tone; and/or add positive words and phrases to give your letter an upbeat tone. Using such personalization techniques ensures customer and client cooperation.

7. *Correct errors.* Finally, before your letter leaves your office, correct any errors you've committed. The most important step of rewriting may be proofreading. Check and double-check your grammar; check and double-check your mathematical computations and scientific notations. Your letter is a legal document. A mistake can cost your company money and you your job. Proofreading is boring, but sitting at home, reading the want ads, and looking for a new job is worse. Most writing handbooks include proofreading tips. Save yourself future problems by proofing your letters now.

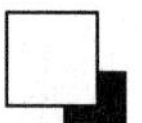

PROCESS LOG

To give you a better idea of how this three-step process approach to letter writing works, we provide the following student-written process log. It includes the student's answers to the reporters' questions (prewriting), her rough draft (writing), her revisions (rewriting), and her finished copy.

☐ Prewriting

First, the student filled in a letter of inquiry reporters' questions checklist (Figure 1.12).

☐ Writing

After the student gathered her data, she wrote a rough draft (Figure 1.13).

☐ Rewriting

Next, with the assistance of a peer review group consisting of two other students, the writer revised the letter (Figure 1.14).

Once the student made the suggested revisions, she submitted the finished copy (Figure 1.15).

1. *Who* is your audience?
   - ☐ High-tech peer Vendor
   - ☐ Low-tech peer
   - ☐ Lay reader
   - ☐ Management
   - ☐ Subordinate
   - ☐ Multiple audiences

2. *Why* are you writing? In response to sales letter – to request information

3. *What* is the general topic of your request? Information about the personal shipping service

4. *What exactly* do you want to know (the specifics itemized in the discussion paragraph of your letter)?
   - ☐ cost of services
   - ☐ number of employees needed
   - ☐ commission?
   - ☐ what department to work with
   - ☐

5. *What* do you want the reader to do next? Respond to questions

6. *When* do you want the reader to act (dated action)? March 15

7. *Why* is this date important? for meeting with management

FIGURE 1.12 Letter of Inquiry Reporters' Questions Checklist

Barney Allis Stores
5000 Main
Omaha, NB 32001

February 15, 1991

Fashion Pace
100 Eby
New York, NY 01034

Dear Ms. Pace:

Thank you for the information abuut your Personal Shopping service. I am interested in Fashion Pace, and would like to receive the following information:

1. Sales figures.
2. Customers serviced.
3. Requirements and costs to start service.

I would appreciate your response by March 1, 1991. Since I will be attending a meeting of the board on March 10, 1991 your early rsponse will allow me to present your service at this time.

Sincerely,

Shirley Chandley, Manager

FIGURE 1.13 Letter of Inquiry Rough Draft

Barney Allis Stores
5000 Main
Omaha, NB 32001

February 15, 1991

add name of contact

Fashion Pace
100 Eby
New York, NY 01034

Dear Ms. Pace:

typo   capitalize?

Thank you for the information abuut your Personal Shopping service. I am interested in Fashion Pace, and would like to receive the following information:

Do you need the periods?

1. Sales figures. too vague - which ones?
2. Customers serviced. Awk! A list of satisfied customers
3. Requirements and costs to start service. too vague

Please... * Add more questions

I would appreciate your response by March 1, 1991. Since I will be attending a meeting of the board on March 10, 1991, your early rsponse will allow me to present your service at this time.

typo

Sincerely,

Shirley Chandley, Manager

move under name

* office space needed
* required training
* # of employees needed

FIGURE 1.14 Letter of Inquiry Revision

Barney Allis Stores
5000 Main
Omaha, NB 32001

February 15, 1991

Ms. Jackie Pace
Fashion Pace
100 Eby
New York, NY 01034

Dear Ms. Pace:

Thank you for the information about your Personal Shopping Service. I am interested in Fashion Pace and would like to receive the following information:

1. Previous sales figures
2. Satisfied customer list
3. Office space needed
4. Number of employees needed
5. Training required for employees
6. Cost of services to customers

Please send the information by March 1, 1991. Your early response will allow me to present your service at our March 10 sales meeting. I look forward to hearing from you.

Sincerely,

Shirley Chandley

Shirley Chandley
Manager

FIGURE 1.15 Letter of Inquiry Final Copy

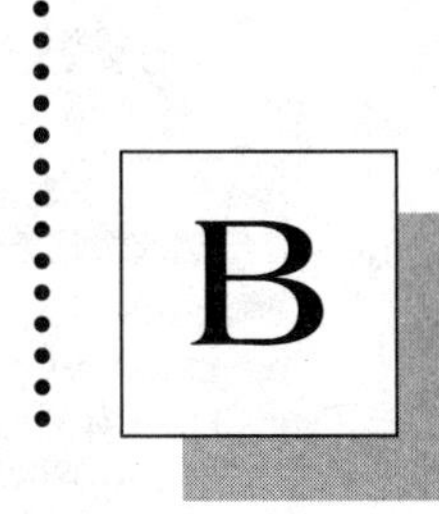

Memos

OBJECTIVES

Memos (correspondence written and read only within the company) are the primary means by which employees communicate with each other. More memos are written than any other type of technical correspondence. Memos are the workhorses of the workplace. A memo is important not only because of its frequency of use and the wide range of subject matter presented in memo form but also because memos represent a major component of your interpersonal communication skills within your work environment.

This chapter presents the following information regarding memos: (a) the difference between memos and letters; (b) criteria for writing successful memos; (c) the process for writing memos (with sample process log); and (d) examples.

THE DIFFERENCE BETWEEN MEMOS AND LETTERS

Before we discuss the criteria for memos, review the differences between memos and letters, shown in Table 1.1.

TABLE 1.1 Memos versus Letters

Memos	Letters
☐ Internal correspondence (written within your company to one of your colleagues)	☐ External correspondence (written outside your business to a vendor or client, for example)
☐ Memo format (Date, To, From, Subject)	☐ Letter format (Letterhead Address, Inside Address, Salutation, Complimentary Close)
☐ Generally high-tech audience (peers)	☐ Generally low-tech or lay audience
☐ High-tech subject matter with abbreviations and acronyms often allowed	☐ Low-tech/layperson's subject matter with abbreviations and acronyms defined clearly
☐ Informal tone (due to peer audience)	☐ More formal tone (due to audience with whom you may not be familiar)

CRITERIA FOR WRITING SUCCESSFUL MEMOS

Although every memo will not look the same, the following page shows an ideal organizational template that works well for most memos.

☐ Subject Line

One hundred percent of your readers read the subject line (after all, we have to start reading any text at its beginning. The beginning of a memo is the subject line). The subject line is where you begin talking to your reader(s). Therefore, you want it to work for you. One-word subject lines don't communicate effectively, as in the following flawed subject line:

Subject: Comptrollers

We've got a topic (a *what*), but we're missing a *focus* (a *what* about the *what*). An improved subject line would read as follows:

Subject: Salary Increases for Comptrollers

This subject line gives us the *topic*—Comptrollers (the *what*)—plus a focus—Salary Increases (the *what* about the *what*)—all linked by a preposition.

DATE:

TO:

FROM:

SUBJECT: Focus + Topic?

Introduction:	A lead-in, warm-up, overview stating ***why*** you're writing and ***what*** you're writing about

Discussion:	Detailed development, made accessible through highlighting techniques, explaining ***exactly what*** you want to say .

Conclusion:	A summation stating ***what's next, when*** this will occur, and ***why*** the date is important

Such a sequence works in all subject lines. For instance, in the following examples, note how the focus alters the meaning of the subject line's topic.

Subject: FOCUS	**plus**	**TOPIC**
Termination	of	Comptrollers
Hiring Procedures	for	Comptrollers
Vacation Schedules	for	Comptrollers
Training Seminars	for	Comptrollers

Although the topic always stays the same, the focus changes and clarifies for the reader the actual subject matter of the memo.

☐ Introduction

Once you've communicated your intent in the subject line, you want to get to the point in the introductory sentence(s). Readers are busy and don't want your memo to slow down their work. To avoid any delays for your audience, you want your first sentence or sentences to communicate immediately. A goal is to write one or two clear introductory sentences which tell your readers *what you want* and *why you're writing.* Remember, until you tell them, they don't know.

> In the third of our series of quality control meetings this quarter, I'd like to get together again to determine if improvements have been made.

This example invites the reader to a meeting, thereby communicating what the writer's intentions are. It also tells the reader that the meeting is one of a series of meetings, thus communicating why the meeting is being called.

> As a follow-up to our phone conversation yesterday (8/12/91), I have met with our VP regarding your suggestions. He'd like to meet with you to discuss the following ideas in more detail.

This introduction reminds the reader why this memo is being written—a follow-up—and tells the reader what will happen next.

☐ Discussion

The discussion section allows you to develop your content specifically. You want to respond to the reporters' questions mentioned in Chapter IA (*who, what, when, why, where, how*), but you also want to make your information accessible. Since very few readers read every line of your memo (tending instead to skip and skim), traditional blocks of data (paragraphing) aren't effective visually. The longer the paragraph, the more likely your audience is to avoid reading. Instead, try to make your text more reader friendly by applying some of the highlighting techniques: (a) itemization, (b) white space, (c) boldface type, (d) headings, (e) columns, and (f) graphics.

Note the difference between the following examples: The first is reader unfriendly, and the second is reader friendly.

Example #1—Unfriendly Text

This year began with an increase, as we sold 4.5 million units in January compared to 3.7 for January 1990. In February we continued to improve with 4.6 compared with 3.6 for same time in 1990. March was not quite so good, as we sold 4.3 against the March 1990 figure of 3.9. April was about the same with 4.2 compared to 3.8 for April of 1990.

Example #2—Reader-friendly Text

Comparative Quarterly Sales (in Millions)

	1990	**1991**	**Increase/Decrease**
Jan.	3.7	4.5	0.8+
Feb.	3.6	4.6	1.0+
Mar.	3.9	4.3	0.4+
Apr.	3.8	4.2	0.4+

The first block of data is unappealing to read and hard to follow due to its complexity. You can't see the relationship between figures and years clearly, nor can you see the variance from year to year easily. On the other hand, the chart in the second example is accessible at a glance. It's clear and concise—perfect technical writing.

□ Conclusion

Conclude your memo with a *complimentary close* and/or a *directive close.*

A complimentary close motivates your readers and leaves them happy as in the following example:

> If our quarterly sales continue to improve at this rate, we will double our sales expectations by 1992. Congratulations!

A directive close tells your readers exactly what you want them to do next or what your plans are (and provides dated action).

> Next Wednesday (12/22/91), Mr. Jones will provide each of you a timetable of events and a summary of accomplishments.

Why is a conclusion important? Without it, the reader senses a lack of closure and does not know what to do next or why the actions requested are important. Without a conclusion, the reader's response is going to be "OK, but now what?" or "OK, but so what?" To write an effective memo, you must sum up and provide closure.

□ Audience

Another criterion for effective memo writing is audience recognition. In memos, audience is both easier and more complex than in letters. Since letters go outside your company, your audience is usually low tech or lay, demanding that you define your terms more specifically. In memos, on the other hand, your in-house audience is easier to define (usually low tech or high tech). Thus, you often can use more acronyms and internal abbreviations.

However, whereas your audience for letters is usually singular—one reader—your audience for memos might be multiple. Studies tell us that memos average six readers. You might be writing simultaneously to your immediate supervisor (high tech), to his or her boss (low tech), to your colleagues (high tech), and even to a CEO (low tech).

This diverse readership presents a problem. How do you communicate to a large and varied audience? How do you avoid offending your high-tech readers with seemingly unnecessary data which your low-tech readers need?

The problem is not easy to solve. Sometimes you can use parenthetical definitions. For instance, don't just write *CIA,* which to most people means Central Intelligence Agency. Provide a parenthetical definition—CIA (Cash in Advance)—if your usage differs from what most people will automatically assume. You are always better off saying too much.

☐ Style

The appropriate style for memos is the same technical writing style discussed in later chapters—conciseness, clarity, and accessibility. Use simple words, readable sentences, specific detail, and highlighting techniques.

In addition, strive for an informal, friendly tone. Memos are part of your interpersonal communication abilities. Just as you should be concerned with how you speak to others on the telephone or at the water cooler, you should assess your tone within a memo. Do you sound natural, normal, informal, and friendly? Does your memo sound like it is written by the kind of person you would want to work with or for? If not, you might be creating a negative image.

Decide which of the following examples has the more positive "feel." Which boss would you prefer working with?

Example 1

We will have a meeting next Tuesday, Jan. 11, 1991. Exert every effort to attend this meeting. Plan to make intelligent comments regarding the new quarter projections.

Example 2

Let's meet next Tuesday (Jan. 11, 1991). Even if you're late, I'd appreciate your attending. By doing so you can have an opportunity to make an impact on the new quarter projections. I'm looking forward to hearing your comments.

Isn't the latter more personal, informal, appealing, and motivational? This tone is achieved through audience involvement (*you* usage), contractions, and positive words, aspects of effective writing.

When you write a memo, you are writing to someone with whom you work every day. The Golden Rule is write as you would like to be written to.

☐ Grammar

Abide by all grammatical conventions when writing memos. Poor grammar or typographical errors destroy your credibility.

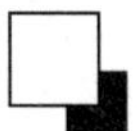

PROCESS

Now that you know what to include in a memo, follow the three-step process to create the correspondence:

- ☐ Prewriting
- ☐ Writing
- ☐ Rewriting

☐ Prewriting

No single method of prewriting is more effective than another. We've already learned the value of reporters' questions—*who, what, when, where, why, how* (earlier in this chapter)—so let's try a new technique called clustering/mind mapping.

The type of prewriting you prefer depends on your unique learning style. Whereas reporters' questions are more systematic and linear (possibly geared toward those who are more analytical), clustering/mind mapping is more visual and free form. Figure 1.16 shows a typical mind map pattern.

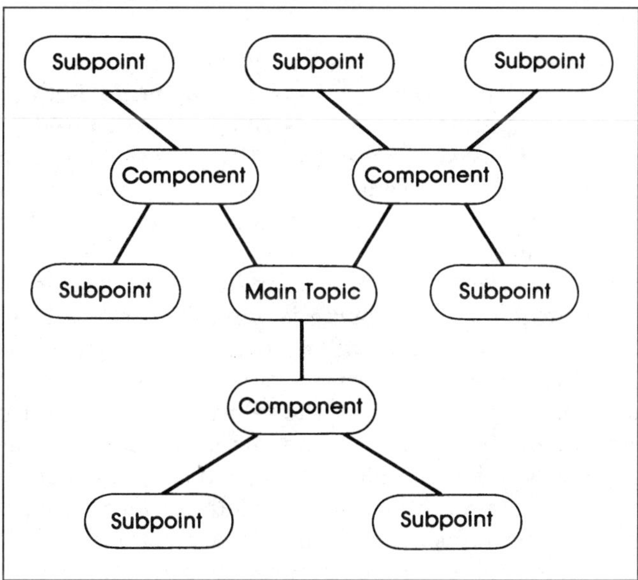

FIGURE 1.16 Clustering/Mind Mapping

The idea of clustering is to start with your main topic, whatever that might be, and then determine what that topic is composed of. For example, if your main topic is a company picnic, the next question is to ask what that picnic should entail. If you're planning such a picnic, you would want to consider food, entertainment, and a schedule for activities. These items represent the major components and are diagrammed in Figure 1.17.

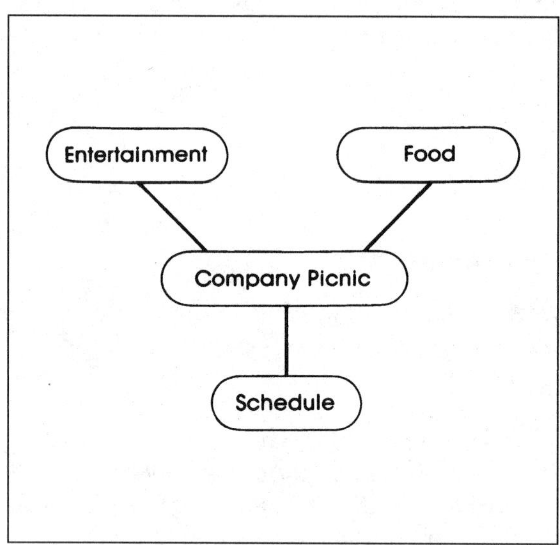

FIGURE 1.17 Major Components of a Company Picnic Mind Map

Writing always requires that you develop your points so you are clear and detailed. Thus, the next step in clustering is to provide more detail through the addition of subpoints. Subpoints clustered around the food component might include the entree (BBQ beef), condiments (pickles, relish, potato salad), drinks (soda and lemonade), and desserts (apple pie). Subpoints clustered around the entertainment component might include a live band and games for both adults and children.

Figure 1.18 shows a mind map including subpoints.

Clustering/mind mapping is valuable because it allows you to sketch your ideas freely without falling prey to the rigid structure of an outline (which often deters some writers' creativity). Clustering/mind mapping also allows you to see graphically the relationship between subpoints and components of an idea. This helps you determine if you've omitted any key concerns or included any irrelevant ideas. If so, you can develop your ideas further by adding new subpoints or delete irrelevancies simply by scratching off one of your subpoint balloons. Thus, clustering/mind mapping is an excellent prewriting technique because it easily allows you to gather information and organize your thoughts.

☐ Writing

Once you've gathered your data and determined your objectives in prewriting, your next step is to draft your memo. In doing so, consider the following drafting techniques:

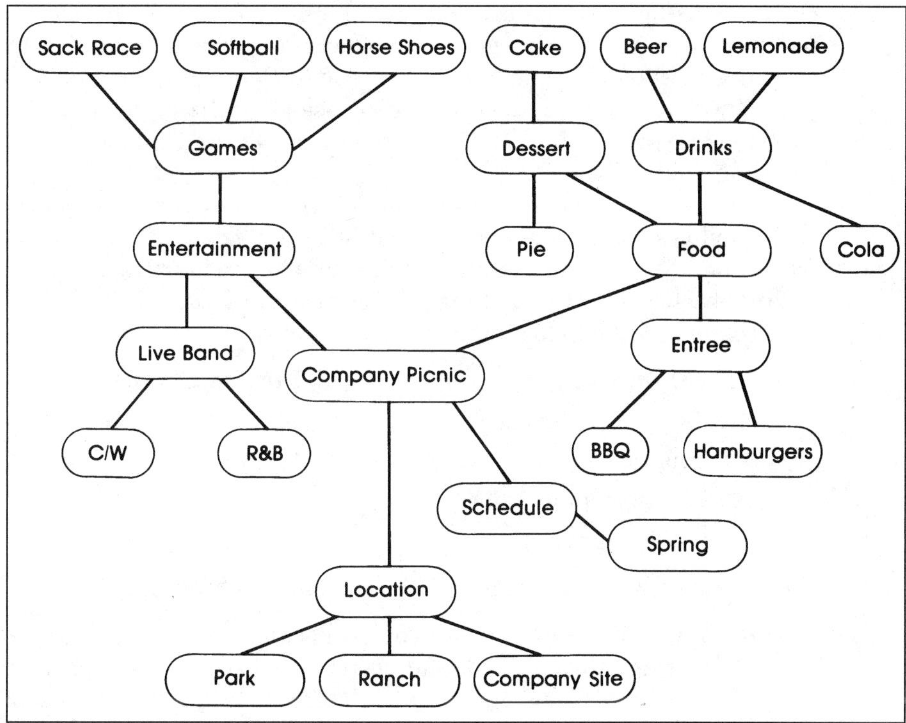

FIGURE 1.18 Company Picnic Mind Map, Including Subpoints

1. Review your prewriting. Before you begin writing, look back over your clustering to see if you've missed anything important. This review also provides one final reminder of what you want to say (the content of the memo) and why you are going to say it (your objectives).

2. Determine your focus (topic sentence, thesis statement, objective of the memo, etc.). Prior to drafting the memo, write down in one or two sentences your objective for this correspondence. For example, regarding the company picnic, you might want to write, "My plan for the picnic includes food, entertainment, and a schedule for activities." Such a sentence provides you with a clear focus for your draft. It helps keep you from straying off course in your memo.

3. Clarify your audience. Again, before writing the draft, be sure that you know who you are writing to. Is your audience high tech, low tech, or lay? Is the audience composed of management, subordinates, or lateral colleagues? Is the audience multiple, consisting of many of the aforementioned levels? Make this determination and then write accordingly.

4. Review your memo criteria. Remember what a memo entails. In addition to Date, To, From, and Subject, try to use the template shown earlier (Introduction, Body, and Conclusion).

5. Organize your ideas. If your supporting details are presented randomly to your audience, your audience will be confused. As a writer, you are obligated to develop your content in a manner which will allow your readers to follow your train of thought easily. Therefore, when you draft your memo, choose a method of organization which will help your readers understand your objectives. In Chapter IA, we discussed organizing by importance (the inverted journalist's pyramid). You may want to use this method of organization in your memo.

Another method of organization is *chronology*. A chronological organization follows a time sequence, from first to last, from 8:00 A.M. to 5:00 P.M., from Monday through Friday, from first quarter to fourth quarter, from step 1 through step 27. This method of organization is useful if your memo focuses on any of the following:

Past Histories	**Future Events**
Incidents or accidents	Instructions
Meeting minutes	Deadlines
Performance appraisals	Agendas
Customer complaints	Itineraries

The following memo in Figure 1.19 is organized chronologically.

6. Write the draft. Once you've decided on content (by reviewing your prewriting), determined your focus, clarified your audience, reviewed your criteria for effective memos, and determined how best to organize your thoughts, all that's left is to draft the text. The key to successful drafting is to avoid worry. When you worry about the end result, you get anxious and you can't write. To draft, you must throw words on the page freely. Don't delay, worry, or procrastinate. Just write it down! Use the sufficing technique mentioned in Chapter IA. Get it on the page and let it suffice, for now. You can go back and revise later.

☐ Rewriting

To revise your memo and make it as good as it can be, follow the revision techniques discussed in Chapter IA:

- ☐ *Add* new detail for clarity. Reread your draft. If you've omitted any information stemming from the reporters' questions (*who, what, when, why, where, how*), insert answers to these questions.
- ☐ *Delete* dead words and phrases for conciseness.
- ☐ *Simplify* words and phrases. For example, *in lieu of* might confuse someone. Why not simplify this to *instead of?* Don't write down to your audience, but a good rule of thumb is to write as you speak, unless you speak poorly. Be more casual.
- ☐ *Move* information from top to bottom or bottom to top for emphasis. Remembering the inverted journalist's pyramid discussed in Chapter IA, place your most important information first, or move information around to maintain an effective chronological order.

DATE: May 1, 1991
TO: Planning Committee
FROM: Adrianne Best *AB*
SUBJECT: Planning Agenda for July 4 Company Picnic

To confirm our decisions reached yesterday at the planning committee meeting, here's the agenda for each of your July 4 Company Picnic responsibilities:

Harry By ***May 10,*** select and book a country-western band.

Susan By ***May 15,*** make arrangements for the picnic food. Since we've already selected the menu, you'll only need to select the caterer (within our budget!).

Adrianne By ***May 20,*** I will mail a schedule of all activities to our coworkers, including where we'll hold the picnic, when to arrive and leave, what the costs will be, and when events will occur.

Thank you all for your support. Together we'll make this team effort a success.

FIGURE 1.19 Memo Organized Chronologically

- ☐ *Reformat* for access. Use highlighting techniques (white space, bullets, numbers, headings, etc.) for reader-friendly appeal.
- ☐ *Enhance* the tone and style of your memo. If you want to sound tough, then revise your memo to sound that way. If you want to tone down your correspondence, now is the time to do so. If you want to personalize the memo (remembering that memos are part of your interpersonal communication skills within the office), then add pronouns and/or names to give the memo a more person-to-person tone.
- ☐ *Correct* for accuracy. Proofread!
- ☐ *Avoid sexist language.* Women and men are equal. Sexist language implies that only men work and have positions of prominence.

Once you have revised your draft in the rewriting stage, review it once more according to the following effective memo checklist.

EFFECTIVE MEMO CHECKLIST

1. ☐ *How does the memo look on the page?* Before your reader reads one word of the memo, he or she will be affected by the look of the text.
   —Is it appealing due to highlighting techniques?
   —Will the look of the memo invite the reader into the correspondence?
   —Or will your use of wall-to-wall words force the reader to skip and skim?
2. ☐ *Is the subject line valid?* A successful subject line requires a topic and a focus.
3. ☐ *Do you get to the point immediately in the first sentence(s)?*
4. ☐ *Is the memo's body developed, answering the reporters' questions?*
5. ☐ *Is the content accessible, through the use of highlighting techniques and organization (importance or chronology)?* You don't want to bury key ideas. You want important ideas to leap off the page. You want your readers to follow your train of thought easily.
6. ☐ *Is your word usage appropriate?*
   —Have you correctly assessed your audience and determined whether you need to define terms?
   —Similarly, have you achieved the correct tone, given your audience's needs?
7. ☐ *Are your words and sentences the appropriate length?* Excessively long words and sentences make your readers work hard. In contrast, manageable words and sentences help your readers grasp your intentions.

8. ☐ *Have you included a directive and/or complimentary close?* If you omit a conclusion, your memo will be forgotten. In contrast, an effective conclusion will make your memo memorable and motivational.
9. ☐ *Have you dated your action?* You don't always need to tell your readers when to act or when to expect a follow-up. However, if a date is important, you must give it.
10. ☐ *Are errors eliminated?* A memo with grammatical or mechanical errors will destroy your credibility. You must prooofread to catch errors like the one in this sentence—*prooofread*

PROCESS LOG

☐ Prewriting

Figure 1.20 shows one student's prewriting, written in response to a request that all students write a memo telling how to write a memo.

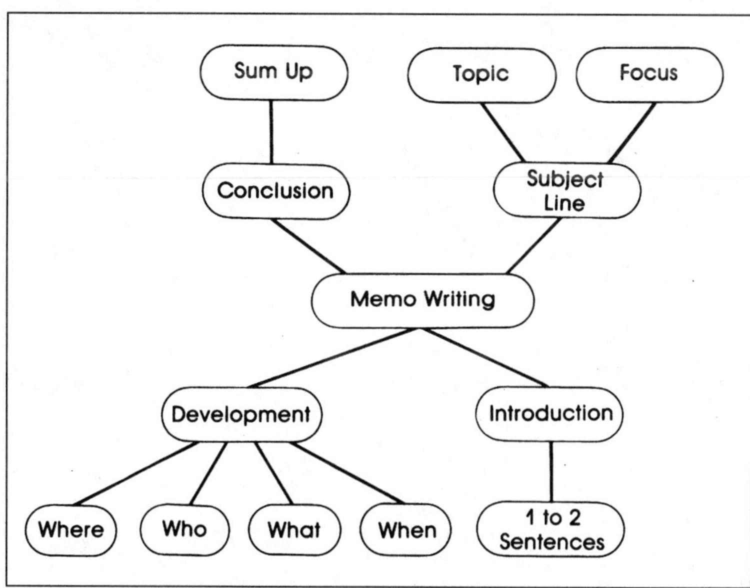

FIGURE 1.20 Student Mind Mapping

☐ Writing

Following is the student's rough draft (Figure 1.21).

```
Subject: Memo Writing

Following are ways to write better memos.

Include a Subject Line, which provides a topic and a focus. Then
have an Introduction to tell your readers what he needs to know.
This Introduction could be about one or two sentences. Next,
develope your ideas in a Discussion. Finally, sum it up in a
Conclusion.

These suggestions should help you write better memos.
```

FIGURE 1.21 Rough Draft

☐ Rewriting

Student peer evaluators suggested the revisions in Figure 1.22. The finished copy is shown in Figure 1.23.

SAMPLE MEMOS

Following are additional examples of both student and professionally written memos (complete with our evaluations of the memos' successes and needed improvements). The first, student-written memo (Figure 1.24) is well organized and developed, but it has several stylistic flaws.

Let's discuss the successes first. We like the way the memo is formatted (indented body for accessibility). It has an introduction, discussion, and conclusion, following our template. The writer also has developed her ideas thoroughly: The introductory paragraph answers the reporters' questions *who* and *what,* the body discusses *why;* and the conclusion focuses on *when.* Finally, the tone of the memo is appropriate for management (especially in the last paragraph).

However, the memo is flawed stylistically. Look how long that first paragraph is! This type of writing requires a high degree of patience on the reader's part. In addition, the writer has committed two punctuation errors. No period is needed in the subject line. The colon after *because* in the body is incorrect. Either no punctuation is needed or the sentence should be rewritten so a colon could be used. For example, if the sentence reads ". . . it would benefit our company for the following reasons," then you could insert a colon after *reasons.*

The example in Figure 1.25 is professionally written. It too has successes and failures. This memo succeeds in the following ways. As with the earlier student-written example, this memo uses the introduction-body-conclusion template. It ends with an excellent series of directives, specifying what is to occur next. The body is formatted for reader-friendly ease of access. The memo answers the reporters' questions *what, who, why,* and *when.*

The memo is flawed, however, in several ways. First, the subject line has a topic (Operating Procedure) but no focus. What about this procedure? Will the memo discuss the termination of the procedure, the writing of a new procedure, or changes in the procedure? A subject line such as "Revision of Operation Procedure 329 dated 5-9-91" would provide the necessary focus.

Next, note that this memo is written to multiple audiences (Distribution). Will each reader recognize that *PQR, OP,* and *EN* are abbreviations for Product Quality Requirement, Operating Procedure, and Engineering Notice? You'd have to guess at an answer, and guessing gets you in trouble in technical writing. When in doubt, spell it out. To avoid any problems with audience recognition, add your abbreviation parenthetically. For example, write, "Operating Procedure (OP) 329." Doing so takes very little time but eliminates any audience doubt.

Finally, the memo uses sexist language in the sentence "They are then to conduct reviews with their supervisors to assure that each supervisor is aware of *his* responsibility." This must read "his or her responsibility."

The student-written memo in Figure 1.26 succeeds in all ways: organization, visual appeal, development, grammar, and tone.

Add Date, To, From

Subject: Memo Writting (NO Focus - what about it ?)
SP

Following are ways to write better memos. Add why! What's their motivation ?

Reformat

Include a Subject Line which provides a topic and a focus.

Reformat agreement ?

Then have an Introduction to tell your readers what he

needs to know. This Introduction could be about one or

SP

two sentences. Next, develope your ideas in a Discussion.

Reformat the text - make it more accessible through Highlighting

Finally, sum it up in a Conclusion.

Your entire memo needs more Development.

These suggestions should help you write better memos. Poor tone - motivate & tell them when (Dated action)

FIGURE 1.22 Suggested Revisions

Memo

Date: Oct. 19, 1991
To: Bob Xidis
From: Candi Millard CM
Subject: Suggestions for Improved Memo Writing

Bob, to help you write even more effective memos, following are some suggestions regarding improved memo writing techniques.

1. ***Subject Line*** Since 100% of all readers read the subject line, this is your first line of communication. To make it work for you, include a topic ("memo writing," for example) and a focus ("suggestions for").

2. ***Introduction*** Your readers are busy people and don't want their time wasted. Use one or two sentences to get to the point; state what you're writing about and why in an introductory paragraph.

2. ***Discussion*** The body of the memo is used to develop your idea. To do so, answer the reporters' questions and use highlighting techniques to make your ideas accessible.

4. ***Conclusion*** End with either a motivational comment, or give your reader direction (time, place, action).

By incorporating these techniques in your memos, you'll be able to communicate more effectively. If you have any questions, let's meet next Tuesday to discuss this matter more thoroughly.

FIGURE 1.23 Final Copy

MEMO

Date: January 19, 1991
To: Tom Lisk
From: Paige Bartel PB PB
Subject: Producing the Annoy-No-More Call Screening Machine

Our product development staff has come up with a break-through new product, a phone answering machine which answers the phone, screens calls, and by voice activation routes the call to an appropriate message and gives a busy signal when the person doesn't want to be bothered.

We have researched this product fully and believe it would benefit our company because:

1. The product has a relatively simple design which occupies no more space than a regular phone and can be designed for wall or desk mount.

2. The cost for manufacturing is low compared to the retail value. The unit costs approximately $100 to produce and retails for $999.99.

3. The unit can be interchanged easily with all phone networks including MBB and Shout.

We would like to begin mass production around April 1, 1991. Our Westport facility could handle the production with the addition of ten technicians and engineers to aid in production. We hope you give this product consideration and endorse it fully.
Thanks.

FIGURE 1.24 Student-written Memo

MEMORANDUM

DATE: June 4, 1991
TO: Distribution
FROM: ADRIENNE TIMMONS AT
SUBJECT: Operating Procedure 329 dated 5-9-91

The reissue of this procedure was the result of extensive changes requested by Quality, Manufacturing, and Engineering. The procedural changes which must be implemented according to Engineering Notice 195 are as follows:

- ☐ The asterisk (*) can no longer be used to identify guidance information or substitutable items in requirement lists. Substitutions must be called out by catalog numbers or descriptive names.
- ☐ Product quality requirements must be included in work directions either by stating the requirement or by referring to the appropriate PQR number.
- ☐ When oral instructions are given by supervisors, all engineers must be present.

Please review this revised OP and EN with your supervisors. They are then to conduct reviews with their supervisors to assure that each supervisor is aware of his responsibility. Advise me by memo when all reviews are complete.

Distribution: H. P. Adams
S. D. Smith
P. R. Braun
A. J. Rogers
T. D. Peters
L. E. Moss

FIGURE 1.25 Professionally-written Memo

MEMORANDUM

Date: December 12, 1991
To: Luann Brunson
From: Juliet Kincaid JK
Subject: Replacement of Maintenance Radios

In response to your request, this memo reports on our evaluation of the RPAD, XPO 1690, and MX16 radios. I issued a purchase order for twelve RPAD radios and summarize my findings below:

1. Performance

During a one-week test period, we found that the RPAD outperformed our current XPO 1690's reception from distant parts of the building.

2. Size

Both the RPAD and the MX16 are easier to carry, due to their reduced weight and size, than our current XPO 1690s.

3. Cost and Specifications

	RPAD	XPO 1690	MX16
Wattage	2	5	1
Size	1 lb.	2 lb.	1 lb.
Cost	$800	$2,600	$1,400

Purchase of the RPAD not only will give us improved performance and comfort, but also we can buy twelve RPAD radios at a cost cheaper than four XPOs. If I can provide you with any further information, please call. I'd be happy to meet with you at your convenience.

FIGURE 1.26 Successful Memo

Techniques for Reports

Three important elements of writing in the technical arena are definitions, descriptions, and instructions. These elements are particularly important when communicating with the non-technical reader. The following three sections provide further detail on each technique.

Definitions

OBJECTIVES

A basic element in writing is to give clear definitions in terms the reader can comprehend. The writer must recognize the level of knowledge held by the reader so that the definition will relate the new word or concept with a familiar one. This section provides guidelines for writing three types of definitions.

DEFINITION

Definitions provide concise, but exact, meanings for unfamiliar words and explain special meanings for familiar words. The words may name a process, object, or concept. Used with other methods of development, definitions introduce new ideas. They are often used to explain technical words and concepts. Definitions can be informal or formal. Informal definitions are synonyms (words that share the same meaning) or explanatory phrases that appear in the same sentence with the unfamiliar word. As shown in parentheses in the previous sentence, an informal definition can be used when the reader does not need much information about the word. Formal definitions are found in dictionaries and glossaries. They also introduce paragraphs or longer sections in a piece of writing. Occasionally they appear as explanatory notes at the bottom of the page. This section is concerned primarily with formal definitions.

What to define and what information to include in a definition depend on the needs of the reader and the purpose of the communication. For customers, you should avoid technical words as often as possible. Customers are interested in hiring someone to do a job for them or in buying a product. They are not interested in learning the special technology of a field. If technical words are essential to justify cost or explain a method, they should be quickly and simply defined. For technicians, you should also avoid needless technical words and their definitions. You should keep definitions of new words and the related explanations of new technology as simple as possible. When asked to remember too many definitions at one time, readers get so tangled in the words that they miss the point of the writing. Depending on the needs of the reader and the purpose of the communication, definitions may be limited to single sentences or expanded to several paragraphs.

□ Sentence Definition

Sentence definitions are written according to an established form: WORD + is + CLASS + DIFFERENCE. WORD is the name of the object, process, or concept defined. "Is" or "are" make the definition into a sentence. CLASS is the general group to which the object, process, or concept belongs. All members of the same CLASS share certain common characteristics. For example, a chair is "a piece of furniture," and changing the oil is "a maintenance procedure." DIFFERENCE is the distinctive feature that separates the object, process, or concept from other members of its class. A chair and a table are both pieces of furniture. However, a chair is different from a table because it has four legs, a seat, and a back and is used by one person for sitting. Changing the oil is different from rotating the tires, another maintenance procedure, because it requires that the dirty, old oil be replaced with new, clean oil.

Look at the class and difference for the words below.

Word	*Class*	*Difference*
time efficiency incentive	promised reward	that encourages a worker to finish a task on schedule or ahead of schedule
embryo transfer	medical procedure	in which a fertilized egg is removed from the reproductive tract of a donor animal and inserted into the womb of a recipient animal
no-tillage planting	farming procedure	in which a crop is planted without turning up the seedbed
acid rain	secondary pollution	that occurs when certain chemicals in the air combine with atmospheric water vapor and fall to the earth as rain

These definitions are easier to read when they are written as sentences.

Time efficiency incentive is a promised reward that encourages a worker to finish a task on schedule or ahead of schedule.

Embryo transfer is a medical procedure in which a fertilized egg is removed from the reproductive tract of a donor animal and inserted into the womb of a recipient animal.

No-tillage planting is a farming procedure in which the crop is planted without turning up the seedbed.

Acid rain is secondary pollution that occurs when certain chemicals in the air combine with atmospheric water vapor and fall to the earth as rain.

Three general rules are important in writing sentence definitions.

The definition must be less technical than the word. A sentence definition will not help a reader understand an unfamiliar word if it is made of equally unfamiliar words.

The class must not be eliminated. Many writers are tempted to skip the class and jump into the difference. They replace the class with the less exact words "where" or "when." For example, "Acid rain is when certain chemicals in the air combine with atmospheric water vapor" leaves out the important information that acid rain is secondary pollution.

Most often, the definition should not contain the word that is defined. When the word is repeated in the class or difference, the definition is circular. For example, "embryo transfer is a medical procedure for transferring embryos" is not informative. In some cases, however, repeating the word is less confusing and more exact than supplying a synonym. In the definition of no-tillage planting, replacing the word "planted" with a phrase such as "put into the ground" lengthens and confuses the sentence. Awkward attempts to avoid repeating a common word—"No tillage planting is a farm procedure in which impregnation by seeds can occur without turning up the ground"—are often difficult to understand as well as silly.

For more examples of sentence definitions, you can consult a dictionary of technical words used in your field. Sentence definitions are also found in manuals, standards, procedures, and textbooks.

□ Expanded Definition

When the reader needs more than a brief explanation, a sentence definition can be added to or expanded. Usually an expanded definition is a paragraph or two long. It gives a general discussion of an object, process, or concept. The methods for expanding a sentence definition include other standard patterns of organization explained later in this chapter. Below is a list of the most typical methods of expansion.

Explanation of use or function. How the object, process, or concept is used, and its benefits and limitations can be given.

Description of parts. If the word defined is an object, the object's parts can be listed and briefly described.

Basic operating principle. If the word defined is an object, a brief explanation of how the object works can be included. If the word defined is a process, the explanation can tell what happens during the process or how the process is performed.

Comparison. The object, process, or concept can be compared to something familiar to the reader. Likenesses and differences can be pointed out.

Origin of the word. The historical background for the word can be given. This method of expansion is particularly effective with medical words or other words derived from Latin roots. It is also effective for new words that name recent technical advancements. For example, osteoporosis is a bone disease which weakens the skeleton and can lead to fractures of the hip, back, or legs. The word "osteoporosis" comes from two Greek words. *Osteo* is the root of the Greek word for bone. *Porosis* is a Greek word that means passage. Literally, osteoporosis is a disease caused by abnormal passageways in the bone.

Examples. Examples of how the object, process, or concept is used or where it occurs can be included. Thls method of expansion helps readers understand the function.

Negation. This method of expansion tells readers what the word does *not* mean or what the object process or concept is *not*. It can be used to warn readers not to confuse the word defined with a similar word.

Visual aids. If the word defined is an object, the object can be illustrated with diagrams or sketches; or, if it is a process, it can be shown with a flowchart.

An expanded definition of a relief valve appears below[1]. This type of introduction to technical words and the devices they name is often found in training manuals. The reader does not read the definition to satisfy a general interest but to gain knowledge that can be used on the job.

Relief valves are controlling devices that open automatically to reduce pressure when it has become dangerously high. They are installed in water, oil, and air lines and in certain machines. Relief valves protect piping much the same way that fuses protect electrical equipment and wiring in a house. They release pressure that could overload the system.

Most relief valves operate with either a disk or a steel ball acting against a coil spring. The disk-type relief valve is shown in Figure 2.1A. It consists of a valve body, a valve disk, a stem, and a steel spring. The spring pushes down on the disk and keeps the valve closed. The force on the bottom of the disk is exerted by the pressure of the fluid in the line. When this force becomes greater than the compression of the spring, the disk is pushed off the seat. The valve opens. The ball-type valve is shown in Figure 2.1B. It operates on the same principle as the disk-type valve. However instead of a stem and disk, it has a ball. When the ball is pushed off the seat, the valve opens. Then the pressure in the line is released.

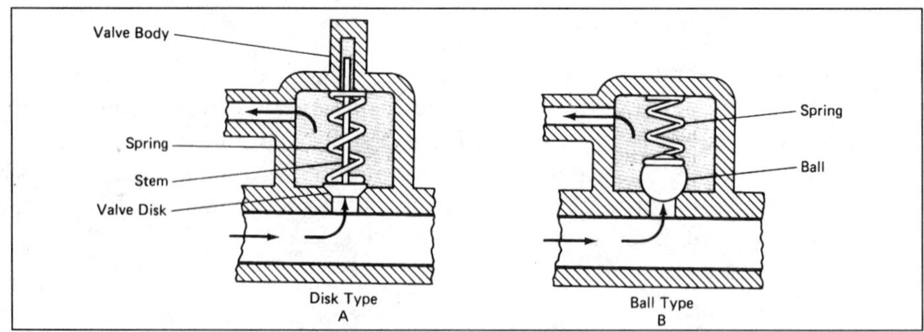

FIGURE 2.1 Two Types of Relief Valves

Notice the first sentence. It is a sentence definition that establishes a clear focus for this excerpt. Also notice the methods of expansion used: explana-

[1]The information and drawing of the relief valve are adapted from the Naval Education and Training Command Rate Training Manual *Fireman*. Washington: Government Printing Office, 1982.

tion of use, comparison with a familiar item (fuse), list of parts, basic operating principle and visual aid.

Here is another expanded definition. Unlike the technicians who read the first example, these readers do not need this writing to perform their jobs. Instead they are similar to the customers who ask for general information about your products.

> Aspirin is an over-the-counter drug used to reduce pain, swelling, and fever. The technical name of aspirin is acetylsalicylic acid. Aspirin belongs to a family of drugs called salicylates. It is a relative of the willow bark Hippocrates gave patients 2300 years ago. Willow bark's principal ingredient is salicin. Salicin occurs in many other trees and shrubs, including the spirea plant. In the nineteenth century, scientists learned to extract salicylic acid from its natural sources. They prescribed salicylic acid to lower fevers and reduce pain. But salicylic acid irritated the mouth, throat, and stomach. In the late 1890s a less harsh compound, acetylsalicylic acid, was developed. Acetylsalicylic acid was called "aspirin." "A" stands for "acetyl" and "spir" for the *Spiraea* genus of plants.
>
> Soon aspirin was being used all over the world. Its major uses today are still for fever, headache, and muscle ache, and the pain and swelling of arthritis. Aspirin lowers fever temperatures rapidly although it does not affect normal temperatures. For a patient with fever, aspirin resets the body's temperature to normal. It also releases the body's excess heat by increasing sweating and blood flow in the skin.

Again notice that the expanded definition begins with a sentence definition. It continues with an explanation of the word's origin along with a brief history of the development of aspirin, examples of its use, and its basic operating principle.

GUIDELINES FOR WRITING DEFINITIONS

Once you know definitions are needed, you must decide on their format and location. Again, consider your readers. How much information do they need? Where is this information best placed within the document? To answer these and other questions, here are five working guidelines for writing good definitions.

□ Definition Guideline 1: Keep It Simple

Occasionally the sole purpose of a report is to define a term. Most times, however, a definition just clarifies a term in a document with a larger purpose. Your definitions should be as simple and unobtrusive as possible. Always present the simplest possible definition, with only that level of detail needed by the reader.

For example, in writing to a client on your land survey of her farm, you might briefly define a transit as "the instrument used by land surveyors to measure horizontal and vertical angles." The report's main purpose is to present property lines and total acreage, not to give a lesson in surveying, so

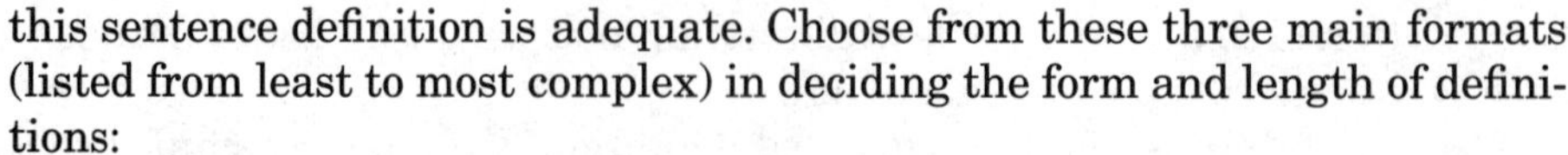

this sentence definition is adequate. Choose from these three main formats (listed from least to most complex) in deciding the form and length of definitions:

- ☐ **Informal definition:** a word or brief phrase, often in parentheses, that gives only a synonym or other minimal information about the term
- ☐ **Formal definition:** a full sentence that distinguishes the term from other similar terms and that includes these three parts: the term itself, a class to which the term belongs, and distinguishing features of the term
- ☐ **Expanded definition:** a lengthy explanation that begins with a formal definition and is developed into several paragraphs or more

Guidelines 2-4 show you when to use these three options and where to put them in your document.

☐ Definition Guideline 2: Use Informal Definitions for Simple Terms Most Readers Understand

Informal definitions appear right after the terms being defined, often as one-word synonyms in parentheses. They give just enough information to keep the reader moving quickly. As such, they are best used with simple terms that can be adequately defined without much detail.

Here is a situation in which an informal definition would apply. An engineering consulting firm has been hired to examine a possible shopping-mall site. The buyers, a group of physicians, want a list of previous owners and an opinion about the suitability of the site. As legal assistant at the company, you must assemble a list of owners in your part of the group-written report. You want your report to agree with court records, so you decide to include real-estate jargon such as "grantor" and "grantee." For your non-technical readers, you include parenthetical definitions like these:

> All **grantors** (persons from whom the property was obtained) and **grantees** (persons who purchased the property) are listed on the following chart by year of ownership.

This same report has a section describing creosote pollution found at the site. The chemist writing the contamination section also uses an informal definition for the readers' benefit:

> At the southwest corner of the mall site, we found 16 barrels of **creosote** (a coal tar derivative) buried under about three feet of sand.

The readers do not need a fancy chemical explanation of creosote. They only need enough information to keep them from getting lost in the terminology. Informal definitions perform this task nicely.

☐ Definition Guideline 3: Use Formal Definitions for More Complex Terms

A formal definition appears in the form of a sentence that lists (1) the **term** to be defined, (2) the **class** to which it belongs, and (3) the **features** that distinguish the term from others in the same class. Use it when your reader needs more background than an informal definition provides. Formal definitions define in two stages:

- ☐ First, they place the term into a *class* (group) of similar items.
- ☐ Second, they list *features* (characteristics) of the term that separate it from all others in that same class.

In the list of sample definitions that follows, note that some terms are tangible (like "pumper") and others are intangible (like "arrest"). Yet all can be defined by first choosing a class and then selecting features that distinguish the term from others in the same class.

Term	*Class*	*Features*
An arrest is	restraint of persons	that deprives them of freedom of movement and binds them to the will and control of the arresting officer.
A financial statement is	a historical report about a business	and is prepared by an accountant to provide information useful in making economic decisions, particularly for owners and creditors.
A triaxial compression test is	a soils lab test	that determines the amount of force needed to cause a shear failure in a soil sample.
A pumper	is a fire-fighting apparatus	used to provide adequate pressure to propel streams of water toward a fire.

This list demonstrates three important points about formal definitions. First, the definition itself must not contain terms that are confusing to your readers. The definition of "triaxial compression test," for example, assumes readers will understand the term "shear failure" that is used to describe features. If this assumption were incorrect, then the term would need to be defined. Second, formal definitions may be so long that they create a major distraction in the text. (See Guideline 5 for alternative locations) Third, the class must be narrow enough so that you will not have to list too many distinguishing features.

☐ Definition Guideline 4: Use Expanded Definitions for Supporting Information

Sometimes a parenthetical phrase or formal sentence definition is not enough. If readers need more information, use an expanded definition with this three-part structure:

- ☐ **An overview at the beginning**—which includes a formal sentence definition and a description of the ways you will expand the definition
- ☐ **Supporting information in the middle**—perhaps using headings and lists as helpful format devices for the reader
- ☐ **Brief closing remarks at the end**—reminding the reader of the definition's relevance to the whole document

Here are seven ways to expand a definition, along with brief examples:

1. **Background and/or history of term**—expand the definition of "triaxial compression test" by giving a dictionary definition of "triaxial" and a brief history of the origin of the test
2. **Applications**—expand the definition of "financial statement" to include a description of the use of such a statement by a company about to purchase controlling interest in another
3. **List of parts**—expand the definition of "pumper" by listing the parts of the device, such as the compressor, the hose compartment, and the water tank
4. **Graphics**—expand the description of the triaxial compression test with an illustration showing the laboratory test apparatus
5. **Comparison/contrast**—expand the definition of a term like "management by objectives" (a technique for motivating and assessing the performance of employees) by pointing out similarities and differences between it and other management techniques
6. **Basic principle**—expand the definition of "ohm" (a unit of electrical resistance equal to that of a conductor in which a current of one ampere is produced by a potential of one volt across its terminals) by explaining the principle of Ohm's Law (that for any circuit the electric current is directly proportional to the voltage and inversely proportional to the resistance)
7. **Illustration**—expand the definition of CAD/CAM (Computer-Aided Design/ Computer-Aided Manufacturing—computerized techniques to automate the design and manufacture of products) by giving examples of how CAD/CAM is changing methods of manufacturing many items, from blue jeans to airplanes

Obviously, long definitions might seem unwieldy within the text of a report, or even within a footnote. For this reason, they often appear in appendices, as noted in the next guideline. Readers who want additional information can seek them out, whereas other readers will not be distracted by digressions in the text.

☐ Definition Guideline 5: Choose the Right Location for Your Definition

Short definitions are likely to be in the main text; long ones are often relegated to footnotes or appendices. However, length is not the main consideration. Think first about the *importance* of the definition to your reader. If you know that decision-makers reading your report will need the definition, then place it in the text—even if it is fairly lengthy. If the definition only provides supplementary information, then it can go elsewhere. You have these five choices for locating a definition:

1. **In the same sentence as the term,** as with an informal, parenthetical definition
2. **In a separate sentence,** as with a formal sentence definition occurring right after a term is mentioned
3. **In a footnote,** as with a formal or expanded definition listed at the bottom of the page on which the term is first mentioned
4. **In a glossary at the beginning or end of the document,** along with all other terms needing definition in that document
5. **In an appendix at the end of the document,** as with an expanded definition that would otherwise clutter the text of the document

Technical Descriptions

OBJECTIVES

Technical descriptions are a part-by-part depiction of the components of a mechanism, tool, or piece of equipment. Technical descriptions are important features in several types of correspondence.

Operations Manuals

Whenever a company manufactures a product, it must enclose an operations manual in the packaging of the mechanism, tool, or piece of equipment. This manual helps the end-user construct, install, operate, and service the equipment. These operations manuals often include technical descriptions.

Technical descriptions provide the end-user with information about the mechanism's features or capabilities. For example, this information may tell the user which components are enclosed in the shipping package, clarify the quality of these components, specify what function these components serve in the mechanism, or allow the user to reorder any missing or flawed components. Here's a brief example of a technical description found in an operations manual:

The Modern Electronics Tone Test Tracer, Model 77A, is housed in a yellow, high-impact plastic case which measures $1^1/_4$" X 2" x $2^1/_4$", weighs 4 ounces, and is powered by a 1604 battery. Red and black test leads are provided. The 77A has a standard four-conductor cord, a three-position toggle switch, and an LED for line polarity testing. A tone selector switch located inside the test set provides either solid tone or dual alternating tone. The Tracer is compatible with the EXX, SetUp, and Crossbow models.

□ Product Demand Specifications

Sometimes a company needs a piece of equipment which does not currently exist. To acquire this equipment, the company must write a product demand specifying its exact needs, as in the following example:

Subject: Requested Pricing for EDM Microdrills

Please provide us with pricing information for the construction of 50 EDM Microdrills capable of meeting the following specifications:

- □ Designed for high-speed, deep-hole drilling
- □ Capable of drilling to depths of 100 times the diameter using .012-inch to .030-inch diameter electrodes
- □ Able to produce a hole through a 1.000-inch thick piece of AISI D2 or A6 tool steel in 1.5 minutes, using a .020-inch diameter electrode

We need your response by January 13, 1991.

□ Study Reports Provided by Consulting Firms

Companies hire a consulting engineering firm to study a problem and provide a descriptive analysis. The resulting study report is used as the basis for a product demand specification requesting a solution to the problem.

One firm, when requested to study crumbling cement walkways, provided the following, technical description in its study report:

> The slab construction consists of a wearing slab over a ½″-thick waterproofing membrane. The wearing slab ranges in thickness from 3½″ to 8½″, and several sections have been patched and replaced repeatedly in the past. The structural slab varies in thickness from 5½ to 9″ with as little as 2″ over the top of the steel beams. The removable slab section, which has been replaced since original construction, is badly deteriorated and should be replaced. Refer to Appendix A, Photo 9, and Appendix C for shoring installed to support the framing prior to replacement.

☐ Sales Literature and Proposals

Not all technical writing is photographically descriptive, depending on quantifiable information. Some descriptions are impressionistic. Note that the following sales piece uses impressionistic adjectives and adverbs (underlined), allowing your imagination to depict the product's components:

> Inside the <u>elegant</u> Zephyr you'll find <u>comfortably designed</u> seats done in <u>rich, tailored</u> cloths. The <u>special</u> suspension system surrounds you with a driving experience quieter than Zephyr's past. Outside you'll find a <u>new bright</u> grille, sport mirrors, and a <u>smart</u> dual pinstripe. Finally, underneath all this <u>comfort</u> and <u>luxury</u> beats the road-hugging heart of an American classic.

Whatever your purpose in writing a technical description, the following will help you write more effectively:

- ☐ **Criteria**
- ☐ **Process (with sample Process Log)**
- ☐ **Technical description examples**

CRITERIA FOR WRITING TECHNICAL DESCRIPTIONS

As with any type of technical writing, there are certain criteria for writing technical descriptions.

☐ Overall Organization

In the *introduction* you specify what *topic* you are describing, explain the mechanism's *functions* or *capabilities*, and list the *major components* of this topic.

Example 1

The Apex Latch (#12004), used to secure core sample containers, is composed of three parts: the hinge, the swing arm, and the fastener.

Example 2

The DX 56 DME (Distance Measuring Equipment) is a vital piece of aeronautical equipment. Designed for use at altitudes up to 30,000 feet, the DX 56 electronically converts elapsed time to distance by measuring the length of time between your transmission and the reply signal. The DX 56 DME contains the transmitter, receiver, power supply, and range and speed circuitry.

In the *discussion* you use highlighting techniques (itemization, headings, underlining, white space) to describe each of the mechanism's components.

Your *conclusion* depends on your purpose in describing the topic. Some options are as follows:

- ☐ Sales—"Implementation of this product will provide you and your company . . ."
- ☐ Uses—"After implementation, you will be able to use this XYZ to . . ."
- ☐ Guarantees—"The XYZ carries a fifteen-year warranty against parts and labor."
- ☐ Testimony—"Parishioners swear by the XYZ. Our satisfied customers include . . ."
- ☐ Comparison/contrast—"Compared to our largest competitor, the XYZ has sold three times more . . ."
- ☐ Reiteration of introductory comments—"Thus, the XYZ is composed of the aforementioned interchangeable parts."

You must use *graphics* in your technical descriptions. Today, many companies use the super comic book look—large, easy-to-follow graphics complementing the text. You can use line drawings, photographs, clip art, exploded views, or sectional cutaway views of your topic, each accompanied by call-outs (labels identifying key components of the mechanism). When using graphics, try one of the techniques shown in Figures 2.2, 2.3, and 2.4.

☐ Internal Organization

When describing your topic in the discussion portion of the technical description, you must itemize the topic's components in some logical sequence. Components of a piece of equipment, tool, or product can be organized by importance (discussed in Chapter IA).

However, *spatial* organization is better for technical descriptions. When a topic is spatially organized, you literally lay out the components as they are seen, as they exist in space. You describe the components either as they are seen from left to right, from right to left, from top to bottom, from bottom to top, from inside to outside, or from outside to inside.

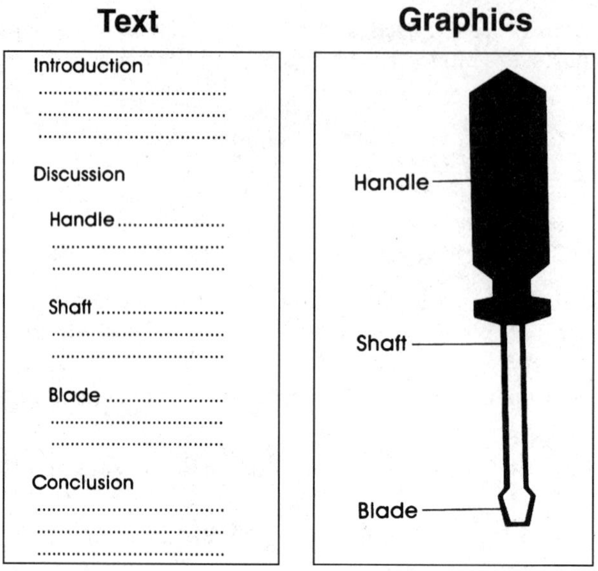

Text
Graphics
Introduction
Discussion
Handle
Shaft
Blade
Conclusion
Handle
Shaft
Blade

FIGURE 2.2 Text and Graphics Separate

Introduction
Discussion
1. Handle
2. Shaft
3. Blade
Conclusion
1
2
3

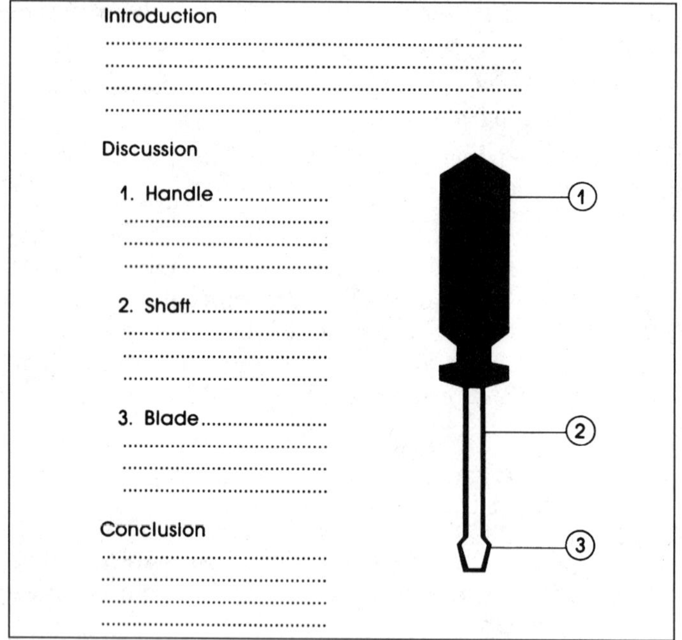

FIGURE 2.3 Text and Graphics Merged

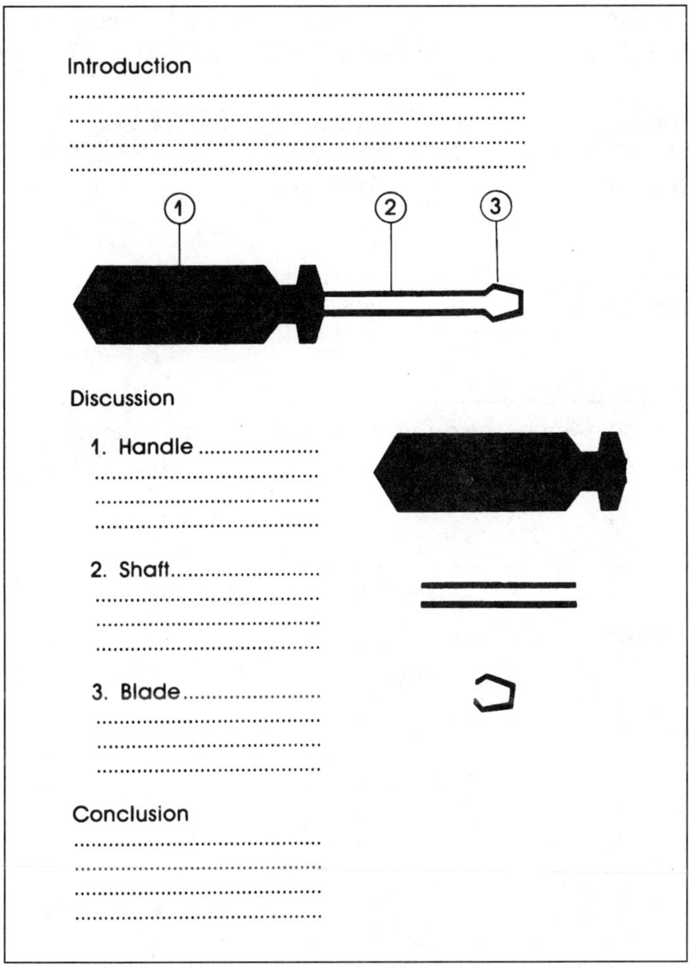

Introduction

1 2 3

Discussion

1. Handle

2. Shaft

3. Blade

Conclusion

FIGURE 2.4 Text and Graphics Merged with Exploded View

☐ Development

To describe your topic clearly and accurately, you must detail the following:

Weight	Materials (composition)
Size (dimensions)	Identifying numbers
Color	Make/model
Shape	Texture
Density	Capacity

☐ Word Usage

Your word usage, either photographic or impressionistic, depends on your purpose. For factual, objective technical descriptions, use photographic words. For subjective, sales-oriented descriptions, use impressionistic words.

Photographic words are denotative, quantifiable, and specific. Impressionistic words are vague and connotative. Table 2.1 shows the difference.

TABLE 2.1 Photographic versus Impressionistic Word Usage

Photographic	**Impressionistic**
6'9"	tall
350 lb.	fat
gold	precious metal
6,000 shares of United Can	major holdings
700 lumens	bright
.030 mm	thin
1966 XKE Jaguar	impressive car

Another way to note the difference between impressionistic words and photographic detail is through the ladder of abstraction, shown in Figure 2.5.

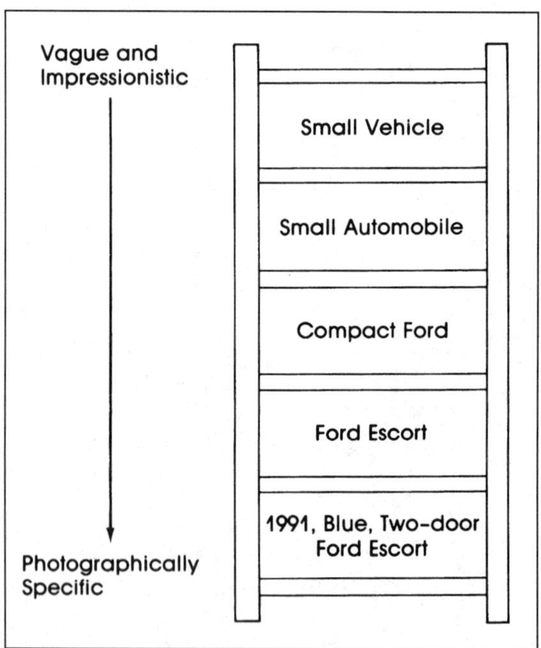

FIGURE 2.5 Ladder of Abstraction

PROCESS

Now that you know what should be included in a technical description, your next question is, "How do I go about writing this type of correspondence?" As always, effective writing follows a systematic, step-by-step process. To write your technical description, (a) *prewrite* to gather data and determine objectives; (b) *write* a draft of the description; and (c) *rewrite* by revising the draft, thereby making it as perfect as possible.

☐ Prewriting

So far we've discussed reporters' questions (Chapter IA) and clustering/mind mapping (Chapter 1B) as techniques for gathering data and determining objectives. Either of these two prewriting tools can be used for your technical description. However, another prewriting technique can be helpful: brainstorming/listing.

Brainstorming/listing, either individually or as a group activity, is a good, quick way to sketch out ideas for your description. To brainstorm/list, do the following:

1. *Title your activity,* at the top of your page, to help you maintain your focus. For example, *Description: XYZ (model 2267) Light Pen.*
2. *List any and all ideas* you might have on the topic. Don't editorialize. Avoid criticizing ideas at this point. Just randomly jot down as many aspects of the topic as possible, without making value judgments.
3. *Edit your list.* Reread the list and evaluate it. To do so, (a) select the most promising features, (b) cross out any that don't fit, and (c) add any obvious omissions.

☐ Writing

Once you've gathered your data and determined your objectives, the next step is writing your description.

1. Review your prewriting. After a brief gestation period (an hour, a half a day, or a day) in which you wait to acquire a more objective view of your prewriting, go back to your brainstorming/listing and reread it. Have you omitted all unneeded items and added any important omissions? If not, do so.

2. Organize your list. Make sure the items in the list are organized effectively. To communicate information to your readers, you must organize the data so readers can follow your train of thought. This is especially important in technical descriptions. You not only want your readers to understand the information, but also to visualize the mechanism or component. This visualization can be achieved by organizing your data spatially.

3. Title your draft. At the top of the page, write the name of your piece of equipment, tool, or mechanism.

4. Write a focus statement. In one sentence, write (a) the name of your topic (plus any identifying numbers), (b) the possible functions of your topic or your reason for writing the description, and (c) the number of parts composing your topic. This will eventually act as the introduction. For now, however, it can help you organize your draft and maintain your focus.

5. *Draft the text.* Use the sufficing technique discussed in earlier chapters. Write quickly without too much concern for grammatical or textual accuracy, and let what you write suffice for now. Just get the information on the page, focusing on overall organization and a few highlighting techniques (headings, perhaps). The time to edit is later.

6. *Sketch a rough graphic of your equipment, component, or mechanism.*

☐ Rewriting

Rewriting is the most important part of the process. This is the stage during which you fine tune, hone, sculpt, and polish your technical description, making it as perfect as it can be. A perfected description ensures your credibility. An imperfect description makes you and your company look bad.

Revise your draft as follows:

1. *Add* any detail required to communicate more effectively. This can involve brand names, model numbers, and/or specificity of detail (size, material, density, dimensions, color, weight, etc.).
2. *Delete* dead words and phrases for conciseness.
3. *Simplify* long-winded, old-fashioned words and phrases for easier understanding.
4. *Move* (cut and paste) information to ensure spatial organization. You don't want to give your reader a distorted view of your mechanism. To avoid doing so, the technical description must maintain a spatial order—left to right, right to left, etc. For example, let's say you are describing a pencil, graphically depicted horizontally so the eraser end is to the left and the graphite tip is to the right. This pencil consists of the eraser, metal ferrule, wooden body, and sharpened point (that's the correct spatial order). If you describe the eraser first, then the tip, then the body, and then the ferrule, you've distorted the spatial order.
5. *Reformat* your text for ease of access through highlighting techniques—headings, boldface type, font size and style, itemization, and so forth. Rewriting is also the time to perfect your graphics. When revising your description, make sure that your graphics are effective. To do so,
   - ☐ Add a figure number and title. Place these beneath the graphic. For example, "Figure 2.6. Exhalation Valve with Labeled Call-Outs."
   - ☐ Draw or reproduce graphics neatly.
   - ☐ Place the graphics in an appropriate location, near where you first mention them in the text.
   - ☐ Make sure that the graphics are an effective size. You don't want the graphics to be so small that your reader must squint to read them, nor do you want them to be so large that they overwhelm the text.

☐ Label the components. Use call-outs to name each part, as in Figure 2.6.

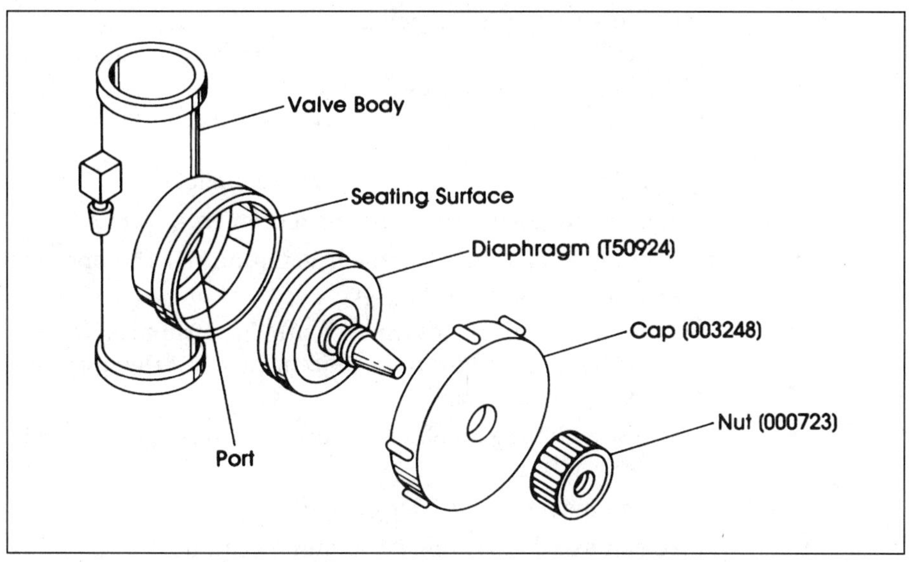

FIGURE 2.6 Exhalation Valve with Labeled Call-Outs
(Courtesy of Puritan Bennett Corp.)

6. *Enhance* the style of your text. Make sure that you've avoided impressionistic words. Instead, use photographic words which are precise and specific. In addition, strive for a personalized tone. Pronoun usage is rare and difficult to achieve in technical descriptions. However, even when writing about a piece of equipment, remember that "people write to people." Although you're describing an inanimate object, you're writing to another human being. Therefore, use pronouns to personalize the text. (Examples later in this chapter clarify how you can accomplish this.)
7. *Correct* your draft. Proofread to correct grammar errors as well as errors in content: measurements, shapes, textures, materials, colors, etc.
8. *Avoid sexist language.*

TECHNICAL DESCRIPTION CRITERIA CHECKLIST

The following checklist will help you in writing technical descriptions.

1. ☐ Does the technical description have a title noting your topic's name (and any identifying numbers)?
2. ☐ Does the technical description's introduction (a) state the topic, (b) mention its functions or the purpose of the mechanism, and (c) list the components?
3. ☐ Does the technical description's discussion use headings to itemize the components for reader-friendly ease of access?

4. ☐ Is the detail within the technical description's discussion photographically precise? That is, does the discussion portion of the description specify the following?

—Colors	—Capacities
—Sizes	—Textures
—Materials	—Identifying numbers
—Shapes	—Weight
—Density	—Make/model

5. ☐ Are all of the calculations and measurements correct?
6. ☐ Do you sum up your discussion using any of the optional conclusions discussed in this chapter?
7. ☐ Does your technical description provide graphics which are correctly labeled, appropriately placed, neatly drawn or reproduced, and appropriately sized?
8. ☐ Do you write using an effective technical style (low fog index) and a personalized tone?
9. ☐ Have you avoided sexist language?
10. ☐ Have you avoided grammatical and mechanical errors?

PROCESS LOG

The following student-written process log clarifies the way process is used in writing technical descriptions.

☐ Prewriting

We asked students to describe a piece of equipment, tool, or mechanism of their choice. One student chose to describe a cash register pole display. To do so, he first had to gather data using listing/brainstorming. He provided the following list:

1. Three parts
2. Pole printed circuit board (PCB)
3. Case assembly
4. Filter
5. Plastic materials

Next, we asked students to go back to their initial lists and edit them. Since this student's list was so sketchy, he didn't need to omit any information. Instead, he had to add omissions and missing detail, as in Figure 2.7.

☐ Writing

After the prewriting activity, we asked students to draft a technical description. Focusing only on overall organization, highlighting, detail, and a sketchy graphic, the aforementioned student wrote a rough draft (Figure 2.8).

☐ Rewriting

Once students completed their rough drafts, we used peer review groups (PRGs) to help each student revise his or her paper. In the following revision, students (a) added new detail for clarity, (b) corrected any errors, and (c) perfected graphics.

The preceding rough draft, complete with student comments, is shown in Figure 2.9.

The student incorporated these suggestions and prepared the finished copy (Figure 2.10).

SAMPLE TECHNICAL DESCRIPTION

Following is a professionally written technical description merging graphic and text (Figure 2.11).

This is a highly effective technical description. It has:

- ☐ A title
- ☐ An excellent introduction that lists topic, function, and components
- ☐ An effectively drawn and placed graphic
- ☐ A reader-friendly discussion with headings exactly corresponding to the call-outs in the drawing
- ☐ A precisely detailed discussion focusing on materials, color, dimensions, etc.
- ☐ An effective conclusion

Pole PCB

- ☐ length--15 mm
- ☐ width--5.1 mm
- ☐ tube length--10.8 mm
- ☐ face plate width--2.3 mm
- ☐ thick--1.7 mm
- ☐ PCB thickness--.2 mm
- ☐ 10" stranded wire with female connectors
- ☐ fiberglass and copper construction

Pole Case Assembly

- ☐ long--15.5 mm
- ☐ bottom width--2.5 mm
- ☐ top width--.9 mm
- ☐ mounting pole--5 mm high x 3.2 mm diameter
- ☐ tounge for mounting--3.1 mm
- ☐ lower mounting tounge--1.5 mm
- ☐ side mounting tounge--.8 mm high
- ☐ high--6.1 mm
- ☐ almond-colored plastic

Filter

- ☐ long--15.6 mm
- ☐ high--6.2 mm
- ☐ thick--.7 mm
- ☐ plastic, blue

FIGURE 2.7 Student's Listing/Brainstorming

The QL 169 Customer Pole Display provides the viewing of all transaction data for the customer. The display consist of a printed circuit board, a case assembly, and a filter display.

Display Circuit Board

- ☐ length--15 mm
- ☐ width--5.1 mm
- ☐ tube length--10.8 mm
- ☐ face plate width--2.3 mm
- ☐ thick--1.7 mm
- ☐ PCB thickness--.2 mm
- ☐ 10″ stranded wire with female connectors
- ☐ fiberglass and copper construction

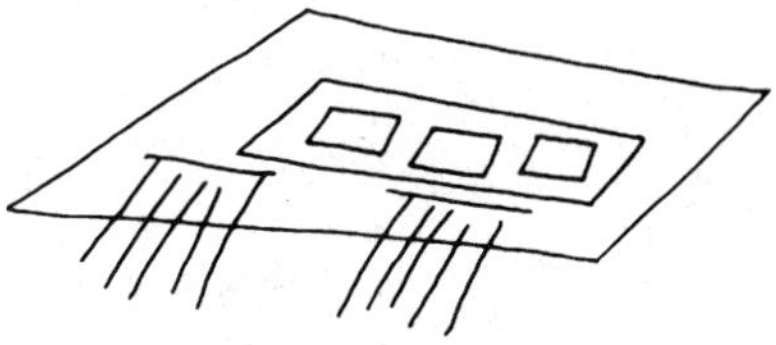

Display Case Assembly

- ☐ long--15.5 mm
- ☐ bottom width--2.5 mm
- ☐ top width--.9 mm
- ☐ mounting pole--5 mm high × 3.2 mm diameter
- ☐ tounge for mounting--3.1 mm
- ☐ lower mounting tounge--1.5 mm wide
- ☐ side mounting tounge--.8 mm high
- ☐ high--6.1 mm
- ☐ almond-colored plastic

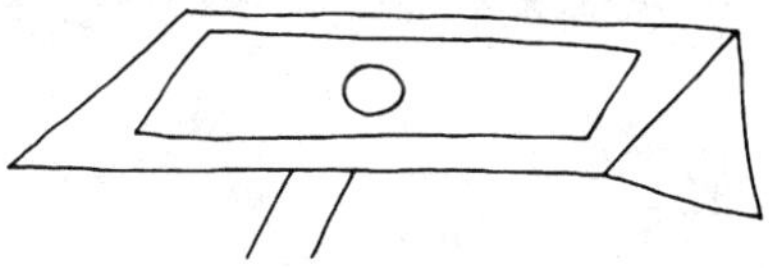

Display Filter

- ☐ long--15.6 mm
- ☐ high--6.2 mm
- ☐ thick--.7 mm
- ☐ plastic, blue

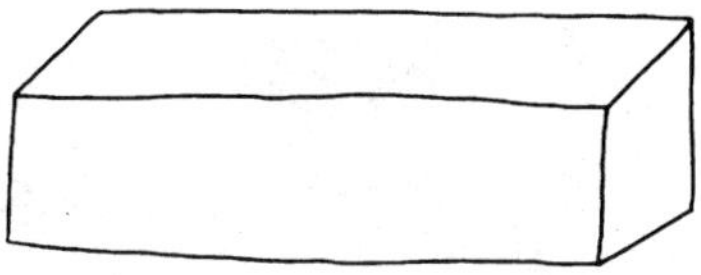

FIGURE 2.8 Student's Rough Draft

No Title

awkward

The QL169 Customer Pole Display provides the viewing of all transaction data for the customer. The display consist of a printed circuit board, a case assembly, and a filter display.

SP

Display Circuit Board

Make all caps

- ☐ length--15 mm
- ☐ width--5.1 mm
- ☐ tube length--10.8 mm
- ☐ face plate width--2.3 mm
- ☐ thick--1.7 mm *thickness*
- ☐ PCB thickness--.2 mm
- ☐ 10″ stranded wire with female connectors
- ☐ fiberglass and copper construction

Number your Components

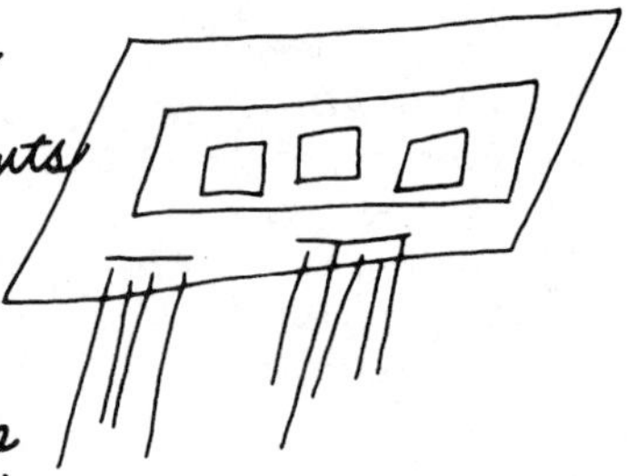

Too vague (specify)

Display Case Assembly

Make all Caps

- ☐ long--15.5 mm *length*
- ☐ bottom width--2.5 mm
- ☐ top width--.9 mm
- ☐ mounting pole--5 mm high × 3.2 mm diameter
- ☐ tounge for mounting--3.1 mm
- ☐ lower mounting tounge--1.5 mm wide
- ☐ side mounting tounge--.8 mm high
- ☐ high--6.1 mm *height*
- ☐ almond-colored plastic

SP

Number Components

vague

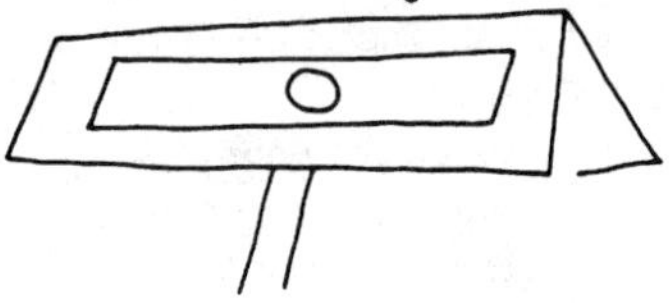

Display Filter

- ☐ long--15.6 mm *length*
- ☐ high--6.2 mm *height*
- ☐ thick--.7 mm *thickness*
- ☐ plastic, blue

what

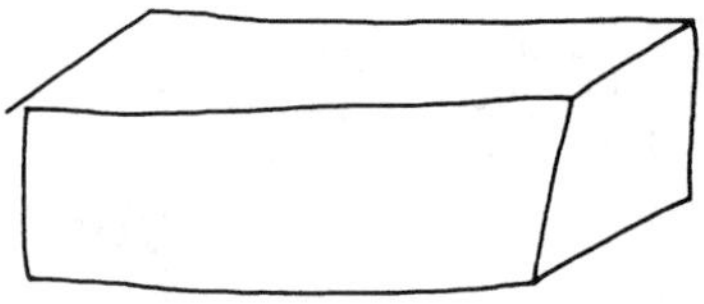

Add a conclusion

FIGURE 2.9 Students' Suggested Revisions

Assembly-Customer Pole Display

Item Description

1. POLE PCB ASSEMBLY
2. POLE CASE ASSEMBLY
3. DISPLAY FILTER

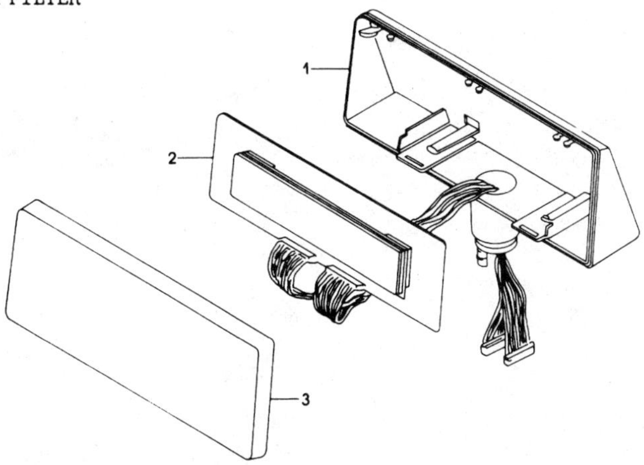

The QL169 pole display provides an alphanumeric display for customer viewing of cash register sales. The display consists of a printed circuit board, a case assembly, and a filter display.

1. Pole Printed Circuit Board

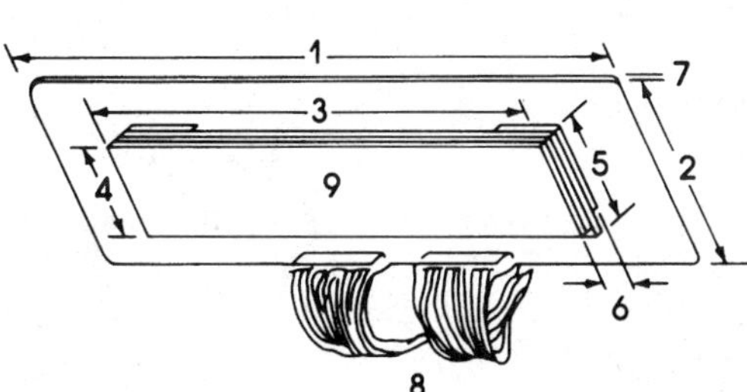

1. Length--15 mm
2. Width--5.1 mm
3. Tube length--10.8 mm
4. Tube faceplate width--2.3 mm
5. Tube total width--2.8 mm
6. Tube thickness--1.7 mm
7. PCB thickness--.2 mm
8. 20 conductor 10″ 22 gauge stranded wire with 2 AECC female connectors (AECC part #7214-001)

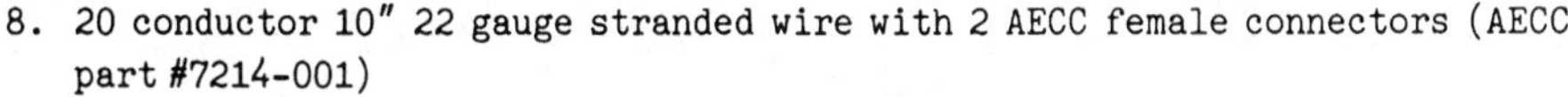

9. American Display Company blue phosphor display tube (ADC part #1172177)

The printed circuit board is constructed of fiberglass with copper etchings.

FIGURE 2.10 Student's Finished Copy

2. Pole Case Assembly

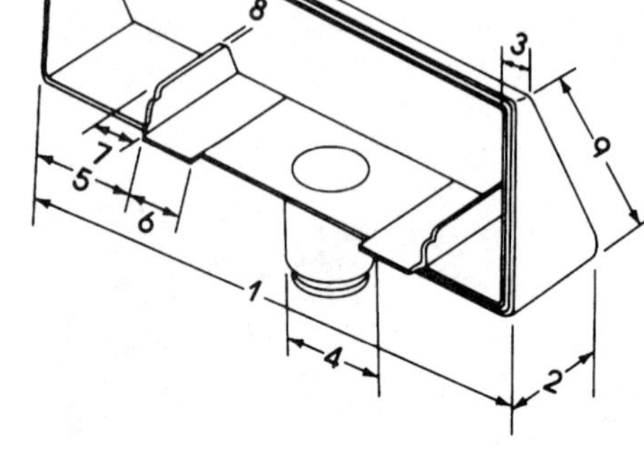

1. Length--15.5 mm
2. Bottom width--2.5 mm
3. Top width--.9 mm
4. Mounting pole--5 mm high and 3.2 mm in diameter
5. Mounting tongue inside width--3.1 mm from side of assembly
6. Lower mounting tongue--1.5 mm wide
7. Side mounting tongue--.8 mm high
8. Tongue thickness--.2 mm
9. Height--6.1 mm

Almond-colored ABS plastic is used in constructing the pole case assembly.

3. Display Filter

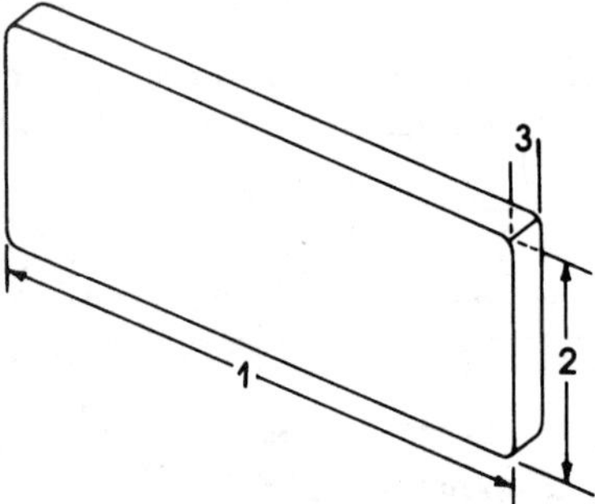

1. Length--15.6 mm
2. Height--6.2 mm
3. Thickness--.7 mm

Transparent blue plastic is used to construct the display filter.

The QL 169 pole display provides easy viewing of clerk transactions and ensures cashier accuracy.

FIGURE 2.10 Continued

Electronic A1 Feed Switch

The Electronic A1 Feed Switch provides an automatic solid-state closure (normally open type) after sensing the lack of presence of food. Figure 1 shows the three principal parts of the feed switch.

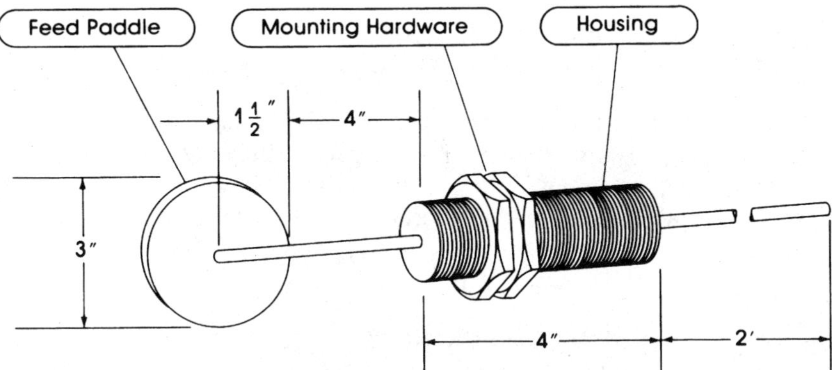

Figure 1. Electronic A1 Feed Switch

- HOUSING: The housing consists of a blue molded polycarbonate cylinder, 4″ in length and 1″ in diameter. Encircling the complete length of the housing are 1″ - 18 threads. At the middle of one end of the housing is a 2′ Belden 6906 cable. Attached to the middle of the other end of the housing is a feed paddle.
- MOUNTING HARDWARE: The mounting hardware consists of two, white, flat, hexagonal, plastic Delryn locking nuts, Grade 2, 1″ ID, $1\frac{1}{4}$″ OD, $\frac{1}{8}$″ thick, and 1″ - 18 EF threads per inch.
- FEED PADDLE: The feed paddle consists of a 3″ diameter, 16 Gauge (.060″) No. 304 galvanized steel, Finish 2D or better, welded to a No. 101 Finish 3D or better galvanized steel shaft $5\frac{1}{2}$″ in length and $\frac{1}{4}$″ in diameter. Exposed threads $\frac{1}{4}$″ - 20 and $\frac{1}{2}$″ in length protrude from the free end of the shaft. Welded on three sides to the middle of the 3″ diameter steel is the $1\frac{1}{2}$″ of the unthreaded shaft end. The feed paddle is white teflon coated to a thickness of $\frac{1}{64}$″.

The Electronic Feed Switch, with its five-year warranty, is reliable in dusty and dirty environments. The easy-to-install, short-circuit-protected switch is internally protected for transient voltage peaks to a maximum of 5 KV, for up to 10 msec duration. Our feed switch can detect dry concentrate, meal, rolled barley, fine and coarse feeds, as well as special feeds such as soybean meal and high-moisture corn.

FIGURE 2.11 Professionally-written Technical Description

GUIDELINES FOR WRITING DESCRIPTIONS

Now that you know how descriptions fit into entire documents, here are some simple guidelines for writing accurate, detailed descriptions. Follow them carefully as you prepare assignments in this class and on the job.

☐ Description Guideline 1: Remember Your Readers' Needs

The level of detail in a technical description depends on the purpose a description serves. Give readers precisely what they need—but no more. Often decision makers do not want too much detail. The level of detail will be reserved for later studies. Always know just how much detail will get the job done.

☐ Description Guideline 2: Be Accurate and Objective

More than anything else, readers expect accuracy in descriptions. Pay close attention to details. (As noted previously, the *degree* of detail in a description depends on the *purpose* of the document.) There are cases in which decision makers must have very specific data in order to make accurate decisions.

Along with accuracy should come objectivity. This term is more difficult to pin down, however. Some writers assume that an objective description leaves out all opinion. This is not the case. Instead, an objective description may very well include opinions that have these features:

- ☐ They are based on your professional background.
- ☐ They can be justified by the time you complete the description.
- ☐ They can be supported by details from the site or object being described.

☐ Description Guideline 3: Choose an Overall Organization Plan

Like other patterns discussed in this chapter, technical descriptions usually make up only parts of documents. Nevertheless, they must have an organization plan that permits them to be read as self-contained, stand-alone sections. Indeed, a description may be excerpted later for separate use.

Following are three common ways to describe physical objects and events. In all three cases, a description should move from general to specific.

That is, you begin with a view of the entire object or event. Then in the rest of the description, you focus on specifics. Headings may be used, depending on the format of the larger document.

1. **Description of the parts:** For many physical objects, like the basement floor and coastal scene in the previous cases, you will simply organize the description by moving from part to part.
2. **Description of the functions:** Often the most appropriate overall plan relies on how things work, not on how they look. In the sonar example, the reader was more interested in the way that the sender and receiver worked together to provide a map of the seafloor. This function-oriented description would include only a brief description of the parts.
3. **Description of the sequence:** If your description involves events, as in a police officer's description of an accident investigation, you can organize ideas around the major actions that occurred, in their correct sequence. As with any list, it is best to place a series of many activities into just a few groups. Four groups of 5 events each is much easier for readers to comprehend than a single list of 20 events.

□ Description Guideline 4: Use "Helpers" Like Graphics and Analogies

The words of a technical description need to come alive. Because your readers may be unfamiliar with the item, you must search for ways to connect with their experience and with their senses. Two effective tools are graphics and analogies.

Graphics respond to the desire of most readers to see pictures along with words. As readers move through your part-by-part or functional breakdown of a mechanism, they can refer to your graphic aid for assistance. The illustration helps you too, of course, in that you need not be as detailed in describing locations and dimensions of parts when you know the reader has easy access to a visual. Note how the diagrams in Figure 2.11 on page 89 give meaning to the technical details in the verbal descriptions.

Analogies, like illustrations, give readers a convenient handle for understanding your description. Put simply, an analogy allows you to describe something unknown or uncommon in terms of something that is known or more common. A brief analogy can sometimes save you hundreds of words of technical description. This paragraph description contains three analogies:

> Our company is equipped to help clean up oil spills with its patented product, SeaClean. This highly absorbent chemical is spread over the entire spill by means of a helicopter, which makes passes over the spill much like a lawn mower would cover the complete surface area of a lawn. When the chemical contacts the oil, it acts like sawdust coming in contact with oil on a garage floor. That is, the oil is immediately absorbed into the chemical and physically transformed into a product that is easily collected. Then our nearby ship can collect the product, using a machine that operates much like a vacuum cleaner.

This machine sucks the SeaClean (now full of oil) off the surface of the water and into a sealed container in the ship's hold.

☐ Description Guideline 5: Give Your Description the "Visualizing Test"

After completing a description, test its effectiveness by reading it to someone unfamiliar with the material—someone with about the same level of knowledge as your intended reader. If this person can draw a rough sketch of the object or events while listening to your description, then you have done a good job. If not, ask your listener for suggestions to improve the description. If you are too close to the subject yourself, sometimes an outside point of view will help refine your technical description.

EXAMPLES OF DESCRIPTION

This section contains two descriptions, one written at a U.S. office and the other produced overseas. The first example includes a description of physical parts and a brief operating procedure. (For a thorough discussion of process descriptions and instructions, see Chapter II.) The second includes only a description of physical parts. Both show the importance of graphics in technical descriptions.

☐ Description 1: Blueprint Machine

The human resources coordinator has been asked to assemble an orientation guide for new secretaries, office assistants, and other members of the office staff. The manual will contain descriptions and locations of the most common pieces of equipment in the office, sometimes with brief instructions for their use.

One section of her manual includes a series of short equipment descriptions organized by general purpose of the equipment. Model 5-2 on pages 94–95 includes a description of the office blueprint machine, which gets used by a wide variety of employees. Because the blueprint machine has an operating procedure that is not self-evident, the description includes a brief procedure that shows the manner in which the machine should be used.

☐ Description 2: Desk Stapler

The director of procurement in Saudi Arabia is changing his buying procedures. He has decided to purchase some basic office and audiovisual supplies from companies in nearby developing countries. For one thing, he thinks this move will save a lot of money. For another, he believes it will help the company get more projects from these nations, for the company name will become known as a firm that pumps back some of its profits into the local economies.

As a first step in this process, the director is sending possible suppliers a set of detailed descriptions of basic products it needs, such as pencils, photocopying paper, staplers, tape dispensers, and transparencies for overhead projectors. The director decides to describe the typical desk stapler in moderate detail so that potential suppliers will know that they must come up with a product that has the basic features of staplers manufactured in developed countries. Model 5-3 on pages 96–97 contains the description included in his report. Later, if need be, he could submit more detailed specifications listing exact measurements, metal grades, and so forth.

DESCRIPTIONS OF MECHANISMS

Descriptions of mechanisms should use ample graphics. Consider an overall drawing with the main parts and dimensions labeled. A sketch of the mechanism in action also will help your reader to envision its use. As you describe each main part or assembly, picture just that portion of the mechanism. Sometimes this will entail exploded or cutaway views. Figure 2.13 contains a list of terms used in mechanism descriptions; use the list to name configurations, materials, shapes, finishes, and methods for attachment of parts of your mechanism.

CONCLUDING DISCUSSION/ASSESSMENT

The concluding discussion assesses the efficiency, reliability, and practicality of the mechanism. This assessment may include an examination of the mechanism's advantages and disadvantages, its limitations, its optional uses, the comparison of one model to another model, and the cost and availability.

Example

The Bostich B8 desk stapler is compact and lightweight, making it easy to store and to transport. The finish is scratch resistant and rustproof. It can be used as a tacker as well as a paper stapler.

No more than 20 pages of copy can be stapled at one time. The Bostich Standard stapler is recommended for larger volume.

The recommended retail price is $8.95. A box of 5,000 staples is approximately $3.00. The Bostich Standard stapler is sold for $16.75. The Bostich staplers are available in most office supply stores.

Figures 2.14 and 2.15 show sample mechanism descriptions. Figure 2.14 is a general description while Figure 2.15 is a specific mechanism description employing far more detail. Be prepared to critique the samples in class.

TECHNICAL DESCRIPTION: BLUEPRINT MACHINE

Starts with a sentence definition and brief overview of two sections that follow.

A blueprint machine is a piece of office equipment used to make photographic reproductions of architectural plans, technical drawings, and other types of figures. The blueprint shows as white lines on blue paper. This description covers the physical parts of the machine and a brief operation procedure.

Physical Description

Begins section with dimensions of machine, before noting two main parts.

The blueprint machine is contained in a metal cabinet measuring 36" wide, 10" tall, and 18" deep. Typically, the machine is placed on a cabinet containing blueprint supplies. The most evident features of the machine are the controls and the paper path.

Uses three perspectives in illustration, for clarity.

Blueprint Machine

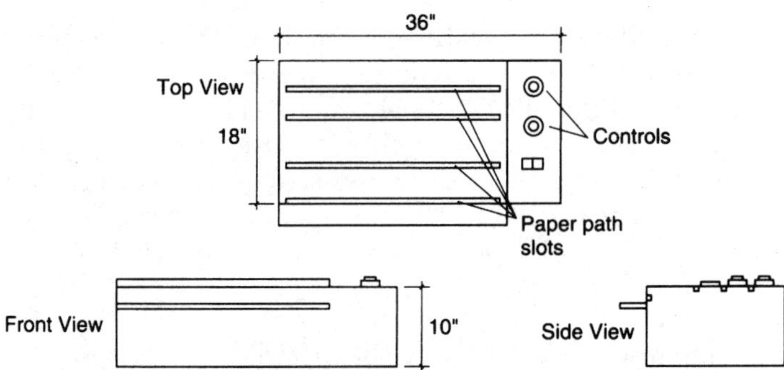

Controls: The controls for the machine are located on the top right-hand side of the case.

Describes three controls in same order that they are viewed—top to bottom.

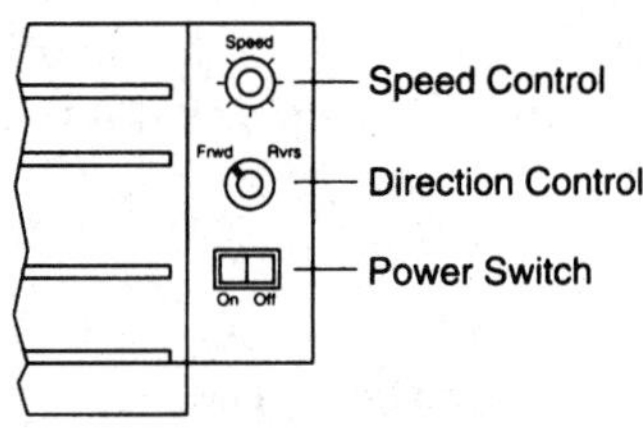

There are two knobs and one power switch. The topmost knob controls the speed of the paper feed. The lower knob changes the direction of the paper. The power switch turns the machine on and off.

MODEL 5-2 Detailed description

Integrates procedure with illustration.

Paper Path: The top of the machine has four horizontal slots. These slots are the openings to the paper path.

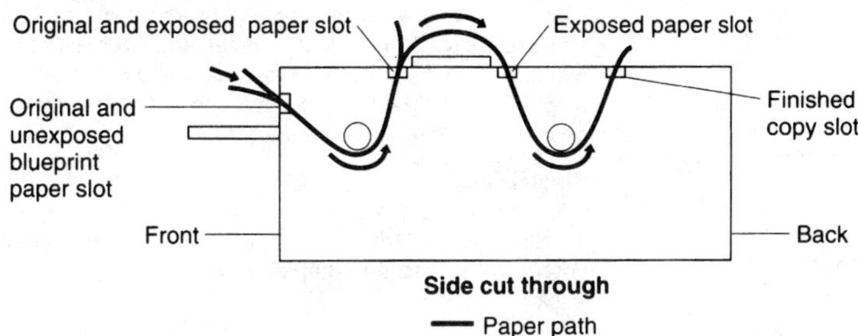

The first slot, beginning at the front of the machine, is the feed slot for the original and the unexposed blue print paper. The second slot is the discharge for the original and the exposed print paper. The third slot is the feed for developing the exposed blueprint paper. The fourth slot is the discharge for the finished blueprint copy.

Operation of the Blueprint Machine

Operating the blueprint machine involves setting the controls and making copies.

Includes brief instructions that help expand upon description of mechanism.

Setting the Controls:

1. Turn on the machine.
2. Set the paper path to forward.
3. Set the speed for the type of paper used.

Making Copies:

1. Place the original, face side up, on top of the blueprint paper, yellow side up.
2. Feed the two pieces of paper into the original feed slot.
3. Separate the original from the copy as they emerge from the discharge slot.
4. Feed the exposed blueprint paper into the developer slot.
5. Collect the copy as it emerges from the discharge slot.
6. Turn power off when desired copies have been made.

Conclusion

Blueprint machines are found in all McDuff offices and are used frequently. If a wide variety of employees understands how these machines function, our office will continue to run smoothly.

MODEL 5-2 Continued

TECHNICAL DESCRIPTION DESK STAPLER

Starts with purpose of mechanism.

Gives general dimensions plus list of main parts.

The stapler is a standard piece of office equipment used to drive a U-shaped piece of metal (staple) through papers, thus binding them together. Although staplers are made in different shapes and sizes, the description here is of the standard desk-use stapler. It is usually 6 to 8 in. long and made out of lightweight strips of metal. The major parts are the head, ejector, and base. The following description covers these main components.

Uses headings to highlight main parts.

Starts section with brief statement of function.

Stapler Head

The head is the part of the stapler that, when compressed, drives the staple from the ejector through the papers. The stapler head has two main parts—the outer casing and the U-shaped driver.

Helps unfamiliar audience by describing parts in terms of common shape.

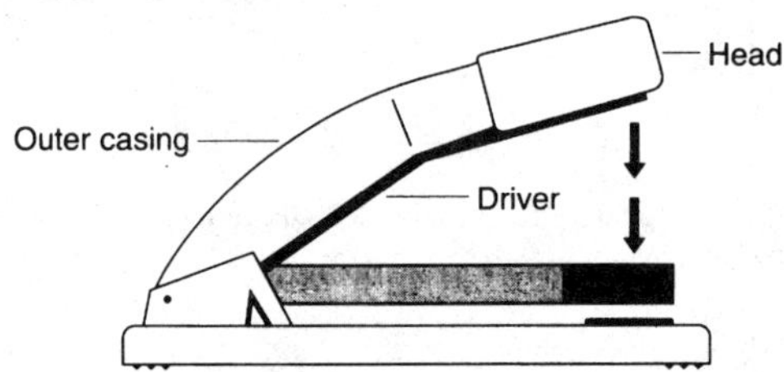

Uses direction ("downward") for clarity.

The outer casing is made of lightweight sheet metal. On a typical stapler it is about 7 in. long, 1 in. wide, and 3/4 in. high. A U-shaped piece with the open portion facing downward, it provides a sheath that wraps around the driver.

States function of part described.

The driver is a metal piece that fits inside the outer casing. On a typical stapler it is about 6 1/2 in. long, 1/2 in. wide, and 1/4 in. high. Like the outer casing, it is U-shaped with the open portion facing downward. The driver is connected to the outer casing at the base by a metal pin. This piece, made of heavier metal than the outer casing, serves to drive the staple out of the ejector.

Mentions function, shape, and general size.

Ejector

The ejector houses the staples that bind the pieces of paper together. Like the outer casing, it is made of U-shaped metal but with the open part of the U facing upward. This piece is about the same size as the driver. Inside the U of the ejector is a tray onto which the row of staples fits. These staples are forced to the front of the tray by a tension-mounted spring.

MODEL 5-3 Detailed description

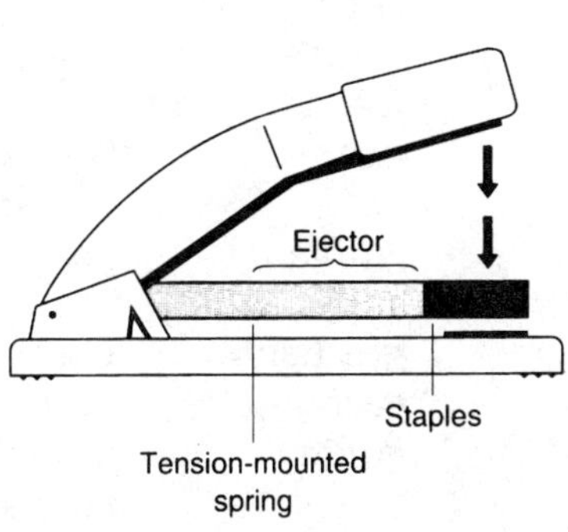

Uses common descriptive term ("tapered").

Base

The base is the heaviest and largest part of the stapler. It is about 8 in. long, 1 1/2 in. wide, and 1 in. thick. The base is tapered somewhat so that the edges closest to the bottom are longer than the edges near the top of the base, thus giving the entire stapler as much stability as possible. On the bottom of the base there are two rubber pieces, one at each end, that are riveted to the base and that cushion

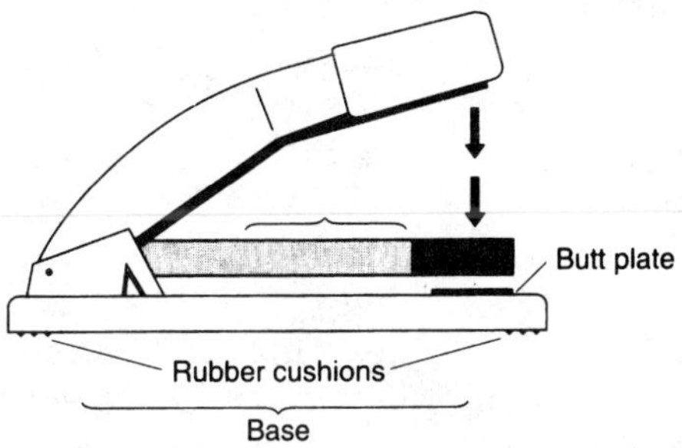

Uses comment on function to identify part.

the stapler from the surface on which it rests. On the top side of the base there is a butt plate that is used to flatten the staples when they are driven from the ejector through the paper. The head and ejector are connected to the base with a pin located at the rear of the stapler.

Ends with "wrap-up" to reinforce earlier points.

Conclusion

The standard stapler is a light-duty machine used mainly for paper binding. Because of its structural simplicity, it usually lasts a long time and can endure a significant amount of abuse (heavy pounding by some users, dropping onto floors, use with excessive amount of paper, etc.).

MODEL 5-3 Continued

TERMS USED IN MECHANISM DESCRIPTIONS

arc
arm
assembly

ball
bar
barrel
bearing
bevels
blade
bolt
bore
bow
brace
bracket
buckle
bushing

calibrations
cap
casing
channel
clamp
clip
coil
collar
cone
cotter pin

diaphragm
disk
dowel

extension arm
eye bolt

face
fin
fitting
flange
frame
funnel

gauge
gear
gradients
groove
guide

handle
hinge
hook
housing
hub

jacket

key

latch
leg
leg ring
lever
lip

marking
matting
mouth

nib
nozzle

nut
  slotted
  square
  wing

O-ring

pad
pin
plate
plug
plunger
pocket clip
point

ratchet
reservoir
ribbing
ring
rivet

screw
  metal
  recess
  wood
shell
sleeve
slot
socket
spline
spool
spring
stem
stopper
switch

teeth
threads
tip
toe plate
tray
trigger
tube

wand
washer
webbing
wedge

yoke plate

<u>Materials</u>

aluminum
copper
non-corroding
  metal
plastic
pot metal
steel
  anodized
  drop-forged
  galvanized
  stainless

FIGURE 2.13 Some terms used in mechanism descriptions

Finishes	Shapes	Attachment Methods
brushed	circular	coiled
buffed	concave	compressed
etched	conical	crimped
glazed	convex	flange/slot attachment
lacquered	cylindrical	glued
lustrous	flared	riveted
matte (dull)	grooved	screwed
stain	hexagonal	soldered
semi-gloss	hollow	welded
	octagonal	
	rectangular	
	solid	
	square	
	tapered	
	triangular	
	u-shaped	

FIGURE 2.13 Continued

A STOP VALVE

Definition and purpose

A screw-down stop valve is a tap which is used to control the flow of liquids and gases. A water faucet is a stop valve.

Operation of parts

A stem or screw spindle is surmounted by a handwheel. The water flows through an opening whose edge forms the valve seat. The stem has a disc which is usually provided with a replaceable sealing washer to make the actual contact with the seat and thus stop the flow of water.

Parts named in text

To open the tap, the disc is raised by rotating the handwheel in a counter-clockwise direction so that the stem is screwed out of the valve body. Clockwise rotation brings the valve disc into contact with the seat and thus closes the tap. Figures 1 and 2 show the screw-down stop valve in the closed and open positions.

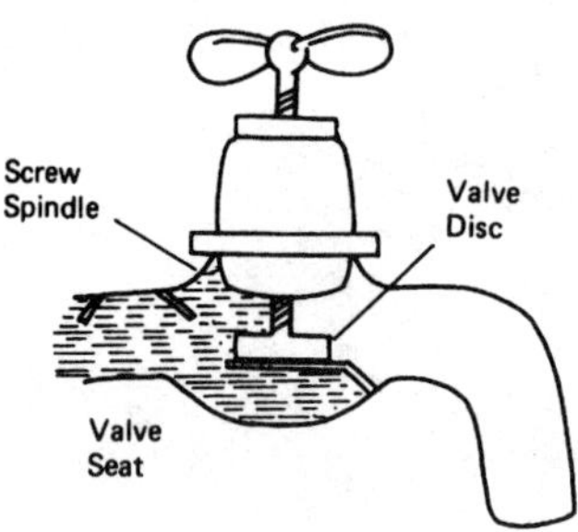

Figure 1 Closed

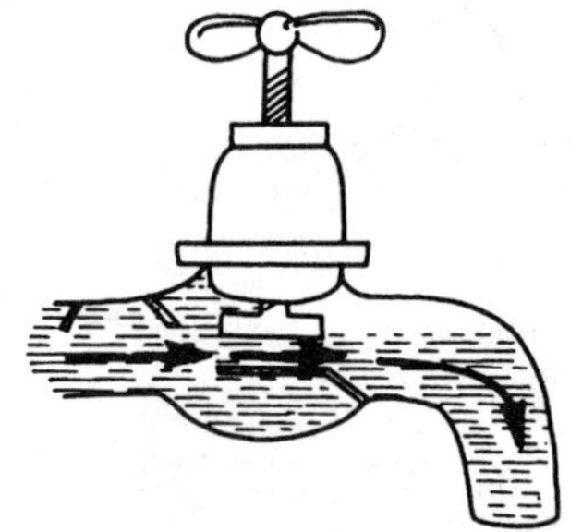

Figure 2 Open

Concluding discussion

Other types of taps are plug cocks and sluice valves. The screw-down stop valve allows for more accurate control of the rate of flow of the fluid than does the plug cock. Sluice valves, which have stuffing boxes to prevent leakage, are used to control the flow in water mains, pipelines, and so forth. Screw-down stop valves are readily available from plumbing supply houses.

FIGURE 2.14 General description of a mechanism

DESCRIPTION OF THE VENOJECT BLOOD COLLECTION SYSTEM

Intended audience

This description of the Venoject Blood Collection System, which is used for obtaining blood specimens for laboratory tests, is intended for medical laboratory students.

General Description

Definition and purpose

The Venoject Blood Collection System obtains blood specimens for laboratory tests. It is designed to obtain multiple blood sample tubes from a patient with only one puncture site required.

Overall description

Assembled, the steel, glass, and plastic parts measure approximately 6 inches long depending upon the length of the selected tube. Figure 1 shows the assembled system:

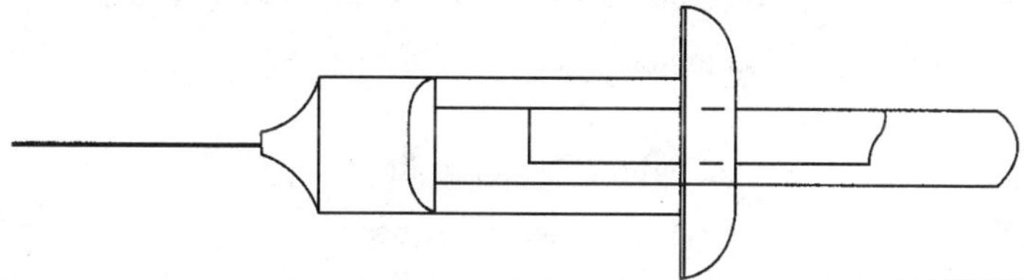

Figure 1 The Venoject Blood Collection System

Theory

Process

The system operates on the principle of a vacuum in the collecting tube. First, the stopper on the top of the tube is punctured by the needle, allowing the blood sample to flow into the tube and stop when the tube is full. Second, when the full tube is removed, the needle stops the blood flow until another tube is punctured by the needle. This procedure can

FIGURE 2.15 Specific description of a mechanism (courtesy of student Joanne Fata)

be repeated for each tube needed for specific blood tests with no discomfort to the patient. Figure 2 shows the Venoject System in a venipuncture procedure:

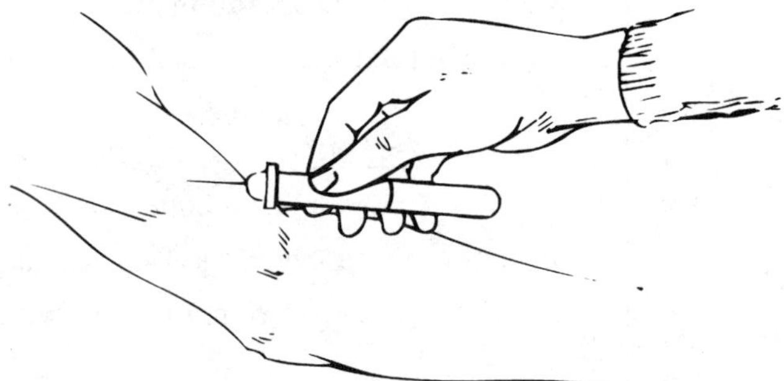

Figure 2 Venoject System in venipuncture procedure

List of parts

The Venoject System consists of three main parts: the double-pointed needle assembly, the adapter, and the blood-collecting tube.

Functional Description

Purpose of first part

Description

The first main part, the needle assembly, functions in two ways: it pierces the skin at the site, and it closes off the blood flow when a collecting tube is not attached. The needle assembly consists of three subparts: the needle, the connector, and the cover. The 2.4-inch sterile needle is hollow steel. A 2.1-inch plastic connector fits securely over the needle at the halfway point. It has threads that screw into the holder and an extended tube to protect the end of the needle which is inserted into the collecting tube. A plastic cover

FIGURE 2.15 Continued

protects the needle until it is to be used. Figure 3 illustrates the needle and plastic cover:

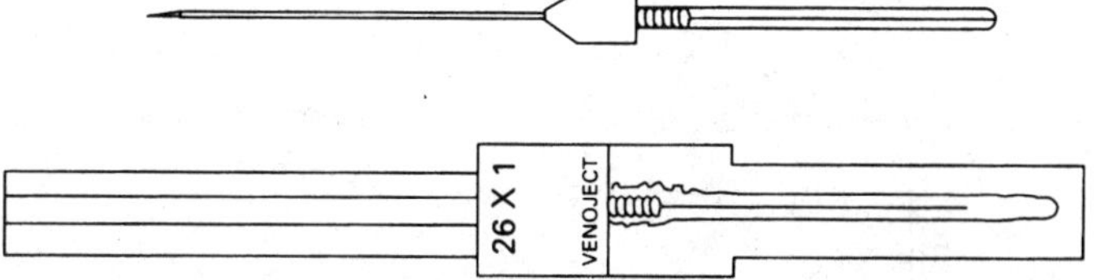

Figure 3 Venoject double-pointed needle with plastic cover

Purpose of second part

Description

The second functional part, the adapter holder, connects the needle and the collecting tube. The 2.8-inch, plastic, cylindrical holder has a diameter of ¾ inch. One end is threaded to receive the needle; the other end is open to receive the collecting tube. Figure 4 shows the holder:

Figure 4 Venoject System holder

Purpose of third part

Description

The third part, the collecting tube, is designed as a vacuum to collect the blood. It consists of three subparts: the tube, a rubber stopper, and a label tape. Hollow, glass tubes are available in 3-inch, 3½-inch, and 4-inch lengths; the two shorter tubes have a ¼-inch diameter while the 4-inch tube has a ½-inch diameter. A color-coded rubber stopper is inserted into or over the open end of the tube. The color of the stopper indicates whether the tube contains an anti-coagulant

FIGURE 2.15 Continued

which is necessary for certain blood tests. The collecting tubes in general use are not sterile; sterile tubes are available when needed for bacterial determinations. A plastic label to record the patient's name and date is taped onto every tube. Figure 5 shows three collecting tubes with rubber stoppers and labels in place:

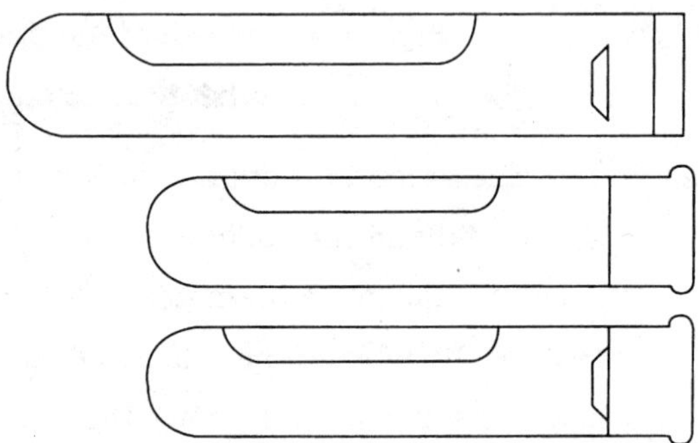

Figure 5 Venoject collecting tubes

Concluding Discussion

Assessment

The Venoject Collecting System is an efficient apparatus for collecting blood for any number of laboratory tests. It allows the technician to obtain multiple samples while preserving the patient's vein. Because it is a disposable system, bacteria and hepatitis cannot be transmitted from one patient to another. It is available at medical supply houses.

FIGURE 2.15 Continued

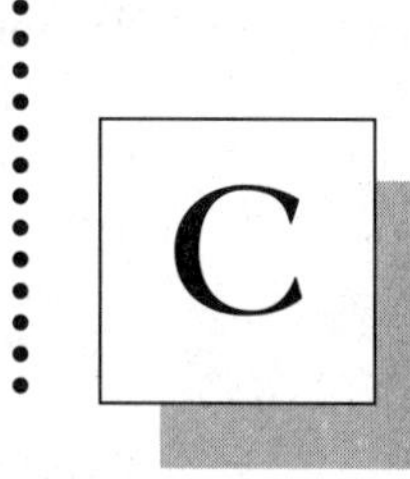

Instructions

OBJECTIVES

Instructions are the heartbeat of technical writing. Every product manufactured comes complete with instructions. You can receive instructions for putting together children's toys, setting up stereo systems, installing automotive parts, constructing electronic equipment, maintaining computers, and operating fighter planes.

There are even instructions for making chicken noodle soup. One major soup manufacturer recently stopped printing instructions for soup preparation on its cans of soup. Executives assumed that such information was unnecessary. They were mistaken. The company received thousands of calls from consumers asking how to prepare the soup. Responding to befuddled customers, the company reverted to printing these instructions. "Pour soup in pan. Slowly stir in one can of water. Heat to simmer, stirring occasionally."

Even pop-top cans of soda include instructions: "1. Lift up. 2. Pull back. 3. Push down." When such simple items as soup and soda need instructions, you can imagine how necessary instructions are for complex products and procedures. You must include instructions whenever your audience needs to know how to:

- Operate a mechanism
- Install equipment
- Manufacture a product
- Package a product
- Restore a product
- Correct a problem
- Service equipment
- Troubleshoot a system

Unpack equipment	Plant
Test components	Harvest
Maintain equipment	Set up a product
Clean a product	Implement a procedure
Monitor a system	Construct anything
Repair a system	Assemble a product

Whatever your objectives are for writing an instruction, the following will help you do so: (a} criteria for writing instructions, (b) process to follow (including sample process log), and (c) examples.

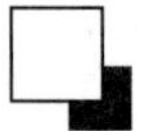

CRITERIA FOR WRITING INSTRUCTIONS

Follow these criteria for writing an effective instruction.

☐ Organization

As the writer of the instruction, you know what your objectives are. You know why you're writing and what you want to accomplish. However, your readers, upon picking up the instruction, are unaware of your intentions. Whereas you know where you're going, they must patiently await further information regarding the destination. To help your readers follow your train of thought, provide them with a road map. One way to do this is through organization. A neatly organized instruction can orient your readers, thereby helping them follow your directions. To organize your instruction effectively, include an *introduction,* a *discussion,* and a *conclusion.*

Introduction

In the first paragraph of your instruction, tell your readers what *topic* you'll be discussing. This could involve mentioning the product's name or commenting about its capabilities and/or ease of use. Next, state *how many steps* are involved in the instruction. Look at the following examples:

Good

The following seven steps will help you operate the Udell PQ 4454 Overhead projector.

Better

The Udell PQ 4454 is an overhead projector for business and school. It's easy to use and requires little maintenance. Follow these eight steps for operating the machine.

Best

The Udell PQ4454 Overhead Projector is used to project written or graphic material onto a screen or wall. Because of its capability to enlarge and project, it is ideal for use in schools or businesses. Six simple steps will help you operate the projector.

The first of the preceding examples includes product plus steps; the second adds ease of use. The third example, however, is best because it mentions product, steps, ease of use, plus capabilities.

In addition to this introductory overview focusing on the topic and steps to be performed, you also might want to tell your readers what tools or equipment they'll need to perform the procedures. You can provide this through a simple list, or perhaps you'll want to add graphics (the type of tool needed plus a picture of that tool). This depends on whether your readers are high tech, low tech, or lay.

Example #1: List of Required Tools
Tools Required
1—2 mm hex wrench
1—pliers

Example #2: List of Required Tools plus Graphic Depiction
Tools Required
1—2 mm hex wrench

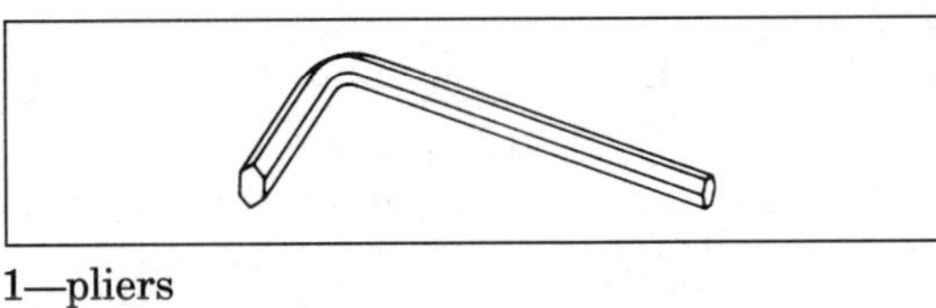

1—pliers

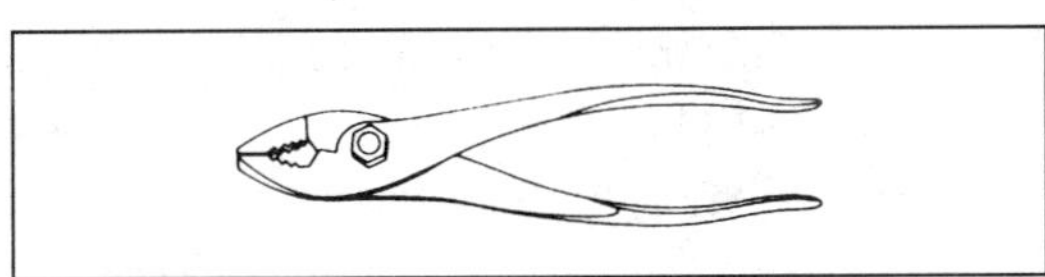

Finally, preface your instructions with warnings. Inform readers about (a} potentially dangerous steps or equipment, (b) precautions regarding appropriate clothing (gloves, work boots, safety glasses), and (c) the need to follow instructions chronologically.

These warnings should be emphatic. To achieve emphasis, use color, boxes, larger font, white space, and/or words such as *danger*, *warning*, *important*, or *caution*. Don't let your readers begin before they are cautioned.

Discussion

Itemize and thoroughly discuss the steps in your instruction. They must be organized *chronologically*—a step-by-step sequence. Obviously, you cannot tell your readers to do step six, then go back to step two, then accomplish step twelve, then do step four. Such a distorted sequence would fail to accomplish your goals. To operate machinery, monitor a system, or construct equipment, your readers must follow a chronological sequence. You must be sure that your instruction is chronologically accurate.

Conclusion

As with a technical description, you can conclude your instruction in various ways. You can end your instruction with a (a) comment about warranties, (b) sales pitch highlighting the product's ease of use, (c) reiteration of the product's applications, or (d) summary of the company's credentials. (For examples, see the discussion on conclusions in Chapter I.)

Another valid way to conclude, however, is to focus on *disclaimers,* as in the following example:

> This operating guide to the Udell PQ 4454 Overhead Projector is included primarily for ease of customer use. Service and application for anything other than normal use or replacement parts must be performed by a trained and qualified technician.

□ Audience Recognition

How many times have you read an instruction and been left totally confused? You were told to "place the belt on the motor pulley," but you didn't know how. Or you were told to "discard the used liquid in a safe container," but you didn't know what was safe for this specific type of liquid. You were told to "size the cutting according to regular use," but you had never regularly performed this activity.

Here's a typical instruction, written without considering audience.

> To overhaul the manual starter, proceed as follows: Remove the engine's top cover. Untie starter rope at anchor and allow starter rope to slowly wind onto pulley. Tie a knot on the end of starter rope to prevent it from being pulled into housing. Remove pivot bolt and lift manual starter assembly from power head.

Although many high-tech readers might be able to follow these instructions, many more readers will be confused. How do you remove the engine's top cover? Where's the anchor? Where's the pivot bolt and how do you remove it? What's the power head?

The problem is caused by writers who assume that their readers have high tech knowledge. This is a mistake for several reasons. First, even high-tech readers often need detailed information because technology changes daily. You can't assume that every high-tech reader is up-to-date on these technical changes. Thus, you must clarify. Second, low-tech and lay readers—and that's most of us—carefully read each and every step, desperate for clear and thorough assistance.

As writer, you must provide your readers with the clarity and thoroughness they require. To do this, recognize accurately who your readers are and give them what they want, whether that amounts to technical updates for high-tech readers or precise, even simple information for low-tech or lay readers. The key to success as a writer of instructions is, "Don't assume anything. Spell it all out—clearly and thoroughly!"

□ Graphics

As with technical descriptions, clarify your points graphically using the super comic book look. Use drawings and/or photographs which are big, simple, clear, keyed to the text, and labeled accurately. Not only do these graphics make your instructions more visually appealing, but also they help your readers and you. What the reader has difficulty understanding, or you have difficulty writing clearly, your graphic can help explain pictorially.

A company's use of graphics often depends on audience. With a high-tech reader, the graphic might not be needed. However, with a low-tech reader, the graphic is used to help clarify. Look at the following examples of instructions for the same procedure. The first example uses text with the super comic book look; the second uses text without graphics.

EXAMPLE 1: TEXT WITH SUPER COMIC BOOK GRAPHICS

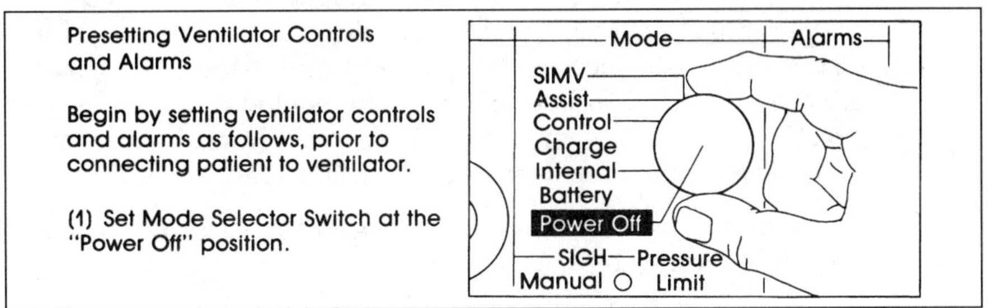

(Courtesy of Puritan Bennett Corp.)

EXAMPLE 2: TEXT WITHOUT GRAPHICS FOR HIGH-TECH READERS

TABLE 1. Operating Instructions

Location Item	Action	Remarks
	NOTE For additional operating instructions, refer to Companion 2800 operator's manual.	
1. MODE switch	Set to POWER OFF.	
2. Rear panel	Ensure that instructions on all labels are observed.	
3. Patient tubing circuit	Assemble and connect to unit.	See Table 2, step 3.
4. Power Cord	Connect to 120/220 V ac grounded outlet.	If power source is external battery, connect external battery cable to unit per Table 2, step 4.
5. Cascade I humidifier	Connect to unit.	See Table 2, step 2.

(Courtesy of Puritan Bennett Corp.)

Note that example 1 uses large, bold graphics to supplement the text, clearly depicting what action must be taken. This is appropriate for a low-tech end-user. On the other hand, example 2, written for a manufacturer's technician (high tech), assumes greater knowledge and, therefore, deletes the graphic.

☐ Style

1. Number your steps. Don't use bullets or the alphabet. Numbers, which you can never run out of, help your readers refer to the correct step. In contrast, if you used bullets, your readers would have to count to locate steps— seven bullets for step seven, etc. If you used the alphabet, you'd be in trouble when you reached step twenty-seven.

2. Use highlighting techniques. Boldface, different size and style font, emphatic warning words, color, italicization, etc. call attention to special concerns. A danger, caution, warning, or specially required technique must be evident to your reader. If this special concern is buried in a block of unappealing text, it will not be read. This could be dangerous to your reader or costly to you and your company. To avoid lawsuits and/or to help your readers see what is important, call it out through formatting.

3. Limit the information within each step. Don't overload your reader by writing lengthy steps, as follows:

1. Start the engine and run it to idling speed while opening the radiator cap and inserting the measuring gauge until the red ball within the glass tube floats either to the acceptable green range or to the dangerous red line.

Instead, separate distinct steps, as follows:

1. Start the engine and run it to idling speed.
2. Open the radiator cap and insert the measuring gauge.
3. Note whether the red ball within the glass tube floats to the acceptable green range or up to the dangerous red line.

4. Develop your points thoroughly. Don't say, "After rotating the discs correctly, grease each with an approved lubricant." Instead, clarify what you mean by correct rotating and specify the approved lubricant, as in the following example:

1. Rotate the discs clockwise so that the tabs on the outside edges align.
2. Lubricate the discs with 2 oz. of XYZ grease.

Unless you tell your readers what you mean, they won't know.

5. Use short words and phrases. Remember the fog index.

6. Begin your steps with verbs—the imperative mood. Note that each of the numbered steps in the following instruction begins with a verb:

1. *Number* your steps.
2. *Use* highlighting techniques.
3. *Limit* the information within each step.
4. *Develop* your points thoroughly.
5. *Use* short words and phrases.
6. *Begin* your steps with verbs.

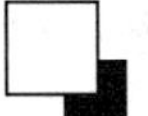

PROCESS

Now that you know what should be included in an instruction, it's time to write. But how do you start? Where do you begin?

As in other technical writing activities, follow a step-by-step process: *prewriting* to gather data and determine objectives, writing to draft your correspondence, and *rewriting* to revise and perfect.

☐ Prewriting

You've already been introduced to three prewriting techniques: reporters' questions, clustering/mind mapping, and brainstorming/listing. For writing an instruction, reporters' questions would be a good place to start gathering data and determining objectives. Ask yourself:

- ☐ *Who* is my reader?
  - —High tech?
  - —Low tech?
  - —Lay?
- ☐ *What* detailed information is needed for my audience? For example, a low-tech or lay reader will be content with "inflate sufficiently" whereas an instruction geared toward high-tech readers will require "inflate to 25 psi."
- ☐ *How* must this instruction be organized?
  - —Chronologically
- ☐ *When* should the procedure occur?
  - —Daily, weekly, monthly, quarterly, biannually, or annually?
  - —As needed?
- ☐ *Why* should the instruction be carried out?
  - —To repair, maintain, install, operate, etc. (See the list of reasons for using an instruction at the beginning of this chapter.)

Once you've gathered this information, you can use brainstorming to sketch out a rough list of the steps required in the instruction and the detail needed for clarity. After that, your major responsibility is to sequence your steps chronologically. To accomplish this goal, use a prewriting technique called *flowcharting*.

Flowcharts chronologically trace the stages of an instruction, visually revealing the flow of action, decision, authority, responsibility, input/output, preparation, and termination of process. Flowcharting is not just a graphic way to help you gather data and sequence your instruction, however. It is two-dimensional writing. It provides your reader content as well as a panoramic view of an entire sequence. Rather than just reading an instruction step by step, having little idea what's around the corner, with a flowchart your reader can figuratively stand above the instruction and see where it's going. With a flowchart, readers can anticipate cautions, dangers, and warnings, since they can see at a glance where the steps lead.

To create a flowchart, use the International Standardization Organization (ISO) flowchart symbols shown in Figure 2.16.

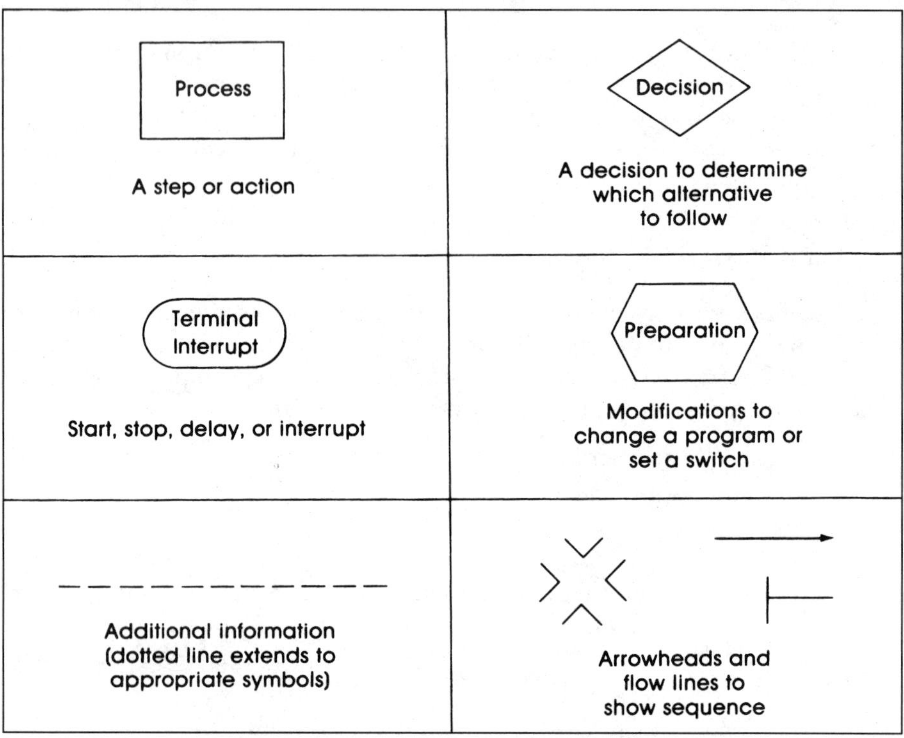

FIGURE 2.16 Flow-charting Symbols

Figure 2.17 shows an excellent example of a flowchart, visually depicting an instruction's sequence.

☐ Writing

Once you've graphically depicted your instruction sequence using a flowchart, the next step is to write a rough draft of the instruction.

1. Review your prewriting. In doing so, you will accomplish the following:

- ☐ *Clarify audience.* Now is a good time to review your reporters' questions and to determine if your initial assumptions regarding audience are still correct. If your attitude toward your audience has changed, redefine your readers and their needs.
- ☐ *Determine your focus.* In your prewriting, you answered the question *why.* Are you still certain of your objectives for writing the instruction? If so, write a one-sentence thesis or statement of objectives to summarize this purpose. For example, you could write, "This instruc-

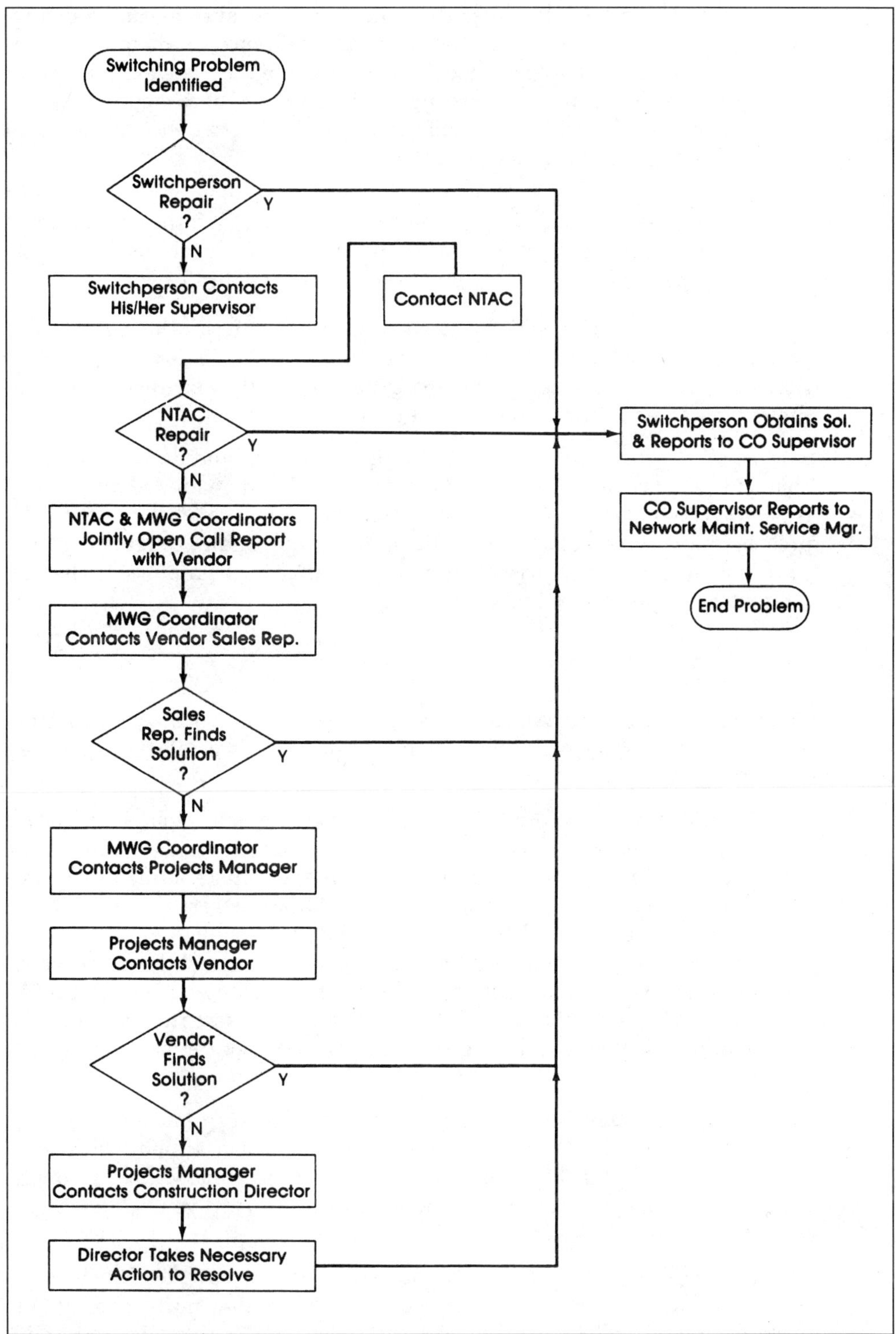

FIGURE 2.17 Flow-chart of Handling Service Problems

tion should be followed so that glitches in the system can be discovered and corrected." This thesis or topic sentence will help you maintain your focus throughout the instruction. If you are uncertain about your purpose for writing the instruction, however, rethink the situation. You will not be able to write an effective instruction until your objectives are clearly stated.

- ☐ *Organize your steps.* Review your flowchart to determine if any steps in the instruction have been omitted or misplaced. If the chronological sequence is incorrect, reorganize your detail. If the chronology is correct, you're ready to move on to the next step in drafting.

2. Review the instruction criteria. Before you write the rough draft, remind yourself what the instruction will consist of. You'll need an introduction, a discussion with itemized steps, graphics to help your reader perform the requested procedures, and a conclusion.

3. Write the draft. You've gathered your data and determined your objectives. You've correctly sequenced the steps and reminded yourself of the instruction criteria. At this point, you should feel comfortable with the prospect of writing. Follow the sufficing technique again, roughly drafting your instruction. Don't worry about perfect grammar or graphics. Perfecting the text comes in the next step, rewriting.

☐ Rewriting

Rewriting, the last stage in the process, is the time to perfect your instruction. To do so, reread your instruction and improve it using the eight-step rewriting procedure.

1. Add detail for clarity. Don't hope you've said enough to clarify your steps. Tell your readers *exactly* how to do it or why to do it. Part of detail involves warnings and cautions, for example. Make sure that you've added all necessary dangers or concerns. In addition, assess each step. Have you added sufficient detail to clarify your intent? For instance, if you are writing to a lay reader, you don't want to say merely "insert the guideposts." You must say, "Before inserting the guide post, dig a 2-ft. deep by 2-ft. wide hole. Pour the ready-mixed concrete into the hole. Insert the post into the hole and hold it steady until the concrete starts to set (approximately one minute)."

2. Delete. Omit unnecessary words and phrases to achieve conciseness. In addition, delete extraneous information which a high-tech reader might not find useful. This, however, could be dangerous. What you might see as extraneous, your reader might see as necessary. If you delete any information, do so carefully.

3. Simplify. Don't overload your steps. If you have too much information in any one stage, divide this detail into smaller units, adding new steps. Doing so will help your readers follow your instructions. Simplify your word usage.

4. Move information. Make sure that the correct chronological sequence has been achieved.

5. Reformat using highlighting techniques. If you include dangers, cautions, warnings, or additional information for clarity, set these off (make them emphatic) through formatting. Use color, windowing, font size and style, emphatic words, graphics, etc.

6. Enhance your text. Use the imperative mood for each step in your instruction. Whenever an action is required, begin with a verb to emphasize the action. In addition, you can enhance your text through personalization. Remember, people write to people. To achieve this person-to-person touch, add pronouns to your instruction.

7. Correct your instruction for accuracy. Proof your text for grammatical correctness as well as for contextual accuracy.

8. Avoid sexist language.

EFFECTIVE INSTRUCTION CHECKLIST

Use the following checklist to make sure that your instruction is effectively written.

1. ☐ *Does the instruction have an effective introduction?*
   —Is the topic mentioned?
   —Are the steps listed?
   —Has a reason for performing the operation been provided?
   —Are ease of use or capabilities mentioned?
   —Has a list of required tools been provided?
2. ☐ *Are the steps in the instruction's discussion effectively developed?*
   —Will a low-tech or lay reader be able to perform the requested operations based on what has been said, or must additional information be added for clarity?
3. ☐ *Is the instruction's discussion effectively presented?*
   —Are the steps overloaded and difficult to follow, or does each step present one clearly defined operation?
   —Are highlighting techniques effectively used? These should include graphics such as comic-book-look photographs or line drawings and correctly placed emphatic warnings (using color and/or universal symbols).
4. ☐ *Does the instruction's discussion contain the same number of steps as mentioned in the introduction?*
5. ☐ *Is the discussion organized chronologically?*
6. ☐ *Do the steps begin with verbs?*
7. ☐ *Does the instruction reveal a correct sense of audience?*
   —High tech?
   —Low tech?
   —Lay readers?

—Sexist language avoided?
—Personalized words (pronouns) used?

8. ☐ *Is the conclusion effective?*
—Have warranties been mentioned?
—Is a sales pitch provided showing the ease of use?
—Has the conclusion reiterated a reason for performing the steps?
—Does the conclusion focus on credentials?
—Are disclaimers provided?

9. ☐ *Is correct technical writing style used?*

10. ☐ *Have grammatical and textual errors been avoided?*

PROCESS LOG

Following is an example of an instruction collaboratively written by a group of students. To write this instruction, the students gathered data, determined objectives and sequenced their instruction through prewriting, drafted an instruction in writing, and finally revised their draft in rewriting.

Their assignment was to write an instruction on how to use an overhead projector, an item readily available in most classrooms.

☐ Prewriting

Figure 2.18 illustrates reporter's questions and students' flowcharting.

☐ Writing

After completing the prewriting, the students composed a draft, complete with sketchy graphics (Figure 2.19).

☐ Rewriting

The students revised the rough draft, considering all the postwriting techniques discussed in this text. The revision is shown in Figure 2.20. The students then prepared their finished copy (Figure 2.21).

SAMPLE INSTRUCTION

Figure 2.22 is an excellent student-written instruction.

Reporter's Questions/Listing

☐ Who is the reader?

Lay Reader - End User

☐ What detail is needed?

- Turn on
- Turn off
- Focus
- Warnings
- Use of transparencies
- Cautions
- Size of viewed image

☐ How must the detail be organized?

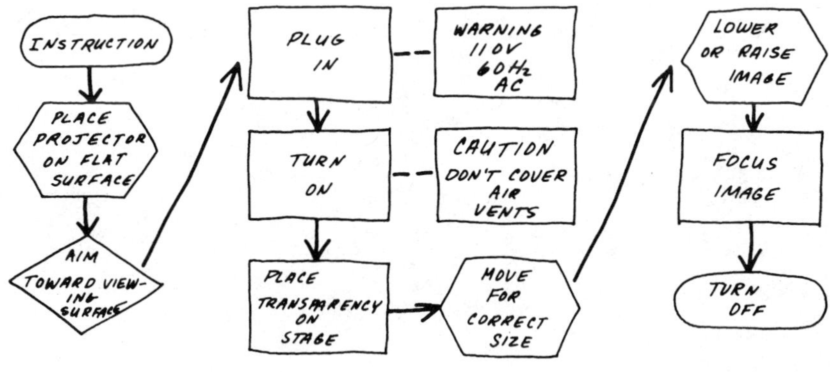

FIGURE 2.18 Students' Prewriting

The Udell Overhead Projector projescts material on a flat surface. Follow these five steps to do so.

1. Place the machine on a flat surface within viewing range of the screen.
2. Plug power plug into a wall outlet and turn the machine on.
3. Put the transparency on the projectors horizontal viewing surface.
4. Move the image up or down for better viewing and focus image by adjusting the focus knob.
5. Turn machine off when completed and umplug.

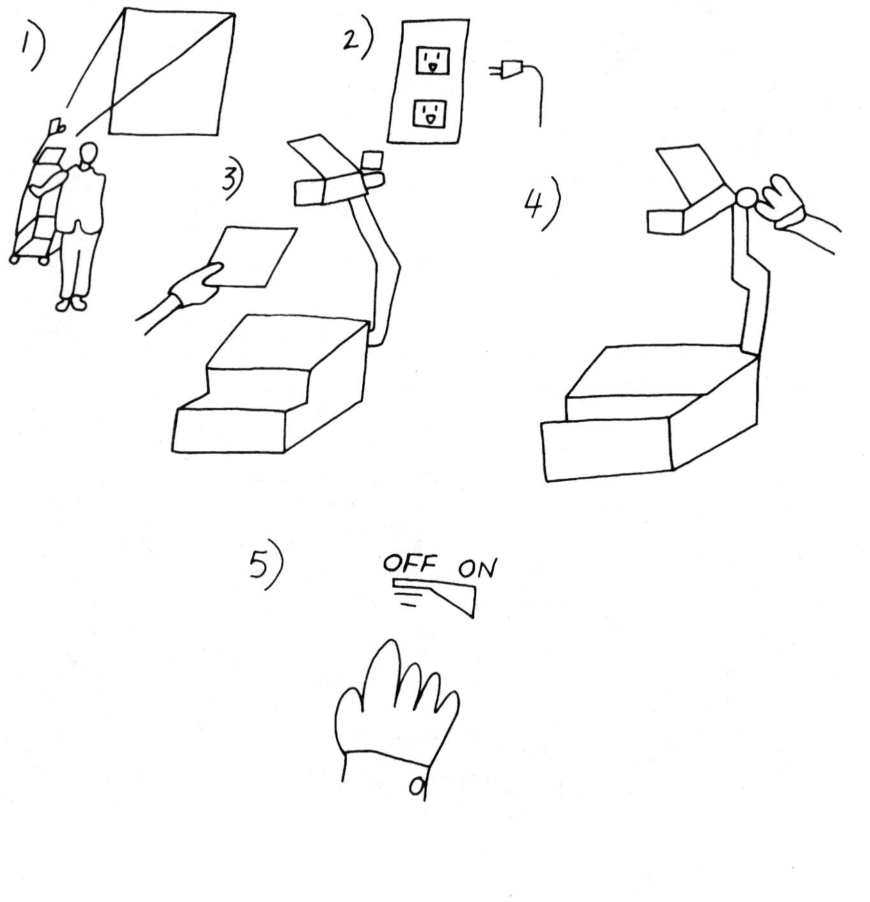

FIGURE 2.19 Students' Rough Draft

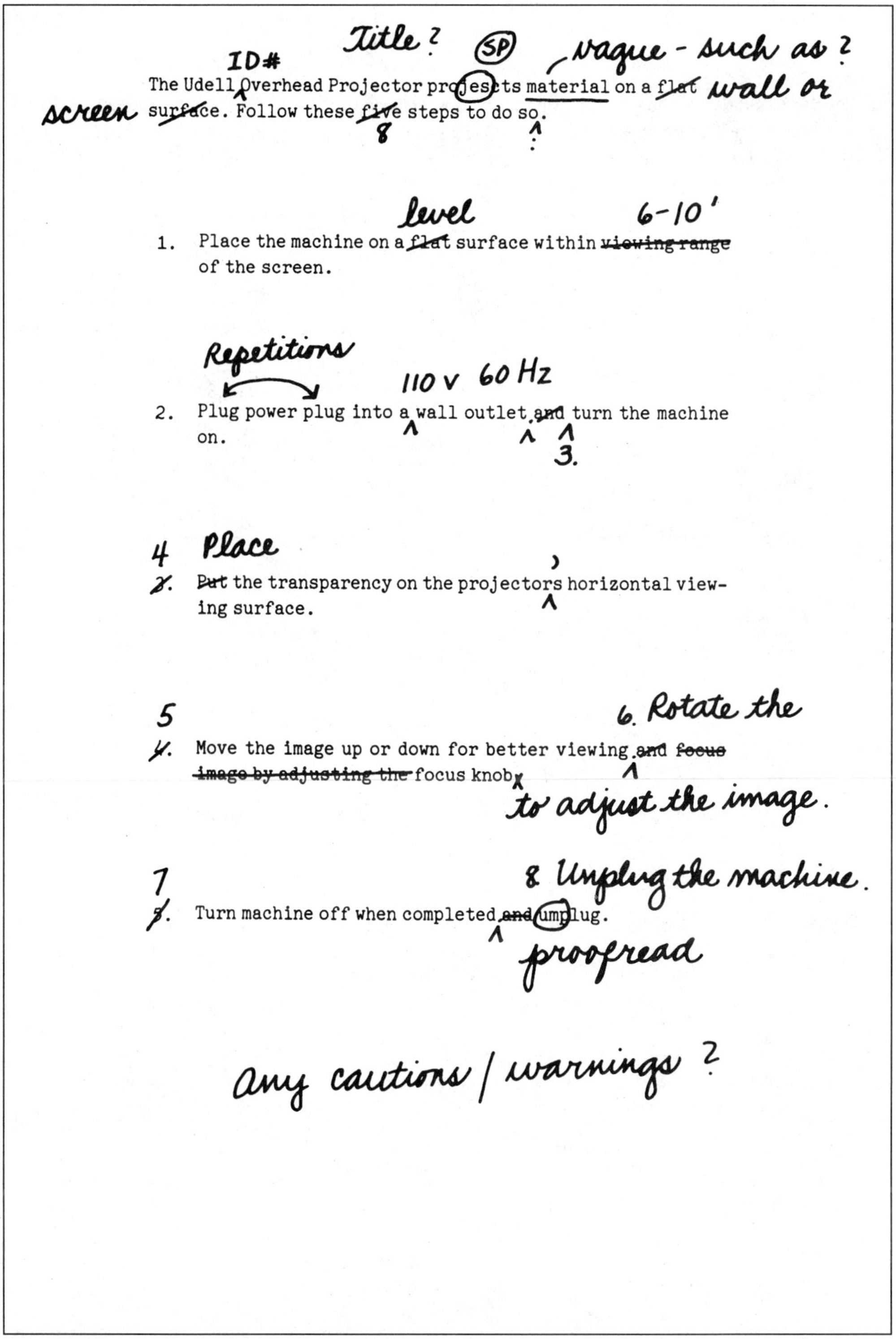

Title? (SP) vague - such as?

ID#

The Udell Overhead Projector projescts material on a ~~flat~~ wall or screen ~~surface~~. Follow these ~~five~~ 8 steps to do so.

level 6-10'

1. Place the machine on a ~~flat~~ level surface within ~~viewing range~~ 6-10' of the screen.

Repetitions 110 V 60 Hz

2. Plug power plug into a wall outlet. ~~and~~ 3. turn the machine on.

4 Place

~~3~~. ~~Put~~ the transparency on the projector's horizontal viewing surface.

5 6. Rotate the

~~4~~. Move the image up or down for better viewing. ~~and focus image by adjusting the~~ focus knob to adjust the image.

7 8. Unplug the machine.

~~5~~. Turn machine off when completed ~~and~~ (unplug).

proofread

Any cautions / warnings?

FIGURE 2.20 Students' Suggested Revisions

THE UDELL 4454 OVERHEAD PROJECTOR

The Udell 4454 Overhead Projector is used to project written or graphic material onto a screen or wall. Because of its capability to enlarge and project, the Udell is ideal for use in school and business.

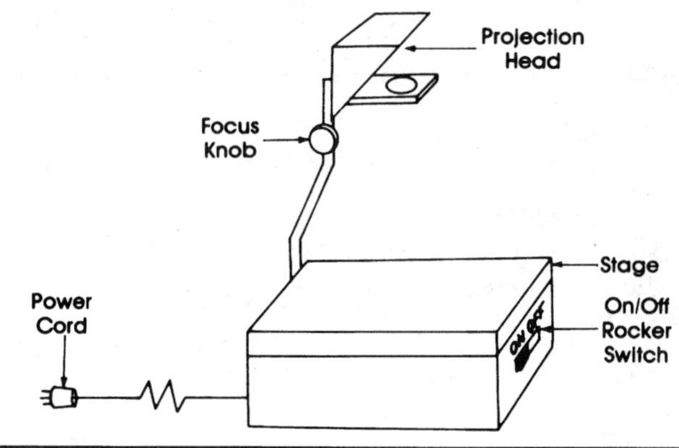

WARNING

The projector bulb heats up during operation. DO NOT TOUCH.

NOTE

Do not touch either the projector lens or glass stage. Smudges will occur.

To operate the Udell, follow these eight simple steps.

1. Place the projector on a level surface, approximately 6-10 feet from a projection screen or blank wall.

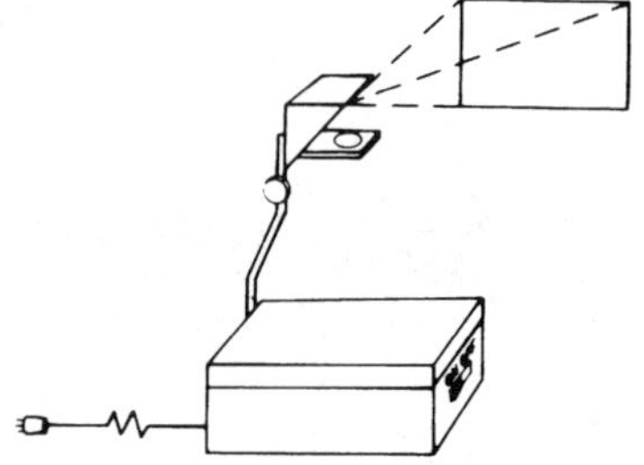

FIGURE 2.21 Students' Finished Copy

2. Plug the power supply cord into a 110 v 60 hz AC wall outlet.

3. Push the rocker switch to the "on" position.

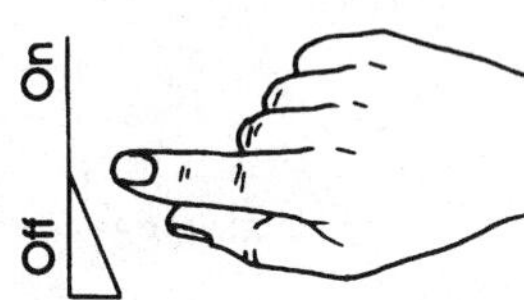

CAUTION

Keep air vents uncovered to allow for proper cooling.

4. Place the material to be viewed squarely on the projector's stage.

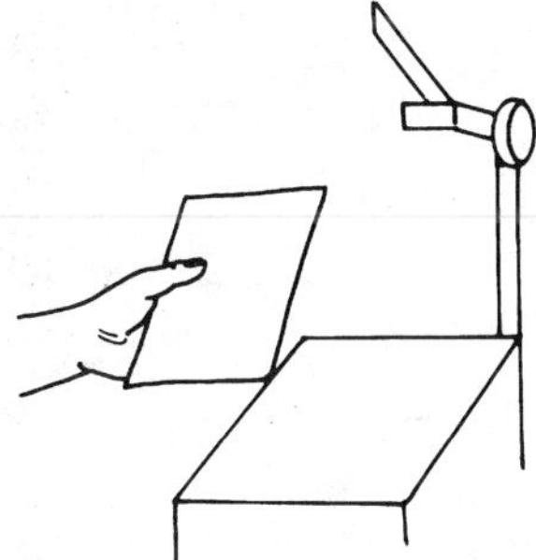

5. Adjust the height of the projected image by lowering or raising the projector's lens head.

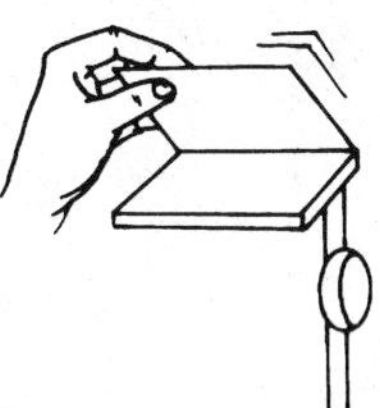

FIGURE 2.21 Continued

6. Rotate the focus knob for clear viewing of the projected image.

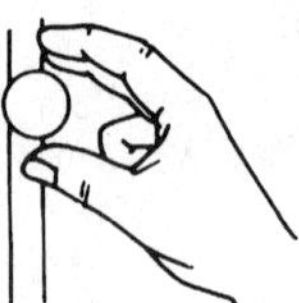

7. Push the rocker switch to the "off" position when you are through viewing your material.

8. Unplug the unit's power cord.

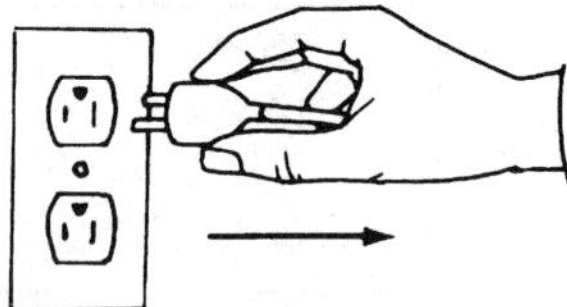

Following these eight simple steps will help you use the Udell overhead projector.

FIGURE 2.21 Continued

HOW TO DRY MOUNT

The best method for mounting photographs is to use dry-mount tissue, a thin sheet coated with an adhesive that becomes sticky when heated.

Dry mounting requires the following materials:

Materials

1. Press
2. Tacking iron
3. Mat knife
4. Mat board
5. Dry-mount tissue
6. Ruler
7. Print (photographed image)

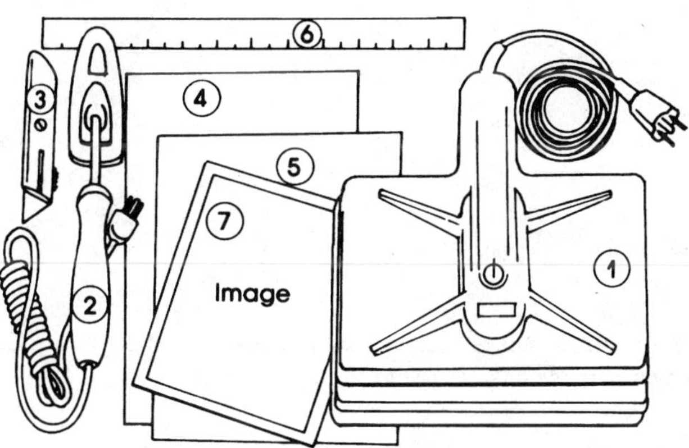

WARNING

Do not touch beyond the handle of the tacking iron. Do not place your fingers inside the press. Be careful when using the mat knife. Burns and cuts may occur.

FIGURE 2.22 Dry Mounting Instruction

Dry mounting involves the following steps:

1. DRY THE MATERIAL.

- ☐ Plug in the press and turn it on. Wait to see the red light.
- ☐ Heat the press to 250 degrees by adjusting the dial on the lid.
- ☐ Predry the mount board and the print.
- ☐ Place them in the press and hold the lid down for 30 seconds.

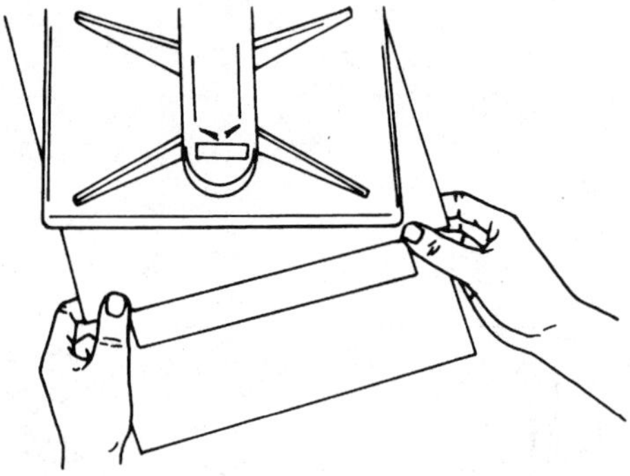

2. WIPE THE MATERIALS CLEAN.

- ☐ After the materials have been baked, let them cool for two to three minutes.
- ☐ Wipe away any loose dust or dirt with a clean cloth.

FIGURE 2.22 Continued

3. TACK THE MOUNTING TISSUE TO THE PRINT.

☐ Plug in the tacking iron and turn it on.
☐ With the print face down and the mounting tissue on top, tack the tissue to the center of the print.

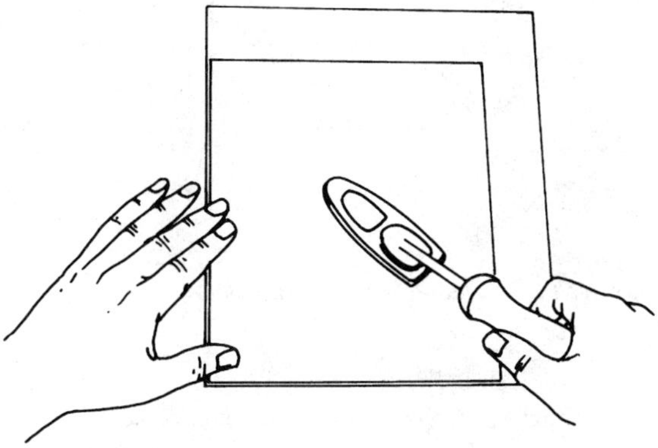

4. TRIM THE MOUNTING TISSUE.

☐ Place a piece of smooth cardboard under the print so that you won't cut your table.
☐ Trim off excess mounting tissue using the ruler.

Caution

Press firmly on the ruler to prevent slipping! Don't cut into the image area of the print!

FIGURE 2.22 Continued

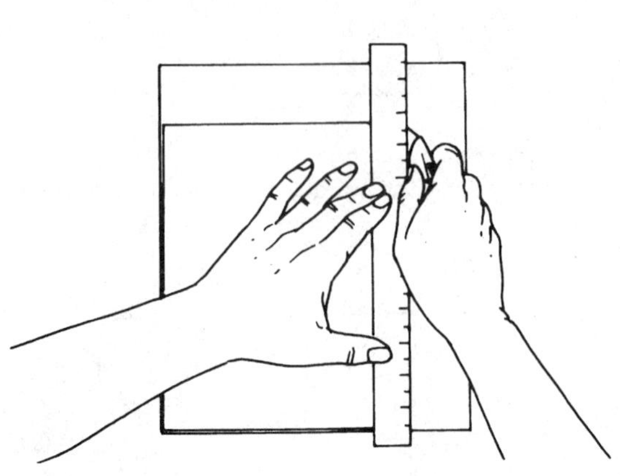

5. ATTACH THE MOUNTING TISSUE AND PRINT TO THE BOARD.

☐ Position the print and the tissue, face up, on the top of the mount board.
☐ Slightly raise one corner of the print and touch the tacking iron to the tissue on top of the board.
☐ Tack each corner down in this manner.

> Note!
>
> The tissue must lie completely flat on the board to prevent wrinkles under the print!

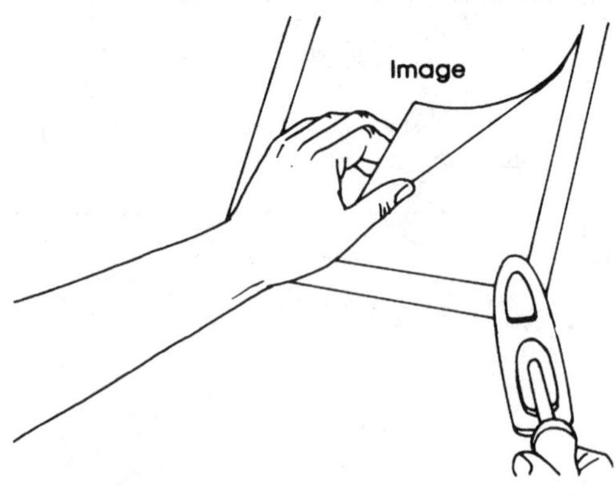

FIGURE 2.22 Continued

6. MOUNT THE PRINT.

☐ Put the board, tissue, and print (with cover sheet on top) into the press.
☐ Hold down the press lid firmly for thirty seconds.

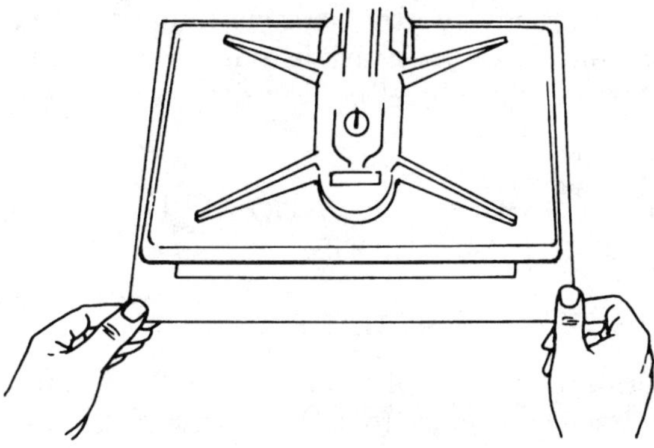

7. TRIM THE MOUNTED PRINT.

☐ Pressing down firmly on the ruler to avoid slipping, trim the edges of the mounted print with a sharp mat knife.

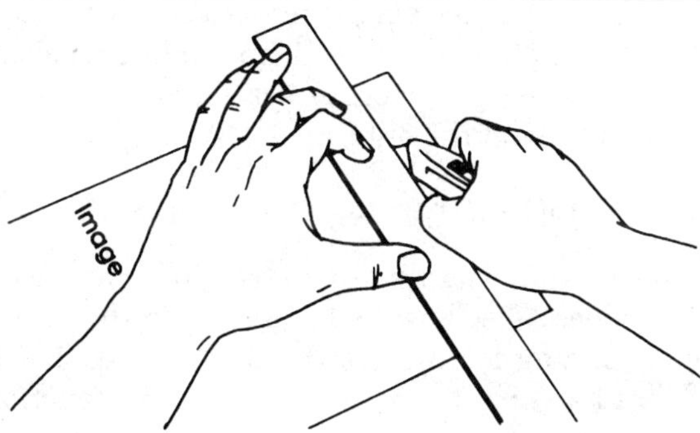

By carefully dry mounting your photographs, they will look beautiful and last longer. Enjoy your artistry.

FIGURE 2.22 Continued

WRITING INSTRUCTIONS

Reasons Instructions Go Unread

Why do so many people avoid reading directions? The humorous statement "As a last resort, read the directions" is humorous mainly because many people do just that. Since your task is to learn to write instructions that can and *will* be read on the job, let us look first at some reasons directions are avoided.

Characteristics of People Who Might Avoid Reading Instructions

INDEPENDENT PERSONALITY

If your readers are the type of people who will drive up and down a 5-mile highway six times and refuse to ask for directions, they will probably avoid reading directions on the job until a disaster occurs. These people will be the hardest to write for because they never want to appear to need advice or help. Reading or listening to instructions will be viewed by them as signs of weakness.

IMPATIENCE OF THE READER OR URGENCY OF THE SITUATION

Reading takes time, so in an emergency it sometimes seems better to risk taking action without stopping to read. To impatient people, every situation seems urgent. These people need to act immediately—even if they must guess and trust to luck on the outcome.

PREFERENCE FOR ORAL INSTRUCTIONS

Some people get used to listening to instructions rather than reading them. They will ask someone else how to do a task and thus take another person's time instead of reading for themselves. They think that listening is easier than reading, but listening to *and remembering* instructions is actually very difficult and often results in their asking for more and more help.

INADEQUATE READING ABILITY

Finally, there are those who are not used to reading or who are not able to read well. They assume the instructions will be too complicated to follow and as a result usually do not even attempt to read them.

Characteristics of Instructions That Might Go Unread

LACK OF BACKGROUND INFORMATION

Most people who write instructions know their subjects very well, so they sometimes write as if their readers have similar training. These writers omit explanations that are necessary for nontechnical readers. As an example, it is obvious that more basic background information is needed before you could begin installing this garage door opener:

> "Before installation, be sure the door is properly balanced and moves without binding throughout its full limit of travel."

(What do you need to know before you even begin installation?)

USE OF UNFAMILIAR TECHNICAL TERMS

Just one term that is confusing is enough to make instructions hard to follow. Many instructions contain terms that only experts would understand. You would have to know some terminology before you could put together the pieces of the bicycle you bought:

> "Remove axle nuts, washers and axle retention device from the ends of the axle. The axle cone bearing adjustment should permit smooth rotation of wheel."

(What words would *you* have trouble with?)

UNCLEAR WRITING STYLE

Sometimes writers of instructions feel it necessary to sound official or very knowledgeable. They may try to impress the reader by using complicated words or sentences instead of familiar words and sentences that anyone could understand. An owner's installation manual for a garage door opener contained this warning:

> "CAUTION: IT IS IMPORTANT TO UNDERSTAND THAT FORCES EXERTED BY THE OPERATOR ON THE DOOR ARE MULTIPLIED AS THE DOOR APPROACHES THE FLOOR. THIS ADJUSTMENT AND TEST PROCEDURE DOES NOT REQUIRE ANY PART OF THE BODY TO REMAIN UNDER A MOVING DOOR AS IT NEARS THE FLOOR."

(The individual words are not so complicated in this quote. What makes the quote so hard to understand?)

INEFFICIENT OR UNATTRACTIVE FORMAT

First impressions are hard to overcome, so instructions that are not attractively presented may not be read. A page of instructions without easy-to-follow steps or clear-cut divisions is easy to dismiss as too complicated to read. The same is true when there are many, many small steps that seem too numerous to complete.

IMPORTANT SAFETY INSTRUCTIONS

WARNING: Follow all the following instructions to reduce the risk of fire, electric shock or other serious injuries to persons using your dryer.

Read these instructions carefully for important health and safety precautions before operating your dryer.

NEVER permit children to operate, crawl inside, or play with or around the dryer. ALWAYS supervise children carefully when the dryer is operating.
NEVER dry items washed, cleaned, or partially dampened with paint, gasoline, or any flammable liquids. AN EXPLOSION or FIRE could result. Hand wash and line dry (outside) all such items.
To prevent accidental injury, ALWAYS remove the door when discarding an old dryer.
DO NOT locate dryer where inclement weather will affect it.
DO NOT put hands or arms into the dryer while it is operating.
DO NOT repair the controls yourself.

It is your responsibility to be sure that a qualified service representative installs, repairs, and replaces parts for your dryer.
DAMAGE can result from harmful fabric softeners. Use only specified fabric softeners. FIRE AND DAMAGE can result if you do the following:
- dry heat-sensitive items such as rubber or plastic
- allow lint to accumulate in the dryer or exhaust pipes

Dryer should be cleaned by a qualified repair person.
ALWAYS clean lint screen every time you use your dryer.
DO NOT allow dust, lint, dirt, papers, chemicals to accumulate around or under your dryer.

• Save these instructions! •

Additional Safety Precautions and Responsibilites of the Owner

NEVER USE THE DRYER WHEN...
- the lint screen is missing or seriously damaged
- parts of the dryer are missing
- the dryer is not working properly (too noisy, lint is escaping)
- it is damaged

WARNING
If you detect the smell of gas:
Put out any open flame.
Open the windows.
Do not touch electrical switches.
Call your local gas company.

WARNING
Do not store or use any flammable materials such as gasoline near this, or any other, appliance.

NEVER leave gas valve turned to "On" when absent from your house for an extended period.
ALWAYS turn off the gas valve before attempting to fix the dryer.
IT IS THE RESPONSIBILITY OF THE OWNER OF THE DRYER TO BE SURE THAT IT:
- is not located next to drapes or flammable furniture.
- is kept clean and operating properly.
- is installed and leveled properly on a floor that can support the weight.
- is installed where the temperature is above 45 degrees.
- is connected to a proper gas or electric supply.
- is not used for drying unsafe items.
- is used only by adults who are able to operate it safely.
- is connected to safe exhaust and fuel outlets.

SEE INSTALLATION INSTRUCTIONS FOR FURTHER INFORMATION.

FIGURE 2.23 Unattractive Format
(What problems do you see with this format? How could the format be improved?)

POOR ILLUSTRATIONS

Sometimes illustrations do not resemble the object as nontechnical readers view it. Small, crowded pictures of parts may be hard to distinguish or labels may not be easy to read. It is difficult to prepare effective illustrations, and even if they are very good, at times the final versions are poorly reproduced.

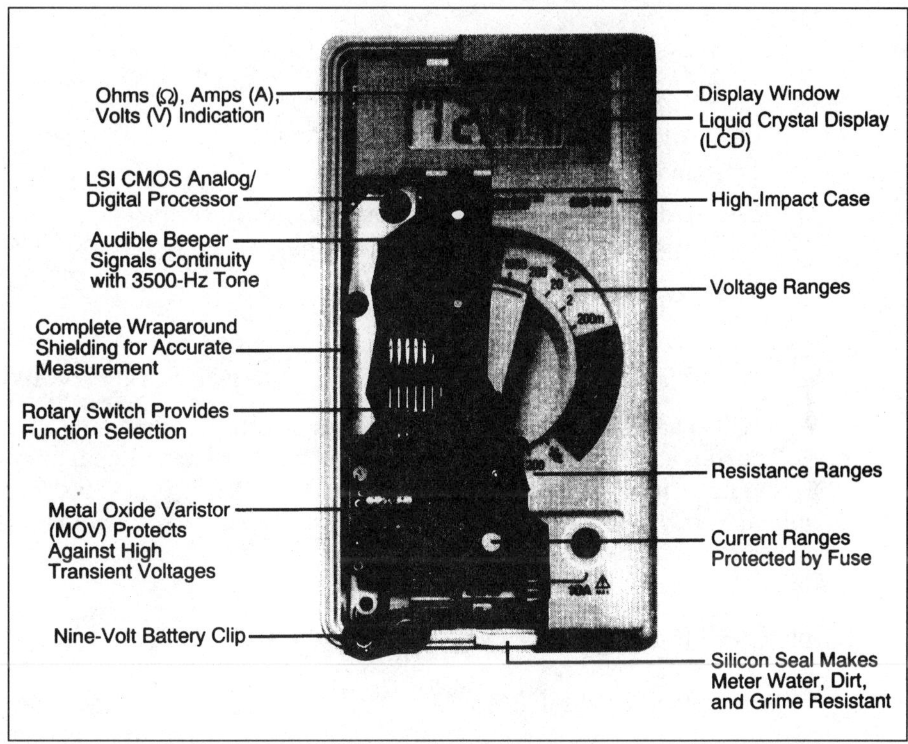

FIGURE 2.24 Hard-to-Distinguish Parts

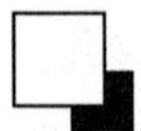

PLANNING INSTRUCTIONS THAT WILL BE READ

Understanding the reasons most people avoid reading instructions should help you to plan instructions that avoid common pitfalls. Here are the planning steps:

- ☐ Assess the readers' previous knowledge.
- ☐ Gather all the necessary information.
- ☐ Outline the basic steps in the process.
- ☐ Plan explanations where needed.
- ☐ Decide whether to define or omit technical terms
- ☐ Anticipate questions and decide where to answer them.
- ☐ Assess the need for illustrations.

☐ Assessing the Readers' Previous Knowledge

Who will read your instructions: members of your department? all employees? customers? Even if you are writing for experienced department members, a new employee may need the instructions. Thus it is safest to *gear the language and information to the least experienced person who might be involved.*

☐ Gathering the Necessary Information

CONSULTING OTHER PEOPLE

Usually the person chosen to write instructions on the job is the one who is most familiar with the procedure. If you are chosen and others are also familiar with the process, be sure to consult them to see how their methods differ from yours. Try to be objective and choose the approach that will be the most efficient for a new person to understand.

DOUBLE-CHECKING THE DETAILS

Now is the time to look for any details that you may have forgotten or that you have taken for granted. Be as specific as possible about information such as amounts, time, or materials needed.

☐ Outlining the Basic Steps in the Process

After the necessary facts are gathered, focus on the intended readers and briefly write down the steps of the process in the proper order. As you do this, jot notes when you think the readers might be confused.

PLANNING EXPLANATIONS

The goal is to provide just enough information so that your instructions will be followed safely and efficiently. Decide whether any of the following explanations are necessary. Do you need to include:

- ☐ A comparison to another procedure?
- ☐ The importance of following the instructions exactly?
- ☐ Safety precautions?

USING TECHNICAL TERMS

Underline any term that may be unfamiliar to the readers. Decide whether they will need to know it and if so determine how and when to teach it. As an example, consider a punctuation rule involving the use of the comma. Review writing handbook on punctuation. If you choose to use technical terminology, the rule might be stated like this:

> When joining two sentences with a ***coordinating conjunction***, put a comma before the coordinating conjunction.

Here are some other ways to deal with that term:

1. Skip it and use a simpler word.

> When joining two sentences with a connecting word (such as ***and, but,*** and ***or***), put a comma before the connecting word.

2. Use an illustration to explain the technical terminology.

> **coordinating conjunction** ⟶
>
> Many large companies have training programs **and** business writing is often included in the courses offered.

3. List all technical words with their definitions at the beginning of the instructions.

> ***coordinating conjunction***—a connecting word, such as ***and, but,*** and ***or.***

4. Write a sentence to define the word when you come to it in the instructions.

> When joining two sentences with a coordinating conjunction, put a comma before the coordinating conjunction. A ***coordinating conjunction*** is a connecting word, such as ***and, but,*** and ***or.***

5. **Briefly give a short definition using commas or parentheses when you come to it in the instructions.**

> When joining two sentences with a coordinating conjunction (a connecting word, such as ***and, but***, and ***or***), put a comma before the coordinating conjunction.

Your choice should be based on the reader's need to know the term and then on the importance of this term in the total process. Too much defining of terms will make the instructions hard to follow. On the other hand, not explaining an important term may make the instructions impossible to follow.

ANTICIPATING QUESTIONS

If you have given the instructions orally before writing them, you may already know where questions will be asked. The most common question is usually "Why?" Plan explanations only for common problems that will make a difference in the outcome. For instance, when instructions state "*Do not* . . . ," the reader may *want* to do that to see what will happen. (Do not open the oven while the cake is baking.) Here is another type of instruction with the "Why?" answered.

> A soldier should have short hair. Female soldiers with long hair must have their hair put up within standards or the protective mask will not seal.

ASSESSING THE NEED FOR ILLUSTRATIONS

If you are providing instructions to operate a piece of equipment and will be using the names of specific parts, an illustration may be necessary to identify the parts. Illustrations must be very clearly drawn and easy to read. Poor illustrations are worse than none at all.

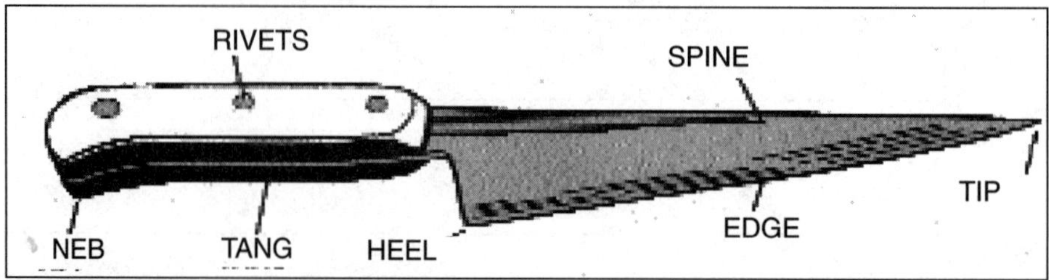

FIGURE 2.25 Clearly Labeled Parts

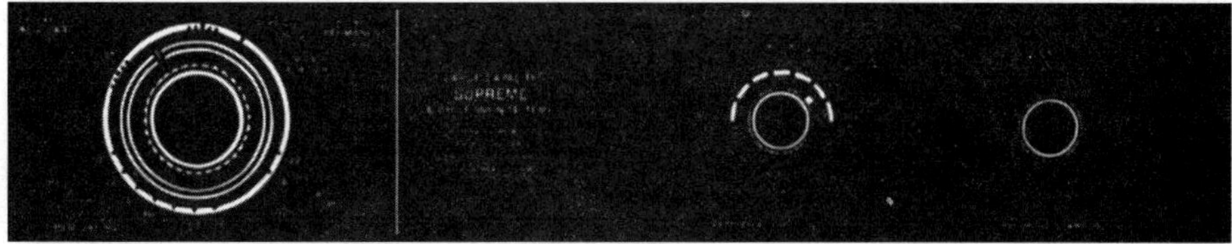

FIGURE 2.26 Poorly Labeled Parts

Be realistic about the resources available to you to prepare and reproduce illustrations. If the quality of the final version will be uncertain, prepare the instructions so the illustrations are not absolutely necessary to understand the procedure.

Before beginning the rough draft, be sure you have done all the necessary planning.

CHECKLIST FOR PLANNING INSTRUCTIONS

I made sure that I:

- ☐ Assessed the reader's previous knowledge.
- ☐ Gathered all the necessary information.
- ☐ Outlined the basic steps in the process.
    - ☐ Planned explanations where needed.
    - ☐ Decided whether to define or omit technical terms.
    - ☐ Anticipated questions and decided where to answer them.
    - ☐ Assessed the need for illustrations.

WRITING THE ROUGH DRAFT

Because it is hard to write instructions that someone else can and will follow, you should expect to make a lot of revisions. If you are a pretty good typist, save time by entering the rough draft on the computer. You can compose quickly and not worry about errors. Write in the same way you speak. Then print a copy and begin making revisions.

☐ The Opening

The beginning sentence or paragraph should contain a clear statement explaining what procedure will be presented. Other information will vary depending on the situation. Decide whether it is necessary to include:

- ☐ Why the procedure is important
- ☐ When the procedure should be followed

- ☐ Restrictions concerning who is permitted to perform the procedure (for example, a licensed technician)
- ☐ A list of equipment or supplies that will be used

☐ The Steps of the Procedure

LISTED FORM

If the steps are clearly separate from one another and very few explanations are needed, each step, or group of similar steps, can be stated separately. *Numbers or symbols should be used* for each one so the order is clear.

Use the same type of wording for each statement. (Review the section on parallel construction in the writing handbook if you need help in wording each step in a similar way.) *Use polite commands*: "Unplug the machine. " "Avoid opening the back of the camera in direct sunlight." "Hold the lever down for exactly 30 seconds." Put the important words at the beginning of the sentences so the readers can follow the directions as quickly as possible.

Try to include the little words (articles) such as "the" and "a" or "an" because leaving words out may cause confusion. Writing "Unplug *the* machine" is a better statement than "Unplug machine." Recipes for preparing food often leave the little words out and so these recipes may not be good models for writing instructions in other fields.

When you become aware of how to write good instructions, you may begin to notice how many instructions are all around us everywhere. Evaluating these instructions will help you see ways to improve your own writing. Here is an example of instructions written in listed form found on the wall above a duplicating machine:

How to Make Copies

1. First Deposit Money
2. Lift Cover.
3. Place Original Face Down.
4. Close Cover.
5. Select Copy Size and Number of Copies.
6. When "Ready" light comes on, Press Print Button.
7. For Change Return, Press the Chrome Coin Return Plunger.
8. Remove your Original from copier.

Are any words or steps unclear to you? If so, what changes would you make? Does the incorrect use of capital letters help or hurt your understanding? Notice that the little words (articles) are sometimes left out. Would you put them in?

PARAGRAPH FORM

When explanations are needed with many of the steps, the listed step format becomes hard to read. Explanations are usually easier to understand when written in paragraph form. The trick is to keep the steps easy to follow even though you have included explanations.

Polite commands should still be used, but more sentence variety is required. In addition, since the steps are not numbered, *a variety of transitions must be used between sentences and between paragraphs.* Paragraphs demand more careful reading than separate numbered statements. *Highlight key words and use headings* where possible to make it easier for readers to find a step quickly.

An example of directions in paragraph form follows.

Cross-country skiing can he a total drag without the right wax. And there's a right way to apply it.

First, remove whatever gobs of wax you already have on the bases with a plastic scraper—a metal one can gouge your ski.

With a lint-free cloth, wipe the skis with wax remover until all the wax is gone. Work in a well-ventilated area and discard all used rags.

Next, sand the skis with aluminum oxide paper or #100 silicon carbide paper. (This step is optional but it helps even the base texture.) A final polish with a fibertex pad removes any burrs.

Now apply the glider wax. If you ski with the skating technique, take an old iron and melt a line of wax from the tips to the tails on both sides of the grooves. If you're a stride-and-glider, don't put wax on the midsection of the skis—from just in front of the binding to just behind the heel plate.

When you spread the glider wax, it's important to set the iron on the lowest temperature that will melt the wax. This is usually in the 60 to 120°C range. Do not use a torch, or you might blister the ski base and cause irreparable damage.

Iron the way you would iron a shirt, and never let the iron rest too long in one spot. When you've covered the base with wax, let it cool for about 30 minutes. For quick drying in cold weather, just set the ski outside.

Once the wax is dry, take a sharp plastic scraper and remove most of the wax so you end up with only a thin coating on the base. The thinner the layer, the faster the ski will be. It's best to scrape with long strokes in one direction.

When finished, apply glider wax to the skis a second time. Then go over the ski with a steel or nylon brush to create a rough textured base. This breaks up the suction that occurs when there's water between the ski and the snow, and lets the ski glide better.

It's important to put on fresh glider wax whenever the base starts to look white or dried out. Skiing without enough wax wears out the polyethylene base.

If you use the diagonal stride, the skis are now ready for grip wax. Rub a good amount onto the midsection area where the ski comes into contact with the snow during the kick phase. Don't be stingy or you'll end up backslipping.

Cork the wax in until smooth with a synthetic cork. Then apply several more layers, corking each one. Now the skis are ready to hit the trails.

Cancian, Anita. OUTDOOR CANADA, March 1990, p. 20. Reprinted with permission.

How do you evaluate these instructions? What changes would you make? Would these instructions be easier to read in listed form?

☐ The Closing

It may be more logical to present certain types of information after the procedure is completed:

- ☐ Sources of additional information or help
- ☐ Uses for a completed project
- ☐ Cost of the project
- ☐ Safety precautions
- ☐ Frequency of performing the procedure
- ☐ Possible future changes in procedure
- ☐ Storage information

Here are some examples of concluding sentences:

These steps should be followed exactly within 15 seconds or less after an order or alarm. If these steps are followed properly, the M17 protective mask should save your life from chemical or biological attack.

For longer-lasting curl, do not shampoo, pull, or stretch the hair for two days after the perm.

The total cost of the supplies for this project should be under $100, and all the items can be purchased at a hardware store or lumberyard.

If the two colors provided with your dishwasher do not match your kitchen decor, optional panels are available from your dealer in a variety of decorator colors.

If you have nothing else to add, be sure your final step is written so the readers know there is no more to do. "Reconnect the power supply" is an example of a final step when one of the first steps was to disconnect the power supply.

☐ Preparing Illustrations

If you decide illustrations are necessary, make them as simple as possible. Details are usually easier to see in a line drawing than in a photograph because the outlines are more distinct. Fancy artwork is not as important as clear outlines and details. The clarity of the labeling is as important as the drawing itself. The example that follows is a computer keyboard. Notice the difference between the photograph and the line drawing.

FIGURE 2.27 Photograph of a Keyboard

FIGURE 2.28 Line Drawing of a Keyboard

When space is limited, enlarge the necessary parts of the illustration. Part of the preceding illustration follows.

Here is an example that includes illustrations. Analyze it and decide if any changes are needed.

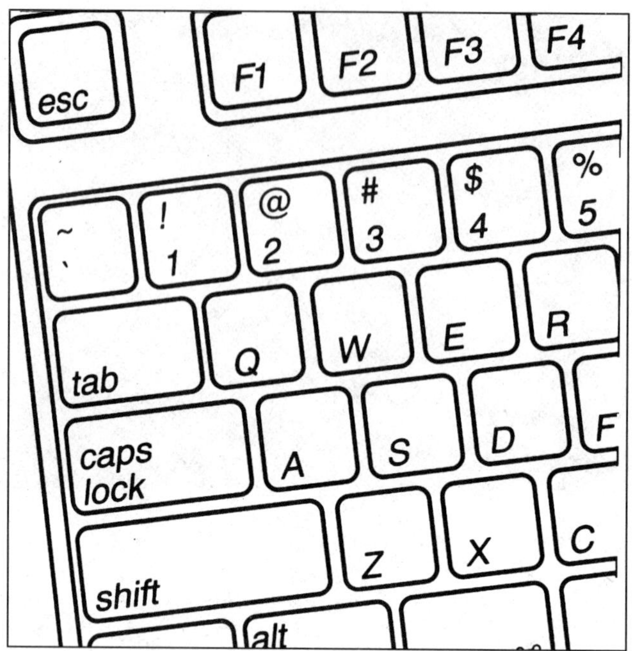

FIGURE 2.29 Enlarged Section from the Line Drawing

You may have already decided that good instructions can be written in more than one way. Your own writing style will influence the way you prefer to present instructions, but the real test comes when your readers try to follow the instructions that you wrote.

PREPARING THE FINAL VERSION

Your goal is to prepare instructions that are accurate, complete, and easy to read. Before you finalize anything, ask other people to try out the instructions from the rough draft. Ask them to look for:

- ☐ Unclear words or sentences
- ☐ Missing steps or steps that are out of order
- ☐ Missing information
- ☐ Unclear illustrations

Now you are ready to prepare the final version. If your rough draft is on a computer disk, changes will be fast and easy. Check off each step as it is completed.

CHECKLIST FOR WRITING INSTRUCTIONS

I made sure that I:

- ☐ Made revisions based on suggestions from readers.
- ☐ Double-checked sentence structure, word use, and spelling.
- ☐ Put in headings for groups of similar steps.
- ☐ Used numbering, underlining, capital letters, or different fonts to make the steps easier to follow.
- ☐ Spaced the steps on the page so the readers can find any step quickly.
- ☐ Placed illustrations so it is always clear which steps they demonstrate.

CHANGING FRONT PANELS

A new look . . .

Your new KitchenAid dishwasher comes with a stainless steel trim kit and one front and lower reversible panel. You can choose from onyx black or almond. The dishwasher has been shipped with the onyx black panel showing.

If you want to change the color of the panels, follow one of the options below. OPTION A may be used if your dishwasher front sticks out several inches from the cabinets. OPTION B may be used if your dishwasher front is flush with the cabinets.

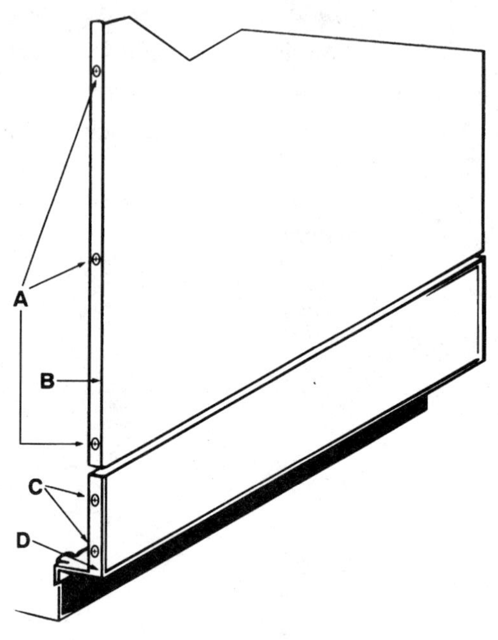

WARNING: TO PREVENT ELECTRIC SHOCK, disconnect electrical power supply to dishwasher before changing panels.

OPTION A

UPPER PANEL:

1. Pull door open and on either side of the dishwasher door, remove the three screws (A) from the trim (B). Remove the loosened piece of trim.
2. Slide the color panel out. Handle carefully so the panel will not be scratched or bent. Turn the panel to the desired color. Place the color panel in position then push the filler panel in behind it.
3. Replace the trim (B) and the three screws (A).

LOWER PANEL:

1. Remove the two screws (C) on either side of the lower panel assembly. Remove the loosened piece of trim (D).
2. Slide the color panel out. Handle carefully so the panel will not be scratched or bent. Turn the panel to the desired color. Place the color panel in position then push the filler panel in behind it.
3. Replace the trim (D) and the two

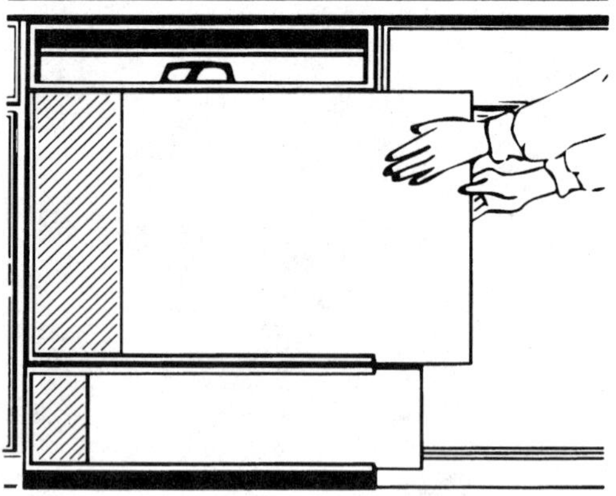

FIGURE 2.30 Listed Paragraphs with Clear Illustrations
(*KitchenAid Use and Care Guide*, p. 24. Reprinted with permission of Whirlpool Corporation)

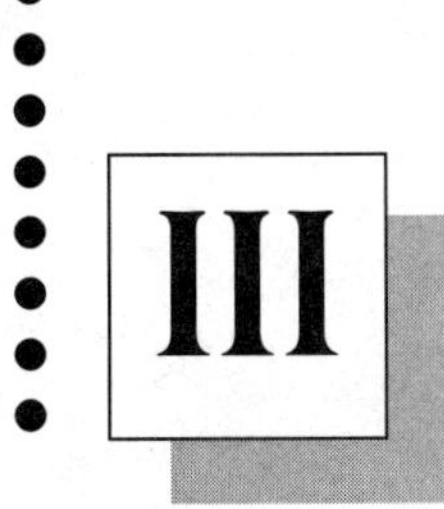

Types of Reports

Written documents most often used in businesses, industry, and governmental, educational, and nonprofit organizations are reports. The type and length of the report will vary from a short form to a comprehensive formal report. This section provides guidance on short reports and long formal reports.

Short Reports

OBJECTIVES

At one time or another, you'll be asked to write a report. This report will satisfy one or all of the following needs:

- ☐ Supply a record of work accomplished
- ☐ Record and clarify complex information for future reference
- ☐ Present information to a large number of people
- ☐ Record problems encountered
- ☐ Document schedules, timetables, and milestones
- ☐ Recommend future action
- ☐ Document current status
- ☐ Record procedures

The most common types of reports include the following:

1. *Accident / incident reports:* What happened, how did it happen, when did it happen, why did it happen, who was involved?
2. *Feasibility reports:* Can we do it, should we do it?
3. *Inventory reports:* What's in storage, what's been sold, what needs to be ordered?
4. *Staff utilization reports:* Is labor sufficient and efficiently used?
5. *Progress / activity reports* (weekly, monthly, quarterly, annually): What's our status?
6. *Travel reports:* Where did I go, what did I learn, who did I meet, etc.?
7. *Lab reports:* How did we do it?

8. *Performance appraisal reports:* How's an employee doing on the job?
9. *Study reports:* What's wrong?
10. *Justification reports:* Here's why we need the material (or will pursue this action) on this date.

Although there are many different types of reports and individual companies have unique demands and requirements, certain traits are basic to all report writing.

CRITERIA FOR WRITING SHORT REPORTS

All reports share certain generic similarities in format, development, and style.

☐ Format

Every short report should contain four basic units: heading, introduction, discussion, and conclusion/recommendations.

Heading

The heading includes the date on which the report is written, the name(s) of the people to whom the report is written, the name(s) of the people from whom the report is sent, and the subject of the report (as discussed in Chapter IB, the subject line should contain a *topic* and a *focus*).

SAMPLE REPORT HEADING

```
DATE:     August 13,1991
TO:       Shelley Stine
FROM:     Judy Simmons JS
SUBJECT:  Report on Trip to Southwest Regional Conference
          on English
          (Fort Worth, TX)
```

Introduction

The introduction supplies an overview of the report. It can include three optional subdivisions:

- ☐ Purpose—a topic sentence(s) explaining why you are submitting the report (rationale, justification, objectives) and exactly what the report's subject matter is.
- ☐ Personnel—names of others involved in the reporting activity.
- ☐ Dates—what period of time the report covers.

INTRODUCTION

Objectives: I attended the National Electronic Packaging Conference in Anaheim, CA, to review innovations in vapor phase soldering.

Dates: September 26-30, 1991

Personnel: Susan Lisk and Larry Rochelle

Some businesspeople omit the introductory comments in writing reports and begin with the discussion. They believe that introductions are unnecessary because the readers know why the reports are written and who is involved.

These assumptions are false for several reasons. First, it is false to assume that readers will know why you're writing the report, when the activities occurred, and who was involved. Perhaps if you are writing only to your immediate supervisor, there's no reason for introductory overviews. However, even in this situation you might have an unanticipated reader because:

- ☐ Immediate supervisors change—they are promoted, fired, retired, or go to work for another company.
- ☐ Immediate supervisors aren't always available—they're sick for the day, on vacation, or off site for some reason.

Second, avoiding introductory overviews assumes that your readers will remember the report's subject matter. This is false because reports are written not just for the present, when the topic is current, but for the future, when the topic is past history. Reports go on file—and return at a later date. At that later date,

- ☐ You won't remember the particulars of the reported subject matter.
- ☐ Your colleagues, many of whom weren't present when the report was originally written, won't be familiar with the subject.
- ☐ You might have outside, lay readers who need additional detail to understand the report.

An introduction—which seemingly states the obvious—is needed to satisfy multiple readers, readers other than those initially familiar with the subject matter, and future readers who are unaware of the original report.

Discussion

The discussion of the report summarizes your activities and the problems you encountered. This is the largest section of the report and involves development, organization, and style (more on these later).

Conclusion/Recommendations

The conclusion allows you to sum up, to relate what you've learned, or to state what decisions you have made regarding the activities reported. The recommendations allow you to suggest future action, to state what you believe you and/or your company should do next.

> CONCLUSION/RECOMMENDATIONS:
>
> The conference was beneficial. It not only taught me how the computer can save us time and money, but also I received hands-on training. Because the computer can assist our billing and inventory control, let's buy and install three terminals in bookkeeping before our next quarter.

☐ Development

Now that you know what subdivisions are traditional in reports, your next question is, "What do I say in each section? How do I develop my ideas?"

First, answer the reporters' questions.

1. *Who* did you meet or contact, who was your liaison, who was involved in the accident, who comprised your technical team, etc.?
2. *When* did the activities documented occur (dates of travel, milestones, incidents, etc.)?
3. *Why* are you writing the report and/or why were you involved in the activity (rationale, justification, objectives)? Or, for a lab report, for example, why did the electrode, compound, equipment, or material act as it did?
4. *Where* did the activity take place?
5. *What* were the steps in the procedure, what conclusions have you reached, or what are your recommendations?

Second, when providing the foregoing information, *quantify!* Don't hedge or be vague or imprecise. Specify to the best of your abilities with photographic detail.

The following justification is an example of vague, imprecise writing.

> Installation of the machinery is needed to replace a piece of equipment deemed unsatisfactory by an Equipment Engineering review.

Which machine are we purchasing? Which piece of equipment will it replace? Why is the equipment unsatisfactory (too old, too expensive, too slow)? When does it need to be replaced? Where does it need to be installed? Why is the installation important?

A department supervisor will not be happy with the preceding report. Instead, supervisors need information *quantified*, as follows:

> The exposure table needs to be installed by 9/91 so that we can manufacture printed wiring products with fine line paths and spacing (down to .0005 inches). The table will replace the outdated printer in Dept. 76. Failure to install the table will slow the production schedule by 27%.

Note that the underlined words and phrases provide detail by quantifying.

☐ Style

Style includes conciseness, simplicity, and highlighting techniques. As already discussed, you achieve conciseness by eliminating wordy phrases. Say *consider* rather than *take into consideration*; say *now* rather than *at this present time*. You achieve simplicity by avoiding old-fashioned words: *utilize* becomes *use, initiate* becomes *begin*, *supersedes* becomes *replaces*.

The value of highlighting has already been shown in this chapter. The parts of reports reviewed earlier use headings (Introduction, Discussion, Conclusion/Recommendation). Graphics can also be used to help communicate content, as evident in the following example. A recent demographic study of Kansas City predicted growth patterns for Johnson County (a large county south of Kansas City):

> Johnson County is expected to add 157,605 persons to its 1980 population of 270,269 by the year 2010. That population jump would be accompanied by a near doubling of the 96,925 households the county had in 1980. The addition of 131,026 jobs also is forecast for Johnson County by 2010, more than doubling its employment opportunity.

This report is difficult to access readily. We are overloaded with too much data. Luckily, the report provided a table (Table 3.1) for easier access to the data.

Through highlighting techniques (tables, white space, headings), the demographic forecast is made accessible at a glance.

TABLE 3.1 Johnson County Predicted Growth by 2010

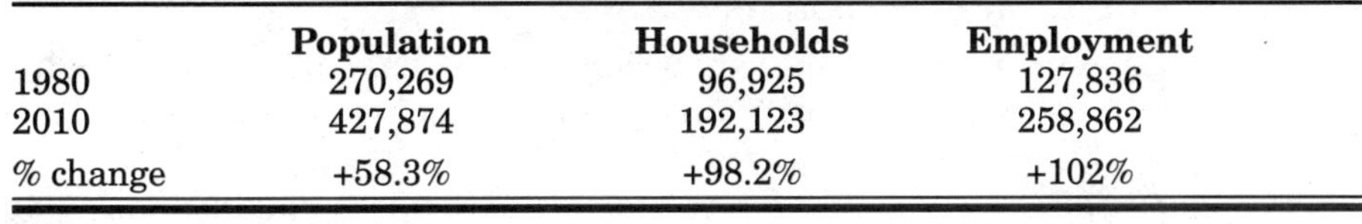

	Population	Households	Employment
1980	270,269	96,925	127,836
2010	427,874	192,123	258,862
% change	+58.3%	+98.2%	+102%

TYPES OF SHORT REPORTS: CRITERIA

All short reports include a heading {date, to, from, subject), an introduction, a discussion, and conclusion/recommendations. However, different types of short reports customize these generic components to meet specific needs. Let's look at the criteria for five common types of short reports: trip reports, progress reports, lab reports, feasibility reports, and incident reports.

Trip Reports

When you leave your work site to go to a conference, analyze problems in another work environment, give presentations, or make sales calls, you must report on these work-related travels. Your supervisors not only require that you document your expenses and time while off site, but they also want to be kept up to date on your work activities. Following is an overview of what you'll include in an effective trip report.

1. **Heading**
   Date
   To
   From
   Subject (Topic + focus)

2. **Introduction (overview, background)**
   Purpose: In the purpose section, document the date(s) and destination of your travel. Then comment on your objectives or rationale. What motivated the trip, what did you plan to achieve, what were your goals, why were you involved in job-related travel?

   You might also want to include these following optional subheadings:

   Personnel: With whom did you travel?

   Authorization: Who recommended or suggested that you leave your work site for job-related travel?

3. **Discussion (body, findings, agenda)**
   Using subheadings, document your activities. This can include a review of your observations, contacts, seminars attended, or difficulties encountered.

4. **Conclusion/ recommendations**
   Conclusion: What did you accomplish—what did you learn, who did you meet, what sales did you make, what of benefit to yourself, colleagues, and/or your company occurred?

   Recommendations: What do you suggest next? Should the company continue on the present course (status quo) or should changes be made in personnel or in the approach to a particular situation? Would you suggest that other colleagues attend this conference in the future, or was the job-related travel not effective? In your opinion, what action should the company take?

Figure 3.1 presents an example of a trip report.

Progress Reports

Your supervisors want to know what you're doing at work. They want to know what progress you're making on a project, whether you're on schedule, what difficulties you might have encountered, and/or what your plans are for the next reporting period. Because of this, supervisors ask you to write progress (or activity or status) reports—daily, weekly, monthly, quarterly, or annually. The following are components of an effective progress report.

1. **Heading**
   Date
   To
   From
   Subject: Include the topic about which you are reporting and the reporting interval (date).

```
Date:    May 31, 1992
To:      Joanna Faulkner
From:    Lupe Salinas LS
Subject: January Progress Report on Sales Calls
```

2. **Introduction (overview, background)**
   Objectives: These can include the following:
   - ☐ Why are you working on this project (what's the rationale)?
   - ☐ What problems motivated the project?
   - ☐ What do you hope to achieve?
   - ☐ Who initiated the activity?

   Personnel: With whom are you working on this project (i.e., work team, liaison, contacts)?

   Previous activity: If this is the second, third, fourth, etc. report in a series, remind your readers what work has already been accomplished. Bring them up-to-date with background data or a reference to previous reports.

3. **Discussion (findings, body, agenda)**
   Work accomplished: Using subheadings, itemize your work accomplished either through a chronological list or a discussion organized by importance.

   Problems encountered: Inform your readers of any difficulties encountered (late shipments, delays, poor weather, labor shortages) not only to justify your possibly being behind schedule but also to show the readers where you'll need help to complete the project.

4. **Conclusion/ recommendations**
   Conclusion: Sum up what you've achieved during this reporting period and provide a prophetic conclusion—tell your readers what work you plan to complete next and what your anticipated date of completion is. Doing so will help your supervisors provide you with needed labor, allocate appropriate funds, and/or reschedule your milestones.

Date: February 26, 1991
To: Pat Berry
From: Juliet Harris *Juliet*
SubJect: Trip Report—Renton West Seminaron Electronic Packaging

INTRODUCTION

On Tuesday, February 23, 1991, I attended the Renton West National Electronic Packaging Seminar, held in Ruidoso, NM. My goal was to acquire hands-on training and to learn new techniques for electronic packaging.

OBSERVATIONS

The following were the most informative seminars attended:

Production Automation—Dr. Wang Hue

- ☐ Reviewed and provided hands-on training for foam-encapsulation automated techniques.

Vapor Phase Soldering—Garth McSwain

- ☐ Provided information on processing double-sided chip components.

Electronics for Extreme Temperatures—Xanadu Rand

- ☐ Presented scientific data on packaging under temperature extremes.

CONCLUSION/RECOMMENDATIONS

1. Dr. Hue's program was the most informative and useful. I suggest that we bring Dr. Hue to our site for further consultation.
2. Vapor phase soldering is too costly. We could not pay back our investment within this quarter.
3. Our new-hires would benefit from Xanadu Rand's scientific overview. Supervisors, however, will find the data remedial.

FIGURE 3.1 Trip Report

Recommendations: Suggest changes to be made which will allow you to meet your deadlines and/or request assistance.

Figure 3.2 presents an example of a progress report.

□ Lab Reports

Professionals in electronics, engineering, medical fields, the computer industry, and other technologies often rank the ability to communicate as highly as they do technical skills. Conclusions derived from a technical procedure are worthless if they reside in a vacuum. The knowledge you acquire from a lab experiment *must* be communicated to your colleagues and supervisors so they can benefit from your discoveries. That's the purpose of a lab report—to document your findings. You write a lab report after you've performed a laboratory test to share with your readers:

- □ Why the test was performed
- □ How the test was performed
- □ What the test results were
- □ What follow-up action (if any) is required

The following are components of a successful lab report.

1. **Heading**
   Date
   To
   From
   Subject (topic + focus)
2. **Introduction (overview, background, purpose)**
   Why is this report being written? To answer this question, provide any or all of the following:
   - □ The rationale (What problem motivated this report?)
   - □ The objectives (What does this report hope to prove?)
   - □ Authorization (Under whose authority is this report being written?)
3. **Discussion (body, methodology)**
   How was the test performed? To answer this question, provide the following:
   - □ Apparatus (What equipment, approach, or theory have you used to perform your test?)
   - □ Procedure (What steps—chronologically organized—did you follow in performing the test?)
4. **Conclusion/ recommendations**
   Conclusion: The conclusion of a lab report presents your findings. Now that you've performed the laboratory experiment, what have you learned or discovered or uncovered? How do you interpret your findings? What are the implications?

Date: April 2, 1991
To: Buddy Ramos
From: Pat Smith PS
Subject: First Quarterly Report—Project 80 Construction

Background:

Department 93 is investigating our capability to support FY1991 build plans for Project 80. This activity is in response to a request from HEW.

Work Accomplished:

In this first quarter, we've studied the following:

1. Shipments: TDDS shipments this quarter have provided us a 30-day lead on scheduled part provisions.
2. Testing: Screening on high-voltage monitors has been completed with a pass/fail ratio of 76.4% pass to 23.6% fail. This meets our 75% goal.
3. Production: Rolanta production is costly ($84 per mil) and two weeks behind schedule.

Problems Encountered:

Rolanta production was delayed due to contamination in the assembly and fill areas, which led to a shutdown. An examination is still pending.

Conclusion:

We anticipate successful build for FY1991.

Recommendations:

We could use your leverage with the Rolanta problem. Please call Chuck Lyons and persuade him that timely production is mandatory to meet our schedules.

FIGURE 3.2 Progress Report

Recommendations: What follow-up action (if any) should be taken?

You might want to use graphics to supplement your lab report. Schematics and wiring diagrams are important in a lab report to clarify your activities, as shown in Figure 3.3.

☐ Feasibility Reports

Occasionally, your company plans a project but is uncertain whether the project is feasible. For example, your company might be considering the purchase of equipment but is concerned that the machinery will be too expensive, the wrong size for your facilities, or incapable of performing the desired tasks. Perhaps your company wants to expand and is considering new locations. The decision makers, however, are uncertain which locations would be best for the expansion. Maybe your company wants to introduce a new product to the marketplace, but your CEO wants to be sure that a customer base exists before funds are allocated.

One way a company determines the viability of a project is to perform a feasibility study and then write a feasibility report documenting the findings. The following are components of an effective feasibility report.

1. Heading
Date
To
From
Subject (topic + focus)

```
Subject: Feasibility Report on XYZ Project
                   (focus)         (topic)
```

2. Introduction (overview, background)

Objectives: Under this subheading, you can answer any of the following questions:

- ☐ What is the purpose of this feasibility report? Until you answer this question, your reader doesn't know. As mentioned earlier in this chapter, it's false to assume prior knowledge on the part of your audience. One of your responsibilities is to provide background data. To answer the question regarding the report's purpose, you should provide a clear and concise statement of intent.
- ☐ What problems motivated this study? To clarify for your readers the purposes behind the study, *briefly* explain either
  —what problems cause doubt about the feasibility of the project (i.e., is there a market, is there a piece of equipment available which would meet the company's needs, is land available for expansion?)

Date: July 18, 1991
To: Dr.Jones
From: Sam Ascendio, Lab Technician *Sam*
Subject: Lab Report on the Accuracy of Decibel Voltage Gain (A) Measurements

Purpose

Technical Services has noted inaccuracies in recent measurements. In response to their request, this report will present results of tested A (gain in decibels) of our ABC voltage divider circuit. Measured A will be compared to calculated A. This will determine the accuracy of the measuring device.

Apparatus

- ☐ Audio generator
- ☐ Decade resistance box
- ☐ 1/2 W resistor: four 470 ohm, two 1 kilohm, 100 kilohm
- ☐ AC millivoltmeter

Procedure

1. Figure A shows a voltage divider. For each value of R (resistances) in Table 1, voltage gain was calculated (table attached).
2. An audio generator was adjusted to give a reading of 0 dB for input voltage.
3. Output voltage was measured on the dB scale. This reading is the measured A and is recorded in Table 1.
4. Step 3 was repeated for each value of R listed in Table 1.
5. Figure B shows three cascaded voltage dividers. A1 = v2/v1, A2 = v3/v2, and A3 = v4/v3. These voltage gains added together give the total voltage, as recorded in Table 2.
6. The circuit in Figure B was connected.
7. Input voltage was set at 0 dB on the 1-V range of the AC millivoltmeter.
8. Values V2, V3, and V4 were read and recorded in Table 3.

FIGURE 3.3 Lab Report

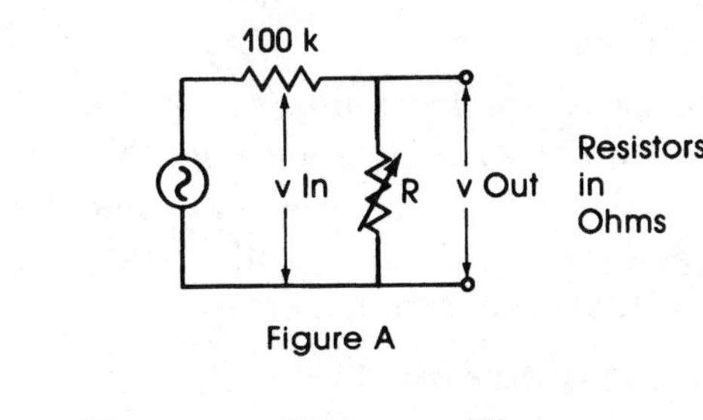

Figure A

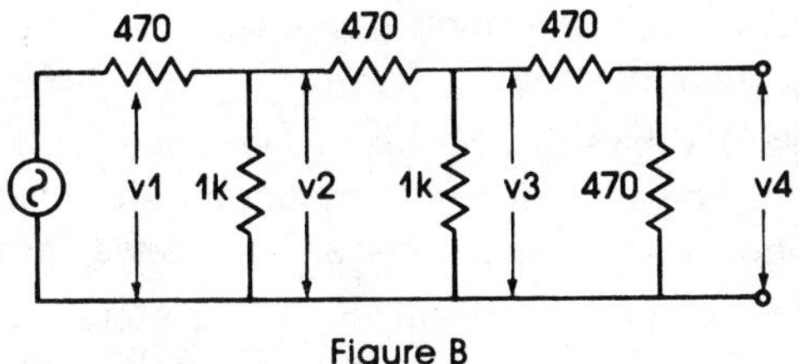

Figure B

TABLE 1

R	Calculated A	Measured A
240 kilohm	-3.02 dB	-3.21 dB
100 kilohm	-6.02 dB	-6.13 dB
46 kilohm	-10.00 dB	-9.71 dB
11 kilohm	-20.00 dB	-20.00 dB
1 kilohm	-40.00 dB	-40.00 dB

TABLE 2

A1	.500
A2	.500
A3	.500
A	.125

TABLE 3

V1	0 dB
V2	-5.97 dB
V3	-11.97 dB
V4	-18.06 dB

Conclusions/Recommendations

Accuracy between measured and calculated A in Table 1 was between .01 and .1 dB. This is acceptable. Accuracy between measured A in Table 3 and calculated voltage gain in Table 2 was between .01 and .1 dB--also very accurate. These tests show minimal error. No further action should be taken.

FIGURE 3.3 Continued

—what problems led to the proposed project (i.e., current equipment is too costly or time consuming, current facilities are too limited for expansion, current net income is limited by an insufficient market)

- ☐ Who initiated the feasibility study? List the name(s) of the managers or supervisors who requested this report.

Personnel: Document the names of your project team members, your liaison between your company and other companies involved, and/or your contacts at these other companies.

3. Discussion (body, findings)

Under this subheading, provide accessible and objective documentation regarding the following:

- ☐ What procedures did you use to analyze the feasibility of your project? Did you use technical research, site evaluations, vendor presentations, computer analyses, interviews, or outside consultants?
- ☐ What did your study reveal? State the facts about your project's cost, specifications, labor requirements, capabilities, availability, etc.

4. Conclusion/ recommendations

Conclusion: In this section, you go beyond the mere facts as evident in the discussion section. You state the significance of the findings. You draw a conclusion from what you've found in your study. What does it mean?

Recommendations: Once you've drawn your conclusions, the next step is to recommend a course of action. What do you suggest that your company do next? Which piece of equipment should be purchased, where should the company locate its expansion, or is there a sufficient market for the product?

Figure 3.4 presents an example of a feasibility report.

☐ Incident Reports

If a problem occurs within your work environment which requires investigation and suggested solutions, you might be asked to prepare an incident report (also called a trouble report or accident report).

Engineering environments requiring maintenance reports rarely provide employees with easy-to-fill-in forms. To write an incident report when you have not been given a printed form, include the following components.

1. Heading

Date
To
From
Subject (topic + focus)

```
Subject: Report on Chilled Water Leaks in D/823
          (focus)             (topic)
```

2. Introduction

Purpose: In this section, document when, where, and why you were called to perform maintenance. What motivated your visit to the scene of the problem?

3. Discussion (body, findings, agenda, work accomplished)

Using subheadings or itemization, quantify what you saw (the problems motivating the activity) and what you did to solve the problem.

4. Conclusion

Explain what caused the problem.

5. Recommendations

Relate what could be done in the future to avoid similar problems.

Figure 3.5 presents an example of an incident report.

☐ Process

Now that you know the criteria for short reports in general and for specific types of short reports (trip reports, progress reports, lab reports, feasibility reports, and incident reports), the next step is to construct these reports. How do you begin? As always, *prewrite, write,* and *rewrite.*

LABORATORY REPORT

There are two kinds of laboratory reports: those written in industry to document laboratory research or tests on materials or equipment, and those written in academic institutions to record laboratory tests performed by students. The former are generally known as test reports or laboratory reports; those written by students are simply called lab reports.

Industrial laboratory reports can describe a wide range of topics, from tests of a piece of metal to determine its tensile strength, through analysis of a sample of soil (a "drill core") to identify its composition, to checks of a microwave oven to assess whether it emits radiation. Academic lab reports can also describe many topics, but their purpose is different since they describe tests which usually are intended to help students learn something or prove a theory rather than produce a result for a client.

Laboratory reports generally conform to a standard pattern, although emphasis differs depending on the purpose of the report and how its results will be used. Readers of industrial laboratory or test reports are usually more interested in results ("Is the enclosed sample of steel safe to use for

Date: October 20, 1991
To: Jack Newton
From: Hal Langston Hal
Subject: Report on the Feasibility of Purchasing an XYZ Mini-Computer

Introduction

Purpose: The purpose of this report is to determine whether three new XYZ 5200 mini-computers can replace our current time-sharing terminals.

Problems motivating the project: Our current time-sharing terminals are costing $2000 a month more than we budgeted due to high initial start-up and annual maintenance costs.

Principal: Kristen Jamberdino

Personnel: Hal Langston, Judi Simmons, and Rick Gambles (project team). Darwin Lawyer (contact at XYZ Corp.).

Discussion

Using research provided by our vendor contact and studies from our accounting department, we concluded the following (all figures in dollars):

	1st Year		2nd Year	
	Time-sharing	Mini-computer	Time-sharing	Mini-compuputer
Initial cost	—	30,000	—	—
Time-Share Chg.	54,000	—	54,000	-
Info. storage	12,000	6,000	12,000	500
Cabinet	—	500	—	—
Maint. contract	—	9,000	—	9,000
Total	66,000	45,500	66,000	9,500

Conclusion

Three mini-computers save as much as 31% in the first year of installation and 85% in the second year.

FIGURE 3.4 Feasibility Report

1st Year $\frac{66,000 - 45,500}{66,000} \times 100 = 31.06\%$

2nd Year $\frac{66,000 - 9,500}{66,000} \times 100 = 85.61\%$

In addition, mini-computers shorten response time, another cost savings.

Recommendations

We should purchase the three XYZ 5200 mini-computers to replace our current time-sharing system.

FIGURE 3.4 Continued

Date: October 16, 1991
To: Tom Warner
From: Carlos Sandia CS
Subject: Report on Chilled Water Leaks in D/823

Introduction

On October 15, 1991, a flood was reported in D/823. I was called in to repair this leak. Following is a report on my findings and maintenance activities.

Agenda

8:15 P.M. The flood was reported.
8:25 P.M. I arrived at D/823 and discovered that the water level in the expansion tank at HVAC unit #253R-01 was 4 feet above normal and the tank valve was open.
8:30 P.M. A second flood was reported at HVAC unit #937-01 in the same department.
8:35 P.M. I shut off the open tank valves.
9:00 P.M. The expansion tank levels and pressure returned to normal.
9:30 P.M. All leaks were secure.

Conclusion

The chilled water leaks were caused by a malfunctioning level switch on the chilled water expansion tanks in the west boiler rooms. This caused the water level in the tanks to rise, which increased the system pressure to 150 lb.

Recommendations

The level control switch will be repaired. An alarm system will be installed by November 1, 1991.

FIGURE 3.5 Incident Report

construction of microwave towers which will be exposed to temperatures as low as -40°C in a North Dakota winter?" a client may ask) than in how a test was carried out. Readers of academic lab reports are usually professors and instructors who are more likely to be interested in thoroughly documented details, from which they can assess the student report writer's understanding of the subject and what the test proved.

A laboratory report comprises several readily identifiable compartments, each usually preceded by a heading. These compartments are described briefly here:

Part	**Section Title**	**Contents**
SUMMARY	**Summary**	A very brief statement of the purpose of the tests, the main findings, and what can be interpreted from them. (In short laboratory reports, the summary can be combined with the next compartment.)
BACKGROUND	**Objective**	A more detailed description of why the tests were performed, on whose authority they were conducted, and what they were expected to achieve or prove.
FACTS		*There are four parts here:*
	Equipment	A description of the test setup, plus a list of equipment and materials used. A drawing of the test hook-up may be inserted here. (If a series of tests is being performed, with a different equipment setup for each test, then a separate equipment description, materials list, and illustration should be inserted immediately before each test description.)
	Test Method	A detailed, step-by-step explanation of the tests. In industrial laboratory reports the depth of explanation depends on the reader's needs: if a reader is nontechnical and likely to be interested only in results, then the test description can be condensed. For lab reports written at a college or university, however, students are expected to provide a thorough description here.
	Test Results	Usually a brief statement of the test results or the findings evolving from the tests.
	Analysis (or Interpretation)	A detailed discussion of the results or findings, their implications, and what can be interpreted from them. (The analysis section is particularly important in academic lab reports.)
OUTCOME	**Conclusions**	A brief summing-up which shows how the test results, findings, and analysis meet the objective(s) established at the start of the report.
BACKUP	**Attachments**	These are pages of supporting data such as test measurements derived during the tests, or documentation such as specifications, procedures, instructions, and drawings, which would interrupt reading continuity if placed in the report narrative (in the test method section).

The compartments described here are those most likely to be used for either an industrial laboratory report or a college/university lab report. In practice, however, emphasis and labeling of the compartments probably will differ slightly, depending on the requirements of the organization employing the report writer or, in an academic setting, the professor or instructor who will evaluate the report.

☐ Prewriting

We've presented several techniques for prewriting—reporters' questions, clustering/mind mapping, flowcharting, and brainstorming/listing. An additional technique is called branching.

As with flowcharting and mind mapping, branching allows you to depict information graphically so you can not only gather data but also visualize it. This type of prewriting benefits both left-brain and right-brain people—those who are linear (outline oriented) as well as those who are more graphically attuned. Figure 3.6 shows an example of branching.

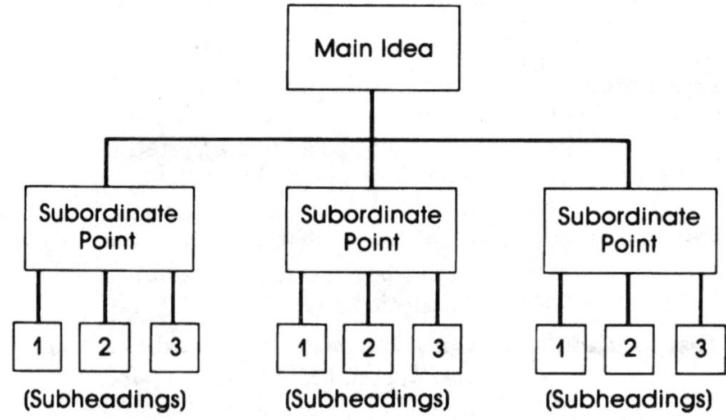

FIGURE 3.6 Branching

Branching is ideally suited for short reports. You can focus on whether the primary subject is a trip report, progress report, lab report, feasibility report, or incident report in the *main idea.* In addition, the *subordinate points* easily correspond to the introduction, discussion, and conclusion/recommendations. Finally, you can develop your ideas more specifically in the *subheadings.* Figure 3.7 shows an example of branching for a trip report.

You can see in Figure 3.7 how branching meshes with reporters' questions. Branching allows you to sketch out your organization and visualize your content. The reporters' questions help you make that content factual, precise, specific, and quantified.

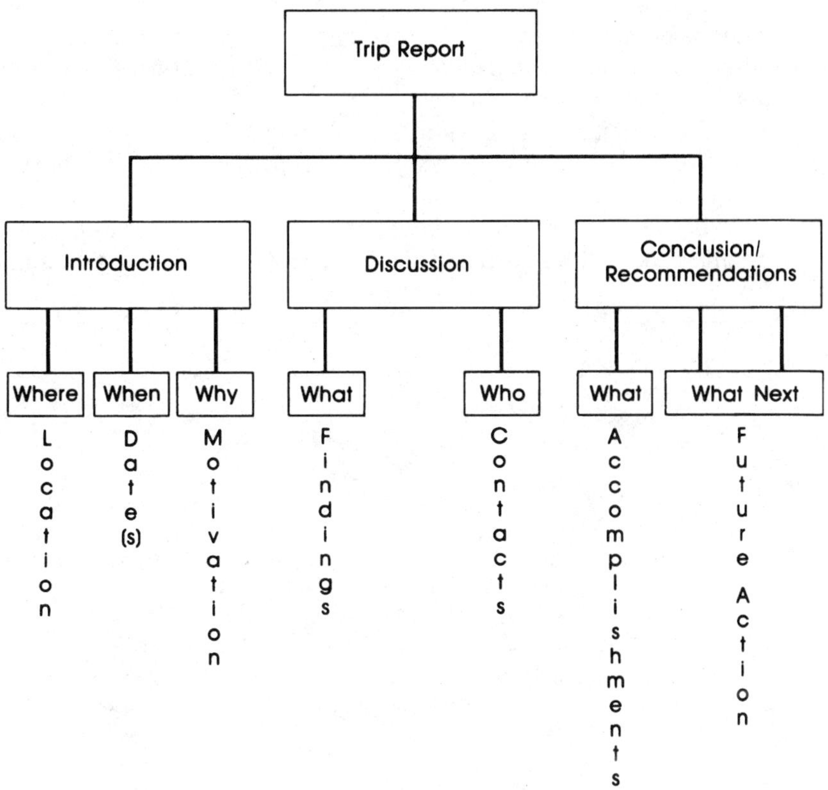

FIGURE 3.7 Branching (Trip Report)

☐ Writing

Once you've sketched an outline for your report using branching, the next step is to write the text. To write your report, do the following:

1. Reread your prewriting. Review what you've sketched in branching. Determine whether you've covered all important information. If you believe you've omitted any significant points, add them for clarity. If you've included any irrelevant ideas, omit them for conciseness.

2. Assess your audience. Your decisions regarding points to omit or include will depend on your audience. If your audience is familiar with your subject, you might be able to omit background data. However, if you have multiple audiences or an audience new to the situation, you'll have to include more data than you might have assumed necessary in your prewriting.

3. Draft the text. Focus on your major headings (introduction, discussion, conclusion/recommendations). Just get your ideas down on paper in a rough draft without worrying about grammar.

4. Organize your content. You can organize the discussion portion of your report using any one of these four modes: *chronology, importance, comparison/contrast,* and *problem/solution.* Which of these modes you use depends on your subject matter.

For example, if the subject of your trip report is a price check of sales items at two stores, comparison/contrast would be appropriate, as in Figure 3.8.

If the subject of your incident report is a site evaluation, chronology might work in the report's discussion, as in the following example:

Findings

8:00 A.M.	I arrived at the site and met with the supervisor to discuss procedures.
9:00 A.M.	We checked the water tower for possible storm damage. Only 10 shingles were missing.
10:00 A.M.	We checked the irrigation channel. It was severely damaged, the wall cracked in six places and water seeping through its barriers. Surrounding orchards will be flooded.
11:00 A.M.	We checked fruit bins. No water had entered.
1:00 P.M.	We checked the freezer units. The storm had disrupted electricity for four hours. All contents were destroyed.
2:00 P.M.	The supervisor and I returned to his office to evaluate our findings.

As discussed in earlier chapters, chronology is an easy method of organization to use and to follow. However, it is not always your most successful choice. Chronology inadvertently buries key data. For instance, in the preceding report findings, the most important discoveries occur at 10:00 A.M. and at 1:00 P.M., hidden in the middle of the list. To avoid making your readers guess where the important information is, use the third method of organization—importance—in which you list the most important point first, lesser points later, as in the following example:

Findings

1. Freezer units: Electricity was out for four hours. All contents were destroyed.
2. Irrigation channel: The wall was cracked in six places. Seepage was significant and sure to affect the orchards.
3. Water tower: Minor damage to shingles.
4. Fruit bins: No damage.

To: Meagan Clem
From: Mary Jane Porter *Mary Jane*
Date: January 12, 1991
Subject: Price Check Report-Handy Sandy Hardware

Introduction

On Thursday,January 8, 1991, I compared our sales prices on plumbing items with those on sale at Handy Sandy Hardware, 1000 W. 29th St., Newtown, WI.

Findings

Item	Hughes's Sale Price	Handy Sandy's Sale Price
1/2" copper tubing	$ 4.89 (10')	$ 4.99 (10')
3/4" copper tubing	10.50 (10')	9.99 (10')
1/2" CPVC pipe	2.39 (10')	2.99 (10')
3/4" CPVC pipe	3.49 (10')	5.99 (10')
1-1/2" PVC pipe	3.99 (10')	4.99 (10')
Acme 800 faucet	40.95	39.95
Acme 700 faucet	22.95	25.95

Conclusion

On five of the seven items (71.4%), Hughes's had the lower price.

Recommendations

We should continue to compare our prices to Handy Sandy's. We should also try to lower our prices which exceed theirs.

FIGURE 3.8 Trip Report Organized by Comparison/Contrast

If you're writing a progress report to document a problem and suggest a solution, use problem/solution to organize your data, as follows:

```
DISCUSSION
```

Problem--Production schedules on our M23 and B19 are behind three weeks due to machinery failures. Our numerical control device no longer maintains tolerance. This is forcing us to rework equipment, which is costing us $200 per reworked piece.

Solution--We must purchase a new numerical control device. The best option is an Xrox 1234. This machine is guaranteed for five years. Any problems with tolerance during this period are covered. Xrox either will correct the errors on site or provide us a loaner until the equipment is fixed. To avoid further production delays, we must purchase this machine by 1/18/92.

☐ Rewriting

After a gestation period in which you let the report sit so you can become more objective about your writing, retrieve the report and rewrite. Perfect your text by using the following rewriting techniques:

1. *Add detail for clarity.* Have you answered the reporters' questions as thoroughly as needed? Don't assume your readers will know the why's and wherefore's. Spell it all out, exactly. You often have multiple readers, many of whom do not know your motivations or objectives. They need clarity.

2. *Delete dead words and phrases for conciseness.* For example, in your recommendations, don't say, "Acme's opinion is that apparently the proposed ideas will not successfully supersede those already implemented." Instead, simply write, "Recommendations: No further action is required."

3. *Simplify old-fashioned words and phrases.* What does *pursuant* mean? And how about *issuance of this report?* The ultimate goal of technical writing is to communicate, not to confuse.

4. *Move information within your discussion for emphasis.* Make sure that you've either maintained chronology (if you're documenting an agenda) or used importance to focus on your main point. If you've confused the two, cut and paste—move information around to achieve your desired goals.

5. *Reformat your text for accessibility.* Highlight your key points with underlining or boldface. Use graphics to assist your readers. Don't overload your readers with massive blocks of impenetrable text.

6. Enhance your text for style. Be sure to quantify when needed, personalize with pronouns for audience involvement, and be positive. Stress words like *benefit, successful, achieved,* and *value* rather than bowing to negative words like *can't, failed, confused,* or *mistaken.*

7. Proofread and correct the report for grammatical and contextual accuracy.

8. Avoid sexist language. Foreman should be *supervisor, chairman* should be *chairperson* or *chair,* and *Mr. Swarth, Mr. James, and Sue* must be *Mr. Swarth, Mr. James, and Ms. Aarons.*

SHORT REPORT CRITERIA CHECKLIST

Use the following short-report criteria checklist to help you in writing your short report.

1. ☐ *Does your subject line contain a topic and a focus?* If you write only "Subject: Trip Report" or "Subject: Feasibility Report," you have not communicated thoroughly to your reader. Such a subject line merely presents the focus of your correspondence. But what's the topic? To provide both topic and focus, you need to write "Subject: Trip Report on Solvent Training Course, Arco Corporation—3/15/91" or "Subject: Feasibility Report on Company Expansion to Bolker Blvd."
2. ☐ *Does the introduction explain the purpose of the report, document the personnel involved, and/or state when and where the activities occurred?*
3. ☐ *When you write the discussion section of the report, do you quantify what occurred?* In this section, you must clarify precisely. Supply accurate dates, times, calculations, and problems encountered.
4. ☐ *Is the discussion accessible?* To create reader-friendly ease of access, use highlighting techniques, such as headings, boldface, underlining, and itemization. You also might want to use graphics, such as pie charts, bar charts, or tables.
5. ☐ *Have you selected an appropriate method of organization in your discussion?* You can use chronology, importance, comparison/contrast, and/or problem/solution to document your findings.
6. ☐ *Does your conclusion present a value judgment regarding the findings presented in the discussion?* The discussion states the facts; the conclusion decides what these facts mean.
7. ☐ *In your recommendations, do you tell your reader(s) what to do next or what you consider to be the appropriate course of action ?*
8. ☐ *Have you maintained a low fog index for readability?*
9. ☐ *Have you effectively recognized your audience's level of understanding (high tech, low tech, lay, management, subordinate, colleague) and written accordingly?*
10. ☐ *Is your report accurate?* Correct grammar and calculations make a difference. If you've made errors in spelling, punctuation, grammar, or mathematics, you will look unprofessional.

PROCESS LOG

Let's look at how one student used the writing process (prewriting, writing, and rewriting) to construct her progress report.

☐ Prewriting

First, the student used branching so she could visually gather data and determine objectives (Figure 3.9).

☐ Writing

Next, the student wrote a quick draft without worrying about correctness. She focused on the main units of the information she discovered in prewriting (Figure 3.10).

☐ Rewriting

After drafting this report, the student submitted her copy to a peer review group, which helped her revise her text (Figure 3.11).

After discussing the suggested changes with her peer review group, the student revised her draft and submitted her finished copy (Figure 3.12).

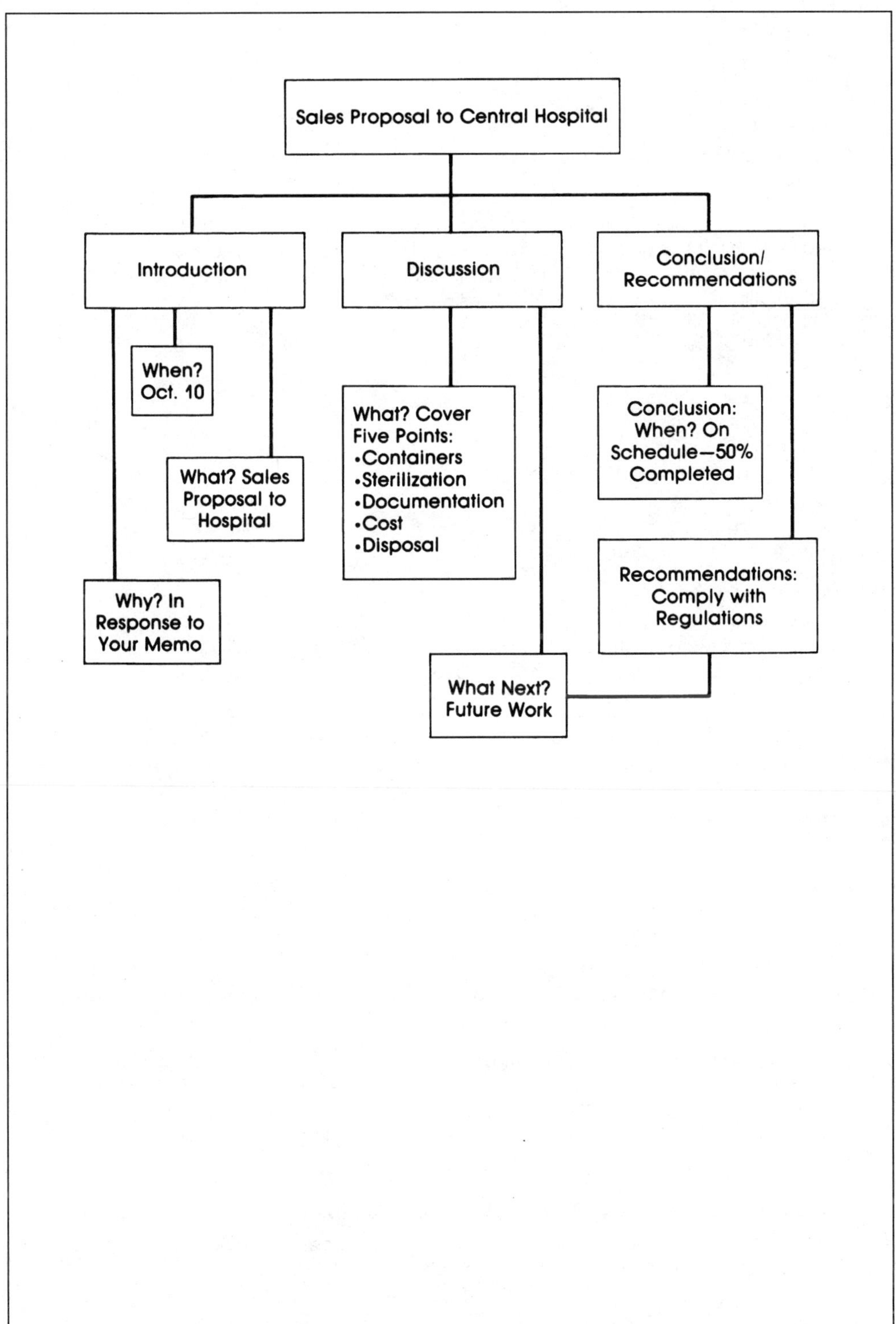

FIGURE 3.9 Student's Branching

November 6, 1991

To: Carolyn Jensen
From: Shuan Wang.
Subject: Progress report.

Purpose: This is a progress report on the status of a sales proposal you requested in your memo of October 10, 1991. The objective of this proposal is the sale of a total program for infectious waste control and disposal to a Central Hospital. The proposal will cover the following five areas.

1. Containers
2. Steam sterilization
3. Cost savings
4. Landfill operating
5. Computerized documentation

Work Completed: The following is a list of items that are finished on the project.

Containers

I have finished a description of the specially designed containers with disposable biohazard bag.

Steam sterilization

I have set a instructions for using the Biological Detector, model BD 12130 as a reliable indicator of sterilization of infectious wastes.

Cost savings

Central Hospital sent me some information on installing a pathological incinerator as well as the constant manpower and maintenance costs to operate them. I ran this information through our computer program "Save-Save". The results show that a substantial savings will be realized by the use of our services.

Future Work: I have an appointment to visit Central Hospital on November 7, 1991. At that time I will make on-site evaluations of present waste handling practices at Central Hospital. After carefully studing this evaluations, I will report to you on needed changes to comply with governmental guidelines.

Conclusion: The project is proceeding on schedule. Approximately 50% of work is done (see graph). I don't see any problem at this time and should be able to meet the target date.

FIGURE 3.10 Student's Rough Draft

November 6, 1991

To: Carolyn Jensen
From: Shuan Wang x
Subject: Progress report x

Needs topic & focus

Redundant ?

Reformat- underline & use CAPS

Purpose: This is a progress report on the status of a sales proposal you requested in your memo of October 10, 1991.

The objective of this proposal is the sale of a total program for infectious waste control and disposal to a Central Hospital.] wordy ?

The proposal will cover the following five areas. weak word

1. Containers
2. Steam sterilization
3. Cost savings
4. Landfill operating — Needs new title
5. Computerized documentation

Reformat

wordy

Work Completed: The following ~~is a list of items~~ that are finished on the ~~project~~.

Containers

I have finished a description of the specially designed containers with disposable biohazard bag. when ?

Steam sterilization

Huh ?

I have set a instructions for using the Biological Detector, model BD 12130 as a reliable indicator of sterilization of infectious wastes. wordy — when ?

Cost savings

vague

Central Hospital sent me some information on installing a pathological incinerator as well as the constant manpower and maintenance costs to operate them. I ran this information through our computer program "Save-Save". The results show that a substantial savings will be realized by the use of our services.

vague

FIGURE 3.11 Peer Group Revisions

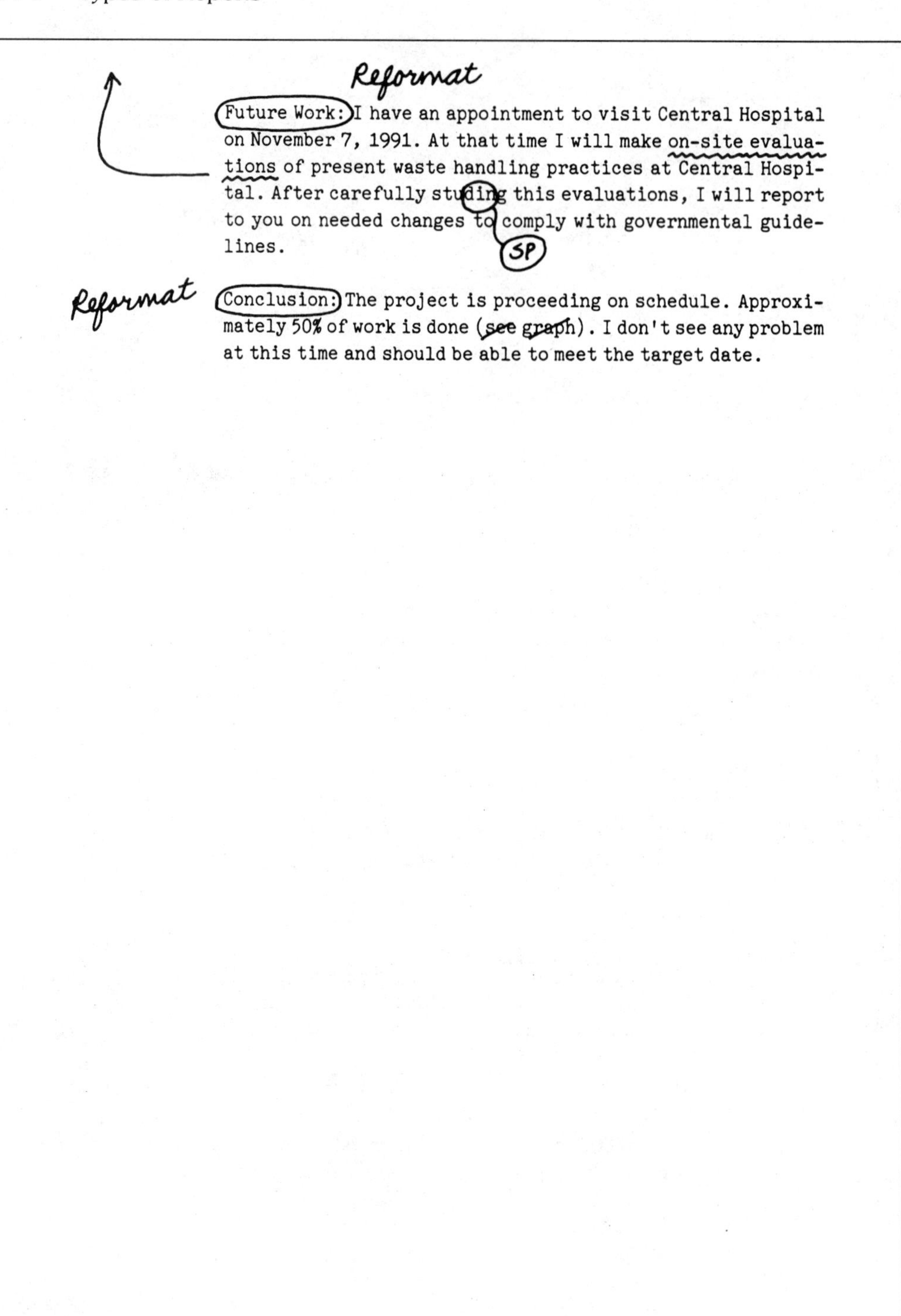
Reformat

Future Work: I have an appointment to visit Central Hospital on November 7, 1991. At that time I will make on-site evaluations of present waste handling practices at Central Hospital. After carefully studing this evaluations, I will report to you on needed changes to comply with governmental guidelines.

SP

Reformat

Conclusion: The project is proceeding on schedule. Approximately 50% of work is done (see graph). I don't see any problem at this time and should be able to meet the target date.

FIGURE 3.11 Continued

Interoffice Correspondence

Date: November 6, 1991
To: Carolyn Jensen
From: Shuan Wang Shuan
Subject: Progress Report on Central Hospital Sales Proposal

PURPOSE

In response to your October 10, 1991, request, following is a report on the status of our Central Hospital sales proposal. This proposal will present Central Hospital our total program for infectious waste control and disposal. The proposal will cover these five topics:

- ☐ Containers
- ☐ Steam sterilization
- ☐ Cost savings
- ☐ On-site evaluations
- ☐ Landfill disposal

WORK COMPLETED

1. ***Containers***—On October 5, I finished a description of the specially designed containers with biohazard bags.
2. ***Steam sterilizations***—On November 4, I wrote instructions for using our Biological Detector, model BG 12130. This detector measures infectious waste sterilization levels.
3. ***Cost savings***—Central Hospital sent me their cost charts for pathological incinerator expenses and maintenance costs. I used our computer program "Save-Save" to evaluate these costs. The program results show that our services can save Central Hospital $15,000 a year on annual incinerator costs, after a two year break-even period.

FUTURE WORK

1. ***On-site evaluations***—When I visit Central Hospital on November 11, 1991, I will evaluate their present waste handling system. After studying these evaluations, I will report changes necessary for government compliance.

FIGURE 3.12 Final Copy

2. ***Landfill disposal***—I will contact the Environmental Protection Agency on November 13, 1991, to receive authorization for disposing of sterilized waste at our sanitary landfill.

CONCLUSION

The project is proceeding on schedule. Approximately 55% of our work is completed. I see no problems at this time. We should meet our December 31, 1991, target date.

FIGURE 3.12 Continued

Long Reports and Proposals

OBJECTIVES

In the preceding section, we discussed various types of short reports, including trip reports, progress reports, lab reports, incident reports, and feasibility reports. The majority of these reports will be limited to no more than five pages. A report on your job-related travel would rarely require multipage documentation. Similarly, most progress reports address only daily, weekly, or monthly activities. The same applies to most lab reports. Since the subject matter will be limited, the report will be short.

However, in some instances, your subject matter might be so complex that a short report will not suffice. For example, your company asks you to write a report proposing the purchase of a new facility. You will have to write a long report—an *internal proposal* for your company's management. Or, perhaps your company is considering offering a new service or manufacturing a new product. Your responsibility is to write a long report—an *external proposal* selling the benefits of this new corporate offering to a prospective client.

In each of these instances, you ask your readers to make significant commitments regarding employees, schedules, equipment, training, facilities, and finances. Only a long report, possibly complete with research, will convey your content sufficiently and successfully. (We discuss research writing in Chapter V.)

To help you write your proposals effectively, this chapter provides the following: criteria for long reports and proposals, a sequential process for writing long reports and proposals, and a sample report.

CRITERIA FOR LONG REPORTS AND PROPOSALS

Since short reports run only a few pages, you can assume that your readers will be able to follow your train of thought easily. Thus, short reports merely require that you use headings such as "Introduction," "Discussion," and "Conclusion/Recommendation" to guide your readers through the correspondence.

Long reports, however, place a greater demand on readers. Your audience will be overwhelmed with numerous pages of information. A few headings won't be enough to help your readers wade through the data. To guide your readers through a proposal, you'll need to provide the following:

- ☐ Cover letter
- ☐ Title page
- ☐ Table of contents
- ☐ List of illustrations
- ☐ Abstract (or executive summary)
- ☐ Introduction
- ☐ Discussion (the body of the long report)
- ☐ Conclusion/Recommendation
- ☐ Glossary
- ☐ Works Cited page (if you're documenting research; this is discussed in Chapter V)
- ☐ Appendix

☐ Cover Letter

Your cover letter prefaces the long report and provides the reader an overview of what is to follow. It tells the reader:

- ☐ Why you are writing
- ☐ What you are writing about (the subject of this report)
- ☐ What exactly of importance is within the report
- ☐ What you plan to do next as a follow-up
- ☐ When the action should occur
- ☐ Why that date is important

Each of these points is discussed in greater detail in Chapter 1A.

☐ Title Page

The title page serves several purposes. On the most simple level, a title page acts as a dustcover or jacket keeping the actual report clean and neat. More importantly, the title page tells your reader the:

- ☐ Title of your report (thereby providing clarity of intent)
- ☐ Name of the company, writer, or writers submitting the report
- ☐ Date on which the report was completed

If the external proposal is being mailed outside your company to a client, you also might include on the title page the audience to whom the report is addressed. If the internal proposal is being submitted within your company to peers, subordinates, and/or supervisors, you might want to include a routing list of individuals who must sign off and/or approve the report.

Following are two sample title pages. Figure 3.13 is for an internal proposal; Figure 3.14 is for an external proposal.

☐ Table of Contents

Proposals are read by many different readers, each of whom will have a special area of interest. For example, the managers who read your reports will be interested in cost concerns, time frames, and personnel requirements. Technicians, in contrast, will be interested in technical descriptions and instructions. Not every reader will read each section of your report.

Your responsibility is to help these different readers find the sections of the report which interest them. One way to accomplish this is through a table of contents. The table of contents should be a complete and accurate listing of the main *and* minor topics covered in the report. In other words, you don't want just a brief and sketchy outline of major headings. This could lead to page gaps; your readers would be unable to find key ideas of interest.

The following table of contents is organized poorly.

```
                    Table of Contents

    I.   List of Illustrations . . . . . . . . . . .iv
   II.   Abstract . . . . . . . . . . . . . . . . . .v
  III.   Introduction . . . . . . . . . . . . . . . .1
   IV.   Proposal . . . . . . . . . . . . . . . . . .3
    V.   Conclusion  . . . . . . . . . . . . . . . .10
   VI.   Appendix  . . . . . . . . . . . . . . . . .11
  VII.   Glossary  . . . . . . . . . . . . . . . . .15
```

In this table of contents, we can see that the proposal section contains approximately eight pages of data. What's covered in those eight pages? Anything of value? We don't know. The same applies to the appendix, which covers four pages. What's in this section?

PROPOSED CABLE TRANSMISSION NETWORK
FROM CHEYENNE, WY
TO
HARTFORD, CT

Prepared by: ______________________________ Date: ________
Pete Niosi
Network Planner

Reviewed by: ______________________________ Date: ________
Leah Workman
Manager, Capital Planning

Recommended by: ____________________________ Date: ________
Greg Foss
Manager, Facilities

Recommended by: ____________________________ Date: ________
Shirley Chandley
Director, Implementation Planning

Approved by: ______________________________ Date: ________
Ralph Houston
Vice President, Network Planning

FIGURE 3.13 Title Page for Internal Proposal

PROPOSAL TO MAINTAIN COMPUTER MAINFRAME EQUIPMENT

For
Acme Products, Inc.
2121 New Tech Avenue
Bangor, ME

Submitted by
Thomas Brasher
Engineering Technician

August 13, 1991

FIGURE 3.14 Title Page for External Proposal

In contrast, an effective table of contents fleshes out this detail so your readers know exactly what's covered in each section. By providing a thorough table of contents, you'll save your readers time and help them find the information they want and need. Figure 3.15 is an example of a successful table of contents.

In the examples, note that the actual pagination (page 1) begins with the introduction section. Your first, Arabic-numbered page begins with your main text, not the front matter. Instead, information prior to the introduction is numbered with lowercase Roman numerals (i, ii, iii, etc.). Thus, the cover letter would be number i, the title page would be number ii, the table of contents number iii, and the list of illustrations (if printed on a page separate from the table of contents) number iv. Since the cover letter is the first page of the long report, you would not need to print the page number on it. Furthermore, a title page is never numbered. Therefore, the first page with a printed number is the table of contents. This lowercase Roman numeral should be printed at the foot of the page and centered.

☐ List of Illustrations

If your long report contains several tables and/or figures, you'll need to provide a list of illustrations. This list can be included below your table of contents, if there is room on the page, or on a separate page. As with the table of contents, your list of illustrations must be clear and informative. Don't waste your time and your reader's time by providing a poor list of illustrations like the following:

List of Illustrations

This list provides your reader with very little information. All the reader can ascertain from this list is that you've used some figures and tables. However, the reader will have no idea what purpose each illustration serves. Instead of supplying such a vague list, you should accompany the table and figure numbers with descriptive titles, as follows:

Table of Contents

FIGURE 3.15 Successful Table of Contents

List of Illustrations

☐ Abstract (or Executive Summary)

As mentioned earlier, a number of different readers will be interested in your proposal. One group of those readers will be management—supervisors, managers, and highly placed executives. How do these readers' needs differ from others? Because these readers are busy with management concerns and might have little technical knowledge, they need your help in two ways: They need information quickly, and they need it presented in low-tech terminology. You can achieve both these objectives through an abstract or executive summary.

The abstract, often called an executive summary, is a brief overview of the report's key points geared toward a low-tech reader. To accomplish the required brevity, you should limit your abstract to approximately three to ten sentences. These sentences can be presented as one paragraph or as smaller units of information separated by headings. Each long report you write will focus on unique ideas. Therefore, the content of your abstracts will differ from report to report. Nonetheless, abstracts should focus on the following: (a) the *problem* necessitating your proposal, (b) your suggested *solution,* and (c) the *benefits* derived when your proposed suggestions are implemented. These three points work for external as well as internal proposals.

For example, let's say you're asked to write an internal proposal suggesting a course of action (limiting excessive personnel, increasing your company's work force, improving your corporation's physical facilities, etc.). First, your abstract should specify the problem requiring your planned action. Next, you should mention the action you're planning to implement. This leads to a brief overview of how your plan would solve the problem, thus benefiting your company.

If you were writing an external proposal to sell a client a new product or service, you would still focus on problem, solution, and benefit. The abstract would remind the readers of their company's problem, state that your company's new product or service could alleviate this problem, and then emphasize the benefits derived.

In each case, you not only want to be brief, focusing on the most important issues, but also you should avoid high-tech terminology and concepts.

The purpose of the abstract is to provide your readers with an easy-to-understand summary of the entire report's focus. Your executives want the bottom line, and they want it quickly. They don't want to waste time deciphering your high-tech hieroglyphics. Therefore, either avoid all high-tech terminology completely or define your terms parenthetically.

The following is an example of a brief and low-tech abstract from an internal proposal.

> ABSTRACT
>
> Due to deregulation and the recent economic recession, we must reduce our work force by 12%.
>
> Our plan for doing so involves
>
> - ☐ Freezing new hires
> - ☐ Promoting early retirement
> - ☐ Reassigning second-shift supervisors to our Desoto plant
> - ☐ Temporarily laying off third-shift line technicians
>
> Achieving the above will allow us to maintain production during the current economic difficulties.

☐ Introduction

Your introduction should include two primary sections: (a) purpose, and (b) problem.

Purpose

In one to three sentences, tell your readers exactly the purpose of your long report. This purpose statement informs your readers *why* you are writing and/or *what* you hope to achieve. This statement repeats your abstract to a certain extent. However, it's not redundant; it's a reiteration. Although numerous people read your report, they all don't read each line or section of it. They skip and skim.

The purpose statement, in addition to the abstract, is another way to ensure that your readers understand your intent. It either reminds them of what they've just read in the abstract or informs them for the first time if they skipped over the abstract. Your purpose statement is synonymous with a paragraph's topic sentence, an essay's thesis, the first sentence in a letter, or the introductory paragraph in your short report.

The following is an effective purpose statement.

> Purpose: The purpose of this report is to propose the immediate installation of the 102473 Numerical Control Optical Scanner. This installation will ensure continued quality checks and allow us to meet agency specifications.

Problem

Whereas the purpose statement should be limited to one to three sentences for clarity and conciseness, your discussion of the problem must be much more detailed.

For example, if you're writing an internal proposal to add a new facility, your company's current work space must be too limited. You've got a problem which must be solved. If you're writing an external proposal to sell a new piece of equipment, your prospective client must need better equipment. Your proposal will solve the client's problem.

Your introduction's focus on the problem, which could average one to two pages, is important for two reasons. First, it highlights the importance of your long report. It emphasizes for your readers the report's priority. In this problem section, you persuade your readers that a problem truly exists and needs immediate attention.

Second, by clearly stating the problem, you also reveal your knowledge of the situation. The problem section reveals your expertise. Thus, after reading this section of the introduction, your audience should recognize the severity of the problem and trust you to solve it.

One way to help your readers understand the problem is through the use of highlighting techniques, especially headings and subheadings.

Figure 3.16 provides a sample introduction stating purpose and problem.

☐ Discussion

The discussion section of your proposal constitutes its body. In this section, you sell your product, service, or suggested solution. As such, the discussion section represents the major portion of the proposal, perhaps 85% of the text.

What will you focus on in this section? Since every proposal will differ, we can't tell you exactly what to include. However, your discussion can contain any or all of the following:

- ☐ Analyses
  - —Existing situation
  - —Solutions
  - —Benefits
- ☐ Technical descriptions of mechanisms, tools, facilities, and/or products
- ☐ Technical instructions
- ☐ Options
  - —Approaches/methodologies
  - —Purchase options
- ☐ Managerial chains of command (organizational charts)
- ☐ Biographical sketches of personnel
- ☐ Corporate and/or employee credentials
  - —Years in business
  - —Satisfied clients
  - —Certifications
  - —Previous accomplishments

I. INTRODUCTION

A. Purpose

This is a proposal for a storm sewer survey for Yakima, WA. First, the survey will identify storm sewers needing repair and renovation. Then the survey will recommend public works projects that would control residential basement flooding in Yakima.

B. Problem

1. Increased Flooding

Residential basement flooding in Yakima, WA, has been increasing. Fourteen basements were reported flooded in 1976, while 83 residents reported flooded basements in 1989.

2. Property Damage

Basement flooding in Yakima, WA, results in thousands of dollars in property damage. The following are commonly reported as damaged property:

a. Washers

b. Dryers

c. Freezers

d. Furniture

e. Furnaces

Major appliances cannot be repaired after water damage. Flooding can also result in expensive foundation repairs.

3. Indirect Costs

Flooding in Yakima is receiving increased publicity. Flood areas, including Yakima, have been identified in newspapers and on local newscasts. Until flooding problems have been corrected, potential residents and businesses may be reluctant to locate in Yakima.

FIGURE 3.16 Proposal Introduction

4. Special-Interest Groups

Citizens over 55 years old represent 40% of the Yakima, WA, population. In city council meetings, senior citizens with limited incomes expressed their distress over property damage. Residents are unable to obtain federal flood insurance and must bear the financial burden of replacing flood-damaged personal and real property. Senior citizens (and other Yakima residents) look to city officials to resolve this financial dilemma.

C. Benefits

Storm sewer surveys are the most cost-effective approach to sewer repairs. You will have an accurate assessment of damages. You will know the ***exact*** location and extent of damages. A survey will allow you to repair the most critical areas first. City officials can plan other repairs based on priority and budget considerations.

FIGURE 3.16 Continued

- ☐ Schedules
  - —Implementation schedules
  - —Reporting intervals
  - —Maintenance schedules
  - —Delivery schedules
  - —Completion dates
  - —Payment schedules
  - —Projected milestones (forecasts)
- ☐ Cost charts

You will have to decide which of these sections will be geared toward high-tech readers, low-tech readers, or a lay audience. Once this decision is made, you'll write accordingly, defining terms as needed. However, one way to handle multiple audience levels is through a glossary (we'll discuss this later in this chapter).

In addition to audience recognition, you should also enhance your discussion with figures and tables for clarity, conciseness, and cosmetic appeal.

☐ Conclusion/Recommendation

As with short reports, you must sum up your proposal, providing your readers with a sense of closure. The conclusion can restate the problem, your solutions, and the benefits to be derived. In doing so, remember to quantify. Be specific—state percentages and amounts.

Your recommendation will suggest the next course of action. Specify when this action will or should occur and why that date is important.

The conclusion/recommendation section can be made accessible through highlighting techniques, including headings, subheadings, underlining, boldface, itemization, and white space.

Your conclusion/recommendation, like your abstract, will be read primarily by executives. Thus, write to a low-tech reader.

Figure 3.17 is an example of a successfully written conclusion/recommendation from an internal proposal.

☐ Glossary

Because you will have numerous readers with multiple levels of expertise, you must be concerned about your use of high-tech language {abbreviations, acronyms, and terms). Although some of your readers will understand your terminology, others won't. However, if you define your terms each time you use them, two problems will occur. You will insult high-tech readers; you will delay your audience as they read your text. To avoid these pitfalls, use a glossary.

A glossary is an alphabetized list of high-tech terminology placed after your conclusion/recommendation. When your first high-tech, unfamiliar abbreviation, acronym, or term is used, follow it with an asterisk (*). Then, at the bottom of the page, in a footnote, write

CONCLUSION

Our line capability between San Marcos and LaGrange is insufficient. Presently, we are 23% under our desired goal. Using the vacated fiber cables will not solve this problem because the current configuration does not meet our standards. Upgrading the current configuration will improve our capacity only 9% and still present us the risk of service outages.

RECOMMENDATION

We suggest laying new fiber cables for the following reasons. They will

- ☐ Provide 63% more capacity than the current system
- ☐ Reduce the risk of service outages
- ☐ Allow for forecasted demands when current capacity is exceeded
- ☐ Meet standard configurations

If these new cables are laid by September 1, 1992, we will predate state tariff plans to be implemented by the new fiscal year.

FIGURE 3.17 Proposal Conclusion/Recommendation

*This and subsequent terms followed by an asterisk are defined on page _ of the glossary.

Subsequent high-tech terms should be followed by an asterisk, but you don't have to place the footnote at the bottom of each page.

A glossary is invaluable. Readers who are unfamiliar with your terminology can turn to the glossary and read your definitions. Those readers who understand your word usage can continue to read without stopping for unneeded information.

Figure 3.18 is a sample glossary.

☐ Works Cited

If you've used research to write your proposal, you will need to include a works cited page. This page documents the sources (books, periodicals, interviews, computer software, etc.) you've researched and quoted or paraphrased. To find more about conducting research, see Chapter V.

☐ Appendix

A final, optional component is an appendix. Appendices allow you to include any additional information (survey results, tables, figures, previous report findings, relevant letters and/or memos, etc.) which you have not built into your proposal's main text.

The contents of your appendix should not be of primary importance. Any truly important information should be incorporated within the report's main text. Valuable data (proof, substantiation, or information which clarifies a point) should appear in the text where it is easily accessible. Information provided within an appendix is buried, simply because of its placement at the end of the report. You don't want to bury key ideas. An appendix is a perfect place to file data which is not essential but which provides documentation for future reference.

PROCESS

Proposals and long reports, which include descriptions, instructions, cost analyses, scheduling assessments, and personnel considerations, are more demanding than other kinds of technical correspondence. Therefore, writing according to a process approach is even more important than for other kinds of writing discussed in this textbook. For your long report, you'll have more data to gather, more information to organize, and more text to revise. To help you tackle these tasks,

- ☐ Prewrite,
- ☐ Write, and then
- ☐ Rewrite.

GLOSSARY

BSCE:	Bachelor of Science, Civil Engineering
Drainage Studies:	The study of moving surface or surplus water
Gb:	Gigabyte
Interface:	Communication with other agencies, entities, and systems to discuss subjects of common interest
POP:	Place of purchase
Smoke Test:	Test using underground smoke bombs to give visual, above-ground signs of sewer pipe leaks
Video Scanner:	A portable video camera which examines the inside surface of sewer pipe
Water Parting:	A boundary line separating the drainage districts of two streams
Watershed Area:	An area bounded by a water parting and draining into a particular watercourse

FIGURE 3.18 Glossary

☐ Prewriting

Throughout this textbook, we have provided numerous prewriting techniques geared toward helping you gather data and determine your objectives. Any or all of these can be used while prewriting your long report. For example, you might want to use:

- ☐ *Listing/brainstorming* to outline the key components of your long report or for your technical description, if you plan to include one.
- ☐ *Reporters' questions (who, what, when, where, why,* and *how)* to help you gather data for any of the sections in your long report.
- ☐ *Flowcharting* to organize procedures and/or schedules.
- ☐ *Branching and mind mapping* to organize your managerial sections (organizational charts for chains of command, personnel responsibilities, etc.).

In addition to these prewriting techniques, you might need to perform research prior to writing. For instance, let's say your engineering firm is submitting a proposal to an out-of-state corporation. Prior to bidding on the job, you'll need to find out what kinds of certifications or licenses this state requires. To do so, you'll have to research the state's requirements and read state laws regarding construction certifications and licenses. (We discuss techniques for doing research in Chapter V.)

Perhaps you'll need to survey residents, clients, or personnel to get their ideas regarding proposed changes. If so, here's what you should do.

Surveys

Before you can take a survey, you must decide what questions to ask. Brainstorming/listing would be an excellent way to gather such data. Follow this procedure:

1. Rapidly jot down whatever questions come to mind regarding your topic.
2. Don't editorialize at this point. Don't try to organize the list; don't delete any questions that emerge.
3. Once you have a list of possible topics, review the list.
   a. Add any omissions (keep in mind your reporters' questions during this stage).
   b. Delete any redundancies or irrelevant ideas.
   c. Organize the list according to some rational order.

Your next step is to format the list into a survey questionnaire, as in Figure 3.19.

☐ Writing

After gathering your data and organizing your thoughts through prewriting, your next step is to draft your proposal.

STUDENT AND STAFF QUESTIONNAIRE
FOR
PROPOSED COLLEGE DAY CARE CENTER

1. Are you male or female?__________
2. Are you married? __________
3. Are you in a single- or double-income family?__________
4. Are you student or staff? __________
5. How many children do you have? __________
6. What are their ages? __________ __________ __________
7. Would you be interested in having a day care at this college?___
8. How much would you be willing to pay per hour for child care at this college? __________
9. Do you think a day care would increase attendance at this college? __________

If student:

10. Are you enrolled full time or part time at this college? _______

11. Do you attend mornings, afternoons, evenings, or a combination of the above (please specify)? __________

12. Would you be willing to work in this day care part time? ______

If staff:

13. What hours do you work at this college (primarily mornings, afternoons, evenings, or a combination of the above—please specify)? ____

14. What hours would you need to use the day care?__________

Optional:

Name: ____

Address: ____________________________________

Phone: ______________________________________

Thank you for your assistance.

FIGURE 3.19 **Questionnaire**

1. Review your prewriting. Double-check your listing, brainstorming, mind mapping, flowcharting, reporters' questions, interviews, research, and/or surveys. Is all the necessary information there? Do you have what you need? If not, now is the time to add new detail or research your topic further. In contrast, perhaps you've gathered more information than necessary. Maybe some of your data is irrelevant, contradictory, or misleading. Delete this information. Focus your attention on only the most important details.

2. Organize the data. Each of your proposal's sections will require a different organizational pattern. Following are several possible approaches:

- ☐ Abstract: problem/solution/benefit
- ☐ Introduction: cause/effect {The problem unit is the cause of your writing; the purpose statement represents the effect.)
- ☐ Main text: This section will demand many different methods of organization, including:
  —Analysis (cost charts, approaches, managerial chains of command, personnel biographies, etc.)
  —Chronology {procedures, scheduling)
  —Spatial (descriptions)
  —Comparison/contrast (options—approaches, personnel, products)
- ☐ Conclusion/recommendation: analysis and importance (Organize your recommendations by importance to highlight priority or justify need.)

3. Write using sufficing techniques. When you draft your text, don't worry about correct grammar, highlighting techniques, or graphics. Just get the information down as rapidly as you can. You can revise the draft during rewriting, the third stage of the writing process.

4. Format your writing according to the criteria for effective long reports and proposals.

☐ Rewriting

After you've written a rough draft of your proposal, the next step is to revise it—fine tune, hone, sculpt, and polish your draft.

1. Add detail for clarity. In addition to rereading your rough draft and adding a missing *who, what, when, where, why,* and *how* where necessary, add your graphics. Go back to each section of your proposal and determine where you could use any of the following:

- ☐ Tables: Your cost section lends itself to tables.
- ☐ Figures: Your introduction's problem analysis and any of the main text sections could profit from the following figures:
  —Line charts /excellent for showing upward and downward movement over a period of time. A line chart could be used to show how a company's profits have decreased, for example.)

—Bar charts (effective for comparisons. Through a bar or grouped bar chart, you could reveal visually how one product, service, or approach is superior to another.)
—Pie charts (excellent for showing percentages. A pie chart could help you show either the amount of time spent or amount of money allocated for an activity.)
—Line drawings (effective for your technical descriptions)
—Photographs (again effective for technical descriptions)
—Flowcharts (a successful way to help readers understand procedures)
—Organizational charts (excellent for giving an overview of managerial chains of command).

Another important addition to your proposal in this rewriting stage is a glossary. Now that you've written your rough draft, go back over each page to decide which abbreviations, acronyms, and high-tech terms must be placed in your glossary. After each of these high-tech words or phrases, add an asterisk. After the first abbreviation, acronym, or high-tech word or phrase, add a footnote stating that subsequent words or phrases followed by an asterisk will be defined in the glossary. Then write your glossary and add it to your proposal.

2. Delete dead words and phrases for conciseness. Because long reports *are* long, you've already made your reader uncomfortable. People don't like wading through massive pages of text. Anything you can do to help your reader through this task will be appreciated. Avoid making the report longer than necessary. Delete dead words and phrases.

3. Simplify old-fashioned words. A common adage in technical writing is to write the way you speak. In other words, try to be more conversational in your writing. We aren't suggesting that you use slang or colloquialisms. But a word like *supersede* should be simplified. Instead, write *replace*. Check your text to see if you've used words that are unnecessarily confusing.

Deleting and simplifying, when used together, will help you lower your fog level. This is especially important in your abstract and conclusion/recommendation sections, which are geared toward low-tech management. Review these sections of your long report to determine if you have written at the appropriate level. If you have used terminology which is too high tech, simplify.

4. Move information. Each section of your proposal will use a different organizational method. Your abstract, for example, should be organized according to a problem/solution/benefit approach. Your introduction will be organized according to cause (the problem) and effect (the purpose). The organization of your main text will vary from section to section. You might analyze according to importance, set up schedules and procedures chronologically, describe spatially, and so forth.

In rewriting, revise your proposal to ensure that each section maintains the appropriate organizational pattern. To do so, move information around (cut and paste).

5. Reformat for reader-friendly ease of access. If you give your readers wall-to-wall words, they will doze off while attempting to wade through your report. To avoid this, revise your long report by reformatting. Indent to create white space. Add headings and subheadings. Itemize ideas, boldface key points, underline important words or phrases. Using graphics (tables and figures) will also help you avoid long, overwhelming blocks of text. By reformatting your proposal, you will make the text inviting and ease reader access.

6. Enhance the tone of your report. Although you want to keep your proposal professional, remember that people write for people. Your reader is a human being, not a machine. Therefore, to achieve a sense of humanity, enhance the tone of your text by using pronouns and positive, motivational words. These are important in your statements of benefit and recommended courses of action. *Sell* your ideas.

7. Correct errors. If you're proposing a sale, you must provide accurate figures and information. Proposals, for example, are legally binding. If you state a fee in the proposal or write about schedules, your prospective client will hold you responsible; you must live up to those fees or schedules. Make sure that your figures and/or data are accurate.

Reread each of your numbers, recalculate your figures, and double-check your sources of information. Correct errors prior to submitting your report. Failure to do so could be catastrophic for your company or your client.

Of course, you must also check for typographical, mechanical, and grammatical errors. If you submit a long report or proposal containing such errors, you will look unprofessional and undermine your company's credibility.

8. Avoid sexist language. As noted throughout this textbook, men and women read your writing. Don't talk about *foremen, manpower,* or *men and girls.* Change *foremen* to *supervisors, manpower* to *work force* or *personnel,* and *men and girls* to *men and women.* Don't address your cover letter to *gentlemen.* Either find out the name of your readers or omit the salutation according to the simplified letter style, discussed in Chapter IA.

SAMPLE PROPOSAL

Following is a sample proposal which you can use as a model for your writing.

Pure Air Medical, Inc.
"Improving the Quality of Life"
12345 College Blvd.
Overland Park, Kansas 66215
(913) 888-4000

December 9, 1991

Dr. Richard Davis, Director
La Habra Retirement Center
220 Cypress
La Habra, CA 90631

Dear Dr. Davis:

Submitted for your review is our proposal regarding the Electronic Demand Cannula oxygen-saving system. This document is in response to your September 25, 1991, letter and our subsequent discussions.

Within our report, you will find the following supporting materials geared toward your requests:

☐ Product specifications ....pages 3-4
☐ Quantity discounts ....page 6
☐ Qualifications ....page 6

Thank you for your interest in our product. We look forward to serving you and will call within the next two weeks to finalize arrangements.

Sincerely,

S. Jeremy Lauren

S. Jeremy Lauren
Marketing Director

Enclosure: Proposal

PROPOSAL FOR
REDUCING OXYGEN EXPENSES

Prepared for
Dr. Richard Davis, Director
La Habra Retirement Center

by
S. Jeremy Lauren
Marketing Director
Pure Air Medical, Inc.

December 9, 1991

TABLE OF CONTENTS

LIST OF ILLUSTRATIONS

ABSTRACT

Expenses for medical oxygen have increased steadily for several years. Now the federal government is reducing the amount of coverage that Medicare allows for prescription oxygen.

These cost increases can be reduced through the use of our new Electronic Demand Cannula (EDC). The EDC delivers oxygen to the patient only when the patient inhales. Oxygen does not flow during the exhalation phase. Therefore, oxygen costs are conserved.

This oxygen-saving feature can reduce your oxygen expenses by as much as 50%. Patients who use portable oxygen supplies can enjoy prolonged intervals between refilling, thus providing more freedom and mobility.

I. INTRODUCTION

A. PURPOSE

This is a proposal to sell the new Electronic Demand Cannula (EDC)* to the La Habra Retirement Center, La Habra, California. This bid to sell offers you a special discount when you purchase our EDCs in the quantities suggested in this proposal.

B. PROBLEM

Since 1980, the price of medical-grade oxygen has skyrocketed. It cost $10 per 1,000 cubic feet (cu ft) in 1980. Today, medical-grade oxygen costs $26 per 1,000 cu ft. Many factors have contributed to this soaring cost, including demand, product liability insurance, and inflation. In 1987, the federal government enacted legislation that reduced the amount that Medicare pays for prescription oxygen. As a result, you can expect your oxygen expenses to double the amount that you spent in 1981. Since few insurance companies offer programs covering long-term prescription oxygen, you, or your patient, will pay the additional expenses.

*This and all subsequent terms marked by an asterisk (*) are defined in the glossary on page 8.

II. PROPOSAL

A. SOLUTION

Since the price of oxygen will not go down, you must try to use less while obtaining the same clinical benefits.

Pure Air Medical, a leader in oxygen-administering technology, proposes the implementation of our new Electronic Demand Cannula* (EDC).Using state-of-the-art electronics, the EDC senses the patient's inspiratory effort*. When a breath is detected, the EDC dispenses oxygen through the patient's cannula*. The patient receives oxygen only when he or she needs it.

Continuously flowing cannulas waste gas during exhalation and rest. Clinical studies have proven that 50% of the oxygen used by cannula patients is wasted during that phase.These same tests also revealed that blood oxygen saturation* does not significantly vary between continuous and intermittent flow cannulas. The patient receives the same benefit from less oxygen. Table 1 explains this in greater detail.

Table 1

BLOOD OXYGEN SATURATION
USING THE ELECTRONIC DEMAND CANNULA
versus
CONTINUOUS FLOW CANNULAS

Prescribed Flowrate	Breaths per Minute (bpm)	Blood Oxygen Saturation %	
lpm*	bpm*	Intermittent	Continuous
0.5 lpm	12	96%	98%
1 lpm	12	98%	99%
2 lpm	12	99%	100%
3 lpm	12	100%	100%
4 lpm	12	100%	100%

We have included a technical description of the EDC to help explain how this system will benefit oxygen cannula users.

B. TECHNICAL DESCRIPTION

The Pure Air EDC (Electronic Demand Cannula) is an oxygen-administering device which is designed to conserve oxygen. The EDC is composed of six main parts: oxygen inlet connector, visual display indicators (LEDS)*, power switch, patient connector, AC adapter connector, and high-impact plastic case (see Figures 1 and 2).

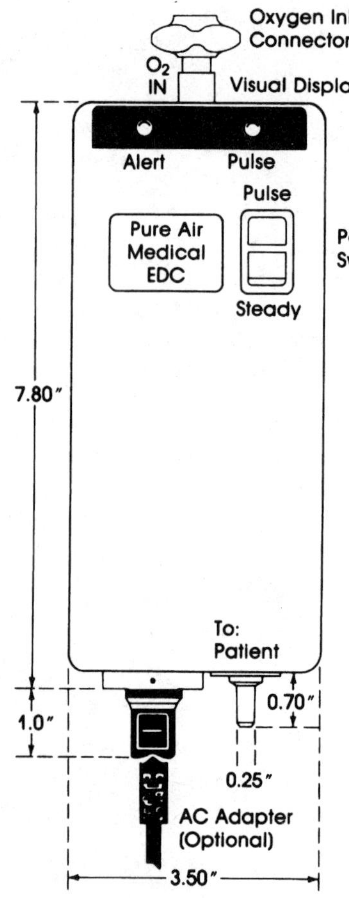

OXYGEN INLET CONNECTOR: The oxygen inlet connector is a DISS No. 1240 (Diameter Index Safety System) and is made of chrome-plated brass.

VISUAL DISPLAY: Two light-emitting diodes (LED) provide visual indications of important functions. Alarm functions are monitored by a red LED, Motorola No. R32454. An indication of each delivered breath is given by the pulse display, which is a yellow LED, Motorola No. Y32454.

POWER SWITCH: The power switch is an ALCO No. A72-3, DPSI slide switch. The dimensions are .5″ X .30″: button height is .20″.

ELECTRICAL SPECIFICATIONS: Dry contact rating is 1 amp, contract resistance is 20 milliohms, and the life expectancy is 100,000 actuations.

FIGURE 1 Front View

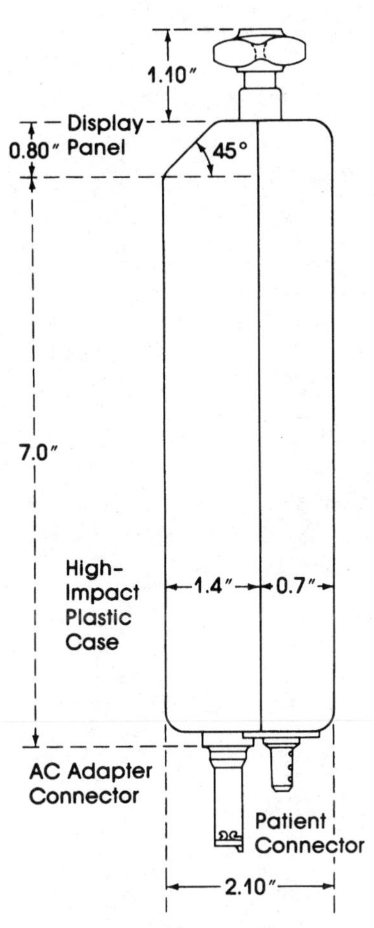

FIGURE 2 Side View

PATIENT CONNECTOR: Attachment of the patient cannula system is made at the patient connector, which is located at the bottom of the case. The white nylon connector, Air Logic No. F-3120-85, is a 10-32, UNF male threaded, straight barbed connector for 1/8″ ID flexible tubing.

AC ADAPTER CONNECTOR: An optional AC adapter* and battery charger assembly, part number PA-32, plugs into the AC adapter connector which is located at the bottom left-hand side of the case. The connector is a male, D-subminiature, 12-pin flush insert which is supplied by Dupont Connector Systems. Their part number is DCS: 68237009.

HIGH-IMPACT PLASTIC CASE: The case housing is made from an impact-resistant, flame-retardant, oxygen-compatible ABS plastic*.

C. OPERATING INSTRUCTIONS

The PURE AIR EDC (electronic demand cannula) is an oxygen-saving and -administering device (see Figures 1 and 2). By following these five easy steps, you will be able to enjoy the benefits of intermittent demand oxygen.

WARNING: Federal law prohibits the sale or use of this device without the order of a physician.

1. Attach your oxygen supply to the Oxygen Inlet Connector located at the top of the case.

2. Move the Pulse-Steady Switch to the Pulse position to begin intermittent demand flow.

3. Connect your nasal cannula to the Patient Outlet Connector located at the bottom of the case.

4. Adjust your oxygen supply to the oxygen flow prescribed by your physician.

5. Put your nasal cannula on and breath normally. The pulse light will turn on when a breath is delivered.

You are now ready to conserve oxygen by as much as 50%. Should you have the need to go back to continuous flow, just push the Pulse-Steady Switch to the "steady" position.

D. QUALIFICATIONS AND EXPERIENCE

Pure Air Medical, Inc., has been an international leader in the field of respiratory therapy since 1947. Pure Air introduced the first IPPB* respirator (Intermittent Positive Pressure Breathing) on the market. In 1960, responding to the needs of doctors and therapists, we produced the first life support volume ventilator, the VV-1. The VV-1 became the industry standard by which all other ventilators were measured.

In 1981, Pure Air Medical introduced the first computer-controlled life support system, the VV-2. Technology developed for this product has found application in other areas as well. Recently, we introduced one such product, the Electronic Demand Cannula.

Pure Air Medical, Inc., is located in Lenexa, Kansas. The main manufacturing and engineering facility employs 450 people. Regional sales and service branch offices are located throughout the United States. Each facility is staffed by trained technical service representatives ready to answer your needs.

E. COST

The Electronic Demand Cannula has a list price of $349. During the introductory phase of this new product, we have reduced the price of the EDC to $310, when purchased in quantities of 25. At this price, and assuming normal use, the oxygen savings will surpass your initial investment in about one year, as seen in Figure 3.

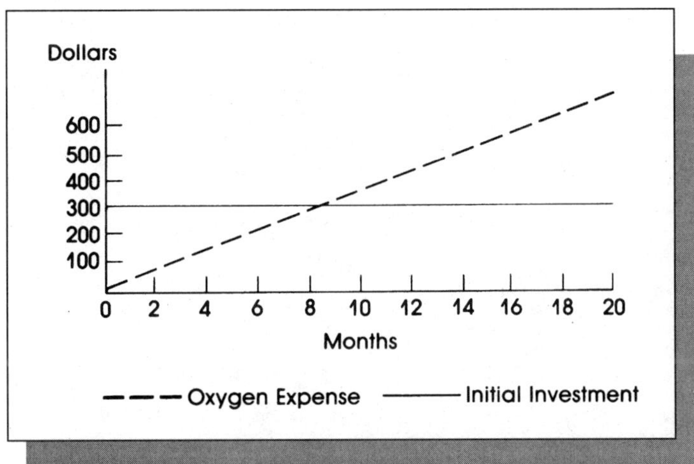

FIGURE 3. Return on Investment

III. CONCLUSION

A. MAJOR CONCERN

Prescription oxygen expenses are escalating while government support has been reduced. The cost increase to the patient and the health care facility will be enormous.

B. CREDENTIALS

Pure Air Medical, Inc., has an outstanding reputation for reliable medical products, specializing in the field of respiratory therapy. Pure Air has recently introduced the Electronic Demand Cannula, which can reduce oxygen consumption up to 50%.

C. RECOMMENDATION

To offset the inevitable rise of oxygen expenses, we recommend the use of the Electronic Demand Cannula.

IV. GLOSSARY

ABS plastic:	Acrylonitrile butadiene styrene. A durable and long-lasting plastic.
AC adapter:	A remote power supply used to convert alternating current to direct current.
Blood oxygen saturation:	The partial pressure of oxygen in alveolar blood recorded in percent.
Cannula:	A small tube inserted into the nose, specifically for administering oxygen.
Electronic Demand Cannula:	(EDC), an electronically controlled device which dispenses oxygen only when triggered by an inspiratory effort.
Inspiratory effort:	The act of inhaling.
Light-emitting diode (LED):	A solid-state semiconductor device which produces light when current flows in the forward direction.

List of Symbols

BPM:	Breaths per minute
DISS:	Diameter index safety system
DPDT:	Double pole double throw
EDC:	Electronic Demand Cannula
IPPB:	Intermittent positive pressure breathing
LPM:	Liter per minute

Guidelines

GUIDELINES FOR THE EIGHT PARTS OF FORMAL REPORTS

What follows is a description of eight parts of the formal report:

1. Cover/title page
2. Letter of transmittal
3. Table of contents
4. List of illustrations
5. Executive summary
6. Introduction
7. Discussion sections
8. Conclusions and recommendations

What could be considered a ninth part, appendices, is mentioned in the context of the discussion section.

Because formal reports can cover such a broad range of material, the guidelines here are rather general. For specific application of these guidelines, see the formal report in Model 3-9 on pages 229–245.

☐ Cover/Title Page

Formal reports are normally bound, usually with a cover used for all reports in the writer's organization. (Reports prepared for college courses, however, are often placed in a three-tab folder, the outside of which serves as the report cover.) Since the cover is the first item seen by the reader, it should be attractive and informative. Usually it contains the same four pieces of information mentioned in the following list with regard to the title page; sometimes it may have only one or two of these items.

Inside the cover is the title page, which should include these four pieces of information:

- ☐ Project title (exactly as it appears on the letter/memo of transmittal)
- ☐ Your client's name ("Prepared for . . .")
- ☐ Your name and/or the name of your organization ("Prepared by . . .")
- ☐ Date of submission

To make your title page or cover distinctive, you might want to place a simple illustration on it. Do not clutter the page, of course. Use a visual only if it reinforces a main point and if it can be simply and tastefully done. For example, assume that a consulting firm has submitted a formal report to a coastal city in California, concluding that an industrial park can be built near the city's bird sanctuary without harming the habitat—if stringent guidelines are followed. The report writer decides to place the picture of a nesting bird on the title page, punctuating the report's point about the industrial park, as in Model 3-1 on page 221.

LETTER/MEMO OF TRANSMITTAL

Letters or memos of transmittal are like an appetizer—they give the readers a taste of what is ahead. If your formal report is to readers outside your own organization, write a letter of transmittal. If it is to readers inside your organization, write a memo of transmittal. Models 3-2 and 3-3 on pages 222-223 show examples of both. Follow these guidelines for constructing this part of your reports:

☐ Transmittal Guideline 1: Place Letter/Memo Immediately After Title Page

This placement means that the letter/memo is bound with the document, to keep it from becoming separated. Some organizations paper-clip this letter or memo to the front of the report, making it a cover letter or memo. In so doing, however, they risk having it become separated from the report.

☐ Transmittal Guideline 2: Include a Major Point From Report

Remember that readers are heavily influenced by what they read first in reports. Therefore take advantage of the position of this section by including a major finding, conclusion. or recommendation from the report—besides supplying necessary transmittal information.

☐ Transmittal Guideline 3: Follow Letter and Memo Conventions

Like other letters and memos, letters and memos of transmittal should be easy to read, inviting readers into the rest of the report. Keep introductory and concluding paragraphs relatively short—no more than three to five lines each. Also, write in a conversational style free of technical jargon and stuffy phrases such as "per your request" or "enclosed herewith." See IA and B for more details and options concerning letter/memo format. For now, here are some highlights about the mechanics of format:

Letters and Memos

- ☐ Use single spacing and ragged-edge copy, even if the rest of the report is double-spaced and right-justified.
- ☐ Use only one page.

Letters

- ☐ Include company project number with the letter date.
- ☐ Correctly spell the reader's name.
- ☐ Be sure the inside address includes the mailing address to appear on the envelope.
- ☐ Use the reader's last name ("Dear Mr. Jamison:") in the salutation because of the formality of the report—unless your close association with the reader would make it more appropriate to use first names ("Dear Bill:").
- ☐ Usually include a project title, as with letter reports. It is treated like a main heading. Use concise wording that matches wording on the title page.
- ☐ Use "Sincerely" as your closing.
- ☐ Include a line to indicate those who will receive copies of the report ("cc" for carbon copy. "pc" for photocopy, or just "c" for copy).

Memos

- ☐ Give a clear description of the project in the subject line of the memo, including a project number if there is one.
- ☐ Include a distribution list to indicate those who will receive copies.

TABLE OF CONTENTS

Your contents page acts as an outline. Many readers go there right away to grasp the structure of the report, and then return again and again to locate report sections of most interest to them. Guidelines follow for assembling this important component of your report. See Model 3-4 on page 224 for an example.

☐ Table of Contents Guideline 1: Make It Very Readable

The table of contents must be pleasing to the eye so that readers can find sections quickly and see their relationship to each other. Be sure to:

- ☐ Space items well on the page.
- ☐ Use indenting to draw attention to subheadings.
- ☐ Include page numbers for every heading and subheading, unless there are many headings in a relatively short report, in which case you can delete page numbers for all of the lowest-level headings listed in the table of contents.

☐ Table of Contents Guideline 2: Use the Contents Page to Reveal Report Emphases

Choose the wording of headings and subheadings with care. Be specific yet concise so that each heading listed in the table of contents gives the reader a good indication of what the section contains.

Readers associate the importance of report sections with the number of headings and subheadings listed in the table of contents. If, for example, a discussion section called "Description of the Problem" contains many more heading breakdowns than other sections, you are telling the reader that the section is more important. When possible, it is best to have about the same number of breakdowns for report sections of about the same importance. In short, the table of contents should be balanced.

☐ Table of Contents Guideline 3: Consider Leaving Out Low-Level Headings

In very long reports, you may want to unclutter the table of contents by removing low-level headings. As always, the needs of the readers are the most important criterion to use in making this decision. If you think readers need access to all levels of headings on the contents page, keep them there. If you think they would prefer a simple contents page instead of a comprehensive one, delete all the lowest-level headings from the table of contents (see Model 3-5 on page 225 compared to Model 3-4 on page 224).

☐ Table of Contents Guideline 4: List Appendices

Appendices include items such as tables of data or descriptions of procedures that are inserted at the end of the report. Typically, they are listed at the end of the table of contents. Often no page numbers are given, since many appendices contain "off-the-shelf" material and are thus individually-paged (for example, Appendix A might be paged A-1, A-2, A-3, etc.). Tabs on the edges of pages can help the reader locate these sections.

☐ Table of Contents Guideline 5: Use Parallel Form in All Entries

All headings in one section, and sometimes even all headings and subheadings in the report, have parallel grammatical form. Readers find mixed forms distracting. For example, "Subgrade Preparation" and "Fill Placement" are parallel, in that they are both the same type of phrase. However, if you were to switch the wording of the first item to "Preparing the Subgrade" or "How to Prepare the Subgrade," parallel structure would be lost.

☐ Table of Contents Guideline 6: Proofread Carefully

The table of contents is one of the last report sections to be assembled; thus it often contains errors. Wrong page numbers and incorrect heading wording are two common mistakes. Another is the failure to show the correct relationship of headings and subheadings. Obviously, errors in the table of contents can confuse the reader and prove embarrassing to the writer. Proofread the section carefully.

LIST OF ILLUSTRATIONS

Illustrations within the body of the report are usually listed on a separate page right after the table of contents. When there are few illustrations, another option is to list them at the bottom of the table of contents page rather than on a separate page. In either case, this list should include the *number, title,* and *page number* of every table and figure within the body of the report. If there are many illustrations, separate the list into tables and figures. See the example in Model 3-6 on page 226.

EXECUTIVE SUMMARY

No formal report would be complete without an executive summary. This short section provides decision-makers with a capsule version of the report. Consider it a stand-alone section that should be free of technical jargon. See Model 3-7 on page 227 for an example. Follow these basic guidelines in preparing this important section of your formal reports:

☐ Executive Summary Guideline 1: Put It on One Page

The best reason to hold the summary to one page is that most readers expect and prefer this length. It is a comfort to know that somewhere within a long report there is one page to which one can turn for an easy-to-read overview. Moreover, a one-page length permits easy distribution at meetings. When the executive summary begins to crowd your page, it is acceptable to switch to single spacing if such a change helps keep the summary on one page—even though the rest of the report may be space-and-a-half or double-spaced.

Some extremely long formal reports may require that you write an executive summary of several pages or longer. In this case, you still need to provide the reader with a section that summarizes the report in less than a page. The answer to this dilemma is to write a brief "abstract," which is placed right before the executive summary. Consider the abstract to be a condensed version of the executive summary, directed to the highest-level decision-makers. (See Chapter IVA for further discussion of abstracts.)

☐ Executive Summary Guideline 2: Avoid Technical Jargon

Include only that level of technical language the decision-makers will comprehend. It makes no sense to talk over the heads of the most important readers.

☐ Executive Summary Guideline 3: Include Only Important Conclusions and Recommendations

The executive summary mentions only major points of the report. An exhaustive list of findings, conclusions, and recommendations can come later at the end of the report. If you have trouble deciding what is most important, put yourself in the position of the readers. What information is most essential for them? If you want to leave them with one, two, or three points about the report, what would these points be? *That* is the information that belongs in the executive summary.

☐ Executive Summary Guideline 4: Avoid References to the Report Body

Avoid the tendency to say that the report provides additional information. It is understood that the executive summary is only a generalized account of the report's contents. References to later sections do not provide the busy reader with further understanding.

An exception is those instances when you are discussing issues that involve danger or liability. Here you may need to add qualifiers in your summary—for example, "As noted in this report, further study will be necessary." Such statements protect you and the client in the event the executive summary is removed from the report and used as a separate stand-alone document.

☐ Executive Summary Guideline 5: Use Paragraph Format

Whereas lists are often appropriate for body sections of a report, they can give executive summaries a fragmented effect. Instead, the best summaries create unity with a series of fairly short paragraphs that flow together well. Within a paragraph, there can be a short listing of a few points for emphasis (see Model 3-7 on page 227), but the listing should not be the main structural element of the summary.

Occasionally, you may be convinced that the paragraph approach is not desirable. For example, a project may involve a series of isolated topics that would not mesh into unified paragraphs. In this case, use a modified list. Start the summary with a brief introductory paragraph, followed by a numbered list of three to nine points. Each numbered point should include a brief explanation (for example, "3. *Sewer Construction:* We believe that seepage influx can be controlled by. . . . 4. *Geologic Fault Evaluation:* We found no evidence of surficial. . . .").

☐ Executive Summary Guideline 6: Write the Executive Summary Last

Only after finishing the report do you have the perspective to write a summary. Approach the task this way. First, sit back and review the report from beginning to end. Then ask yourself, "What do my readers really need to know if they had only three to five minutes to read?" The answer to that question becomes the core of your executive summary.

INTRODUCTION

View this section as your chance to prepare both technical and nontechnical readers for the discussion ahead. You do not need to summarize the report, for your executive summary has accomplished that goal. Instead, give information on the report's purpose, scope, and format, as well as a project description. Follow these basic guidelines, which are reflected in the Model 3-8 example on page 228:

☐ Introduction Guideline 1: State Your Purpose and Lead-in to Subsections

The purpose statement for the document should appear immediately after the main introduction heading ("This report presents McDuff's foundation design recommendations for the new Hilltop Building in Franklin, Maine"). Follow it with a sentence that mentions the introduction subdivisions to follow ("This introduction provides a description of the project site and explains the scope of activities we conducted").

☐ Introduction Guideline 2: Include a Project Description

Here you need to be precise about the project. Depending on the type of project, you may be describing a physical setting, a set of problems that prompted the report study, or some other data. The information may have been provided to you or you may have collected it yourself. Accuracy in this section will help prevent any later misunderstandings between you and the reader. (When the project description would be too long for the introduction, sometimes it is placed in the body of the report.)

☐ Introduction Guideline 3: Include Scope Information

This section must outline the precise objectives of the study. Include all necessary details, using bulleted or numbered lists when appropriate. Your listing or description should parallel the order of the information presented in the body of the report. Like the project description, this subsection must be accurate in every detail. Careful, thorough writing here can prevent later misunderstanding about the tasks you were hired to perform.

☐ Introduction Guideline 4: Consider Including Information on Report Format

Often the scope section lists information as it is presented in the report. If this is not the case, end the introduction with a short subsection on the report format. Here you can give readers a brief preview of the main sections that follow. In effect, the section acts as a condensed table of contents and may list the report's major sections and appendices.

DISCUSSION SECTIONS

Discussion sections compose the longest part of formal reports. In general, they are written for the most technically oriented members of your audience. You can focus on facts and opinions, demonstrating the technical expertise that the reader expects from you. General guidelines for writing the report discussion are listed here. For a complete example of the discussion component, see the formal-report example in Model 3-9 on pages 231–247.

☐ Discussion Guideline 1: Move From Facts to Opinions

As you have learned, the ABC format requires that you start your formal report with a summary of the most important information. That is, you skip right to the essential conclusions and recommendations the reader needs and wants to know. Once into the discussion section, however, you back up and adopt a strategy that parallels the stages of the technical project itself. You begin with hard data and move toward conclusions and recommendations (that is, those parts that involve more opinion).

One way to view the discussion is that it should follow the order of a typical technical project, which usually involves these stages:

First, you collect data (samples, interviews, records, etc.).

Second, you subject these data to verification or testing (lab tests or computer analyses, for example).

Third, you analyze all the information, using your professional experience and skills to form conclusions (or convictions based on the data).

Fourth, you develop recommendations that flow directly from the conclusions you have formed.

Thus, the body of your report gives technical readers the same movement from fact toward opinion that you experience during the project itself. There are two reasons for this approach, one ethical and the other practical. First, as a professional, you are obligated to draw clear distinctions between what you have observed and what you have concluded or recommended. Second, your reports will usually be more persuasive if you give readers the chance to draw conclusions for themselves. If you move carefully through the four-stage process just described, readers will be more likely to reach the same conclusions that you have drawn.

☐ Discussion Guideline 2: Use Frequent Headings and Subheadings

Headings give readers handles by which to grasp the content of your report. They are especially needed in the report body, which presents technical details. Your readers will view headings, collectively, as a sort of outline by which they can make their way easily through the report.

☐ Discussion Guideline 3: Use Listings to Break Up Long Paragraphs

Long paragraphs full of technical details irritate readers. Use paragraphs for brief explanations, not for descriptions of processes or other details that could be listed.

☐ Discussion Guideline 4: Use Illustrations for Clarification and Persuasion

A simple table or figure can sometimes be just the right complement to a technical discussion in the text. Incorporate illustrations into the report body to make technical information accessible and easier to digest.

☐ Discussion Guideline 5: Place Excessive Detail in Appendices

Today's trend is to place cumbersome detail in appendices that are attached to formal reports, rather than weighing down the discussion with this detail. In other words, you give readers access to supporting information without cluttering up the text of the formal report. Of course, you need to refer to appendices in the body of the report and label appendices clearly so that readers can locate them easily.

Tabbed sheets are a good way to make all report sections, including appendices, very accessible to the reader. Consider starting each section with a tabbed sheet so that the reader can "thumb" to it easily.

CONCLUSIONS AND RECOMMENDATIONS

This final section of the report should give readers a place to turn to for a *comprehensive* description—sometimes in the form of a *listing*—of all conclusions and recommendations. The points may or may not have been mentioned in the body of the report, depending on the length and complexity of the document. Conclusions, on the one hand, are convictions or beliefs based on the findings of your study. Recommendations, on the other hand, are actions you are suggesting based on your conclusions. For example, your conclusion may be that there is a dangerous level of toxic chemicals in a town's water supply. Your recommendation may be that the toxic site near the reservoir should be immediately cleaned.

What distinguishes this last section of the report text from the executive summary is the level of detail and the audience. The conclusions and recommendations section provides an *exhaustive* list of conclusions and recommendations for technical and management readers. The executive summary provides a *selected* list or description of the most important conclusions and recommendations for decision-makers, who may not have technical knowledge.

In other words view the conclusions and recommendations section as an expanded version of the executive summary. It usually assumes one of these three headings, depending of course on the content:

1. Conclusions
2. Recommendations
3. Conclusions and Recommendations

Another option for reports that contain many conclusions and recommendations is to separate this last section into two sections: (1) Conclusions and (2) Recommendations.

FORMAL REPORT EXAMPLE

Model 3-9 (pp. 229-245) provides a long, formal technical report from McDuff, Inc. It contains the main sections discussed previously, with the exception of the list of illustrations. (Because the report's figures are in the appendices, they are listed at the end of the table of contents.) Marginal annotations indicate how the model reflects proper use of this chapter's guidelines for format and organization.

The report results from a study that McDuff completed for the City Transit Authority (CTA) of Alba, Texas. The CTA wants to install part of its light-rail transit system along a right-of-way now owned by the Southern Pacific Railroad. Before it begins the project, however, it needs to know what environmental hazards exist along the corridor. McDuff completes what it calls a "Phase I Environmental Site Assessment."

Members of the CTA come from both technical and nontechnical backgrounds. Some are full-time professionals hired by the city, whereas others are part-time, unpaid citizens appointed by the mayor. The paid professionals include engineers, environmental specialists, accountants, city planners, managers, lawyers, real estate experts, and public-relations specialists. The part-time appointees include citizens who work in a variety of blue-collar and white-collar professions or who are homemakers.

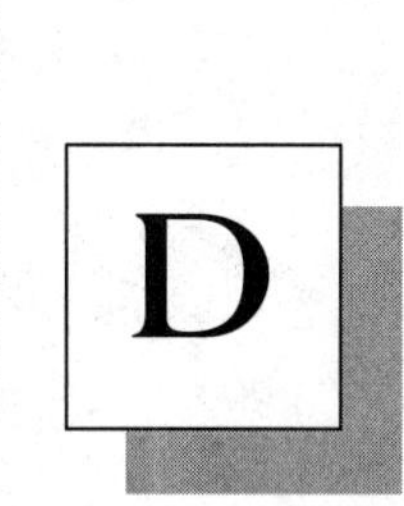

Models

Oceanside's New Industrial Park

Prepared for: City Council
Oceanside, California

Prepared by: McDuff, Inc.
San Francisco, California

Date: March 3, 1994

MODEL 3-1 Title page with illustration

12 Post Street
Houston, Texas 77000
(713) 555-9781

Report #82–651

July 19, 1994

Belton Oil Corporation
P.O. Box 301
Huff, Texas 77704

Attention: Mr. Paul A. Jones

GEOTECHNICAL INVESTIGATION
DREDGE DISPOSAL AREA F
BELTON OIL REFINERY
HUFF, TEXAS

This is the second volume of a three-volume report on our geotechnical investigation concerning dredge materials at your Huff refinery. This study was authorized by Term Contract No. 604 and Term Contract Release No. 20–6 dated May 6, 1994.

This report includes our findings and recommendations for Dredge Disposal Area F. Preliminary results were discussed with Mr. Jones on July 16, 1994. We consider the soil conditions at the site suitable for limited dike enlargements. However, we recommend that an embankment test section be constructed and monitored before dike design is finalized.

We appreciate the opportunity to work with you on this project. We look forward to assisting you with the final design and providing materials-testing services.

Sincerely,

George Fursten

George H. Fursten
Geotechnical/Environmental Engineer

GHF/dnn

MODEL 3-2 Letter of transmittal

MEMORANDUM

DATE: March 18, 1994
TO: Lynn Redmond, Vice President of Human Resources
FROM: Abe Andrews, Personnel Assistant *aa*
SUBJECT: Report on Flextime Pilot Program at Boston Office

As you requested. I have examined the results of the six-month pilot program to introduce flextime to the Boston office. This report presents my data and conclusions about the use of flexible work schedules.

To determine the results of the pilot program, I asked all employees to complete a written survey. Then I followed up by interviewing every fifth person off an alphabetical list of office personnel. Overall, it appears that flextime has met with clear approval by employees at all levels. Productivity has increased and morale has soared. This report uses the survey and interview data to suggest why these results have occurred and where we might go from here.

I enjoyed working on this personnel study because of its potential impact on the way McDuff conducts business. Please give me a call if you would like additional details about the study.

MODEL 3-3 Memo of transmittal

TABLE OF CONTENTS

MODEL 3-4 Table of contents (all subheadings included)

TABLE OF CONTENTS

PAGE

MODEL 3-5 Table of contents (third-level subheadings omitted)

LIST OF ILLUSTRATIONS

MODEL 3-6 List of illustrations—formal report

Gives brief background of project.

Keeps verbs in *active voice*, for clarity and brevity.

Uses short list to emphasize major findings.

Emphasizes major conclusion in separate paragraph. (Note that this major point *could* have been placed after first paragraph, for a different effect.)

EXECUTIVE SUMMARY

Quarterly monitoring of groundwater showed the presence of nickel in Well M–17 at the Hennessey Electric facility in Jones, Georgia. Nickel was not detected in any other wells on the site. Hennessey then retained McDuff's environmental group to determine the source of the nickel.

The project consisted of four main parts. First, we collected and tested 20 soil samples within a 50-yard radius of the well. Second, we collected groundwater samples from the well itself. Third, we removed the stainless steel well screen and casing and submitted them for metallurgical analysis. Finally, we installed a replacement screen and casing built with Teflon.

The findings from this project are as follows:

- The soil samples contained *no* nickel.
- We found *significant* corrosion and pitting in the stainless steel screen and casing that we removed.
- We detected *no* nickel in water samples retrieved from the well after replacement of the screen and casing.

Our study concluded that the source of the nickel in the groundwater was corrosion of the stainless steel casing and screen.

MODEL 3-7 Executive summary—formal report

Gives purpose of report and overview of introduction (as lead-in).

Describes the task the writer was given.

Denotes the major activities that were accomplished.

Provides reader with a preview of main sections to follow (as a sort of "mini" table of contents).

INTRODUCTION

This document examines the need for a McDuff, Inc., Human Resources Manual. Such a manual would apply to all U.S. offices of the firm. As background for your reading of this report, I have included (1) a brief description of the project, (2) the scope of my activities during the study, and (3) an overview of the report format.

Project Description

Three months ago, Rob McDuff met with the senior staff to discuss diverse human resources issues, such as performance appraisals and fringe benefits. After several meetings, the group agreed that the company greatly needed a manual to give guidance to managers and their employees. Shortly thereafter, I was asked to study and then report on three main topics: (1) the points that should be included in a manual, (2) the schedule for completing the document, and (3) the number of employees that should be involved in writing and reviewing policies.

Scope of Activities

This project involved seeking information from any McDuff employees and completing some outside research. Specifically, the project scope involved:

- Sending a survey to employees at every level at every domestic office
- Tabulating the results of the survey
- Interviewing some of the survey respondents
- Completing library research on the topic of human resource manuals
- Developing conclusions and recommendations that were based on the research completed

Report Format

To fulfill the report's purpose of examining the need for a McDuff Human Resources Manual, this report includes these main sections:

Section 1: Research Methods
Section 2: Findings of the Survey and Interviews
Section 3: Findings of the Library Research
Section 4: Conclusions and Recommendations

Appendices at the end of the text contain the survey form, interview questions, sample survey responses, and several journal articles of most use in my research.

MODEL 3-8 Introduction—formal report

Phase 1 Environmental Site Assessment
Inner Corridor
Benton Junction to Craft
Alba, Texas

Prepared for
City Transit Authority
Alba, Texas

Prepared by
McDuff, Inc.
Houston, Texas

March 18, 1991

MODEL 3-9 Formal report

12 Post Street
Houston, Texas 77000
(713) 555-9781

March 18, 1991

City Transit Authority
500 State Street
Alba, Texas 75001

ATTENTION: Mr. Ralph Letson
Manager of Engineering Support Services

Lists project title as it appears on title page.

PHASE I ENVIRONMENTAL SITE ASSESSMENT
INNER CORRIDOR
BENTON JUNCTION TO CRAFT
ALBA, TEXAS

Gives brief project description and authorization information

We have now completed our Phase I environmental site assessment for the proposed City Transit Authority (CTA) Inner Corridor. The project was authorized on January 6, 1991. We performed the work in accordance with our revised proposal letter, McDuff Proposal No. 88-P34, dated December 16, 1990, and under the provisions of CTA Contract #601.

The enclosed report presents a preliminary evaluation of possible environmental risks at sites located within 300 ft of the proposed CTA Inner Corridor. The corridor is within the Southern Gulf Railroad right-of-way near West Drive. We have considered about 2.75 miles of the alignment located between Benton Junction and Craft.

Provides single most important finding or conclusion

In this Phase I environmental site assessment. we identified 24 sites along the alignment that may have *some* potential for environmental risks, 13 of which are considered to have a *high* potential for such risks. We have outlined an additional scope of work (Phase 2) to evaluate the possibility that these 13 sites have affected the proposed CTA project.

Thank you for the opportunity to work with you on this Phase I environmental site assessment. If we may be of further assistance, please call us.

Sincerely,
Marie S. Harris
Marie S. Harris, P.E.

MODEL 3-9 Continued

Uses white space and indenting to accent organization of report.

TABLE OF CONTENTS

MODEL 3-9 Continued

EXECUTIVE SUMMARY

Summarizes scope of work.

The City Transit Authority (CTA) hired McDuff. Inc., to perform a preliminary environmental site assessment of a 2.75-mile segment of the Inner Corridor alignment. The section of alignment addressed in this study is along the Southern Gulf Railroad right-of-way between Benton Junction and Craft. For this study, we have considered a 300-ft wide band along both the north and south boundaries of the right-of-way.

Describes major finding or conclusion.

McDuff has identified 24 sites with *some* potential for environmental risks that could affect the CTA alignment. Of the 24 sites, we believe that 13 have a *high* potential for environmental risk. These professional opinions are based on a review of environmental site listings, a review of historical aerial photographs, and fieldwork at the site.

Includes major recommendation also.

McDuff recommends that a Phase 2 sampling and analytical testing program be performed near these high-risk sites. This program will help assess the possible impact of environmental problems on the proposed CTA alignment.

1

MODEL 3-9 Continued

States purpose of study.

Gives a brief project description.

Uses bulleted list to emphasize scope of activities

Leads into rest of report with list of main sections to follow

INTRODUCTION

McDuff, Inc., performed a Phase 1 environmental site assessment for a 2.75-mile segment of the Inner Corridor. We reviewed a variety of potential risks at the site. The rest of this introduction describes the project site, work scope, and report format.

Project Description

The proposed CTA Inner Corridor is located along the Southern Gulf Railroad right-of-way near West Drive in Alba, Texas. The portion of the Inner Corridor alignment addressed in this study is located between Benton Junction and Craft, as shown in Figure 1. The alignment is about 2.75 miles long.

Scope

The purpose of the Phase 1 environmental site assessment was to evaluate the potential for selected environmental risks. The project sites were located within 300 ft north and 300 ft south along the alignment. Selected environmental risks considered for this project include:

- Nearness to sites and hazardous waste spills documented by the regulatory agencies
- Current and former land-use activities associated with waste disposal or industrial operations

To accomplish this purpose, our study included four main tasks:

- A search for listed and potential environmental sites within 300 ft north and south of the 2.75-mile alignment
- A review of historical aerial photographs to evaluate former land-use activities associated with waste disposal, oil and gas explorations, or industrial operations
- A site reconnaissance to evaluate current land use and to evaluate any anomalies observed during the aerial photograph review
- A report to present our preliminary evaluation for sites located within 300 ft north and south of the project alignment

Report Format

This report includes these four main sections:

1. **Technical Approach:** a complete discussion of our activities in completing the project
2. **Results:** a presentation of the data accumulated on the sites, particularly with regard to previous and current use
3. **Site Risk Evaluation:** a description of the criteria for evaluating risk
4. **Conclusions and Recommendations:** a summary of the potential effects of the result of this study, along with recommendations for further study

2

MODEL 3-9 Continued

Gives overview of sections to follow.

Lists items in *exact* order of appearance below.

Uses subheadings to help reader find information quickly.

TECHNICAL APPROACH

The technical approach used for this Phase 1 study consisted of an environmental site search, a review of aerial photographs, and a site reconnaissance. A description of each task follows:

Environmental Site Search

McDuff reviewed possible environmental hazards located within 300 ft north and 300 ft south of the alignment. We collected information from the following selected sources:

- Texas Water Commission (TWC)
- Region VI U.S. Environmental Protection Agency (EPA)
- Texas Department of Health (TDH)
- Geomap Company (GC)
- Alba Fire Department (AFD)

Texas Water Commission (TWC) Listing. The TWC listing includes the generator's list, the underground storage tank (UST) registration list, and the Texas Registry List.

The generator's list typically includes sites that generate, transport, store, or dispose of potential industrial solid waste materials. A TWC generator's listing does not imply that a listed site has documented hazardous waste problems. The TWC generator's file dated May 17, 1988, was used in our site search (TWC Industrial Solid Waste System, General Information Report).

The UST registration list typically includes underground storage tanks that have been registered with the TWC. A UST listing does not imply that the underground storage tank leaks. The UST registration list, dated October 1985, was used in our search .

The Texas Registry List includes a listing of sites published in the January 22, 1991, Texas Registry and includes "hazardous waste facilities or areas which may constitute an imminent and substantial endangerment to public health and safety or to the environment." The Texas Registry is more commonly known as the Texas Superfund sites.

Region VI EPA Listing. The Region VI EPA listing consists of two lists: RCRA and CERCLIS. (These acronyms refer to two legislative acts that help identify, control, and clean up environmental waste.) The RCRA list is composed of sites that generate, transport, store, or dispose of regulated hazardous materials. The RCRA notifiers listing, dated May 31, 1989, was used in our search. A RCRA listing does not imply that the site has documented hazardous waste problems.

3

MODEL 3-9 Continued

The CERCLIS list is composed of sites that have documented on-site hazardous waste problems. The CERCLIS listing, dated September 29, 1988, was used in our search. The CERCLIS listing also includes National Priorities List (NPL) sites, or Superfund sites.

Texas Department of Health (TDH) Listing. The TDH listing includes sites that have been permitted or for which applications have been submitted to receive municipal solid wastes. The TDH listing, dated September 30, 1990, was used in our search.

Geomap Company Map. Geomap Company provides a map that locates documented oil and gas wells and provides the well name and operator. This map is constructed at a 1 in.-4000 ft scale. The Geomap, dated April 15, 1988, was used in our search for documented oil and gas wells.

Alba Fire Department Listing. The Alba Fire Department-Hazardous Materials Division provides a listing of documented hazardous materials spills. The approximate spill location, spill type, and spill date are provided. This listing is updated daily by the Hazardous Materials Division. Spill records from 1980 through January 11. 1991, were included in this search.

Aerial Photograph Review

McDuff reviewed photographs for surficial anomalies indicative of possible fill areas, oil and gas exploration activities, and industrial development. Photographic coverage throughout the proposed alignment was obtained from the U.S.D.A. Agricultural Stabilization and Conservation Service (ASCS) for the following years:

Incorporates simple, informal table into text of report

Year Scale	Photograph Number	Approximate Scale
1953	BQY-16M-33R	1 in.-200 ft.
1953	BQY-16M-33L	1 in.-200 ft.
1957	BQY-6T-32R	1 in.-200 ft.
1957	BQY-6T-32L	1 in.-200 ft.
1957	BQY-6T-57R	1 in.-200 ft.
1964	BQY-3FF-71R	1 in.-200 ft.
1964	BQY-3FF-71L	1 in.-200 ft.
1964	BQY-3FF-14R	1 in.-200 ft.
1973	48201-173-172X	1 in.-200 ft.
1981	48201-281-78X	1 in.-200 ft
1981	48201-281-96X	1 in.-200 ft

4

MODEL 3-9 Continued

Uses *action* verbs and maintains parallel structure in listing.

Site Reconnaissance

We performed site visits on January 13, 1991, and February 8, 1991. They consisted of traveling along the alignment from Benton Junction to Craft. The purposes of the site visits were as follows:

- Observe sites that were identified during the environmental site search
- Observe currently operating businesses along the alignment and identify those businesses associated with potential environmental risks
- Observe anomalies identified from the aerial photograph review
- Document the existing condition of the alignment with photographs

Potential Environmental Sites. A reconnaissance of the sites identified during the environmental site search was performed from adjacent properties. Access to these sites was not attempted. The approximate distance from the proposed CTA alignment was also checked.

Current Businesses. The site reconnaissance also included observations of the types of currently operating businesses located within about 300 ft north and south of the CTA alignment. Observations were made from adjacent properties. These observations were aimed at identifying nonlisted sites that may have the potential for high environmental risk operations.

Aerial Photograph Anomalies. The site reconnaissance was also aimed at field observation of anomalous areas disclosed from the aerial photograph review.

Site Photographs. Photographs were taken during the February 8, 1991, site reconnaissance to document the existing condition of the alignment. After completion of the environmental site risk evaluation, a site reconnaissance was made on March 15, 1991, to photograph the high-risk sites.

5

MODEL 3-9 Continued

States main point up front in section.

RESULTS

We have based our findings on our environmental site search, aerial photograph review, and site reconnaissance. We consider 24 sites located within about 300 ft north and 300 ft south of the alignment to have potential for selected environmental risks.

A list of the potential sites is presented in Appendix A. The following section presents the results of our Phase 1 study and provides a preliminary evaluation of environmental sites, historical land use, and current land use.

Environmental Sites

Eleven sites were documented as having registered underground storage tank (UST) facilities, as indicated on Appendix A. None of the registered tank facilities is listed within the TWC active leaking underground storage tank data base, dated December 15, 1990. Seven AFD spill sites were documented and are indicated on Appendix A. No registered TDH facilities were documented within the alignment area. The Geomap Company did not document any oil and gas wells located within the project alignment. Seven sites were identified within the TWC generator's listing and the Region VI EPA RCRA listing, as indicated on Appendix A.

Regulatory agency site files for the TWC and RCRA sites were reviewed for possible compliance violations and enforcement actions. Available files were received from the TWC district office in Deer Park, Texas, and the EPA Region VI headquarters in Dallas, Texas. What follows is a summary of the pertinent findings for each site for which files were available:

- **J. S. Jones Company**—EPA files show that this facility generates hazardous wastes. The materials are ink wastes. A Generators Biennial Hazardous Waste Report dated 1988 indicated that the firm had generated about 55 gal. of ink wastes since 1982. No violations were noted.

- **XYZ Type Compositors**—EPA file information shows that this facility was not registered by the EPA as a hazardous-waste generator. All records were transmitted to the Texas Department of Health. No violations were noted.

Uses expanded listing to organize information from sites.

- **Jack Parch Ford**—EPA file information shows that this facility generates less than 1000 kg per month of ignitable wastes. No violations were noted.

- **Manoplate**—EPA file information shows that this facility is a small-quantity generator that produces nonspecific ignitable, corrosive, and toxic wastes. No violations were noted. TWC file information indicates that the facility engages in printing, developing, and color manufacturing. A letter to Manoplate from the TWC, dated June 4, 1987, cited violations for not registering all generated hazardous wastes. TWC lists the facility as a small-quantity generator.

6

MODEL 3-9 Continued

- **Paste-Randall Printing**—EPA file information indicates that this facility generates hazardous wastes. Typical wastes include formic acid, trichlorethylene sludge, cooling oil, and naptha. No violations were noted. TWC file information included diazo coating wastes and indications of an aboveground and a belowground storage tank. No violations were noted.
- **Tansley Palms Chrysler/Plymouth**—EPA file information indicates that this facility generates small quantities of ignitable wastes. No violations were noted.
- **Buck Service Station**—EPA file information indicates that this facility generates small quantities of ignitable, corrosive, and toxic wastes. A letter from Buck Oil to the EPA, dated February 23, 1988, stated that after evaluating the station, Buck finds that it is not a hazardous-waste generator and has canceled the generator number. No acknowledgment by the EPA was noted. No violations were noted.

Historical Land Use

McDuff reviewed aerial photographs to evaluate historical land use throughout the alignment. Aerial photographs indicated that the Southern Gulf Railroad right-of-way was established before 1953. We observed that land along the alignment is used for a mixture of undeveloped, commercial, industrial, and residential purposes.

We observed no significant surficial anomalies that would indicate possible waste ponds, dumps, or oil and gas well sites. However, we observed an electrical substation located next to the alignment at Wakeforest on the 1957 photographs.

Our review of historical aerial photographs suggests that most of the adjacent land use to the north included commercial and industrial operations. Sites located south of the alignment generally were used for residential purposes. However, in the vicinity of Narden Speedway to Gilbert, the land use immediately south of the alignment is typically more commercial and industrial. Most residential land use in this area is located south of the 300-ft area included in this study.

Current Land Use

We conducted a site reconnaissance on January 13, 1991, to assess current land use. The findings from our site reconnaissance indicate that three sites, in addition to the environmental site listings, could have a potential for environmental risks. These sites include the A&L Substation, Quansi-Cola Bottling Co., and SDS Electronics. The sites were previously identified during the aerial photo review and relisted on Appendix A because of the industrial/commercial nature of the site operations. The A&L Substation was noted on the 1957 aerial photographs.

During the site reconnaissance we noted no evidence of significant waste or remnant product spillage at the documented AFD sites, at the regulatory agency sites, or at other industrialized areas along the alignment. We did not observe other significant industrial or commercial areas identified on the 1981 aerial photographs.

7

MODEL 3-9 Continued

Uses section to identify *criteria* used in evaluation.

Prepares reader for conclusions and recommendations to follow.

SITE RISK EVALUATION

After identifying the 24 potential environmental sites, we screened each site into two environmental risk classifications—high and low. This section outlines the screening criteria and discusses the ranking of sites.

Environmental Screening Criteria

Criteria used in the environmental site screening included:

- Presence of registered underground storage tanks (UST)
- Presence of unregistered UST
- Presence of potential PCB-containing electrical equipment
- Documented EPA CERCLIS sites
- Regulatory compliance violations and enforcement actions
- Presence of oil and gas wells
- Presence of hazardous material spill remnants
- Presence of industrial and selected commercial operations

A high environmental risk potential was assigned to each site meeting one or more of the screening criteria.

Several screening criteria deserve special mention. First, note that we considered the possible presence of leaking underground storage tanks (USTSs) and polychlorinated byphenyls (PCBs). Either one can cause soil contamination. Second, note that we also considered any listing on EPA's CERCLIS list, for such a listing indicates that a site has documented hazardous waste problems. However, our study did not evaluate the type or extent of any actual soil contamination or migration of hazardous waste.

Site Risk Ranking

On the basis of the results of our environmental site screening, a total of 13 out of the 24 environmental sites were classified as having a high potential for preexisting environmental liabilities. A summary of the high-risk environmental sites is presented in Appendix B. A site reconnaissance was made on March 15, 1991, to obtain photographic documentation of the 13 high-risk sites. (Photographs of each high-risk site are available upon request.)

We observed no indications of on-site underground storage tanks or waste handling practices at SDS Electronics and Quansi-Cola Bottling Co.; therefore, these sites were not included as high-risk sites. Documented underground storage tanks were present at 11 of the 13 high-risk sites. The remaining two high-risk sites have the potential for PCB contamination.

8

MODEL 3-9 Continued

Uses narrative form for section, given *detail* of conclusions and recommendations.

Starts with most important conclusion.

Explains limitations of study.

Suggests need for more intensive study of 13 sites.

Gives reader necessary *details* of recommended study (fieldwork, lab work, report.)

CONCLUSIONS AND RECOMMENDATIONS

What follows are the conclusions of our current study and some recommendations for further work at some of the sites.

Conclusions

High-risk environmental sites located within about 300 ft north and south of the proposed alignment may affect the condition of the property being considered by CTA. We consider the 13 high-risk sites identified during our preliminary study to have a greater likelihood of environmental impact than other properties located within the 600-ft study band. (See Appendix B for list.)

Potential environmental impacts from the high-risk sites may result from transporting contaminants from adjacent properties onto the proposed CTA alignment. Contaminant transport may occur by surface water runoff, groundwater migration, airborne particulate emissions, and physical soil/waste removal.

Because of the nature of our preliminary study, we have identified sites that *may* affect the CTA alignment. Further evaluation of high-risk sites is necessary to assess whether environmental impacts are *probable*.

Recommendations for Phase 2 Evaluation

We recommend a Phase 2 study to evaluate the potential for environmental risks along the CTA alignment. The Phase 2 study would consist of these tasks:

- A field exploration along the alignment with approximate boring locations at the projections of the high-risk sites on the alignment
- A laboratory test program to analyze selected samples for possible hydrocarbon and/or PCB contamination
- The preparation of a report documenting our findings and our opinion of probable environmental damage

General Scope of Work. Underground fuel storage tanks were present at 11 of the 13 high-risk sites. Therefore, we consider hydrocarbons the primary contaminant of concern. Possible PCB compounds may be present at the remaining two high-risk sites. The general scope of work for each high-risk site located next to the alignment right-of-way is presented as follows.

The field exploration will consist of drilling soil borings and collecting soil samples to evaluate the potential presence of shallow subsurface and surface hydrocarbon contaminants. Borings will be drilled within the alignment right-of-way near the high-risk sites. Boring depths will extend to the first water-bearing zone where hydrocarbons, if present, are typically encountered.

9

MODEL 3-9 Continued

We will sample the individual borings at 2-ft intervals throughout the borehole depth. The soil sampler will be cleaned between each sampling interval with a trisodium phosphate (TSP) wash followed by a deionized-water rinse, to reduce the potential for cross-contamination. Upon completion of soil sampling activities, the boreholes will be backfilled with a bentonite-cement grout. All field activities will be conducted in accordance with an OSHA site safety plan using personnel trained for hazardous-waste site work, in accordance with 29 CFR Part 1910.120.

The laboratory test program will consist of screening the recovered samples to select representative soil samples for analytical testing. Each recovered sample will be screened for volatile organic response using a portable photoionization detector (PID). On the basis of the field observations and the PID headspace screening results, we will select representative soil samples from each borehole for testing. The laboratory analysis will be concerned with (1) total petroleum hydrocarbons (TPH), in accordance with EPA Method 418.1; (2) benzene, toluene, ethylbenzene, and total xylenes (BTEX), in accordance with EPA Method 5030; and/or (3) polychlorinated biphenyls (PCBs) in accordance with EPA Method 608.

We will prepare an engineering report documenting the data and findings of our field exploration and laboratory testing. The report will describe the work tasks and procedures we used to complete these tasks. We will also provide our opinions about the potential for on-site environmental damage from the 13 high-risk sites.

Scope Quantities. We propose to drill 42 borings to evaluate the 13 high-risk sites. These borings will be located along the alignment at the approximate projection of the high-risk environmental sites. For estimating purposes, we assumed that most boring depths will be 25 to 30 ft. We based this assumption on limited subsurface information from our previous geotechnical report of the System Connector (McDuff File No: 88-139; dated May 27, 1990). The boring depths may be adjusted depending on the actual depths of target soil strata. The proposed Phase 2 work scope is presented in Appendix C. Supporting price estimates are presented in Appendix D.

10

MODEL 3-9 Continued

APPENDIX A: POTENTIAL ENVIRONMENTAL SITES

Facility Name	Location	File
1. J. S. Jones Company	304 South St.	RCRA/TWC
2. XYZ Type Compositors	102 South St.	RCRA/TWC
3. Jack Parch Ford	304 South Street	RCRA/TWC/UST
4. Jack Parch Ford Paint and Body Shop	26 Mill Street	Recon/UST
5. Manoplate	15 South St.	RCRA/TWC
6. Paste-Randall Printing	32 Greenbriar	RCRA/TWC/UST
7. Tansley Paints Chrysler/Plymouth	35 Kirb Drive	RCRA/TWC/UST
8. Buck Service Station	39 South St.	RCRA/TWC/UST
9. Tex Service Station	67 South St.	UST
10. Barnes Building Material	45 Greenbriar	UST
11. Monser Auto Rental	988 Wakeforest	UST
12. Alba Van Lines	488 South St.	UST
13. Phil's Gas Station	766 Anster Place	UST
14. Argo 44 Service Station	66 South St.	UST
15. A&L Substation	877 Wakeforest	Recon
16. SDS Electronics	430 South St.	Recon
17. Quansi-Cola Bottling	26 Bisonet	Recon
18. Transformer explosion	Wakeforest at Gren	AFD
19. Diesel spill	South St. at Bender Ave.	AFD
20. Diesel spill	South St. at Yazo St.	AFD
21. Gasoline spill	229 South St.	AFD
22. Hydrochloric acid spill	34 South St.	AFD
23. Methane	South St. at Kirb	AFD
24. Diesel spill	South St. at Bisonet	AFD

11

MODEL 3-9 Continued

APPENDIX B: POTENTIAL HIGH-RISK ENVIRONMENTAL SITES

Facility (number and name from Appendix A)	Files
3. Jack Parch Ford	RCRA/TWC/UST
4. Jack Parch Ford Paint and Body Shop	Recon/UST
6. Paste-Randall Printing	RCRA/TWC/UST
7. Tansley Palms Chrysler/Plymouth	RCRA/TWC/UST
8. Buck Service Station	RCRA/TWC/UST
9. Tex Service Station	UST
10. Barnes Building Material	UST
11. Monser Auto Rental	UST
12. Alba Van Lines	UST
13. Phil's Gas Station	UST
14. Argo 44 Service Station	UST
15. A&L Substation	Recon
18. Transformer explosion	AFD

12

MODEL 3-9 Continued

APPENDIX C: PHASE 2 WORK SCOPE

	No. of Borings	Total Footage	No. of Headspace Readings	Laboratory Tests TPH	BTEX	PCB
3. Jack Parch Ford	4	120	60	4	4	—
4. Jack Parch Ford Paint and Body Shop	3	90	45	3	3	—
6. Paste-Randall Printing	3	90	45	3	3	—
7. Tansley Palms Chrysler/Plymouth	4	120	60	4	4	—
8. Buck Service Station	3	90	45	3	3	—
9. Tex Service Station	3	90	45	3	3	—
10. Barnes Building Material	3	90	45	3	3	—
11. Monser Auto Rental	2	60	30	2	2	—
12. Alba Van Lines	3	90	45	3	3	—
13. Phil's Gas Station	3	90	45	3	3	—
14. Argo 44 Service Station	3	90	45	3	3	—
15. A&L Substation	4	40	20	—	—	10
18. Transformer explosion	4	40	20	—	—	10
	42	1100	550	34	34	20

MODEL 3-9 Continued

APPENDIX D: PHASE 2 COST ESTIMATES

Task 1—Soil Borings	Item	Units	Rate	Total
Field Coordination	Project Engineer	30	43.58	1,307
Borehole Staking	Senior Soil Tech.	25	26.80	670
Utility Clearances	Senior Soil Tech.	20	26.80	536
Drilling & Sampling	Contract Driller	140	94.00	13,160
Borehole Logging	Senior Soil Tech.	140	26.80	3,752
Site Safety Supplies	Disposables	expense	cost	700
Decontamination Supplies	Disposables	expense	cost	1,100
Borehole Backfill	Grouting	1,100	1.50	1,650
			Total Task 1:	$22,875

Task 2—Laboratory Testing				
Sample Screening	Staff Engineer	40	30.17	1,207
Sample Delivery	Staff Engineer	35	30.17	1,056
TPH Tests	Soil	34	40	1,360
BTEX Tests	Soil	34	75	2,550
PCB Tests	Soil	20	70	1,400
			Total Task 2:	$ 7,573

Task 3—Evaluation and Report				
Project Administration	Principal	30	76.64	2,299
Project Management	Project Manager	75	57.83	4,337
Report Preparation	Project Engineer	90	43.58	3,922
	Staff Engineer	70	34.75	2,433
	Draftsman	30	15.51	465
	Typist	50	19.94	997
Miscellaneous	Reproduction	expense	cost	350
			Total Task 3:	$14,803
			Total Phase 2 Budget:	$45,251

14

MODEL 3-9 Continued

IV SUMMARY

The information age requires the ability to write a concise short version of a more comprehensive document. This may be an executive summary or abstract of a long or formal report or may be a summary of an article from a magazine or a book. Part A provides details on writing summariesy. Part B includes twelve sample works with corresponding activities. The art of summarizing the key points in a readable interesting manner is essential in today's business world.

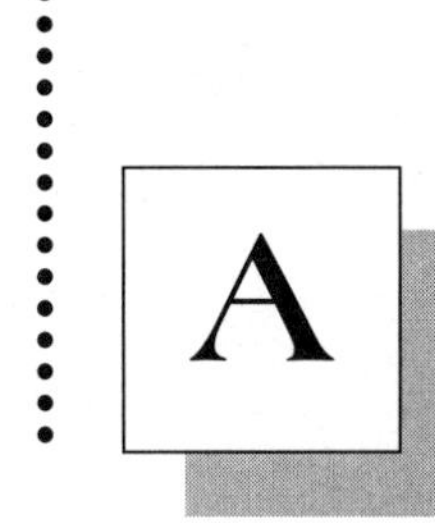

The Summary

OBJECTIVES

You might be required to write a summary if, for example, your boss is planning to give a speech at a civic meeting (Better Business Bureau, Rotary Club, or Businesswomen's Association) and needs some up-to-date information for his or her presentation. Bosses often are too busy to perform research, wade through massive amounts of researched data, or attend a conference where new information might be presented. Therefore, your boss asks you to research the topic and provide the information in a shortened version. He or she wants you to provide a summary of your findings. Similarly, your boss might need to give a briefing to upper-level management. Again, time is a problem. How can your boss get the appropriate information and digest it rapidly? The answer is for *you* to read the articles, attend the conference or meeting, and then summarize your research.

Finally, as a class assignment, your teacher might want you to write a summary instead of a formal research report. The summary, though shorter than a research report, would still require that you practice research skills, such as reading, note taking, and writing with paraphrases.

To write a summary, you'll need to study the research material. Then, in condensed form (a summary is no longer than five to fifteen percent the length of the original source), you'll report on the author's main points. Preparing a summary puts to good use your research, analyzing, and writing skills.

The following will help you to write a summary:

- Criteria for writing summaries
- Process to follow
- Process log with examples

CRITERIA FOR WRITING SUMMARIES

A well-constructed summary, though much shorter than the original material being summarized, highlights the author's important points. A summary is like a *Reader's Digest* approach to writing. Although the summary will not cover every fact in the original, after reading the summary you should have a clear overview of the original's main ideas. There are several criteria for accomplishing this.

Overall Organization

As with any good writing, a summary contains an introduction, a discussion, and a conclusion.

Introduction

Begin with a topic sentence. This sentence will present the primary focus of the original source and list the two or three major points to be discussed. You must also tell your reader what source you are summarizing. You can accomplish this in one of three ways. You can either list the author's name and article title in the topic sentence; preface your summary with a works cited notation providing the author's name, title, publication date, and page numbers; or follow your topic sentence with a footnote and give the works cited information at the bottom of the page.

NAME/TITLE IN TOPIC SENTENCE

> In "Robotics: Tactile Sensing" (***Radio Electronics***, August 1986: 71–72), Mark J. Robillard states that since robots move to do their jobs, they need to be equipped with an assortment of tactile sensors.

WORKS CITED PREFACING TOPIC SENTENCE

Robillard, Mark J. "Robotics: Tactile Sensing." ***Radio Electronics***. August 1986: 71–72.

Because robots must move around to do their jobs, they need to be equipped with an assortment of tactile sensors.

TOPIC SENTENCE FOLLOWED BY EXPLANATORY FOOTNOTE

Because robots move around to do their jobs, they need to be equipped with an assortment of tactile sensors.*________________

____
____
____
____
____
____
____
____
____
____
____
____

*This paragraph summarizes Mark J. Robillard's "Robotics: Tactile Sensing," found in ***Radio Electronics***, August, 1986, pages 71–72.

Discussion

In this section, briefly summarize the main points covered in the original material. To convey the author's ideas, you can paraphrase, using your own words to restate the author's point of view.

Conclusion

To conclude your summary, you can either reiterate the focus statement, reminding the reader of the author's key ideas; highlight the author's conclusions regarding his or her topic; or state the author's recommendations for future activity.

☐ Internal Organization

How will you organize the body of your discussion? Since a summary is meant to be objective, you should present not only what the author says but also how he or she organizes the information. For example, if the author has developed his or her ideas according to a problem/solution format, your summary's discussion should also be organized as a problem/solution. This would give your audience the author's content and method of presentation. Similarly, if the author's article is organized according to cause/effect, comparison/contrast, or analysis (classification/division) this would determine how you would organize your summary.

☐ Development

To develop your summary, you'll need to focus on the following:

- ☐ *Most important points:* Since a summary is a shortened version of the original, you can't include all that the author says. Thus, you should include only the two or three key ideas within the article. Omit irrelevant details, examples, explanations, or descriptions.
- ☐ *Major conclusions reached:* Once you've summarized the author's key ideas, then state how these points are significant. Show their value or impact.
- ☐ *Recommendations:* Finally, after summarizing the author's major points and conclusions, you'll want to tell your audience if the author recommends a future course of action to solve a problem or to avoid potential problems.

☐ Style

The summary. like all technical writing, must be clear, concise, accurate, and accessible. Therefore, you'll want to abide by the fog index. Watch out for long words and sentences. Avoid technical jargon. Most importantly, be sure that your summary truly reflects the author's content. Your summary must be an unbiased presentation of what the author states and include none of your opinions.

☐ Length

As mentioned earlier, the summary will be approximately five to fifteen percent the length of the original material. To achieve this desired length, omit references to the author (after the initial reference in the works cited or topic sentence). You'll also probably need to omit from your summary the following:

- ☐ Past histories
- ☐ Definitions
- ☐ Complex technical concepts

- ☐ Statistics
- ☐ Tables and/or figures
- ☐ Tangential information (such as anecdotes and minor refutations)
- ☐ Lengthy examples
- ☐ Biographical information

☐ Audience Recognition

You must consider your audience in deciding whether to omit or include information. Although you usually would omit definitions from a summary, this depends on your audience. Technical writing is useless if your reader does not understand your content. Therefore, determine whether your audience is high tech, low tech, or lay.

☐ Grammar and Mechanics

As always, flawed grammar and mechanics will destroy your credibility. Not only will your reader think less of your writing and research skills, but also errors in grammar and mechanics might threaten the integrity of your summary. Your summary will be inaccurate and, therefore, invalid.

PROCESS

Writing your summary will be easiest if you follow the same step-by-step process detailed throughout this text.

☐ Prewriting

To gather your data and determine your objectives, do the following:

1. Locate your periodical article, book chapter, or report. If you are summarizing a meeting or seminar, take notes. If your boss or instructor gives you your data, one major obstacle has been overcome. If, however, you need to visit a library to research your topic, refer to Chapter V for helpful hints on research skills.

2. Write your works cited information. Once you've found your research material, *immediately* write down the author's name, the article's title, the name of the periodical or book in which this source was found, the date of publication, and the page numbers. Doing so will save you frustration later. For example, if you lose your copy of the article and have not documented the source of your information, you'll have to begin your research all over again. Instead, spend a few minutes at the beginning of your assignment documenting your sources. This will ensure that you do not spend several harried hours the night before the summary is due frantically scouring the library for the missing article. (Chapter V provides the correct works cited format.)

3. Read the article to acquire a general understanding of its content.

4. Reread the article, this time taking notes. Determine exactly what the author's thesis is and what main points are discussed. You can take notes in one of two ways. You can either underline important points, or you can take marginal or interlinear notes on the photocopy. For a summary of an article or chapter in a book, we suggest that you take notes directly on the photocopy. To do so, read and reread a paragraph. After you've read and understood the paragraph, write a one- or two-word notation in the margin which sums up that paragraph's main idea.

☐ Writing

Once you've gathered your data and determined your author's main ideas, you're ready to write a rough draft of your summary.

1. Review your prewriting. Look back over your marginal notes and your underlining. Have you omitted any significant points? If you have, now is the time to include them. Have you included any ideas which are insignificant or tangential? If so, delete these to ensure that your summary is the appropriate length.

2. Write a rough draft, using the sufficing technique. Once you've reviewed the data you've gathered, *quickly* draft the text of your summary. Follow the criteria for writing an effective summary discussed earlier in this chapter, including:

- ☐ A topic sentence clearly stating the author's main idea. Also provide the works cited information here, in a title, or in an explanatory footnote.
- ☐ Organization paralleling the author's method of organization (comparison/contrast, argument/persuasion, cause/effect, analysis, chronology, spatial, importance, etc.).
- ☐ Clear transitional words and phrases.
- ☐ Development through paraphrases. Restate the author's ideas in your own words.
- ☐ A conclusion in which you either reiterate the main points discussed, state the significance of the author's findings, and/or recommend a future course of action.

☐ Rewriting

Once you've written a rough draft of your summary, it's time to revise. Follow the six-step revision checklist to ensure that your finished product will be acceptable to your readers.

1. Add detail for accuracy. When looking over your draft, be sure that you've covered all of the author's major points. If you haven't, now is the time to add any omissions. Be sure that your summary accurately covers the author's primary assertions.

2. Delete unnecessary information, biased comments, and/or dead words and phrases. Deleting is especially important in a summary. Because a summary must be no more than five to fifteen percent of the length of the original source, your major challenge is brevity. Therefore, review your draft to see if you have included any of the author's points which are *not* essential. Such inessential information may include side issues which are interesting but not mandatory for your reader's understanding.

Another type of information you'll want to delete will be complex technical theories. Although such data might be valuable, a summary is not the vehicle for conveying this kind of information. If you have included such theories, delete them. These deletions serve two purposes. First, your summary will be stronger since it will focus only on key ideas and not on tangential arguments. Second, the summary will be briefer due to your deletions.

Delete biased comments. If you inadvertently have included any of your attitudes toward the topic, remove these biases. A summary should not present your ideas; it should reflect only what the author says.

Finally, as with all good technical writing, conciseness is a virtue. Long words and sentences are not appreciated. Reread your draft and delete any unnecessary words and phrases. Strive for an average of fifteen-word sentences and one- or two-syllable words. We're not suggesting that every multisyllabic word is incorrect, but keep them to a minimum. If an author has written about telecommunications or microbiology, for example, you shouldn't simplify these words. You should, however, avoid long words which aren't needed and long sentences caused by wordy phrases.

3. Simplify "impressive" words and complex technical terms. Good technical writing doesn't force the reader to look up words in a dictionary. Your goal in a summary is to present complex data in a brief and easily understandable package. This requires that you avoid difficult words. In a summary, *difficult* means two things. First, as with all good technical writing, you want to use words which readers understand immediately. Don't write *supersede* when you mean *replace*. Don't write *remit* when you mean *pay*. Second, you'll also need to simplify technical terms. To do so, you can define them parenthetically or merely replace the technical term with its definition.

4. Move information within the summary to parallel the author's organization. Does your summary reflect the order in which the author has presented his or her ideas? Your summary must not only tell the reader what the author has said but also how the author has presented these ideas. Make sure that your summary does this. If your summary fails to adhere to the author's organization, move information around. Cut and paste. Maintain the appropriate comparison/contrast, argument/persuasion, cause/effect, etc. sequence.

5. Correct errors. Reread your draft and look for grammatical and mechanical errors. Don't undermine your credibility by misspelling words or incorrectly punctuating sentences. In addition, accurate information is mandatory. You might be writing this summary for your boss who is giving a speech at a civic meeting or briefing upper-level management. Your boss is trusting you to provide accurate information. Therefore, to ensure that your boss is not embarrassed by errors, review your text against the original source. Make sure that all the information is correct.

6. Avoid sexist language. Sexist language is always inappropriate.

As one of our regular rewriting tips, we ask you to enhance the text by adding pronouns and positive words. For summaries, however, such enhancements would be incorrect. Since the summary must only restate what the author has written and be devoid of your attitude, total objectivity is necessary.

Use the summary's criteria checklist to help you write an effective summary.

Summary Criteria Checklist

1. ☐ Does your summary provide the works cited information for the article that you're summarizing?
2. ☐ Is the works cited information correct?
3. ☐ Does your summary begin with an introduction clearly stating the author's primary focus?
4. ☐ Does your summary's discussion section explain the author's *primary* contentions and omit secondary side issues?
5. ☐ In the discussion section, do you explain the author's contentions through pertinent facts and figures while avoiding lengthy technicalities?
6. ☐ Is your content accurate? That is, are the facts that you've provided in the summary exactly the same as those the author provided to substantiate his or her point of view?
7. ☐ Have you organized your discussion section according to the author's method of organization?
8. ☐ Did you use transitional words and phrases?
9. ☐ Have you omitted direct quotations in the summary, depending instead on paraphrases?
10. ☐ Does your conclusion either reiterate the author's primary contentions, reveal the author's value judgment, or state the author's recommendations for future action?
11. ☐ Is your summary completely objective, avoiding any of your own attitudes?
12. ☐ Have you used an effective technical writing style, avoiding long sentences and long words?

13. ☐ Are your grammar and mechanics correct?
14. ☐ Have you avoided sexist language?

PROCESS LOG

Following is one student's successful summarization of an article, including the student's prewriting, rough draft, revisions, and finished copy.

☐ Prewriting

First, the student found an article. wrote down the required works cited information, read the article, and then took marginal notes and underlined key points.

☐ Writing

The student wrote a rough draft from the notes and underlining (Figure 4.1).

☐ Rewriting

Student peer evaluators suggested revisions (Figure 4.2).

The student made these changes and prepared a finished version of the summary (Figure 4.3).

In "Robotics" (Radio Electronics, August 1986), Mark J. Robillard states that "Most robots musts move around to accomplish their tasks" (71). The information that is needed to accomplish these tasks is gathered through an assortment of sensors--touch sensors, sound sensors, and light sensors. Depending on what type of tactile information is obtained through these sensors, objectives of the robot can be met. A robot's gripper could crush an object or not exert enough force to hold on to an object if it doesn't have sensors to determine the amount of force needed. Microswitches are used in the form of touch sensors. They are the simplest form of sensors used for this purpose. To eliminate weight and space used for switches, LED/phototransistor pairs can be used. "If you've ever been bowling, that setup should look familiar" (71). The phototransistor is then interfaced to a computer or other type of controller. The pairs of sensors provide more than just a there/not there signal. "The amount of light that is reflected provides an indication of how close the object is" (72). This approach is patented by "*Heath's Hero 2000*" (72) and uses optical encoder disks. Integrated circuits that use "strain guages and pressure sensitive pain" (72) are yet another way to detect the amount of force applied to an object.

All of these different methods of allowing a robot to interface with the real world "comprise a field of inquiry that is as large as robotics itself" (72).

FIGURE 4.1 Rough Draft

Could you separate Bibliography from your topic sentence? underline periodical titles

In "Robotics" (Radio Electronics, August 1986), Mark J. Robillard states that "Most robots musts move around to accomplish their tasks" (71). The information that is needed to accomplish these tasks is gathered through an assortment of sensors--touch sensors, sound sensors, and light sensors. Depending on what type of tactile information is obtained through these sensors, objectives of the robot can be met. [A robot's gripper could crush an object or not exert enough force to hold on to an object if it doesn't have sensors to determine the amount of force needed.] Microswitches are used in the form of touch sensors. They are the simplest form of sensors used for this purpose. To eliminate weight and space used for switches, LED/phototransistor pairs can be used. "If you've ever been bowling, that setup should look familiar" (71). The phototransistor is then interfaced to a computer or other type of controller. The pairs of sensors provide more than just a there/not there signal. "The amount of light that is reflected provides an indication of how close the object is" (72). This approach is patented by "Heath's Hero 2000" (72) and uses optical encoder disks. Integrated circuits that use "strain guages and pressure sensitive

Avoid quotes- Paraphrase instead

Repetitious

Do you need this?

Combine these sentences

Don't quote

Combine these sentences

Don't quote

Do you need this?

Don't quote

Check spelling

FIGURE 4.2 Rough Draft with Editing

pain"(72) are yet another way to detect the amount of force applied to an object. Write just one ¶

All of these different methods of allowing a robot to interface with the real world "comprise a field of inquiry that is as large as robotics itself"(72). Don't quote

FIGURE 4.2 Continued

Robillard, Mark J. "Robotics." *Radio Electronics* August 1986: 71-72.

Robots, which must move to do their jobs, require an assortment of tactile sensors. These sensors help the robots locate items and use the appropriate amount of force for gripping an object. Microswitches, in the form of touch sensors, are the simplest sensing devices. These microswitches can be used to grip an object. In addition, microswitches can help the robot maintain contact with the ground to avoid falling down stairs. LED/phototransistors, similar to those used on bowling alley foul lines, are less bulky than microswitches. The phototransistor, when interfaced with a computer, provides more than a there/not there signal. The light reflected indicates the exact placement of the object. The above sensors, however, have difficulty gauging the appropriate force required for gripping. This problem could be solved by using optical encoder disks and integrated circuits to determine the appropriate force. All of the above tactile sensing devices constitute an important part of successful robotics.

FIGURE 4.3 Revised Summary

B

The Natural Sciences and Technology

SUBJECTS AND METHODS OF STUDY IN THE NATURAL SCIENCES AND TECHNOLOGY

Natural science, as a field of study, is defined very clearly by its methodology. Physical and biological scientists the world over share a basic approach to their work. Even though they may give conflicting answers to important questions in their disciplines, they rarely argue about the methods of conducting scientific investigation. The specific method by which researchers discover, collect, and organize these facts is called the scientific method. It involves questioning, observing, experimenting, and theorizing. We will discuss briefly each of these aspects of science.

□ The Scientific Method

Scientific investigations usually begin with questions that need answers. Drawing on previous knowledge and prior investigations, scientists ask questions not only about things that are unknown but also about things that are supposedly understood. Often, the questions they ask challenge commonly accepted beliefs. Scientists also question the work and conclusions of other scientists. Indeed, no fact or theory is exempt from legitimate inquiry. Even the most widely accepted ideas are continually reexamined. This questioning process helps make science self-correcting. Errors made by scientists can be detected and corrected by subsequent investigation.

To answer questions and determine what is true, scientists rely heavily on direct observation of the world. For example, Ulric Neisser in his article on artificial intelligence (Chapter IV, Section B) records many concrete observations of human and machine behavior upon which he bases his conclusion that computers reason differently than humans do. Like Neisser, other scientists rely on their five senses to collect information about the world, but they also use instruments to go beyond their sensory limits. Ideas must be confirmed through observation before they are considered fact. Assertions that cannot be supported by direct observation are generally greeted with skepticism by the scientific community.

For phenomena that cannot be observed readily in nature, scientists design experiments that make events stand out more clearly. Information derived from observation, experimental findings are continually reexamined. Experiments are considered valid only if they can be repeated with identical results by different investigators.

Scientists build theories to account for direct observations and experimental results. Theories are rules or models that explain a large body of separate facts. An example is the Bohr model of the atom in which electrons orbit around the nucleus like moons around a planet. Scientists use the Bohr atom model since it explains so many basic observations made by physicists and chemists. Theories are continually abandoned or modified as new observations are made. Also, scientists often weigh competing theories that purport to explain the same body of facts. The scientists that are best remembered for their creative genius, Newton, Galileo, Einstein, and others, came up with new theories to account for facts that were already known. The other aspects of the scientific method, questioning, observing, and experimenting, all contribute to the process of constructing and testing theories.

☐ Writing About Science

Natural science writing can be separated into two groups: (1) reports of original research, usually focusing on a narrow topic, and (2) summary or speculative articles, usually generalizing about a body of specific information. Research reports are usually written for experts in particular scientific disciplines. Summary and speculative articles are often directed to less specialized audiences. Some of the articles you read were written for an audience of professional scientists, but most will be summary and speculative articles written for a general audience.

Organization

Most research reports share a common rhetorical pattern. Scientists within specific disciplines have established standard methods for organizing research reports, and most journals that publish research results accept only articles written according to these formats. However, summary and speculative articles vary widely in rhetorical structure. Nonscientists who think the only aim of science writing is to relate established facts fail to recognize that much science writing argues a point. As you read through the next three chapters, notice that the majority of the articles are organized as arguments. For example, the title of Carl Sagan's article "In Defense of Robots" indicates that the essay will present an argument. The pursuit of science often gives rise to intense debate over what questions should be investigated, what observations are accurate, and what theories best explain particular observations. Thus, argumentative writing is common in science. In addition to argumentation, the full range of rhetorical patterns can be found in popular science writing.

Writing research reports according to a set organizational formula does have its drawbacks. In some cases, scientists may become so obsessed with fitting their work into a research report formula that they lose sight of the true nature of research: an active pursuit of the truth. A similar problem sometimes surfaces in popular science writing where the rhetorical pattern becomes more important than scientific accuracy. For example, Joseph Weizenbaum states that most essays about the societal impact of computers follow a set formula.[1] First, they survey the benefits to society of computers; then, they consider some of the potential dangers of widespread computer use; finally, they claim that these dangers can be overcome with new technology and argue for a vigorous program to expand computer development and use. Weizenbaum implies that this simplistic, problem/solution approach to writing about computers may obscure the truth. Much popular writing about controversial science and technology follows a pattern similar to the one Weizenbaum describes. To fit a set format, the science writer may ignore important facts or pass over alternative interpretations of certain facts. Consequently, analyzing rhetorical structure is an important element in comprehending science writing.

As we mentioned earlier, the scientific method involves questioning, observing, experimenting, and theorizing. A given article may focus on one or two aspects of this methodology. For example, in "The Imitation of Man by Machine," Ulric Neisser lists a number of observations about the behavior of humans and computers and then uses these observations as a basis for theorizing about the comparative nature of human and computer intelligence. Articles that draw on only one aspect of the scientific method are often useful, but a careful reader understands that the entire methodology is important in evaluating any issue.

[1]Joseph Weizenbaum. "The Impact of the Computer on Society," *Science, 176* (1972): 609-14.

Style

Although the tone of research report writing is almost always unemotional and authoritative, popular science writing varies considerably in tone and style. Once free from professional research report constraints, scientists express emotions and personal attitudes as do writers in other fields. As you read the article by Gina Kolata, notice that even a respected academic journal *(Science)* publishes articles that are personal in tone.

No matter what the tone, a science writer establishes authority by providing concrete evidence. Even the most eminent scientists must support their theories with verifiable observations. As you read the following articles, you will find that most of the authors include objective evidence to support major assertions. This evidence often comes from scientific experiments, also from anecdotes and hypothetical cases. Most science writers are careful to build on evidence, even when they are writing for a general audience. Consequently, it is important for readers of science writing to identify and evaluate the evidence authors provide in support of their claims.

Nonscientists are often amazed to find that different sources may present conflicting versions of scientific "fact." Two scientists may look at the same body of experimental evidence and come away with entirely different notions of what the facts are. For instance, as you read the articles on Artificial Intelligence, you will find that experts disagree on the extent to which a computer can model human intelligence. When you find that the experts disagree, try to describe precisely the various versions of the facts, and if possible try to explain the reasons for the difference of opinion.

Sometimes, differences of opinion among scientists have nothing to do with scientific fact but rather reflect conflicting personal or social values. Science is not immune to the political and moral controversy that is part of other human activity. As you read the articles on technological decision making, you will see that both scientists and nonscientists address social and moral issues. When writers do not support scientific claims with objective evidence, you should consider the moral, ideological, or emotional motivations behind their assertions.

Even nonscientists can evaluate intelligently many summary and speculative articles about science. As you read and think about the material, keep in mind that many of the articles will be organized as arguments and can be analyzed like other forms of argumentative writing. Also, ask yourself whether the article involves questioning, observing, experimenting, or theorizing, the basic components of the scientific method. Be sensitive to the author's tone. Look for evidence that supports the author's claims. Note the specific points on which the experts disagree and try to account for these differences of opinion. Finally, consider the social or ethical questions that scientific advances raise. These procedures will help you read about science and technology with more understanding and better critical judgment.

HUMAN INTELLIGENCE VS HEURISTICS

Since the invention of electronic digital computers in the 1940s, experts have speculated on how these machines might be programmed to model human thought processes. Early in the development of computers, researchers programmed machines to perform various mathematical and clerical tasks. However, scientists also worked to develop computers that could attack more intellectually challenging problems. As the technology advanced, scientists created computer programs that contained problem-solving strategies called "heuristics." Armed with these heuristics, computers could respond to new tasks in ways that were not entirely preprogrammed. Heuristics allowed computers to divide complex problems into manageable subunits and identify potential routes to solutions. They could decide which subproblems to attack first, use models and analogies, and make educated guesses at solutions when necessary. Eventually, computer scientists claimed that these heuristic-based programs possessed an "artificial intelligence."

Today, powerful computers use sophisticated heuristics along with vast information banks to solve problems in ways that appear very humanlike. For example, medical computer systems provide advice to doctors who practice in remote locations and thus cannot consult specialists in particular medical fields. Similar "expert" computers help forecast the weather, locate oil reserves, and predict business trends. On the drawing board is the Strategic Defense Initiative calling for a vast computer-commanded weapons system. Indeed, some computer scientists argue that machines will one day equal or surpass humans in all areas of decision making.

However, some scientists maintain that computer intelligence will always be essentially different from human intelligence. They point out that it is difficult to imagine a machine that has wisdom, compassion, cultural values and other attributes that are essential to human decision-making processes. In addition, they claim failing to recognize the limitations of artificial intelligence opens the door for allowing computers to make socially important decisions that are best made by humans.

The sources in this chapter cover both enthusiastic and cautious attitudes toward artificial intelligence. Carl Sagan's essay, "In Defense of Robots," describes the advantages of developing highly intelligent machines. Sagan argues that humans should not feel threatened by mechanical intelligence. Next, Ulric Neisser, an experimental psychologist, argues in his article "The Imitation of Machine by Man" that human and computer intelligences are profoundly and necessarily different. He maintains that some crucial aspect of human thought processes can never be duplicated by machines. In contrast to Neisser, Gina Kolata, in "How Can Computers Get Common Sense?" describes two divergent approaches to developing machines that have humanlike reasoning powers. One approach is based on modeling basic human behavior and the other on using mathematical logic.

Next, "Designing Computers that Think the Way We Do," by William Allman, focuses on efforts to design computer circuitry that mimics the neural networks in the human brain. In an excerpt from his book *Computer Power and Human Reason,* Joseph Weizenbaum, a prominent computer scientist, urges restraint in applying machine intelligence to problems that he feels only humans should handle. Weizenbaum maintains that computers will never have "wisdom" comparable to that of human beings.

Activities

PREREADING

1. Brainstorm for a few minutes on your prior knowledge of computer and robot intelligence. Consider information from math and computer courses, newspapers, magazines, and science fiction. Briefly list what you already think or know about this topic.
2. Drawing on the list that you made for question one, freewrite a one- to two-page paper on what impact computer and robot intelligence may have on society in the future.

CLOSE READING

1. Scan the articles in this chapter for titles, headings, thesis statements, topic sentences, and organizational clues. Jot down topics, assertions, theses, and proposals that you will encounter in this chapter.
2. As you read other writers' observations about computer intelligence, try to relate them to your experience and knowledge of the topic.

TAKING NOTES AND ORGANIZING IDEAS

1. After you have read the articles, note the similarities between your experiences and perspectives on computer and robot intelligence and the views of the authors of the sources.
2. Try to place your experiences and previous knowledge about computer and robot intelligence into the larger context that the articles in this chapter provide.
3. Consult the Additional Readings at the end of this chapter and determine whether you should pursue some of them. If you have decided to write on the use of robotics in manufacturing, for example, determine whether you will need more information and ideas that further reading might provide. Go to the library, look up the books and journals in the card catalogue, browse through them and others on the same topic located near them, and consult the relevant reference works.

WRITING

1. Taking into account your own and the source author's knowledge, observations, and perspectives, write a brief paper on one issue or problem that this chapter's articles raise.

IN DEFENSE OF ROBOTS

Carl Sagan

The author is a professor of astronomy and space science at Cornell University and a Pulitzer Prize-winning science writer.

PREREADING

1. Sagan's title indicates that his essay will discuss robots. Consider both actual and fictitious robots that you are aware of. In ten minutes of free-writing, compare and contrast robots and humans.
2. Read the last paragraph of Sagan's essay. What organizational pattern for the entire essay does his summary paragraph suggest? What would you predict Sagan's thesis will be?
3. In the last sentence of this essay, Sagan states, "There is nothing inhuman about an intelligent machine . . . ." What might he mean by this statement?

CLOSE READING

1. The first sentence in Sagan's concluding paragraph lists several categories of advantages that robots provide. As you read the article, annotate each specific example of computer or robot activity with the appropriate category from this list. Create additional categories if necessary.
2. As you read the beginning of the essay, enumerate the common criticisms of robots that Sagan mentions. As you read the rest of the essay, ask whether Sagan responds adequately to these criticisms. Which ones does he explain in depth? Which ones does he dismiss?
3. Mark each text passage that discusses machine intelligence. In the margin, note the aspect of human intelligence that the computer or robot supposedly models.

The word "robot," first introduced by the Czech writer Karel Capek, is derived from the Slavic root word for "worker." But it signifies a machine rather than a human worker. Robots, especially robots in space, have often received derogatory notices in the press. We read that a human being was necessary to make the terminal landing adjustments on Apollo 11, without which the first manned lunar landing would have ended in disaster; that a mobile robot on the Martian surface could never be as clever as astronauts in selecting samples to be returned to Earthbound geologists; and that machines could never have repaired, as men did, the Skylab sunshade, so vital for the continuance of the Skylab mission.

(Carl Sagan, "In Defense of Robots." *Broca's Brain* (New York: Ballantine, 1980): pp. 280-292.

But all these comparisons turn out, naturally enough, to have been written by humans. I wonder if a small self-congratulatory element, a whiff of human chauvinism, has not crept into these judgments. Just as whites can sometimes detect racism and men occasionally discern sexism, I wonder whether we cannot here glimpse some comparable affliction of the human spirit—a disease that as yet has no name. The word "anthropocentrism" does not mean quite the same thing. The word "humanism" has been preempted by other and more benign activities of our kind. From the analogy with sexism and racism I suppose the name for this malady is "speciesism"—the prejudice that there are no beings so fine, so capable, so reliable as human beings.

This is a prejudice because it is, at the very least, a prejudgment, a conclusion drawn before all the facts are in. Such comparisons of men and machines in space are comparisons of smart men and dumb machines. We have not asked what sorts of machines could have been built for the $30-or-so billion that the Apollo and Skylab missions cost.

Each human being is a superbly constructed, astonishingly compact, self-ambulatory computer—capable on occasion of independent decision making and real control of his or her environment. And, as the old joke goes, these computers can be constructed by unskilled labor. But there are serious limitations to employing human beings in certain environments. Without a great deal of protection, human beings would be inconvenienced on the ocean floor, the surface of Venus, the deep interior of Jupiter, or even on long space missions. Perhaps the only interesting results of Skylab that could not have been obtained by machines is that human beings in space for periods of months undergo a serious loss of bone calcium and phosphorus—which seems to imply that human beings may be incapacitated under 0 g for missions of six to nine months or longer. But the minimum interplanetary voyages have characteristic times of a year or two. Because we value human beings highly, we are reluctant to send them on very risky missions. If we do send human beings to exotic environments, we must also send along their food, their air, their water, amenities for entertainment and waste recycling, and companions. By comparison, machines require no elaborate life-support systems, no entertainment, no companionship, and we do not feel any strong ethical prohibitions against sending machines on one-way, or suicide, missions.

Certainly, for simple missions, machines have proved themselves many times over. Unmanned vehicles have performed the first photography of the whole Earth and of the far side of the Moon; the first landings on the Moon, Mars and Venus; and the first thorough orbital reconnaissance of another planet, in the Mariner 9 and Viking missions to Mars. Here on Earth it is increasingly common for high-technology manufacturing—for example, chemical and pharmaceutical plants—to be performed largely or entirely under computer control. In all these activities machines are able, to some extent, to sense errors, to correct mistakes, to alert human controllers some great distance away about perceived problems.

The powerful abilities of computing machines to do arithmetic—hundreds of millions of times faster than unaided human beings—are legendary. But what about really difficult matters? Can machines in any sense think through a new problem? Can they make discussions of the branched-contingency tree variety which we think of as characteristically human? (That is, I ask Question 1; if the answer is A, I ask Question 2; but if the answer is B, I ask question 3; and so on.) Some decades ago the English mathematician A. M. Turing described what would be necessary for him to believe in machine intelligence. The condition was simply that he could be in teletype communication with a machine and be unable to tell that it was not a human being. Turing imagined a conversation between a man and a machine of the following quality:

INTERROGATOR: In the first line of your sonnet which reads "Shall I compare thee to a Summer's day," would not "a Spring day" do as well or better?

WITNESS: It wouldn't scan.

INTERROGATOR: How about "a Winter's day"? That would scan all right.

WITNESS: Yes, but nobody wants to be compared to a Winter's day.

INTERROGATOR: Would you say Mr. Pickwick reminded you of Christmas?

WITNESS: In a way.

INTERROGATOR: Yet Christmas is a Winter's day, and I do not think Mr. Pickwick would mind the comparison.

WITNESS: I don't think you're serious. By a Winter's day one means a typical Winter's day, rather than a special one like Christmas.

No device of this sophistication has yet been built, although I am not sure how many humans would pass Turing's human test. But the amount of effort and money put into artificial intelligence has been quite limited, and there are only about a half-dozen major centers of such activity in the world. One of the more striking results obtained in a very limited universe of discourse—that of children's blocks—has come from the work of Terry Winograd, then at the Massachusetts Institute of Technology. Here is a dialogue between man and machine, the machine having been programmed by Winograd:

Q: What does the box contain?

A: The blue pyramid and the blue box.

Q: How many blocks are not in the box?

A: Four of them.

Q: Is at least one of them narrower than the one which I told you to pick up?

A: Yes, the red cube.

Q: Is there a steeple?

A: Sorry, I don't know the word "steeple."

Q: A steeple is a stack which contains two green cubes and a pyramid, for example.

A: I understand.

Q: Are there any steeples now?

A: No.

Q: Build one.

The machine does. It reaches out its mechanical hand, moves the cubes and builds the structure that has just been described.

Q: When did you pick up the pyramid?

A: While I was stacking up the red cube, the large red block and the large green cube.

Q: Why?

A: To get rid of it.

Q: Why did you clear off that cube?

A: To put it on the large green cube.

As another example, a machine psychiatrist has been developed by Joseph Weizenbaum, also at MIT. This is a much simpler program than Winograd's, since it involves nondirective psychotherapy, which, generally speaking, requires extremely simple-minded computer programs. Here is a striking dialogue between a human being and a computer psychotherapist. (There is certainly a selection effect here. Many other such machine/human psychiatric dialogues are not nearly so striking. But I suppose most human/human psychiatric dialogues are not very striking either.) In this interaction, in order to spell out clearly the respective roles of therapist and patient, the computer therapist types upper case while the patient types lower case:

men are all alike
IN WHAT WAY
they're always bugging us about something or other
CAN YOU THINK OF A SPECIFIC EXAMPLE
well, my boy friend made me come here
YOUR BOY FRIEND MADE YOU COME HERE
he noticed that i'm depressed much of the time
I AM SORRY TO HEAR YOU ARE DEPRESSED
he's right. i am unhappy
DO YOU THINK COMING HERE WILL HELP YOU NOT TO BE UNHAPPY
i need some help, that much is clear
WHAT WOULD IT MEAN TO YOU IF YOU GOT SOME HELP
perhaps i could learn to get along with my mother
TELL ME MORE ABOUT YOUR FAMILY
my mother takes care of me
WHO ELSE IN YOUR FAMILY TAKES CARE OF YOU

my father
YOUR FATHER
you are like my father in some ways
WHAT RESEMBLANCE DO YOU SEE
you are not very aggressive, but i don't think you want me to notice that
WHAT MAKES YOU THINK I AM NOT VERY AGGRESSIVE
you don't argue with me
WHY DO YOU THINK I DON'T ARGUE WITH YOU
you are afraid of me
DOES IT PLEASE YOU TO BELIEVE I AM AFRAID OF YOU
it pleases my father to think i am afraid of him
WHAT ELSE COMES TO MIND WHEN YOU THINK OF YOUR FATHER
bullies
DOES THAT HAVE ANYTHING TO DO WITH THE FACT THAT YOUR BOY FRIEND MADE YOU COME HERE

This astonishing—one is very tempted to say "perceptive"— response from the computer is, of course, preprogrammed. But, then, so are the responses of human psychotherapists. In a time when more and more people in our society seem to be in need of psychiatric counseling, and when time-sharing of computers is widespread, I can even imagine the development of a network of computer psychotherapeutic terminals, something like arrays of large telephone booths, in which, for a few dollars a session, we are able to talk to an attentive, tested and largely nondirective psychotherapist. Ensuring the confidentiality of the psychiatric dialogue is one of several important steps still to be worked out.

Another sign of the intellectual accomplishments of machines is in games. Even exceptionally simple computers—those that can be wired by a bright ten-year-old—can be programmed to play perfect tic-tac-toe. Some computers can play world-class checkers. Chess is of course a much more complicated game than tic-tac-toe or checkers. Here programming a machine to win is more difficult, and novel strategies have been used, including several rather successful attempts to have a computer learn from its own experience in playing previous chess games. Computers can learn, for example, empirically the rule that it is better in the beginning game to control the center of the chessboard than the periphery. The ten best chess players in the world still have nothing to fear from any present computer. But the situation is changing. Recently a computer for the first time did well enough to enter the Minnesota State Chess Open. This may be the first time that a nonhuman has entered a major sporting event on the planet Earth (and I cannot help but wonder if robot golfers and designated hitters may be attempted sometime in the next decade, to say nothing of dolphins in free-style competition). The computer did not win the Chess Open, but this is the first time one has done well enough to enter such a competition. Chess-playing computers are improving extremely rapidly.

I have heard machines demeaned (often with a just audible sigh of relief) for the fact that chess is an area where human beings are still superior.

This reminds me very much of the old joke in which a stranger remarks with wonder on the accomplishments of a checker-playing dog. The dog's owner replies, "Oh, it's not all that remarkable. He loses two games out of three." A machine that plays chess in the middle range of human expertise is a very capable machine; even if there are thousands of better human chess players, there are millions who are worse. To play chess requires strategy, foresight, analytical powers, and the ability to cross-correlate large numbers of variables and to learn from the experience. These are excellent qualities in those whose job it is to discover and explore, as well as those who watch the baby and walk the dog.

With this as a more or less representative set of examples of the state of development of machine intelligence, I think it is clear that a major effort over the next decade could produce much more sophisticated examples. This is also the opinion of most of the workers in machine intelligence.

In thinking about this next generation of machine intelligence, it is important to distinguish between self-controlled and remotely controlled robots. A self-controlled robot has its intelligence within it; a remotely controlled robot has its intelligence at some other place, and its successful operation depends upon close communication between its central computer and itself. There are, of course, intermediate cases where the machine may be partly self-activated and partly remotely controlled. It is this mix of remote and *in situ* control that seems to offer the highest efficiency for the near future.

For example, we can imagine a machine designed for the mining of the ocean floor. There are enormous quantities of manganese nodules littering the abyssal depths. They were once thought to have been produced by meteorite infall on Earth, but are now believed to be formed occasionally in vast manganese fountains produced by the internal tectonic activity of the Earth. Many other scarce and industrially valuable minerals are likewise to be found on the deep ocean bottom. We have the capability today to design devices that systematically swim over or crawl upon the ocean floor; that are able to perform spectrometric and other chemical examinations of the surface material; that can automatically radio back to ship or land all findings; and that can mark the locales of especially valuable deposits—for example, by low-frequency radio-homing devices. The radio beacon will then direct great mining machines to the appropriate locales. The present state of the art in deep-sea submersibles and in spacecraft environmental sensors is clearly compatible with the development of such devices. Similar remarks can be made for off-shore oil drilling, for coal and other subterranean mineral mining, and so on. The likely economic returns from such devices would pay not only for their development, but for the entire space program many times over.

When the machines are faced with particularly difficult situations, they can be programmed to recognize that the situations are beyond their abilities and to inquire of human operators—working in safe and pleasant environments—what to do next. The examples just given are of devices that are largely self-controlled. The reverse also is possible, and a great deal of very preliminary work along these lines has been performed in the remote handling of highly radioactive materials in laboratories of the U.S. Department of Energy. Here I imagine a human being who is connected by radio link with a mobile machine. The operator is in Manila, say; the machine in the Mindanao Deep. The operator is attached to an array of electronic relays, which transmits and amplifies his movements to the machine and which can, conversely, carry what the machine finds back to his senses. So when the operator turns his head to the left, the television cameras on the machine turn left, and the operator sees on a great hemispherical television screen around him the scene that machine's searchlights and cameras have revealed. When the operator in Manila takes a few strides forward in his wired suit, the machine in the abyssal depths ambles a few feet forward. When the operator reaches out his hand, the mechanical arm of the machine likewise extends itself; and the precision of the man/machine interaction is such that precise manipulation of material at the ocean bottom by the machine's fingers is possible. With such devices, human beings can enter environments otherwise closed to them forever.

In the exploration of Mars, unmanned vehicles have already soft-landed, and only a little further in the future they will roam about the surface of the Red Planet, as some now do on the Moon. We are not ready for a manned mission to Mars. Some of us are concerned about such missions because of the dangers of carrying terrestrial microbes to Mars, and Martian microbes, if they exist, to Earth, but also because of their enormous expense. The Viking landers deposited on Mars in the summer of 1976 have a very interesting array of sensors and scientific instruments, which are the extension of human senses to an alien environment.

The obvious post-Viking device for Martian exploration, one which takes advantage of the Viking technology, is a Viking Rover in which the equivalent of an entire Viking spacecraft, but with considerably improved science, is put on wheels or tractor treads and permitted to rove slowly over the Martian landscape. But now we come to a new problem, one that is never encountered in machine operation on the Earth's surface. Although Mars is the second closest planet, it is so far from the Earth that the light travel time becomes significant. At a typical relative position of Mars and the Earth, the planet is 20 light-minutes away. Thus, if the spacecraft were confronted with a steep incline, it might send a message of inquiry back to Earth. Forty minutes later the response would arrive saying something like "For heaven's sake, stand dead still." But by then, of course, an unsophisticated machine would have tumbled into the gully. Consequently, any Martian Rover requires slope and roughness sensors. Fortunately, these are readily available and are even seen in some children's toys. When confronted with a precipitous slope or large boulder, the spacecraft would either stop until receiving instructions from the Earth in response to its query (and televised picture of the terrain), or back off and start off in another and safer direction.

Much more elaborate contingency decision networks can be built into the onboard computers of spacecraft of the 1980s. For more remote objectives, to be explored further in the future, we can imagine human controllers in orbit around the target planet, or on one of its moons. In the exploration of Jupiter, for example, I can imagine the operators on a small moon outside the fierce Jovian radiation belts, controlling with only a few seconds' delay the responses of a spacecraft floating in the dense Jovian clouds.

Human beings on Earth can also be in such an interaction loop, if they are willing to spend some time on the enterprise. If every decision in Martian exploration must be fed through a human controller on Earth, the Rover can traverse only a few feet an hour. But the lifetimes of such Rovers are so long that a few feet an hour represents a perfectly respectable rate of progress. However, as we imagine expeditions into the farthest reaches of the solar system—and ultimately to the stars—it is clear that self-controlled machine intelligence will assume heavier burdens of responsibility.

In the development of such machines we find a kind of convergent evolution. Viking is, in a curious sense, like some great outsized, clumsily constructed insect. It is not yet ambulatory, and it is certainly incapable of self-reproduction. But it has an exoskeleton, it has a wide range of insectlike sensory organs, and it is about as intelligent as a dragonfly. But Viking has an advantage that insects do not: it can, on occasion, by inquiring of its controllers on Earth, assume the intelligence of a human being—the controllers are able to reprogram the Viking computer on the basis of decisions they make.

As the field of machine intelligence advances and as increasingly distant objects in the solar system become accessible to exploration, we will see the development of increasingly sophisticated onboard computers, slowly climbing the phylogenetic tree from insect intelligence to crocodile intelligence to squirrel intelligence and —in the not very remote future, I think— to dog intelligence. Any flight to the outer solar system must have a computer capable of determining whether it is working properly. There is no possibility of sending to the Earth for a repairman. The machine must be able to sense when it is sick and skillfully doctor its own illnesses. A computer is needed that is able either to fix or replace failed computer, sensor or structural components. Such a computer, which has been called STAR (self-testing and repairing computer), is on the threshold of development. It employs redundant components, as biology does—we have two lungs and two kidneys partly because each is protection against failure of the other. But a computer can be much more redundant than the human being, who has, for example, but one head and one heart.

Because of the weight premium on deep space exploration ventures, there will be strong pressures for continued miniaturization of intelligent machines. It is clear that remarkable miniaturization has already occurred: vacuum tubes have been replaced by transistors, wired circuits by printed circuit boards, and entire computer systems by silicon-chip microcircuitry. Today a circuit that used to occupy much of a 1930 radio set can be printed on the tip of a pin. If intelligent machines for terrestrial mining and space exploratory applications are pursued, the time cannot be far off when household and other domestic robots will become commercially feasible. Unlike the classical anthropoid robots of science fiction, there is no reason for such machines to look any more human than a vacuum cleaner does. They will be specialized for their functions. But there are many common tasks, ranging from bartending to floor washing, that involve a very limited array of intellectual capabilities, albeit substantial stamina and patience. All-purpose ambulatory household robots, which perform domestic functions as well as a proper nineteenth-century English butler, are probably many decades off. But more specialized machines, each adapted to a specific household function, are probably already on the horizon.

It is possible to imagine many other civic tasks and essential functions of everyday life carried out by intelligent machines. By the early 1970s, garbage collectors in Anchorage, Alaska, and other cities won wage settlements guaranteeing them salaries of about $20,000 per annum. It is possible that the economic pressures alone may make a persuasive case for the development of automated garbage-collecting machines. For the development of domestic and civic robots to be a general civic good, the effective reemployment of those human being displaced by the robots must, of course, be arranged; but over a human generation that should not be too difficult—particularly if there are enlightened educational reforms. Human beings enjoy learning.

We appear to be on the verge of developing a wide variety of intelligent machines capable of performing tasks too dangerous, too expensive, too onerous or too boring for human beings. The development of such machines is, in my mind, one of the few legitimate "spin-offs" of the space program. The efficient exploitation of energy in agriculture—upon which our survival as a species depends—may even be contingent on the development of such machines. The main obstacle seems to be a very human problem, the quiet feeling that comes stealthily and unbidden, and argues that there is something threatening or "inhuman" about machines performing certain tasks as well as or better than human beings, or a sense of loathing for creatures made of silicon and germanium rather than proteins and nucleic acids. But in many respects our survival as a species depends on our transcending such primitive chauvinisms. In part, our adjustment to intelligent machines is a matter of acclimatization. There are already cardiac pacemakers that can sense the beat of the human heart; only when there is the slightest hint of fibrillation does the pacemaker stimulate the heart. This is a mild but very useful sort of machine intelligence. I cannot imagine the wearer of this device resenting its intelligence. I think in a relatively short period of time there will be a very similar sort of acceptance for much more intelligent and sophisticated machines. There is nothing inhuman about an intelligent machine; it is indeed an expression of those superb intellectual capabilities that only human beings, of all the creatures on our planet, now possess.

TAKING NOTES AND ORGANIZING IDEAS

1. Paraphrase Sagan's definition of "speciesism" in paragraph 2.
2. Summarize the criticisms of robots and computers that Sagan responds to in his essay.
3. List the tasks that Sagan suggests we will assign to intelligent machines in the future.

4. List the advantages that robots and computers provide over human workers.
5. List the aspects of human intelligence that Sagan feels can be copied by machines.
6. What organizational plan does Sagan use to develop his argument?
7. How would you characterize the style of Sagan's essay? Is this style appropriate for his intended audience? Why?
8. What feelings does Sagan want his audience to develop toward computers? Does he achieve this effect on you? Why?
9. Why do you think Sagan chooses a pacemaker as his concluding example of an intelligent machine? Is this a good example? Why?
10. Sagan stresses the use of robots for space exploration, one of his personal and professional interests. Does Sagan convince you that robots have more practical, everyday applications? Which everyday applications impress you the most?
11. What does Sagan attempt to achieve with his opening paragraph? How does this paragraph fit in with the rest of the essay?

WRITING

1. Agree or disagree with Sagan's position that current machines do possess a form of intelligence. Do his examples of intelligent machines convince you? If not, what further evidence would you need?
2. Using Sagan's essay as a source, write a two-page description of what our society will be like fifty years from now. Focus on the social roles that humans and robots will occupy and on what the interaction between people and machines will be like. Write for an audience of sociology students.
3. In paragraph 28, Sagan suggests that robots may take over from human workers such tasks as garbage collection. Describe some social problems that might arise from robotization of the work force. Can these problems be solved? Are the social costs of robotization worth the potential social benefits?
4. Paragraph 6 describes the Turing Test, a widely cited standard for detecting artificial intelligence. Imagine that you are a governmental official studying the possibility of using computers to make low-level bureaucratic decisions. Would you accept the Turing Test as an adequate indicator that computers could make an intelligent decision? Defend your answer drawing on the examples of computer intelligence in Sagan's essay.
5. In our current society, psychotherapists are trained for many years, and they charge their patients substantial fees for one-on-one therapy sessions. Respond to Sagan's suggestion in paragraph 14 that an intelligent machine could provide low-cost psychotherapy for human patients. Describe what it might do, analyze its possibilities, and evaluate its effectiveness. Write for an audience of psychology majors.

THE IMITATION OF MAN BY MACHINE

Ulric Neisser

The author is a professor of psychology at the University of Georgia. He is widely known for his classic textbook Cognitive Psychology *and for his research on human cognition.*

PREREADING

1. Two of the subheadings in Neisser's article contain the word "cognitive." Make sure you know the meaning of this word before you begin to read the passage.
2. Note that Neisser is a psychologist rather than a computer scientist. How would you anticipate that a psychologist would react to the idea of artificial intelligence?
3. In the middle of the essay, Neisser indents and enumerates three points. Read these three points carefully. How do you think these three points are connected to Neisser's title, "The Imitation of Man by Machine"? Now speculate on what Neisser's thesis might be.

CLOSE READING

1. In the margins of the text, enumerate the similarities between computer and human intelligence that Neisser notes. Also enumerate the differences between computer and human intelligence that Neisser emphasizes. Which seem most striking to you, the similarities or the differences? Why?
2. Neisser draws on psychological terminology that may not be familiar to you. You will find most of the terms he uses in a standard dictionary. As you read, pause to look up unfamiliar terms and write the definitions in the margin of the article.
3. Neisser mentions the psychologist Jean Piaget several times. If you are not familiar with Piaget, consult a general reference book to learn something about his work. In the margin of the text, briefly summarize what you learned about Piaget. What might Piaget's work have to do with artificial intelligence?
4. As you read, mark the sections of the text that contain objective evidence and the sections of the text that contain Neisser's interpretation of this evidence. Does either evidence or interpretation dominate the article?

Popular opinion about "artificial intelligence" has passed through two phases. A generation ago, very few people believed that any machine could ever think as a man does. Now, however, it is widely held that this goal will be reached quite soon, perhaps in our lifetimes. It is my thesis that the second of these attitudes is nearly as unsophisticated as the first. Yesterday's skepticism was based on ignorance of the capacities of machines; today's confidence reflects a misunderstanding of the nature of thought.

There is no longer any doubt that computing machines can be programmed to behave in impressively intelligent ways. Marill[1] does not exaggerate in saying, "At present, we have, or are currently developing, machines that prove theorems, play games with sufficient skill to beat their inventors, recognize spoken words, translate text from one language to another, speak, read, write music, and learn to improve their own performance when given training." Nevertheless, I will argue that the procedures which bring about these results differ substantially from the processes which underlie the same (or other) activities in human beings. The grounds for this assertion are quite different from the "classical" reasons for skepticism about thinking machines, but the latter should be considered first. This amounts to reviewing the similarities between men and computers before stressing the differences.

First of all, it was formerly maintained that the actions of a mechanism would never be purposive or self-directed, whereas human behavior can be understood only in terms of goals and motives. Two counterexamples will be enough to show that this argument has become untenable. In the realm of action, it is difficult not to be impressed with the "homing" missile, which pursues its target tenaciously through every evasive action until it achieves its destructive goal. On the intellectual level, the "Logic Theorist" of Newell, Simon, and Shaw[2] is just as persistent: determined to prove a theorem, it tries one logical strategy after another until the proof is found or until its resources are exhausted. If anything, the argument from purpose cuts the other way: machines are evidently *more* purposive than most human beings, most of the time. This apparently excessive persistence reflects one of the fundamental differences to be elaborated later—one that could, however, be superficially eliminated by disconnecting the goal-setting part of the program at random intervals.

Secondly, machines were once believed to be incapable of learning from experience. We now know that machine learning is not only possible but essential in the performance of many tasks that might once have been thought not to require it. Simple problems of pattern recognition, such as the identification of hand-printed capital letters, have been solved only by programs which discover the critical characteristics of the stimuli for themselves.[3] The success of Samuel's[4] checker-playing program is based on its capacity to store and use experience from previous games; no program without the ability to learn has been nearly as successful. This argument, too, is

[1]T. Marill, *IRE (Inst Radio Engineers) Trans. Human Factors Electron., 2* (1961): 2.
[2]A. Newell, J. C. Shaw, and H. A. Simon, *Psychol. Review, 65* (1958): 151.
[3]O.G. Selfridge and U. Neisser. *Scientific American* 203 (1960): 60.
[4]L. Samuel, *IBM J. Res. Develop,* 3 (1959): 211.

more interesting when viewed the other way. In a sense, computers learn more readily than people do: you can teach checkers to a 3-year-old computer, but not to a 3-year-old child. The reason will appear later; it is evidently not just that the computer is the more intelligent of the two.

Finally, it has often been asserted that machines can produce nothing novel, spontaneous, or creative—that they can "only do what they have been programmed to do." This is perhaps the most widely held of the negative beliefs, yet it is the first to be relinquished by anyone who actually tries to write programs for a digital computer. Long before a programmer succeeds in getting the machine to learn anything, or to behave purposefully, he repeatedly encounters its capacity to act in astonishing, unpredicted, and (usually) frustrating ways. For example, he may change a few steps in a familiar program involving thousands of instructions and find that the output printer produces reams of unintelligible gibberish. Careful diagnostic procedures are needed to discover that one comma was omitted in a single instruction. As a result the computer interpreted two small adjacent numbers as a single large number, executed the wrong instruction in the program, and continued blithely on from a point where it was never expected to be.

Such an event may seem trivial, both because the reason for the unpredicted outcome can be discovered in retrospect and because the effect was maladaptive rather than useful. But neither of these are necessary properties of unpredicted computer output. Existing programs have found original proofs for theorems, made unexpected moves in games, and the like. The belief that a machine can do nothing qualitatively novel is based on a false dichotomy between quality and quantity. What has become a truism in physics also applies to information processes: large changes in the magnitude of phenomena always imply major changes in the "laws" through which these phenomena can be understood. The result of 200,000 elementary symbolic operations cannot be readily predicted from knowledge of the elements and the program. The sheer *amount* of processing which a computer does can lead to results to which the adjective *novel* may honestly be applied. Indeed, complexity is the basis for emergent qualities wherever they are found in nature.

Some Observable Differences

It appears, then, that computers can learn, and can exhibit original and purposive behavior. What can they not do? At first reckoning, their intellectual defects seem trivial and nearly irrelevant. Nevertheless, a list of the inadequacies of present-day artificial intelligence is worth making for its suggestive value. Two or three of the inadequacies have already been mentioned. When a program is purposive, it is too purposive. People get bored; they drop one task and pick up another, or they may just quit work for a while. Not so the computer program; it continues indomitably. In some circumstances the program may be more effective than a man, but it is not acting as a man would. Nor is such single-mindedness always an advantage: the computer is very likely to waste its time on trivialities and to solve problems which are of no importance. Its outlook is a narrow one: with Popeye, it says, "I am what I am," and it lets the rest of the world go hang while it plays chess or translates Russian relentlessly. The root of the difference seems to be more a matter of motivation than of intellect. Programs have goals, but they do not acquire or use their goals as a man would.

Computers are more docile than men. They erase easily: an instruction or two can wipe out anything ever learned, whether pernicious or useful. The decision to acquire new knowledge or to destroy old memories is a deliberate one. Usually it must be taken by the programmer, though in principle the program could decide for itself. Human memory seems much less flexible. A man rarely has single-minded control over what he will learn and forget; often he has no control at all. Thus, he lives willy-nilly in an accumulating context of experience which he cannot limit even if he would. The result is both stupidity and serendipity; if he is inefficient, he also can become wise in unexpected ways. Youth is not doomed to ignorance even though it would like to be, and no one can entirely avoid growing up. A program or a programmer, in contrast, can easily prevent any change that appears superficially undesirable.

By the same token, any apparently desirable change in a program can be carried out, at least if the necessary techniques are known. There is no need to embed it in an orderly sequence of growth, no resistance from an organism that has other things to do first. In this respect artificial intelligence is conformist, and precociously so. Again this is a problem of motivation, but it is a developmental question as well. We would be rightly worried about a child who played chess before he could talk; he would seem "inhuman."

Growth is a process of self-contradiction, but computer programs are never at cross-purposes with themselves. They do not get tangled up in conflicting motives, though they may oscillate between alternative courses of action. Thus, they are good at problem solving but they never solve problem *B* while working on *A*.

Artificial intelligence seems to lack not only breadth but depth. Computers do not dream, any more than they play. We are far from certain what dreams are good for, but we know what they indicate: a great deal of information processing goes on far beneath the surface of man's purposive behavior, in ways and for reasons that are only very indirectly reflected in his overt activity. The adaptive significance of play is much clearer. In playing, children (and adults) practice modes of thought and action that they do not yet need. Free of any directing immediate necessity, skills can develop into autonomous units that can later serve a variety of ends.

Taken one at a time, these differences between natural and artificial intelligence are not impressive. All together, they give rise to the suspicion that the cognitive activities of machines and men are still substantially different. In stressing the differences, my purpose is not to disparage current work in artificial intelligence. The research that has been done and is being done has important practical implications; it is also providing us with valuable models for some kinds of human thinking. Its incompleteness is emphasized here for two reasons. For *psychologists,* I wish to stress that contemporary computer models are oversimplified in the same sense that early stimulus-response psychology and early psychoanalytic theory were oversimplified. It may be well to regard "artificial intelligence" with the same mixture of hopefulness and suspicion that was appropriate to those earlier efforts. For *programmers,* I make a prediction. As computers are used for increasingly "human" activities, either directly (as in simulation) or indirectly (as in situations where the criteria of performance are psychological and social), new and difficult problems will arise. The focus of difficulty will no longer be in pattern recognition, learning, and memory but in an area which has no better name than "motivation". In support of these assertions, I describe, in the remainder of this article, three fundamental and interrelated characteristics of human thought that are conspicuously absent from existing or contemplated computer programs.

1. Human thinking always takes place in, and contributes to, a cumulative process of growth and development.
2. Human thinking begins in an intimate association with emotions and feelings which is never entirely lost.
3. Almost all human activity, including thinking, serves not one but a multiplicity of motives at the same time.

Cognitive Development

The notion of "development" involves more than the obvious fact that a newborn baby has a great deal to learn. The intricacies of adult behavior cannot be acquired in just any order, to suit the convenience of the environment. Certain attitudes and skills must precede others. In part this is a matter of simple prerequisite learning: one must know how the pieces move before one can invent winning chess combinations. Moreover, the cumulation of learning is interwoven at every point with inborn maturational sequences. It may or may not be true that one must walk before he can run, but it is clear that neither skill can be taught to a 6-month-old baby. Therefore, no baby of that age can have the adequate conceptions of space and localization that genuinely do depend on experience. By the time a child has the opportunity to discover other rooms and other worlds, he already has a year's worth of structure with which to assimilate them. He will necessarily interpret his own exploration in terms of experience that he already has: of losing love or gaining it, of encountering potential disaster, joy, or indifference. These preconceptions must affect the kind of explorations he makes, as well as the results of his ventures; and these consequences in turn help to shape the conceptual schemes with which the next developmental problem is met. A child who could move about from the very beginning would grow into an adult complexly different from any of us.

In Piaget's[5] useful terminology, human development consists of two reciprocal phases: "assimilation" and "accommodation." The first is the transformation and recoding of the stimulus world which is performed by the child's cognitive equipment of the moment. Computers also assimilate in this sense; for example, they reduce photographs to bit-patterns through specialized input devices. Accommodation is harder to imitate. It refers to

[5]J. Piaget, *The Origins of Intelligence in Children* (New York: W. W. Norton, 1952).

change in the cognitive apparatus itself, as a result of the attempt to assimilate novel material.

In a loose way, accommodation may be equated to learning, and it is evident that computers can learn (for example, by optimizing probability weights or other internal parameters). But the most important accommodations in human development are changes in the structure of the processing itself. The child's visual and physical exploration of space does not result merely in the assignment of specific quantitative values to an innate spatial schema. On the contrary, the weight of the evidence suggests that such fundamental concepts as objective permanence, three-dimensionality, and tangibility must themselves be formed by development. And we do not yet have any realistic hope of programming this type of growth into an artificially intelligent system.

It is instructive to consider game playing from this point of view, because it has been a focus of interest for both programmers and developmental psychologists. Young children cannot be taught to play games such as checkers and chess because they cannot be reconciled to the restrictions imposed by the rules. Having grasped the idea that he should try to capture pieces, a young child proceeds to do so with any "move" and any piece of his own that comes to hand. He will avoid the loss of his own piece by every possible maneuver, including removing it from the board and putting it in his mouth. If the piece is taken nevertheless, the child may have a tantrum and stop playing. According to Piaget[6] there is an interesting later stage in which the schoolchild thinks of the rules as sacrosanct and eternal; it takes an adult to admit that what was arbitrarily established may be arbitrarily altered. Such a history must leave its mark on a human chess player, in the form of a hierarchical organization of purposes as well as strategies. Nothing comparable exists for the computer program, which works steadily toward its fixed goal of legal victory. There is no obvious reason to doubt that a specialized program may some day play chess as well as a man or better, but the intellectual processes of the two are likely to remain fundamentally different.

Emotional Basis of Cognitive Activity

The activity of a newborn baby is very largely organized around the satisfaction of needs. While there are intervals dominated by visual or tactile exploration, major events in the baby's life are hunger and sucking, irritability and sleep, pain and relief, and the like. This suggests that stimulus information is assimilated largely with reference to its need-satisfying and need-frustrating properties. The first accommodations to such basic features of the world as time, distance, and causality are interwoven with strongly emotional experiences. Moreover, the fluctuations of the child's internal states do not have any very obvious relation to the logic of his environment, so that months and years are needed before his thinking and his actions become well attuned to the world around him. To put it another way: the pleasure principle yields to the reality principle only slowly.

[6]J. Piaget, *The Moral Judgment of the Child* (Glencoe, Ill: Free Press, 1948).

Many psychologists, such as Robert White,[7] have recently stressed the opposite point: that activity directed toward mastering reality is present from the very beginning. They are surely right, but even the beginning of competence and esthetic pleasure depend heavily on internal structures. What the baby explores, and how he reacts to it, is not determined only by realistically important features of the environment but by the schemata with which that environment is assimilated.

Needs and emotions do not merely set the stage for cognitive activity and then retire. They continue to operate throughout the course of development. Moreover, they do not remain constant but undergo growth and change of their own, with substantial effects on intellectual activities. Some emotional growth, such as the gradual differentiation of specific fear from general anxiety, is the result of interaction with the environment. Other changes, like those of puberty, seem to be relatively autonomous. It would be rash indeed to believe that events so important to the individual's life play no role in his thinking. One fundamental way in which they exert their influence is discussed in the next section. In addition, it is worth nothing that one of the most common and frequently discussed modes of learning—that of reward and punishment—operates through an open involvement of strong and historically complicated emotions.

To think like a man, a computer program would need to be similarly endowed with powerful internal states. We must imagine these states, which have both short- and long-term dynamics of their own, to be in almost complete control of information processing at first. Later their influence must become more subtle, until their final role is a complex resultant of the way in which preset internal patterns have interacted with the flow of experience. Perhaps such programs can be written, but they have not been, nor do they appear to be just around the corner.

Multiplicity of Motives

Human actions characteristically serve many purposes at once. Any activity whatever could serve as an example, but it will be instructive to consider chess playing again. Typically, a computer which has been programmed to play chess has one overriding goal—to win—and establishes subordinate goals (capturing pieces, controlling open files, and the like) when they may be useful to that end. Human chess players do this also, but for them winning is itself only one goal among many, to which it is not always related in a simply subordinate way.

For instance, a chess player may also seek the esthetic pleasure which comes from an unexpected and elegant combination. This desire has surely been responsible for the achievement of many spectacular victories in the history of chess; the search for such a combination is also responsible for an uncountable number of defeats. It is likely, too, that most players seek the experience of success, either for the internal satisfactions or for the public acclaim which it brings, or for both of these reasons. The avoidance of the inner or outer humiliation which defeat brings must also play a frequent

[7]R. White, *Psychol. Review,* 66 (1959): 297.

role. None of these motives is fully interchangeable with any other. Each has its own attendant retinue of potential substitute satisfactions, reactions to frustration, and interactions with the concrete reality of the game. However, it is very possible for all of them to exist in the same chess player at the same time.

Chess can serve other purposes as well, which are certainly not without their effect on the actual sequence of moves. It is a social occasion, and serves as a vehicle for a relationship to another person. As such, chess can be an instrument of friendship, but it is double-edged because each friend is trying to defeat the other. Thus, the game becomes an outlet for aggression, in which one may aim for destruction of his opponent in an entirely nonphysical (and so nonpunishable) way. It is not only the opponent who may be symbolically destroyed. Reuben Fine, who is both grand master and psychoanalyst, has argued[8] that the presence of a "king" and a "queen" on the board may give chess a deeply symbolic value, so that very primitive fantasy goals can become relevant to the progress of the game.

Apart from considerations of winning and losing, playing chess may reflect many other human motives. One man may adopt what he considers to be a "daring" style of play because he wants to think of himself as a bold person; another may play conservatively for analogous reasons. Both men may be *playing* because (that is, partly because) chess is only a *game*—an activity in which they can succeed and be respected without growing up or competing in what they regard as more adult, and thus more frightening, realms. Some people probably play chess because it is at least something to do and a means of avoiding the anxiety-laden or self-destructive thoughts they might otherwise have. Others, of both sexes, may play because they somehow think of chess as a masculine rather than a feminine activity and playing it makes them more certain of their own sex identity. And so on; the list is endless.

Every sort of human behavior and thought is open to this type of analysis. No person works on a mathematical problem as contemporary computer programs do: simply to solve it. No person writes a scientific paper merely to communicate technical information, nor does anyone read such a paper merely to be better informed. The overt and conscious motives are important, but they never operate in isolation. In the early days of psychoanalysis it was fashionable to devalue the obvious motives in favor of the unconscious ones, and to assume that cognitive activity was "nothing but" a way to placate instinctual demands. This tendency is happily no longer common; "rational" activities are unquestionably important in their own right to the person who engages in them. But we must be careful not to let the availability of computer models seduce us into the 19th-century view of a man as a transparently single-minded and logical creature.

Elsewhere I have discussed the multiplicity of thought,[9] suggesting that much in human thinking is better conceptualized as "parallel" than as "sequential" in nature. The manifold of motives that I am describing here goes beyond that assumption, although it certainly presupposes a capacity

[8]R. Fine. *Psychoanalysis* 4 (3) 7 (1956): 7.
[9]U. Neisser, *British Journal of Psychology*. 54 (1963): 1.

for parallel processing. The motivational complexity of thought is more easily seen as depth than as breadth. It is what makes people interesting, and it is also what gives them the capacity for being bored. It is what the "shallow" characters of poor fiction lack, and it is the source of the inventive spontaneity of real people. People succeed in using experience with one problem in solving another because, after all, they want to solve both; and both solutions are only parts of an intricate system of needs and goals. Miller, Galanter, and Pribram[10] have emphasized the hierarchical structure that human intentions often exhibit. Such a multiplicity of motives is not a supplementary heuristic that can be readily incorporated into a problem-solving program to increase its effectiveness. In man, it is a necessary consequence of the way his intellectual activity has grown in relation to his needs and his feelings.

The future of artificial intelligence is a bright one. The intellectual achievements of computer programs are almost certain to increase. We can look forward with confidence to a time when many complex and difficult tasks will be better performed by machines than they now are by men, and to the solution of problems which men could never attempt. Moreover, our understanding of human thinking may well be furthered by a better understanding of those aspects of intelligence which the programs display. This process has already begun: many psychologists, myself included, are indebted to computer technology for a wealth of new ideas which seem to be helpful in understanding man. But two systems are not necessarily identical, or even very similar, because they have some properties in common.

The deep difference between the thinking of men and machines has been intuitively recognized by those who fear that machines may somehow come to regulate our society. If machines really thought as men do, there would be no more reason to fear them than to fear men. But computer intelligence is indeed "inhuman": it does not grow, has no emotional basis, and is shallowly motivated. These defects do not matter in technical applications, where the criteria of successful problem solving are relatively simple. They become extremely important if the computer is used to make social decisions, for there our criteria of adequacy are as subtle and as multiply motivated as human thinking itself.

The very concept of "artificial intelligence" suggests the rationalist's ancient assumption that man's intelligence is a faculty independent of the rest of human life. Happily, it is not.

TAKING NOTES AND ORGANIZING IDEAS

1. Summarize in one paragraph the similarities between human and computer intelligence that Neisser points out.
2. In paragraphs 16 to 19, Neisser explains that humanlike "cognitive development" or mental growth is not found in machines. He uses the comparison between human and computer game playing to illustrate this difference. Discuss another human mental activity that demonstrates what Neisser means by cognitive development.

[10]G. A. Miller, E. Galanter, and K. Pribram, *Plans and the Structure of Behavior* (New York: Holt, 1960).

3. Summarize Neisser's explanation in paragraphs 20 and 21 of how infants' needs and emotions influence their cognitive development.
4. In paragraphs 24 to 29, Neisser states that all human activity has multiple motives. Explain his idea using your own examples.
5. Why does Neisser think that the differences between human and computer intelligence are important to recognize?
6. What organizational plan does Neisser use? Explain how the first six paragraphs of the essay function within this plan.
7. What is Neisser's intended audience? Does it include both psychologists and computer scientists?
8. Respond to Neisser's argument that human mental activity has complex motives. Support your point of view with specific examples from your own experiences.
9. Evaluate Neisser's claim that we would have nothing to fear from machines that think exactly as humans do.

WRITING

1. Based on Neisser's article, compare and contrast human and machine intelligence. You may also draw on Sagan's article if you wish. What human intellectual activities can computers master? How could the differences between computers and humans limit the potential applications of computers?
2. In paragraph 31, Neisser warns against using machines to make "social decisions." However, he does not give any specific examples of these decisions. Based on Neisser's discussion of the limitations of machine intelligence, suggest specific examples of social decisions that machines should not make. Explain why they should not make those decisions and indicate the social consequences if they did make them. Write for an audience of students in a political science course.
3. In a two- to three-page paper illustrate with your own examples Neisser's characterization of human intelligence. Make sure you include all the essential features of human intelligence that Neisser mentions. Write for an audience of psychology majors.
4. Compare and contrast the views of Neisser and Sagan on the future of artificial intelligence. How significant are the differences between their views? Can you account for these differences? Do they disagree on matters of science? Write for an audience of computer science majors.

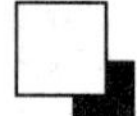

HOW CAN COMPUTERS GET COMMON SENSE?

Gina Kolata

The author is a member of the research report staff of Science, *an academic journal.*

PREREADING

1. The title of the article indicates the author will discuss efforts to develop the equivalent of human common sense in computers. How do you define common sense? Freewrite on this question for ten minutes.
2. Try to envision a commonsense problem that you don't think a computer could solve. Then try to list the steps you would go through to solve the problem. Could a computer be given the information and logical thought processes contained in your series of steps? Explain your answer.

CLOSE READING

1. Annotate the text to differentiate between various theories of how computers can develop common sense. Which of these views do you think the author favors? Why? As you read, which views do you favor? Why?
2. As you read, mark each passage that contains evidence supporting a particular approach to developing artificial intelligence. In the margin, label each piece of evidence as either anecdotal or experimental. Which theory has the strongest supporting evidence?
3. As you read about the circumscription theory, make sure you look up the following words: variable, monotonic, nonmonotonic, premise, and predicate.

Despite all the marvelous things that computers can do today, they simply lack many of the qualities that are present in human intelligence—they don't even have common sense. And it is not at all clear on how to program computers to give them common sense. Or, as experts in artificial intelligence put it, it isn't clear how to represent common sense knowledge in a computer. "I think the AI [artificial intelligence] problem is one of the hardest science has ever undertaken," says Marvin Minsky of Massachusetts Institute of Technology, who is one of the founders of the field of AI.

There are, of course, computer programs that frequently are described as possessing artificial intelligence. Such programs can perform medical diagnosis, for example, or can predict where mineral deposits lie. These so-called expert systems are developed by computer scientists who glean a list

---

Gina Kolata, "How Can Computers Get Common Sense?" *Science,* 217 (1982): 1237-1238.

of rules and procedures from human experts, such as doctors or mineral prospectors. And often the systems are quite useful. But they also are quite limited. "Much of the ordinary common sense ability to predict the consequences of actions requires going beyond the rules present in expert systems," says John McCarthy of Stanford University.

Theoreticians, however, have reached no consensus on how to solve the AI problem—on how to make true thinking machines. Instead, there are two opposing philosophical viewpoints and a flurry of research activity along these two directions. The different viewpoints were represented at a recent meeting[1] of the American Association for Artificial Intelligence by Minsky and by McCarthy, who also is a founder of the AI field and is an inventor of the term "artificial intelligence."

McCarthy believes that the way to solve the AI problem is to design computer programs to reason according to the well worked out languages of mathematical logic, whether or not that is actually the way people think. Minsky believes that a more fruitful approach is to try to get computers to imitate the way the human mind works which, he thinks, is almost certainly not with mathematical logic.

"I really think of myself as a psychologist," says Minsky, who reports that he gets his inspiration for attempting to represent knowledge in a computer by thinking about thinking, talking to psychologists and by going to playgrounds and questioning children who have not yet learned to conceal their thinking process by couching their explanations in logical terms. From these investigations, he has become convinced that there is no single, simple way to explain human reasoning. "I think human intelligence is an accumulation of many different mechanisms and methods," he remarks. "I bet the human brain is a kludge."

So how do you put a jumble of poorly understood mechanisms and methods into a computer? Minsky believes that trying to represent the whole system with mathematical logic gets you into too many difficulties. "I've become convinced that the idea of 'fact' and the idea of 'truth' are no good. I think facts and truth are only good in mathematics and that's an artificial system. Logical systems work very well in mathematics, but that is a well-defined world. The only time when you can say something like, If a and b are integers, then a plus b always equals b plus a is in mathematics."

Minsky gives an example of the kind of difficulties that can occur if mathematical reasoning is applied to the real world. "Consider a fact like, 'Birds can fly.' If you think that common-sense reasoning is like logical reasoning then you believe there are general principles that state, 'If Joe is a bird and birds can fly then Joe can fly.' But we all know that there are exceptions. Suppose Joe is an ostrich or a penguin? Well, we can axiomatize and say if Joe is a bird and Joe is not an ostrich or a penguin, then Joe can fly. But suppose Joe is dead? Or suppose Joe has his feet set in concrete? The problem with logic is that once you deduce something you can't get rid of it. What I'm getting at is that there is a problem with exceptions. It is very hard to find things that are always true."

---

[1]The National Conference on Artificial Intelligence, sponsored by the American Association for Artificial Intelligence was held on 18 to 22 August at Carnegie-Mellon University and the University of Pittsburgh.

An alternative approach that Minsky developed is a system called frame (for framework) systems. It is a psychological approach. The idea is to put large collections of information into a computer—much more information than is ever needed to solve any particular problem—and then to define, in each particular situation, which details are optional and which are not. For example, a frame for "birds" might include feathers, wings, egg-laying, flying, and singing. In a biological context, flying and singing are optional; feathers, wings and egg-laying are not.

In frame systems, there is a collection of frame definitions which set the scene for common-sense reasoning. But the importance of the details in a frame can change if there is a change in purpose or goal. If you are walking in the woods, the importance of "flying" in your bird frame is substantial. If you are in Antarctica its importance is minimal. Or, in another type of example, you may have two different images of another person—one is as a business associate and the other is as a friend. If you cannot understand the person's behavior when you are viewing him as a business associate, you switch frames and try to understand his behavior by viewing him as a friend. In a sense, frame systems are like logic, but there is one important difference. Ordinarily, logic would not say which things are most important in which frame.

Minsky himself never actually sat down to program a computer to use frame systems, but one of his students did. Ira Goldstein, who is now at Hewlett-Packard in Palo Alto, developed a computer language which he calls FRL, for frame representation language, which he and his colleagues use in developing expert systems.

Originally, FRL represented only static objects. But Steven Rosenberg at Hewlett-Packard recently began extending the language so that it also represents the rules people employ for reasoning. With Rosenberg's extension of FRL, says Goldstein, "You can tie rules of reasoning to a particular domain of discourse. With FRL, we emphasize more the use of specific knowledge to guide reasoning. We place less emphasis on general reasoning mechanisms devoid of heuristic guidance."

"Minsky never liked logic," says McCarthy. "When difficulties with mathematical reasoning came up, he felt they killed off logic. Those of us who did like logic, and there weren't many, thought we should find a way of fixing the difficulties." Whether logical reasoning is really the way the brain works is beside the point, McCarthy says. "This is AI and so we don't care if it's psychologically real."

What McCarthy would like to do is to express common sense facts in the language of first order mathematical logic, meaning a language consisting only of variables and relation symbols such as "less than" or "mother of." "A proper axiomatization is one in which a proof exists for all conclusions that are ordinarily drawn from these facts," McCarthy remarks. "But what we know now about common sense is that that's asking for too much. You need another kind of reasoning—nonmonotonic reasoning."

Ordinary mathematical reasoning is monotonic in that if you have a set of premises and a set of conclusions, the set of conclusions is monotonic in the premises. If you add more facts, any conclusions you could draw without the additional facts are still valid with them. But common sense reasoning is often quite different from this mathematical logic. McCarthy explains, "If you know I have a car, you may conclude that you can ask me for a ride. If I tell you the car is in the shop, you may conclude you can't ask me for a ride. If I tell you it will be out of the shop in 2 hours, you may conclude you can ask me." As more premises are added, the conclusion keeps changing. "What's new is the possibility of formalizing nonmonotonic reasoning." That is, the possibility of using rules like those of mathematical logic to represent even nonmonotonic reasoning in a computer.

McCarthy calls his version of nonmonotonic reasoning circumscription. Unlike frame systems, circumscription is not yet being applied. "Circumscription is new and is still changing continuously as a theoretical idea. There is still more theory to be done before it can be used in applications."

Circumscription is used to restrict a predicate as much as possible compatible with the facts that are being taken into account. After this has been done, the desired conclusions may follow by mathematical logic. For example, in the "Birds can fly" problem, McCarthy would use a predicate called "prevented from flying." In it, he would put any facts preventing flying that were being taken into account. These could include, for example, birds that are penguins or ostriches, as well as dead birds, or birds with their feet in concrete. Then the computer would reason, "If Joe is a bird and Joe is not a member of the set 'prevented from flying' then Joe can fly."

But is this circumscription a substitute for common sense? It certainly cannot take into account every contingency. It is easy to think of examples of nonflying birds, such as a bird with a broken wing, that a person with common sense would recognize as unable to fly but the computer would not.

"The conclusions we draw are risky, but that's inevitable," says McCarthy. "We can't invent all the hypotheses that might come to mind although we would like to take into account all the obvious things or, if a nonobvious fact becomes apparent, to take it into account. There is no reason to suppose we can make an omniscient computer program. We only want to make it as good as people."

Yet, McCarthy observes, "I admit that there are difficulties with circumscription. Suppose someone says, 'This bird is in a cage and is only prevented from flying on occasion.' That way lies madness. You can be forced to keep elaborating. The key thing about trying to formalize common sense is to avoid being forced to haggle."

Alternatives to logical reasoning also have their difficulties. Nils Nilsson of SRI International, who is president elect of the American Association for Artificial Intelligence, believes that "alternatives to logic all seem to be somewhat fuzzy and mushy. Some people think that's a virtue—they think that's what intelligence is all about. I don't see the evidence for that." In addition, says Nilsson, many of the people who try to develop systems that are alternatives to logic simply don't know much about logic. (Nilsson emphatically excludes Minsky from this group.) As a result, their alternative systems turn out to be mere subsets of logic. "Some of the things they invent are pale imitations of what logic can do," Nilsson remarks. "In some cases, there may be a little something extra, they may stick a little finger out. But the way to handle that is to extend logic. I think we should stand on the foundation that's been developed."

All efforts to solve the knowledge representation problem share two major obstacles, McCarthy explains. "The preliminary problem is to decide what knowledge to represent. The key thing that we have not got formulated is the facts of the common sense world." Then, even if researchers do manage to represent knowledge in computers, they are still faced with the problem of getting answers out of the computer in a reasonable time.

It is both Minsky's and McCarthy's opinion that the problem of common sense will need many new ideas to go further. But in the meantime, Minsky predicts, there will be immensely valuable spin-offs from attempts to solve the AI problem. This has been the pattern so far. Time sharing, word processing, the computer language LISP, symbolic manipulations by computers, all were developed by AI researchers in the course of their work on more basic problems. Minsky and McCarthy make an analogy with physics. Minsky says, "It took 300 years from the time of Galileo to the discovery of quantum mechanics. You might ask, 'What took those guys so long?'" Yet all along there were important practical consequences of basic research in physics.

Of course, if the AI problem is solved, it will have enormous social consequences which Minsky, for one, worries about. "Do we need AI? There certainly is a dark side to any kind of advance and that's the question of whether societies can tolerate new systems. One of the things that AI threatens to do is to make work unnecessary. The dark question is, what will we do instead of work?"

Is it even possible to solve the AI problem—to design a computer that has common sense and intelligence? Minsky, McCarthy, and others in the field are convinced that the problem will be solved eventually. Asked why he holds this view, McCarthy answers, "The alternative is to say that there is an area of nature that is not reachable by science. And nothing in the history of science supports that hypothesis."

TAKING NOTES AND ORGANIZING IDEAS

1. Write one-paragraph explanations of Minsky's frame system and of McCarthy's circumscription theory.
2. What is Kolata's organizational plan for her article? How does this plan reflect her attitude toward Minsky's and McCarthy's work?
3. Paraphrase Minsky's explanation of why artificial intelligence should be modeled after human intelligence. Then, paraphrase McCarthy's explanation of why it should not.
4. The article describes both Minsky's and McCarthy's approaches to the "birds fly" problem. Which approach seems best? Why?
5. If we did develop machines that could make our common sense decisions for us, how might this affect our culture?
6. Paraphrase Kolata's conclusion about the future of artificial intelligence.

7. Analyze Kolata's article as an argument. What is Kolata's goal? To what extent is Kolata arguing a point?
8. Characterize the tone of Kolata's article. How is this achieved? Is this article typical of the other articles you have read from *Science* in this anthology? Explain your answer, keeping in mind the general characteristics of science writing.

WRITING

1. Drawing on the ideas in Kolata's article, define "common sense." Argue whether or not it is exclusively a human attribute.
2. In a three- to five-page paper, argue in favor of either Minsky's or McCarthy's approach to developing artificial intelligence. Decide which scientist presents the most convincing argument and evaluate the merits and flaws of each position. Write for an audience of science majors.
3. Assume that you need to program a computerized robot chauffeur to make safe right turns on red lights. What are the errors that the robot might make? Describe in general terms how to use a frame system approach to this problem. Then, describe how you might use circumscription to solve the problem. Write for an audience of computer science students.
4. Respond to Minsky's suggestion in paragraph 23 that artificial intelligence may make it unnecessary for humans to work. Argue whether a reduction in human labor would benefit humankind or whether it would deter human initiative. Consider some of the social, political, psychological, and ethical implications of your argument.

DESIGNING COMPUTERS THAT THINK THE WAY WE DO

William F. Allman

Formerly a staff writer for Science '86, *William F. Allman is a Washington, D.C.-based free-lance writer.*

PREREADING

1. React to Allman's title. What attributes would a computer need to "think the way we do?" Freewrite on this topic for ten minutes.
2. Before you read the article, make sure that you understand how a human nerve cell, or neuron, works. Consult an encyclopedia or other general reference book if you need an explanation of neuron function.

CLOSE READING

1. Read the subheadings that Allman provides in his article. Note in the margin the characteristics of neural nets that each subheading suggests.
2. Annotate the text to indicate which paragraphs contain predictions for the future and which describe current technology. Is the article predominately fact or prediction? Is the evidence for each attribute based on anecdotes or experimental results?
3. Label in the margin sections that describe logical thinking and the sections that describe common sense and intuitive thinking.
4. Enumerate in the margin the attributes of human intelligence that Allman suggests machine can or will duplicate.

It doesn't look like much: a chunk of wood the size of a chessboard, festooned with wires and electronic components. Still, it's something that physicist John Hopfield keeps in his office and displays with a broad smile. Built by Hopfield and his colleagues at the California Institute of Technology, the board is a physical manifestation of an idea that a handful of theorists have kicked around for years. Their dream is to build a computing machine that operates on an entirely different principle than the step-by-step symbol processing of conventional computers. This machine would be modeled after the brain: a vast network of neuron-like units that operate on data all at once.

Cognitive scientists have succeeded in simulating such "neural nets" on powerful conventional computers, and Hopfield's crude board is one of

---

William F. Allman. "Designing Computers That Think the Way We Do," *Technology Review* May-June 1987, pp. 58-65. Reprinted with permission from *Technology Review,* M.I.T. Alumni Association, copyright 1987.

the first real neural-net machines. It represents a radical shift in designing computers that think, and it might even change the way we think about thinking.

For decades most artificial intelligence (AI) experts believed that thinking involved the manipulation of symbols—letters or numbers that were in themselves abstract but could be used to express specific ideas or concepts. Take the equation $f = ma$. If you know that f is force and m is the mass of an object, and a is the object's acceleration, these symbols assume a powerful meaning in the real world. Furthermore, there is a consistent set of operations that applies to these symbols. Using algebra, for example, $f = ma$ can be changed to $a = f/m$ and still be true.

If the physical realm of motion and mass can be captured in a set of symbols and rules, then why not the mind? the theorists asked. Might not our cognitive abilities be formalized as a set of operations that would work on a symbolic representation of the world? If we know that everyone at a convention is a lawyer, and that Jane is at the convention, then we can conclude that Jane is a lawyer. This reasoning can be expressed formally as symbols and operations: if all *p's* are *q's*, and x is a p, then x is also a q. It doesn't matter if we're talking about lawyers or farmers, conventions or state fairs, Jane or Jack. The same rules apply. Theorists believed they would simply translate the world into symbols, manipulate the symbols, and translate the results back into the language of the real world.

Formal systems appealed to engineers and mathematicians as well. In 1937 Claude Shannon, then a graduate student at M.I.T., showed in his master's thesis how the true/false proposition of symbolic logic could be simulated in the on/off states of electronic switches. The mathematician John von Neumann showed how a machine could store data in such switches and use a processor to do one operation at a time. The excitement came to a head in 1955, when Herbert Simon is said to have told his class at the Carnegie Institute of Technology, "Over Christmas, Allen Newell and I invented a thinking machine."

Newell and Simon did not believe that their computer imitated what actually happens when humans think. Rather, they suggested that the workings of the mind might be better understood if scientists studied the process of thinking at a more general, theoretical level.

The Limits of Logic Machines

Newell and Simon believed that the main task for AI enthusiasts was figuring out the nature of the symbols and rules the mind uses. For example, what are the rules by which we change words from the present to past tense? What rules do we use to distinguish a table from a chair? Newell and Simon assumed that once the mind's symbols and rules were known, neuroscientists could then figure out how the brain physically produced them.

The people who build neural nets are challenging that long-held assumption. Conventional computers, after all, are having a terrible time making the transition from number and symbol crunching to more formidable tasks such as speech and vision. In fact, computers are awful at these tasks. This failure has led to a growing suspicion that perhaps the people who brought us "I symbol process, therefore I think" might have been putting Descartes before the horse, as it were.

Since some types of thinking such as formal logic and arithmetic involve symbol manipulation, it's not unreasonable to conclude that all other types of thinking do, too—even if we aren't consciously aware of it. But might it not be the other way around? Perhaps the lion's share of what we call thinking is something else. Processing symbols could be a sideline, more the exception than the rule, icing on the cognitive cake.

A quick look at the human mind makes you think so. "Our attempts at general-purpose computation [that is, doing arithmetic or logic] are often inconsistent," says Brown University cognitive scientist James A. Anderson. "Far more complex tasks that are biologically relevant [such as using language or rapidly recognizing faces] are so effortless that we do not realize how hard they are until we try to make a machine do them. On the other hand, the pitiful mess most humans make of formal logical reasoning or arithmetic would embarrass a $10 pocket calculator."

In other words, using a human brain to do symbol processing may be like using the head of a wrench to drive a nail. Though it might do the job, a hammer would probably do it better. But unfortunately, if the only tool you owned happened to be a hammer, you might begin to see every problem as a nail to be driven.

So if thinking isn't symbol processing at its basic level, then what is it? Hopfield and a growing number of computer scientists, cognitive researchers, psychologists, and physicists are trying to find out. Instead of building bigger and faster hammers, they are designing machines based on the hunch that the mind is more wrench-like. For inspiration on how to build the hardware of their thinking machines, they are looking to the hardware of that other thinking machine, the brain.

Neuroscientists have come to realize that the architecture of the brain—how its billions of neurons are connected in a complex, three-dimensional maze—is central to its function. Individual neurons aren't especially smart by themselves, but when they are connected to each other they become quite intelligent. The problem is, nobody knows how they do it. It isn't that neurons are fast: in sending their electrochemical message to other neurons, they are roughly 100,000 times slower than a typical computer switch. But what our brains lack in speed they make up in "wetware," as it is sometimes called. The brain contains from 10 billion to a trillion neurons, each of which may be connected to anywhere from 1,000 to 100,000 others. If this vast net of interconnected neurons forms the grand collective conspiracy we call our minds, maybe a vast interconnected net of mechanical switches can make a machine that thinks.

Simple elements often display complicated behavior when they come in large groups. Imagine that you put 2 molecules of gas such as hydrogen in an otherwise empty, closed container at room temperature. Because hydrogen is a gas, the molecules float around, colliding with the walls and, rarely, with each other. "Every once in a while the molecules collide, and that's an exciting event in the life of someone studying molecular collisions," Hopfield says. "If we put 10 or even 1,000 molecules in the box, all we get is more collisions. But if we put a billion billion molecules in the box, there's a new phenomenon—sound waves. Sound waves wouldn't exist without collisions. There was nothing in the behavior of 2 molecules in the box, or 10 or 1,000 molecules, that would suggest to you that a billion billion molecules would be able to produce sound waves. Sound waves are collective phenomenon of a complex system."

Hopfield and other scientists who loosely call themselves connectionists are not trying to make machines that mimic the action of neurons. Nerve cells are far too complex for that. Rather, these researchers prefer to think of their machines as "neuron-inspired," using "neuronal units" that share some of the brain's properties.

Like neurons, these units are connected to one another in a huge net. Each unit consists of electronic circuitry that responds to input from the others either by switching on and off or by amplifying and diminishing a signal. The units receive incoming electrical or optical messages, add them up, and decide whether to send messages of their own. In the simplest device, the inputs are added up and compared to a certain value. If the sum of inputs is below that value, there is no output.

The conventional von Neumann-type computer takes a few bits of data at a time from a separate memory storage and then operates on them with a central processor, but in neural nets the interconnected units all act on data at once. Like the human brain, they engage in what is called massively parallel computation.

In a seminal paper published in the *Proceedings of the National Academy of Sciences* in 1982, Hopfield showed that the way a network of switches behaves could be mathematically analyzed with the same tools that physicists use to analyze dynamic physical systems. His thesis is complex, but to make a rough analogy: Like a heated bar of metal that hardens as it cools off, a neural net whose switches have started to turn on and off at random will also go through a stabilizing process.

As its units communicate, the net eventually will settle into a state where each switch is permanently set in either the on or the off position. The significance of this becomes clear when we remember that neural nets, like conventional computers, encode information in such switches. For instance, the letter A could be represented as 10001, and 10001 can be stored in on/off switches as on/off/off/off/on. A neural net could recognize the letter A through an array of sensors that signal on or off depending on the data they receive. The final output would be a series of 1s and 0s. Because neural nets work like that, the stabilizing process can indicate the answer to a particular problem.

A Computer That Guesses Right

This process also gives neural nets the data-sorting characteristic of a "content-addressable," associative memory. Our own memories are content-addressable. We can fetch a whole set of facts from a fragmented or even partially incorrect input. When we think of our friend Sally, for example, we also remember that she is a doctor, lives in Pittsburgh, and has red hair. Sally may also come to mind when we think of redheads or doctors or people who live in Pittsburgh. So if someone asks, "Don't you know a redheaded doctor who lives in Philadelphia?" there is enough correct information to conjure up Sally and say, "No, Pittsburgh."

It's tough to make a conventional computer do this, but for neural nets it's natural. If one stable arrangement of the net's on/off switches represents an assortment of related information—*Sally, doctor, red hair, lives in Pittsburgh*—the whole memory can be retrieved by putting in any part of it. Given the input *Sally* and *doctor,* the units will settle into that configuration that represents *red hair* and *Pittsburgh.* In fact, only 5 percent of the memory is enough to make the rest of the system settle into a stable state representing the whole memory.

The net will even make a good guess on the basis of faulty input. Thus if it is given *a red-headed doctor who lives in Philadelphia,* it might still come up with *Sally.*

Again unlike a conventional computer—and very much like our minds—neural nets produce answers that are pretty good but not always the very best. With some tasks, perfection may not be worth the extra time and effort, especially if there are good answers that can be found quickly.

The Traveling Salesman Problem

One such task is solving the "traveling salesman problem," which crops up in everyday situations ranging from deciding on routes to making up airline schedules to designing microchips. Suppose you were a sales representative and had to visit 10 cities. What would be the shortest route you could take to visit them all? It turns out that it is mathematically possible to take 181, 440 different routes to visit any 10 cities. To find the shortest one might be manageable, but as the number of cities to visit goes up, the number of possible routes skyrockets. If you want to visit 100 cities, for example, and there are more than 10^{100} routes. Though digital computers can solve this problem with sophisticated programs, their strategy is to simply measure each route one by one, and that takes a lot of time.

With a neural net, you need only adjust the connections between units to represent the distances between cities. On the few neural-net machines that actually exist—like Hopfield's board—these adjustments are made by hand. The varying strength of connections is manifested as resistance in a wire or some other electronic trickery that reduces or amplifies currents. In neural nets simulated on conventional computers—which is far more common at this stage—a simple factor in multiplication or addition does the job. Within a few millionths of a second, the switches will settle into a stable state, indicating a short route—and a solution to the traveling salesman problem.

In one experiment by Hopfield and his associate at Bell Labs, David Tank, a neural net found answers to traveling salesman problems 1,000 times faster than a conventional computer did. While these answers were the very best only 50 percent of the time, the net came up with one of the two best answers 90 percent of the time.

Absolute accuracy may not always be ideal. Reaching a good working solution fast—rather than struggling for a long time for the best answer—may be more effective in finding the shortest way to route telephone lines or creating a compact design for a microchip. Speed would also be more important than perfection for machines designed to recognize patterns and make generalizations.

The same principle applies to the way we think. "Biology by and large is not interested in finding the best things, just things that are pretty good that can be found quickly," Hopfield says. For example, speech experts estimate that we actually understand only 70 percent of the words we hear. Our minds fill in the rest from the context of what's being said.

Another mind-like trait neural nets display almost borders on intuition. The system can, for instance, make inferences from ambiguous language. "If you hear the words *bat, ball,* and *diamond,* you think of one thing," says Brown University's Anderson, who works with neural nets. "And if you hear the words, *bat, vampire,* and *blood,* you think another." Given *bat* or *diamond* alone, Anderson's machines will respond with characteristic qualities of animals or geometric shapes. But if *bat* and *diamond* are put together, the machine comes up with *baseball.*

It is possible to program a conventional computer to make some of these inferences. However, a neural-net system has a natural ability to form categories and associations, because information about specific objects is spread out among the connections. The net stores the facts that a bat is both an animal and an instrument used in baseball, and the fact that a diamond is both a geometric shape and a baseball-playing field. As a result, the system is able to associate bat and diamond as being two common traits in baseball.

Neural nets have the potential to produce a new kind of artificial intelligence. Instead of relying on the rules an expert might use to make decisions, these machines can learn from a series of examples. For instance, a network repeatedly shown the present and past tense of certain verbs will eventually learn to change the tenses on its own—even for words it hasn't seen before.

It accomplishes this by following a series of "algorithms," or learning rules. Such rules work roughly on the principle that if two neural units cooperate to produce the right answer, the strength of the connection between them is increased. Likewise, if two units produce a wrong answer, then the connection between them is decreased.

Machines That Make Their Own Rules

NETalk is one machine that can learn through algorithms. Built recently by Johns Hopkins biophysicist Terry Sejnowski and Charles Rosenberg of Princeton, NETalk is a 200-unit neural net that has learned to read aloud. With a conventional computer, a programmer would have to sit down and write a series of rules, such as "when you come to an *s,* make an *s* sound; an *n* makes an *n* sound." Of course, there are exceptions to the rules as well: for example, making the *s* silent when it's next to another, as in "passing." And that doesn't explain what to do with the *s* in "passion." But it's possible, with enough perseverance, to track down most of the rules and most of the exceptions, though a word like "knack" might send the system into paroxysms. Most speaking machines take a shortcut, consulting first a pronouncing dictionary of 10,000 or so most-used words, then switching to rules if a word is not in the dictionary.

NETalk, on the other hand, started with an input of written text and the ability to drive a speaker. But it didn't have any rules for matching letters with sounds. It had a learning algorithm instead.

For its first training session, NETalk was given a 500-word text of a first-grader's recorded conversation. The correct sounds for the child's speech—divided into units called phonemes—were already known because they had been transcribed by a linguist. As NETalk read the text, it's network chose phonemes to represent the letters. Meanwhile, its learning algorithm compared those phonemes with the ones the linguist had transcribed. Whenever differences appeared, the algorithm adjusted the strength of the connections between various neural units to try to make the network produce a phoneme that was a better match.

At first, NETalk could only babble. But after a day of training it could read any text with about 90 percent accuracy. In a way, NETalk still has rules for pronunciation. But it makes them itself, adjusting the myriad connections in the machine to make the best fit. "The rules aren't put there," says Sejnowski. "They emerge."

Computers That Don't Crash

Cognitive scientists are using neural nets to explore not only associative memory but other aspects of thinking as well. At Carnegie Mellon University, Geoffrey Hinton is working on a network that makes generalizations about the relationships in a family tree. Cognitive scientists David Rumelhart of the University of California at San Diego and Carnegie Mellon's Jay McClelland are looking at the ways networks perform language-related tasks, such as changing the tense of verbs. And Carnegie Mellon's David Touretzky, collaborating with Geoffrey Hinton, is demonstrating that neural nets can even do the kind of sequential symbolic processing that ordinary computers do.

At this stage, connectionist machines are usually simulated on conventional computers because no one is sure what the best configuration for neural nets might be. However, researchers at Bell Labs have constructed an experimental "neural net" chip that has 75,000 transistors in an area the size of a dime. Furthermore, the concept has piqued the interest of the Pentagon's Advanced Research Projects Agency, the Jet Propulsion Laboratory, AT&T Bell Laboratories, and Los Alamos National Laboratory. Researchers at all of these organizations are now attempting to put theory into practice and build neural-net machines that are more sophisticated than Bell Labs' chip or Hopfield's board.

Defense agencies are particularly interested in neural nets because such systems have a brain-like property known as "graceful degradation."

Since information and processing are distributed among many neural units, a neural net can still function—though somewhat less efficiently—when as much as 15 percent of its units are damaged. A similar occurrence would be disastrous for a conventional computer. "Cut 1 percent of the wires in a computer," says Hopfield, "and it will grind to a halt."

Such resilient networks would be ideal for spacecraft, nuclear power plants, or Star Wars, where a sudden breakdown could be catastrophic. And because of their potential strengths in speedy pattern recognition, neural nets are being considered as vision and speech-recognition systems for robots.

Neural nets are still very much in the experimental stage, and many cognitive scientists remain skeptical about their potential. Stanford AI researcher Terry Winograd, for one, says the machines are receiving attention now because "they have a higher percentage of wishful thinking."

Even with all the excitement over the promise of neural-net computers, it's unlikely they will replace the good old number crunchers that we've grown so used to over the decades. As traditional AI proponents point out, relying on machines that think the way we do may not be such a great idea. You certainly wouldn't want to balance your bank account or figure out a company payroll with a computer that does not consistently produce the best answer.

Yet many researchers feel neural nets will enhance our understanding of how the brain works and help us build better AI systems. Indeed, if these systems really can recognize patterns and make good inferences from sketchy and partially incorrect data, they might serve as bridges between the sloppy, intuitive human world and the more literal and precise realm of conventional computers. Sometime in the distant future, when we ask our personal robot to go fetch a bat, its neural net might be responsible for determining whether we are about to go to a Halloween costume party or a baseball game.

TAKING NOTES AND ORGANIZING IDEAS

1. What is a "neural net" as embodied in the human brain?
2. How does the organization and operation of a computer designed on the neural net pattern differ from that of a traditional computer?
3. Write a one-paragraph explanation of what Allman refers to as "content-addressable, associative memory."
4. Describe what Allman indicates are the "limits of logic machines."
5. Explain the sense in which NETalk has "learned" to talk as opposed to being preprogrammed to talk.
6. Does Allman overlook any potential disadvantages of neural net machines?
7. What is Allman's goal in writing? Is his article predominantly informative or argumentative? What passages best indicate Allman's goal?
8. Summarize Allman's predictions for the future of artificial intelligence. How confident does he seem in these predictions?

WRITING

1. React to Allman's suggestion that a neural network machine, such as NETalk, may be able to generate its own rules rather than merely follow a programmer's instructions. What are the wider implications of developing a computer that can make significant modifications in its own programming?
2. In a three- to five-page essay, compare and contrast Allman's and Neisser's predictions for the future development of artificial intelligence. What accounts for the differences between their predictions? Do they disagree on matters of science? On political or social values?
3. Compare and contrast traditional computers and neural net machines. Explain the advantages of neural networks over traditional computer designs. Write for an audience of computer science majors.
4. What future applications can you envision for neural net computers? How might society change once we have these machines? Consider options beyond those suggested by Allman. Are there any potential negative impacts of this new technology? Write for an audience of social science majors.

THE LIMITATIONS OF EXPERT SYSTEMS

Joseph Weizenbaum

The author, a professor of computer science at the Massachusetts Institute of Technology, is widely recognized as a pioneer in the field of artificial intelligence.

PREREADING

1. Read carefully the first and last paragraphs of the article. Based on this preview, anticipate what Weizenbaum's thesis might be.
2. Read carefully the last sentence in the excerpt. Think over the other articles in this chapter that suggest ways to make computers "wise." With the other articles in mind, freewrite for ten minutes in response to Weizenbaum's last sentence.

CLOSE READING

1. As you read, search for Weizenbaum's answer to the question he poses in his first sentence. Underline possible answers as you find them.
2. Annotate the text noting passages that contain scientific facts and those that contain the author's opinions.

From *Computer Power and Human Reason* by Joseph Weizenbaum (New York: W. H. Freeman, 1976). pp. 207-227.

3. As you read, underline words and phrases that seem particularly significant in setting the tone of the article. In the margin, characterize Weizenbaum's tone. How is the tone different from that of other articles you have read in this chapter?

The question I am trying to pursue here is, "What human objectives and purposes may not be appropriately delegated to computers?" We can design an automatic pilot, and delegate to it the task of keeping an airplane flying on a predetermined course. That seems an appropriate thing for machines to do. It is also technically feasible to build a computer system that will interview patients applying for help at a psychiatric out-patient clinic and produce their psychiatric profiles complete with charts, graphs, and natural-language commentary. The question is not whether such a thing *can* be done, but whether it is appropriate to delegate this hitherto human function to a machine.

The artificial intelligentsia argue . . . that there is no domain of human thought over which machines cannot range. They take for granted that machines can think the sorts of thoughts a psychiatrist thinks when engaged with his patient. They argue that efficiency and cost considerations dictate that machines ought to be delegated such responsibilities. As Professor John McCarthy once put it to me during a debate, "What do judges know that we cannot tell a computer?" His answer to the question—which is really just our question again, only in different form—is, of course, "Nothing." And it is, as he then argued, perfectly appropriate for artificial intelligence to strive to build machines for making judicial decisions.

The proposition that judges and psychiatrists know nothing that we cannot tell computers follows from the much more general proposition subscribed to by the artificial intelligentsia, namely, that there is nothing at all which humans know that cannot, at least in principle, be somehow made accessible to computers . . . .

Human language in actual use is infinitely more problematical than those aspects of it that are amenable to treatment by information theory, of course. But . . . language involves the histories of those using it, hence the history of society, indeed, of all humanity generally. And language in human use is not merely functional in the way that computer languages are functional. It does not identify things and words only with immediate goals to be achieved or with objects to be transformed. The human use of language manifests human memory. And that is a quite different thing than the store of the computer, which has been anthropomorphized into "memory." The former gives rise to hopes and fears, for example. It is hard to see what it could mean to say that a computer hopes.

These considerations touch not only on certain technical limitations of computers, but also on the central question of what it means to be a human being and what it means to be a computer.

I accept the idea that a modern computer system is sufficiently complex and autonomous to warrant our talking about it as an organism. Given that it can both sense and affect its environment, I even grant that it can, in an extremely limited sense, be "socialized," that is, modified by its experiences with its world. I grant also that a suitably constructed robot can be made to develop a sense of itself, that it can, for example, learn to distinguish between parts of itself and objects outside of itself, that it can be made to assign a higher priority to guarding its own parts against physical damage than to similarly guarding objects external to itself, and that it can form a model of itself which could, in some sense, be considered a kind of self-consciousness. When I say therefore that I am willing to regard such a robot as an "organism," I declare my willingness to consider it a kind of animal. And I have already agreed that I see no way to put a bound on the degree of intelligence such an organism could, at least in principle, attain.

I make these stipulations, as the lawyers would call them, not because I believe that what any reasonable observer would call a socialized robot is going to be developed in the "visible future"—I do not believe that—but to avoid the unnecessary, interminable, and ultimately sterile exercise of making a catalogue of what computers will and will not be able to do, either here and now or ever. That exercise would deflect us from the primary question, namely, whether there are objectives that are not appropriately assignable to machines.

If both machines and humans are socializable, then we must ask in what way the socialization of the human must necessarily be different from that of the machine. The answer is, of course, so obvious that it makes the very asking of the question appear ludicrous, if indeed not obscene. It is a sign of the madness of our time that this issue has to be addressed at all . . . .

The concept of an intelligence alien to certain domains of thought and action is crucial for understanding what are perhaps the most important limits on artificial intelligence. But that concept applies to the way humans relate to one another as well as to machines and their relation to man. For human socialization, though it is grounded in the biological constitution common to all humans, is strongly determined by culture. And human cultures differ radically among themselves. . . .

Profound differences in early training crucially affect the entire societies involved. And they are, of course, transmitted from one generation to the next and thus perpetuated. They must necessarily also help determine what members of the two societies know about their worlds, what are to be taken as "universal" cultural norms and values, hence what in each culture is and is not to be counted as fact. They determine, for example (and this is particularly relevant to the contrast between Japanese and American social norms), what are private as opposed to public conflicts, and hence what modes of adjudication are appropriate to the defense of what human interests. The Japanese traditionally prefer to settle disputes, even those for which relief at law is statutorily available, by what Westerners would see as informal means. Actually, these means are most often themselves circumscribed by stringent ritualistic requirements that are nowhere explicitly codified but are known to every Japanese of the appropriate social class. This sort of knowledge is acquired with the mother's milk and through the whole process of socialization that is itself so intimately tied to the individual's acquisition of his mother tongue. It cannot be learned from books; it cannot be explicated in any form but life itself.

An American judge, therefore, no matter what his intelligence and fairmindedness, could not sit in a Japanese family court. His intelligence is simply alien to the problems that arise in Japanese culture. The United States Supreme Court actively recognized this while it still had jurisdiction over distant territories. For example, in the case of Diaz v. Gonzales, which was originally tried in Puerto Rico, the court refused to set aside the judgment of the court of original jurisdiction, that is, of the native court. Justice Oliver W. Holmes, writing opinion of the Court, stated,

> This Court has stated many times the deference due to understanding of the local courts upon matters of purely local concern. This is especially true when dealing with the decisions of a court inheriting and brought up in a different system from that which prevails here. When we contemplate such a system from the outside it seems like a wall of stone, every part even with all the others, except so far as our own local education may lead us to see subordinations to which we are accustomed. But to one brought up within it, varying emphasis, tacit assumptions, unwritten practices, a thousand influences gained only from life, may give to the different parts wholly new values that logic and grammar never could have got from the books.[1]

Every human intelligence is thus alien to a great many domains of thought and action. There are vast areas of authentically human concern in every culture in which no member of another culture can possibly make responsible decisions. It is not that the outsider is unable to decide at all—he can always flip coins, for example—it is rather that the *basis* on which he would have to decide must be inappropriate to the context in which the decision is to be made.

What could be more obvious than the fact that, whatever intelligence a computer can muster, however it may be acquired, it must always and necessarily be absolutely alien to any and all authentic human concerns? The very asking of the question, "What does a judge (or a psychiatrist) know that we cannot tell a computer?" is a monstrous obscenity. That it has to be put into print at all, even for the purpose of exposing its morbidity, is a sign of the madness of our times.

Computers can make judicial decisions, computers can make psychiatric judgments. They can flip coins in much more sophisticated ways than can the most patient human being. The point is that they *ought* not be given such tasks. They may even be able to arrive at "correct" decisions in some cases—but always and necessarily on bases no human being should be willing to accept.

There have been many debates on "Computers and Mind." What I conclude here is that the relevant issues are neither technological nor even mathematical; they are ethical. They cannot be settled by asking questions beginning with "can." The limits of the applicability of computers are ultimately stable only in terms of oughts. What emerges as the most elementary insight is that, since we do not now have any ways of making computers wise, we ought not now to give computers tasks that demand wisdom.

---

[1]*Diaz v. Gonzales,* 261 U.S. 102 (1923), Per Holmes, O. W. I owe this reference to Professor Paul Freund of the Law School of Harvard University.

TAKING NOTES AND ORGANIZING IDEAS

1. Paraphrase Weizenbaum's explanation of how a computer can be seen as an organism.
2. What exactly does Weizenbaum mean when he says in paragraph 8 that both computers and humans are "socializable"? Illustrate with your own examples how both people and machines can be socialized.
3. Explain what Weizenbaum sees as the essential difference between human language and memory on the one hand and computer language and memory on the other.
4. How does Weizenbaum's brief discussion of Japanese culture function in his essay?
5. To what extent is Weizenbaum's argument based on scientific analysis? What other concerns does he raise?
6. What is Weizenbaum's organizational pattern? How does the tone of the essay fit with the organizational pattern?
7. Where would Wiezanbaum draw the line between decisions that are appropriate for computers to make and decisions that only humans should make?
8. In his attack on the notion of computerized judges, does Weizenbaum overlook any weaknesses in our present judicial system? If so, what are these weaknesses?
9. List any unproven assumptions upon which Weizenbaum bases his argument. Do you think these assumptions are reasonable?

WRITING

1. Weizenbaum suggests in paragraph 6 that computers can be viewed as organisms. In what way or from what perspective does this make sense? React to Weizenbaum's suggestion from as many perspectives as possible. How would a biochemist respond to this suggestion? A physicist? A physician? A psychologist? A zoologist? A philosopher?
2. Argue for or against Weizenbaum's position that we need to consider what is wise rather than what is possible in making technological decisions. Can scientists evaluate what is wise as well as what is possible? Do they have a responsibility to make this determination? What are the criteria for deciding whether or not something is wise? Write for an audience of computer science students.
3. Analyze the Weizenbaum excerpt as a scientific argument. Consider how he handles his opposition and how he presents his basic assumptions. How fair is he to opposing arguments? Are his assumptions scientifically verifiable through research? Write for an audience of science majors.
4. Where would you draw the line between what a computer should do and what a human should do? Write a two- to three-page paper in which you differentiate between tasks that only humans should do and

those that could be safely assigned to computers. Identify any assumptions and values on which you base your judgment. Make sure that you respond to Weizenbaum's ideas in your discussion.

TECHNOLOGICAL DECISION MAKING

Before 1945, technological innovations were developed and implemented as fast as advances in the basic sciences would allow. Little thought was given to the ultimate consequences of technology. Except in cases where technology had extremely obvious effects, such as the horrible suffering caused by gas warfare during World War I, few attempts were made to control the use of new technology.

The Hiroshima and Nagasaki atomic bomb blasts in the final days of World War II demonstrated modern military technology's horrifying potential. In the years that followed, more subtle effects of technological development, such as human cancers caused by synthetic chemicals, showed that new technology should not be applied indiscriminately. Consequently, scientists and the public began to study the technological decision-making process. The debate that followed raised a number of important questions: Who is competent to make correct technological decisions? What are appropriate criteria and procedures for making technological decisions? Who is responsible for the adverse consequences of technology? None of these questions have obvious answers.

The readings in this chapter all focus on technological decision making. In the first article, Matthew L. Wald discusses the potential impact of the greenhouse effect and outlines the technological decisions that need to be made in response to this threat. The next two sources concern the AIDS crisis. In his discussion of policy decisions concerning an experimental AIDS treatment, M. Mitchell Waldrop explains the conflict of interest between AIDS researchers, federal regulatory agencies, and AIDS patients. David R. Zimmerman describes a controversial plan to produce and distribute to drug addicts self-destruct needles, a plan that raises important questions concerning the motives behind technological decisions. The AIDS discussion is followed by two articles concerning the international impact of technological decision making. Abdus Salam advocates a worldwide program of technological development directed at the problems of Third World nations. In "The Human Dimension of Science and Technology," James Gudaitis argues that social concerns should impact strongly on technological decision making. He stresses the dire consequences of technological decisions made in the West for people the world over. In his article on White House science advisors, Colin Norman examines the impact of the scientific community on federal decision making. Finally, George Orwell's short article "What Is Science?" maintains that study in the humanities and arts is central to making good technological decisions.

FIGHTING THE GREENHOUSE EFFECT

Matthew L. Wald

Matthew L. Wald is a reporter for The New York Times.

PREREADING

1. What is the "greenhouse effect?" In what contexts have you heard the term used? Freewrite for ten minutes in response to these questions.
2. What are the major means of generating power used by the industrialized world? What have you read about the environmental consequences of generating power? Freewrite for ten minutes in response to these questions.

CLOSE READING

1. As you read Wald's article, label both the sections that describe the potential problems associated with the greenhouse effect and the sections that describe possible solutions to these problems. Does Wald devote more time to problems or to solutions?
2. Identify the paragraph(s) in which Wald defines the greenhouse effect. In what ways, if any, does this definition differ from the one you produced in your freewriting?
3. Label the sections of the article that describe the views of environmentalists and those that describe the views of industrialists.

The worst of this summer's searing heat may be over, but the concerns that it raised about a global warming trend—known as the greenhouse effect—seem certain to linger.

Whether the earth is really warming is still a matter of debate. One thing is clear, however, finding a way to slow or stop the accumulation of gases thought to be responsible for the greenhouse effect would involve a drastic change in the amount of fuel we burn and in our sources of energy. The shifts could ultimately affect the cost of availability of all types of energy and be felt in every corner of society, changing manufacturing processes, construction techniques, even driving habits.

"The implications go very deeply into modern industrial society," said William R. Moomaw, director of the climate, energy and pollution program of the World Resources Institute, a Washington-based study group that has played a prominent role in the greenhouse debate.

"In many ways we're talking about changing the quality of life of everyone in the world," said Carl Crawford, a spokesman for the American Electric Power Company of Columbus, Ohio, the nation's biggest user of coal.

Matthew L. Wald "Fighting the Greenhouse Effect," *The New York Times* (28 Aug. 1988). Sec.

The burning of coal, oil and other combustion energy sources produces carbon dioxide, a natural constituent of the atmosphere. Elevated levels of carbon dioxide are thought to be responsible for half the greenhouse effect. There is good reason to do something now to curb that production, many experts argue; enough carbon dioxide has been sent into the atmosphere already, they say, to cause a significant temperature increase—and energy use continues to grow.

Indeed, scientists are already scrambling to think of ways to limit the potential effects. And Congress is weighing what it can do. Curiously, business, which produces most of the energy used and whose products are so energy-dependent, seems largely to have stayed out of the debate.

Perhaps for good reason. Barring some futuristic technological solution that scientists can now only fantasize about, the choices facing business—as well as policy makers—are tough ones.

Indeed, the magnitude of the changes could easily dwarf the conservation efforts of the early 1970's sparked by the oil embargo. This time around, cutbacks in energy use and the search for alternative energy sources would be just the beginning.

The main event would likely involve a fundamental restructuring of every industry that is dependent on energy, as well as the energy industry itself. In particular, the warming trend poses critical problems for coal producers and users, unless cost-effective pollution control techniques can be developed. At the same time, it could provide new life for nuclear power, which produces virtually no greenhouse gases.

The gases thought to be responsible for the greenhouse effect—besides carbon dioxide, they include methane, nitrous oxide and chlorofluorocarbons—are a byproduct of many industrial processes. But mostly they are produced when fossil fuels are burned in boilers, furnaces and car engines. The gases cause the earth's surface to warm by trapping the infrared radiation that otherwise would be reflected back into space, just as a greenhouse keeps in heat that would otherwise escape.

A change of just a few degrees in atmospheric temperature over the next century could be catastrophic. A parade of scientists appearing before a Senate committee in June painted a graphic picture of what that could mean: melting icecaps and rising sea levels that would inundate seaboard cities and drown thousands in fierce storms; rainfall shifts that would make the deserts bloom and turn breadbaskets into dustbowls; and, of course, heat everywhere.

Proposals are coming from various camps to meet the potential threat. Senator Timothy E. Wirth, a Colorado Democrat, has introduced a bill to spend $4.3 billion to study ways to combat the greenhouse effect. The bill, which would provide more money for conservation research and for a new generation of nuclear plants, is sure to have a host of competitors.

But the challenge confronting all the planners is the scope of the greenhouse issue. "If this is a problem," American Electric's Mr. Crawford said, "it is so global and so diffuse in our economy, it's going to be very hard to come up with a strategy."

The heart of the problem, said Jay Agarwal, vice president for technology assessment of Charles River Associates, a consulting firm based in Boston, is that energy consumption is fundamental to the economy. "You can't make steel without energy, or make copper, or aluminum, or food, or clothing," he said. "The transformation of things we eat, things we consume, all takes energy."

And energy, to a large degree, currently means the combustion of hydrocarbons in coal, oil and gas—and the resulting production of carbon dioxide. Combustion provides nearly 90 percent of the energy needs of the United States. The balance comes from hydroelectric power, which has a limited potential for expansion, and nuclear fission, which has been consigned to slow extinction in this country because of its high cost and safety concerns.

Before concerns about global warming, carbon dioxide was considered a harmless byproduct of combustion. But if it comes to be considered a pollutant, a new pecking order could emerge among energy sources.

The two criteria that have determined the choice of fossil fuels for more than a century are price and availability. The new standard would be how much carbon dioxide a fuel produces. For the amount of heat that results in four pounds of carbon dioxide when coal is used, oil would produce only three pounds and natural gas, two.

Switching to fuels that produce less carbon dioxide would require huge dislocation. The Shell Oil Company, for example, estimates that in 1987, total world energy production of hydrocarbon fuels was the equivalent of 135 million barrels of oil a day. Of that amount, 32 percent was coal, 45 percent was oil and only 23 percent was natural gas, the best of the lot.

Shifts are possible, but they would create new strategic problems. The United States has enough coal to last more than 300 years, but there are just a few decades' worth of gas reserves at current rates of consumption. While there is more gas to be discovered, the total would still be a small fraction of the coal supply.

At the moment, some utilities are interested in gas, especially for a new generation of power plants that produces more electricity and useful steam from a given quantity of fuel. Over all, however, energy users have considered natural gas unattractive because of questions about availability and whether the price will remain competitive in years to come. Demand is low and production has fallen by more than 25 percent since the early 1970's; recently natural gas has lost market share to cheaper oil. And coal is far cheaper than either.

The biggest users of coal—and therefore, perhaps, the biggest greenhouse targets—are the electric utilities. American utilities alone contribute 7.5 percent of the world's carbon dioxide output, according to the Electric Power Research Institute, a nonprofit consortium based in Palo Alto, California. If the utilities could curb their carbon dioxide production, the benefits would be twofold. Their own electricity would be "cleaner," and more electricity could be used to heat homes and run factories, replacing fossil fuels burned in boilers and furnaces. With a few advances in battery technology and provisions for easy recharging, electricity could begin to replace gasoline to power cars.

But producing "clean" electricity now is not practical. The utilities have already spent billions of dollars to install equipment to capture the sulfur dioxide created by their plants that is linked to acid rain. In theory, they could install equipment to capture carbon dioxide, as well. The cost would be staggering, however.

A study earlier this year by the Brookhaven National Laboratory, commissioned by the Department of Energy, estimated that the capital cost of installing the technology would be 70 to 150 percent of the cost of the original plant. The average cost of electricity itself, the study estimated, would rise 75 percent. And there are equally daunting concerns about storing the millions of tons of carbon dioxide gas that would be captured each year.

Another possibility for the utilities would be more nuclear plants. There are 109 nuclear plants licensed to operate in the United States, but the technology became uneconomic in the early 70's and the accident at Three Mile Island in 1979 raised safety concerns that have not receded. As a result, all plants ordered after 1974 were canceled or abandoned during construction.

The manufacturers, not surprisingly, think it is time to bring them back, especially in light of the greenhouse effect. At the Westinghouse Electric Corporation, for example, Richard J. Slember, vice president and general manager of the energy system unit, ran down the list of technologies his division, the energy systems business unit, is doing business and research in: photovoltaics (or electricity directly from sunlight), windmills, coal, waste-to-energy plants, fuel cells (which combine oxygen and hydrogen to make water and electricity) and coal-bed methane production (in which a burnable gas is made in coal mines).

"It seems that the major solution that's available presently is to stop burning," he said. "The only one you're really left with, in a very pragmatic sense, is nuclear."

Westinghouse, which has sold some plants overseas during the long hiatus in American orders, is working on what it calls "a new half-generation" of reactors, with more backup safety systems and a "user friendly" standardized design. Besides offering improved safety, the new design would be far more economical, the company said.

To some, the Westinghouse program and similar ideas from other reactor builders make nuclear energy more attractive than it used to be. Senator Wirth said at a hearing early this summer that it might be time for the country to get over its case of "nuclear measles," and his bill calls for spending $500 million on research for a reactor that would be "passively safe," with non-mechanical features to prevent meltdown, and which would minimize the volume of nuclear waste.

"We have to re-think nuclear," he said. "We really have to start all over again, but we've got time to do it." Some climate changes may already be inevitable, he said, and mankind will be fighting the greenhouse problem for decades. "The environmentalists will come around." he added. "They can't help but come around."

But some experts are not convinced. "Let's remember why nuclear power died before we suddenly say let's restart it," said John Ahearne, a former member of the Nuclear Regulatory Commission and now a vice president of Resources for the Future, a Washington study group. "Costs were rising rapidly, a number of plants were seen to be operated very poorly and electricity demand wasn't there."

"How does the greenhouse effect change that?" Mr. Ahearne asked. "It's really only the electricity issue. The greenhouse question for the first time says, maybe all those coal plants should be significantly cut back or closed. But the first two problems don't automatically go away."

Some environmentalists are reviewing their options. "I think it's time to re-think our energy policy as a whole," said Jan Beyea, a scientist at the Audubon Society, which is based in New York. "I don't think the current generation of nuclear plants is a viable option, even if one wanted to solve the greenhouse problem that way. With public fears, you're just not going to get enough built."

But Mr. Beyea said, "There certainly should be research into inherently safe nuclear power plants, provided that an equal amount is put into photovoltaics." He added that photovoltaic cells were likely to be a cheaper energy source.

Others believe the construction of new reactors should be made contingent on solving the nuclear waste problem. "The waste problem is of overwhelming importance," says Lynn A. Greenwalt, vice president for resources conservation of the Washington-based National Wildlife Federation.

Even without safety concerns, the higher costs of nuclear power would appear to be prohibitive.

But nuclear energy has the edge over a conservation approach to the problem in at least one respect, said David G. Hawkins, a senior attorney at the Natural Resource Defense Council in Washington. "You're dealing with human beings whose psychology tends to be dominated by what appears to be the easiest fix," he said. "How do you get attention focused on more diverse issues like energy efficiency, when you're sitting at a table with nuclear people who say, 'Here, we're willing to sell you the answer, in a technological box'?"

A general increase in energy efficiency, from gas mileage in autos and trucks to foot-candles per watt in light bulbs, would be a faster and cheaper answer to the greenhouse effect than building more nuclear plants, environmentalists say. And the conservation route is certainly within reach. "In West Germany today, per capita energy consumption is just about half what it is in the U.S.," Mr. Hawkins said.

Scott G. Denman, director of the Safe Energy Communication Council, a coalition of environmental and anti-nuclear groups in Washington, made a similar point, "Today we spend 10 percent of our G.N.P. on energy," he said. "Japan, our primary competitor in many areas of the economy, spends only 5 percent on energy."

The group favors increasing the Federal standards for car and truck mileage, which were scheduled to rise to 27.5 miles per gallon but which the Reagan Administration lowered to 26. "If we want to mine for oil, Detroit is the biggest field we have," Mr. Denman said. "We can be contributing to a healthier economy and a healthier environment," he added, suggesting that the standard be doubled over the next few decades.

Efficiency can also be achieved by getting more power from each ton of fuel used to produce energy. Mr. Moomaw of the World Resources Institute, for example, foresees a strong future for a new model of generators, of a type under development by the General Electric Company. The generators are expect to be about 25 percent more efficient than current models.

In the long term, many existing technologies may benefit from the fear of the greenhouse effect. Mr. Moomaw points to the burning of trash to make electricity, an idea that cities are turning to as they exhaust their landfill space.

Trash burning has environmental hazards of its own, producing carbon dioxide and other greenhouse gases. But the landfill process produces methane gas, which also contributes to the greenhouse effect. As long as garbage results in greenhouse gases of one kind or another, Mr. Moomaw suggested, society should try to get the maximum energy benefit from it; the electricity generated by burning trash could replace some generated from coal or oil.

Another obvious technology is photovoltaic solar power, whose cost is dropping but is still not competitive. Engineers at the Electric Power Research Institute have recently made enough progress in the fabrication of photovoltaic cells to suggest that the technology will soon be competitive with the more expensive fossil-fired electric plants.

The importance of future technological innovation is difficult to measure. "It's hard to imagine powering 20th century industry with sunshine," said Gerald Kraft, an analyst at Charles River Associates. "But maybe we can. Nobody knows."

And nobody knows, as the long hot summer of '88 draws to a close, just how serious the greenhouse effect will prove to be.

But while it is too soon for a scientific consensus about the extent of the warming trend, most experts say enough evidence already exists to place everyone—business included—on the alert.

TAKING NOTES AND ORGANIZING IDEAS

1. In three or four sentences, summarize Wald's main points.
2. According to Wald's article, can scientists prove that the greenhouse effect has already begun to influence the earth's climate?
3. Describe the physical process that gives rise to the greenhouse effect.
4. What are the major sources of greenhouse gases?
5. What energy sources that do not produce greenhouse gases are mentioned in the article? According to the article, how viable are these options?
6. Summarize the estimates Wald presents for the cost of minimizing greenhouse gas production.
7. Describe Wald's organizational plan. Why is this plan used frequently in articles that discuss the impact of advanced technology?

8. What is Wald's purpose in writing? Does he argue for a particular perspective on the greenhouse issue?

WRITING

1. Based on the information in Wald's article, what should we do, if anything, to respond to the greenhouse effect? Write for an audience of science majors.
2. Over the last two decades, the air pollution problem has received considerable attention from the news media and has been the subject of many state and federal laws and regulations. Compare air pollution with the greenhouse effect. In what ways are the two problems similar? In what ways do they differ? Can they be solved through the same means?
3. Who is responsible for responding to the greenhouse effect? Scientists? Government officials? Private industries? Everyday citizens? Write for students in a public policy course.
4. As Wald indicates, the greenhouse effect is international in scope. What are the possible impacts of the greenhouse effect on U.S. foreign policy?
5. Assuming that the greenhouse effect is an actual problem, should the solution involve cutting back on technology or creating new technology? Defend your position based on the information in Wald's article.
6. Drawing on Wald's article, compare and contrast the views of environmentalists and industrialists on the greenhouse effect. Which of these perspectives is the most reasonable?

AN UNDERGROUND DRUG FOR AIDS

William Booth

William Booth is on the news staff of Science, *a publication of the American Association for the Advancement of Science.*

PREREADING

1. Review what you know about AIDS. Consider what causes the disease, what its effects are on its victims, and how it is spread.
2. Review what you know about AIDS treatment. What have you read in newspapers or magazines about how AIDS is currently treated or how it might be treated in the future?

William Booth, "Underground Drug for AIDS," *Science,* 241 (1988): 1279-1281.

3. What do you know about the Food and Drug Administration (FDA)? What other controversies involving the FDA have you read about in the newspapers or magazines?
4. Freewrite for ten minutes on how you think the federal government should respond to the AIDS crisis.

CLOSE READING

1. Locate and mark arguments in favor of the new FDA ruling described in the first paragraph. Also, locate and mark arguments against this ruling.
2. As you read, imagine your responses to the article if you were an AIDS patient, an AIDS researcher, or an FDA official. Record these responses in the margin.

Determined not to go down in history as the heartless bureaucrat who robbed AIDS patients of hope, Frank Young, commissioner of the Food and Drug Administration (FDA), recently decided to allow individuals to import small quantities of unapproved drugs for their personal use. The policy applies not only to AIDS patients, who fought to receive shipments of an experimental AIDS drug called dextran sulfate, but to any person suffering from any ailment.

The directive stunned some AIDS researchers. One official in the federal government's AIDS Program went so far as to suggest that the FDA commissioner had gone "temporarily insane."

There are grave concerns among investigators that if the government allows unapproved drugs to circulate freely it will make rigorous drug testing far more difficult to do. They fear that if patients are allowed to take a variety of unproven drugs in unknown combinations, it will be impossible to untangle the subtle signs of their efficacy or toxicity. Critics of the FDA policy say they sympathize with the need for compassion, but add that in the long run, Young's decision will only prolong the time needed to develop new AIDS drugs, while sending a confused message to patients and opening the door to charlatans selling snake oil.

Young maintains that the policy simply recognizes the fact that a large number of AIDS patients and people infected with the human immunodeficiency virus (HIV) are smuggling experimental drugs into the country from Mexico, Europe, and now Japan.

"Desperately ill people are going to be searching for anything that might offer hope. It's a fact of life and clinical trials should take this into account," says Young. The only drug approved by the FDA for AIDS is azidothymidine or AZT, which extends life but extracts a heavy price both in cost and toxicity.

Young adds that the new policy is not really new, but only makes official a long-standing but informal system for allowing patients to bring small quantities of drugs with them when they enter the country from abroad. Young stresses that the FDA will not allow the importation of dangerous drugs or drugs that are being actively marketed as cures for AIDS or other illnesses.

Young asks researchers what they would do if they were in his shoes? "We're not prepared to march into people's homes like the Gestapo and take drugs away from desperately ill people," says Young. But it is one thing to march into someone's home and quite another for the government to allow people to receive parcels of drugs about which virtually nothing is known.

"I can't see how having an unevaluated and unapproved drug floating around is good for anybody," says Thomas Merigan, an AIDS researcher at Stanford University and a member of the government's AIDS drug development committee.

"People must remember that individual self-experimentation is extremely unlikely to yield meaningful results," says Samuel Broder of the National Cancer Institute. "The only way to know whether or not a drug really works is to put it through a series of carefully controlled and scientifically sound clinical trials."

"The FDA is saying: 'We can't regulate anymore. So who cares? Let the patients take whatever they want! Just get them off our backs,'" says Donald Abrams, an AIDS researcher at San Francisco General Hospital.

At the center of this storm is the experimental AIDS drug dextran sulfate, a potential antiviral agent that has shown promise in a test tube. In many ways, the story of this drug tells much about the roiling world of AIDS today, where emotions and politics continue to play as large a role as science, and where a sophisticated but desperate patient population composed of gay men is changing the way that drugs move through the scientific and regulatory pipeline.

The story of dextran sulfate begins with a Japanese investigator named Ryuji Ueno, the son of a food additive mogul who owns a company called Ueno Fine Chemicals Industry in Osaka, Japan. In the summer of 1986, the young Ueno told Abrams of San Francisco General that dextran sulfate could stop the AIDS virus from binding with its target cell in a laboratory dish. Impressed by the simple elegance of Ueno's data and the potent antiviral effect of dextran sulfate in vitro, Abrams agreed to test the drug for Ueno's company in a small number of patients with AIDS and HIV-related illness.

While Abrams sought approval from the FDA to do a small Phase 1 clinical trial to gauge the maximum tolerated dose of the drug, he also convinced Ueno to publish something in the scientific literature. Why? Abrams knew that any news of a potential AIDS drug would travel quickly around the network that joins AIDS patients with researchers and physicians sympathetic to their plight. An article in a scientific journal would help Abrams accrue the patients he needed.

It was a move that Abrams and Ueno may have come to regret. For Ueno's publication did far more than help Abrams attract a few new patients to his study. It set in motion the whole series of events that led to the change in the FDA's approach toward unproven AIDS drugs.

On 13 June 1987, Ueno and his colleague Sachiko Kuno published a letter in the British medical journal *Lancet* that reports that dextran sulfate blocks the binding of HIV to the white blood cells called T lymphocytes. Old hands in retrovirology were not completely surprised by the news. In fact, Erik De Clercq of the Rega Institute for Biomedical Research in Belgium had suggested in 1986 that a large negatively charged molecule not unlike dextran sulfate might inhibit the absorption of retroviruses.

How the drug accomplishes this neat trick is not yet known. Dextran sulfate is basically a big polymer of glucose that contains about 20% sulfur. Ueno suspects that the negative charge of the macromolecule and the amount of sulfur play a critical role in inhibiting infection, perhaps interfering with the virus particle as it tries to attach itself to the surface of its target cell.

More tantalizing to patients, however, was the passing mention in the *Lancet* paper that dextran sulfate has been used in Japan for 20 years as a drug to repress coagulation and to lower cholesterol in the blood. It is assumed that the drug is relatively safe. And because the Japanese Ministry of Health does not regulate drugs in the same way that the FDA does, it was possible for patients or their loved ones to simply step up to the counter at a pharmacy in Japan, slap down their yen, and buy the drug for about 20 cents a pill.

Aided by FAX machines, national hotlines, a dozen "buyers clubs," and several newsletters, word spread quickly on dextran sulfate. Within weeks of Ueno's scientific publication, the first AIDS patients began flying to Tokyo to purchase the drug. Airline stewards flying in the Orient began mailing it to friends in the United States. One AIDS patient convinced a chemical company in the United States to manufacture 80 pounds of the stuff, which he then coated in pill form and distributed up and down the West Coast. Soon, a male nurse from Los Angeles with the nickname "Dextran Man" began smuggling the drug back to the United States in bulk.

A group of AIDS patients being treated by a physician in Los Angeles named Michael Scolaro were getting their pills from Dextran Man. Scolaro is one of a growing number of physicians who aggressively treat AIDS and HIV infection with a variety of drugs. While Scolaro did not prescribe dextran sulfate, he was willing to monitor the first patients who took it on their own. "I cannot honestly say whether dextran sulfate makes any dent in this disease," says Scolaro. "But the patients who take it do seem to be doing better."

Scolaro's patients were also telling their friends that they were feeling better. And for AIDS patients, this is enough. Soon, trips to Tokyo for dextran sulfate became so routine that detailed subway maps to certain pharmacies in Tokyo began to circulate around New York City, San Francisco, and Los Angeles.

Martin Delaney of Project Inform, a San Francisco-based AIDS education and advocacy group, estimates that as many as 700 shipments left Japan for the United States and that as many as 2500 people were taking dextran sulfate before the FDA changed its mail policy.

International smuggling of dextran sulfate was a development that Ueno had never dreamed of. Not only did Ueno fear that the sudden popularity of dextran sulfate in the AIDS underground would disrupt his clinical trials, but his company had nothing to gain from it. The Ueno Fine Chemicals Industry does not even make dextran sulfate. A large pharmaceutical company in Japan does.

For reasons that are not entirely clear, dextran sulfate suddenly became extremely difficult for Americans to buy in Tokyo in the early spring. In January, Ueno's U.S. representative had notified the FDA that someone in Los Angeles was bringing in at least $10,000 worth of the drug every month. That someone was Dextran Man. Ueno himself expressed concern to the Japanese Ministry of Health that too many Americans were buying the drug through the underground.

Not only was the drug getting difficult to buy in Japan, but the FDA was detaining packages of dextran sulfate at Customs. The combination of events caused the gay community to start howling. FDA Commissioner Young was told by gay advocates that the more vocal groups in the community would be used to stage "political funerals" outside the FDA's office in suburban Maryland.

"We were talking real coffins with real bodies inside," says Curtis Ponzi, a San Francisco attorney who represents a club that buys AIDS drugs. Ponzi told FDA officials that he himself would try to bring back a large supply of dextran sulfate, and that he would alert the media of his intention. If the FDA or Customs stopped him at the airport, Ponzi would read off the names of every patient who was being denied the drug. It would have made for dramatic footage.

"I take the simple position that it's unethical and immoral to deny this drug to terminally ill patients," says Ponzi. Apparently, Ponzi and his allies got their point across. Young agreed to allow patients to receive small quantities of the unapproved drug from overseas and the Japanese agreed to allow Americans to buy dextran sulfate at three pharmacies in Tokyo as long as they showed their passport and bought only enough for a 3-month supply.

Because of the intense interest in the drug among AIDS patients and their allies, dextran sulfate has also become an issue for legislators. It was a hot topic for congressional hearings held in April and July by Representative Ted Weiss (D-NY) and Senator Ted Kennedy (D-MA), who keep asking officials from the National Institutes of Health (NIH) why it is taking them so long to get an experimental drug like dextran sulfate into their sick and desperate constituents.

Why indeed? Anthony Fauci, head of NIH's AIDS Program, admits that the government should have moved faster on dextran sulfate. But Fauci adds that part of the problem is that dextran sulfate is being developed as an AIDS drug by a small Japanese firm more familiar with producing food additives than with taking a product through the bureaucratic jungle of Washington. Ueno Fine Chemicals is represented in the United States by one person.

Staffers from Fauci's AIDS Program did meet with Ueno in August 1987, 3 months after his paper appeared. At that time it was agreed that Ueno's company would sponsor the Phase 1 clinical trial under way at San Francisco General Hospital. If things looked promising, the AIDS Program would then take dextran sulfate through larger, more extensive Phase 2 trials at a number of institutions.

In November, the AIDS drug development committee at NIH awarded dextran sulfate a high priority, based on Ueno's in vitro experiment and a few details provided by Paul Volberding of San Francisco General Hospital, who was following the work of his colleague Abrams.

But the drug committee identified several problems in November that continue to plague the development of dextran sulfate today. The group discovered that even though the drug has been used for 20 years in Japan, there are virtually no data on whether or not dextran sulfate is absorbed by the blood stream when taken orally. "The committee wanted to know what happened to the drug after people ate it," says Maureen Myers of NIH's AIDS Program. "And nobody seemed to know."

Producing an answer has not been easy. Until very recently, there has been no good assay to detect dextran sulfate in blood. Yet this is a critical piece of information, because some researchers suspect that the large size of the dextran sulfate molecules means that the drug is not absorbed from the stomach, making oral doses of dextran sulfate about as efficacious against AIDS as drinking a glass of water.

In December and again in March, various AIDS committees at NIH kept pressing Ueno and Abrams about the assay. Where were the data? Abrams told NIH he was drawing blood and sending it to Japan. On questions about the assay, Abrams deferred to Ueno, who replied that he was developing a more sensitive way to analyze the drug in the blood, and that as soon as he had the data, he would submit them.

Unfortunately, Abrams was required to heat-treat the blood specimens before shipping them to Japan, because Japanese lab workers refused to handle the live AIDS virus, says Armond Welch, the U.S. representative for Ueno Fine Chemicals. In turn, this made developing an assay in Japan even more difficult, since during heat treatment, dextran sulfate has a nasty tendency to precipitate.

Ueno now says that he finally has an assay that will settle once and for all the question of whether or not dextran sulfate is absorbed—even in blood that has been heat-treated. He is busy analyzing samples now and expects results in the coming weeks. Frustrated with the lack of data on bioavailability, the FDA recently developed another assay that will be used to confirm Ueno's data.

If dextran sulfate is indeed absorbed, there is still the question of whether or not the drug works. Of the 29 people in Abrams' clinical trial who took dextran sulfate for 8 weeks, Abrams observed no statistically significant changes in T cell counts or other markers of disease progression, such as the production of p24 antigen, a sign that the virus is active. "I saw no demonstrable effect for this agent," says Abrams.

Still, Abrams has agreed to pursue the investigation of dextran sulfate in a larger, federally sponsored Phase 2 clinical trial that is just now getting under way. With more patients, Abrams and his colleagues hope to get a clearer answer about any efficacy dextran sulfate may have for people with HIV infections and AIDS.

But whatever effect dextran sulfate turns out to have in the human body, it has certainly had a profound effect on the body politic.

TAKING NOTES AND ORGANIZING IDEAS

1. Summarize the FDA's new position on unapproved AIDS drugs. What does Booth suggest are the motives behind this ruling?
2. Why are scientists concerned over the FDA's new ruling on unapproved AIDS drugs?
3. Why did Abrams advise Ueno to publish the initial finding that dextran sulfate might combat the AIDS virus? What was the unexpected result of this publication?
4. As the article indicates, dextran sulfate was smuggled into the United States before the FDA ruling that allows unapproved drugs. Were these smugglers justified in their actions?
5. How have AIDS patients organized to protect their own interests?
6. What indications are given in the article that FDA procedures for testing new drugs are too slow?
7. Draw a diagram or idea map that reflects the organization of Booth's article. What organizational plan ties the article together?
8. Where does Booth stand on the dextran sulfate controversy? Upon which passages do you base your answer?

WRITING

1. Argue for or against the FDA's new ruling that allows AIDS patients to use unapproved drugs. Consider legal and ethical aspects of this issue. Write for an audience of students majoring in the humanities.
2. As Booth's article indicates, the FDA is responsible for regulating drugs that are used by physicians in the United States. The broadest goal of the agency is to safeguard public welfare. In light of the issues raised in Booth's article, is it appropriate for the FDA to decide what drugs will be used in the treatment of AIDS? Write for an audience of political science majors.
3. Booth points out that if AIDS patients are allowed to use unapproved drugs, it will make it difficult to conduct meaningful tests of experimental AIDS treatments. This may hinder efforts to develop more effective treatments that could save lives in the future. However, advocates for current AIDS patients maintain that those facing imminent death from AIDS have a right to pursue any treatment available. How should we, as a society, resolve this dilemma?
4. Imagine that you are a physician treating an AIDS patient who is considering the use of unapproved drugs. Write a letter to your patient in which you give advice on this issue. Use specific examples to illustrate your points.
5. Are AIDS patients justified in organizing their own treatment networks? Write for an audience of students majoring in health care administration.

AN ENGINEER'S ROLE IN HALTING AIDS

David R. Zimmerman

David R. Zimmerman, a free-lance journalist, has written widely on AIDS in relation to technology and public policy.

PREREADING

1. Speculate on the meaning of the article's title. How might an engineer contribute to the battle against AIDS?
2. Read the first paragraph of Zimmerman's article. What does this paragraph suggest the article might say about AIDS?

CLOSE READING

1. As you read Zimmerman's article, label in the margin each reason he presents to support the development of self-destruct needles.
2. Mark any passages where Zimmerman characterizes past and current attempts to curb the spread of AIDS. Does Zimmerman feel these efforts have been successful?

When a terrible cholera outbreak erupted in London in 1854, Dr. John Snow suspected that sewage was contaminating the district's drinking water and spreading the disease. When Snow found that cases were clustered around a water pump on Broad Street, he persuaded skeptical authorities to remove the pump handle, forcing residents to draw water elsewhere. The epidemic stopped as suddenly as it had started.

Today we are in a similar situation with AIDS. We need to isolate the narrowest and most vulnerable link of the disease's chain of transmission—and interrupt it. Nationwide, hypodermic needles used by drug addicts will soon be the main route for the spread of AIDS. In New York City and northern New Jersey, they already are. Before larger percentages of addicts are infected in communities across the country, we should promote the development of needles that can be used only once, and induce or coerce addicts to use them.

This would be a simple solution to a complex problem, yet it has not been vigorously pursued. Until very recently, the federal government has refused to grasp the nettle and deal with AIDS' spread among addicts as a technical problem, on the grounds that to do so would be to condone drug abuse. Instead, Washington urges addicts to "Just say no!" Most can't, and there are too few treatment slots for addicts who wish to quit.

A few enlightened communities have bucked this political and moral agenda. Public agencies in San Francisco and some New Jersey communi-

---

David R. Zimmerman, "An Engineer's Role in Halting AIDS," *Technology Review* (Oct. 1988), pp. 22-23.

ties distribute vials of household bleach to allow addicts to disinfect their "works." And a program in Portland, Oregon, lets addicts exchange dirty needles for clean ones. Data reported at the Fourth International Conference on AIDS, held in Stockholm in June, suggested that needle-exchange programs, in particular, slow the spread of the virus.

These epidemic control methods have picked the right target, the shared needle. But they leave too much to chance or choice among notoriously self-destructive people. An addict who really needs a fix will use any needle, clean or dirty. At this critical—and frequent—moment, addicts won't protect themselves, their lovers, or society at large from AIDS.

Needles that self-destruct after a single use would be a better solution. Yet in the report by the presidential commission on the epidemic, which contains hundreds of proposals for stepping up the war against AIDS, there is no demand that the government help develop such needles. Indeed, the concept is not even mentioned.

The private sector has been only a little less reticent about self-destruct needles. Representatives of two major medical instrument makers, Abbott Laboratories and Becton-Dickinson, say their biomedical engineers believe such needles can be made. But, they maintain, their companies are stumped by problems such as how to test-market and merchandise a product intended for illicit use. Becton-Dickinson also worries about how a self-destruct syringe could compete in price with the company's simple disposable syringe, which costs less than a dime wholesale.

These do not seem to be insurmountable obstacles. But the only people who appear not to be waiting for others to act are a few free-lance inventors. For example, San Diego physicist and psychologist Philip Kaushall has invented a self-destruct valve that he says can be built into the barrel or needle of a syringe. The valve allows a user to draw a drug up once through the needle and into the barrel. Injecting the drug permanently closes the valve, says Kaushall, who is reluctant to discuss more details until his device is patented and developed.

Meanwhile, Carl R. Sahi of Coventry, Connecticut, a chemist and former assistant medical examiner, has developed a syringe in which a thin, blunt-ended metal rod is automatically thrust down through the needle as an injection is finished. The rod, which will not penetrate the skin, locks in place about 0.02 of an inch past the needle point, preventing reuse.

These individual efforts are poorly financed. But they and others like them support the view that the technological challenge can be met.

How could addicts be induced to use self-destruct needles? The most politically feasible solution could grow out of the safer needle design being developed to protect health workers from accidental transmission of AIDS. These changes will be mandated under federal occupational safety laws. If the federal government stipulates that the safer needles should also self-destruct, AIDS transmission among addicts will drop as the more dangerous needles fall out of the market. Other simple answers also come to mind: self-destruct needles could be government subsidized and sold cheaply or given away, without a prescription.

The laws making it a criminal offense to carry a syringe without medical reason—common to many jurisdictions—could be amended. Possession of a self-destruct needle could be made legal, while the penalty for carrying reusable equipment could be greatly toughened.

Our failure to seize a technological opportunity to combat AIDS transmission by needles raises an old question with new urgency: how can critical advances that are not obviously profitable be developed? We need laws to promote such work. The model could be the Orphan Drug Act, which offers incentives to develop drugs with markets too small to be profitable.

The more immediate issue is how the war against AIDS will be fought. Will the agenda be set by rational calculations? If so, the prospects are good, because the spread of the AIDS virus is governed by fathomable natural rules. Or will it be set by politics and morality? If that is the case, control efforts will fail—for humans respond to moral law inconsistently, viruses not at all. Technology's advocates can no longer afford to be silent.

TAKING NOTES AND ORGANIZING IDEAS

1. In one sentence, state Zimmerman's main point. In what paragraphs, if any, does Zimmerman directly state this thesis?
2. Summarize Zimmerman's view of the federal government's current response to the spread of AIDS among drug addicts.
3. Describe how a self-destruct needle might work.
4. According to Zimmerman, why are private companies reluctant to develop self-destruct needles?
5. How does Zimmerman suggest that addicts could be encouraged to use self-destruct needles?
6. Does Zimmerman's article succeed as an argument? How well does he support his thesis? Is the evidence he presents adequate?
7. What is the organizational pattern for Zimmerman's article? How does he signal this pattern in the first two paragraphs?

WRITING

1. Argue for or against development and distribution of self-destruct needles.
2. Respond to Zimmerman's statement in his final paragraph. Does technology offer more hope in battling AIDS than either politics or morality? As you frame your response, consider Booth's article as well as Zimmerman's.
3. Does the government have an obligation to protect drug addicts from the consequences of their own self-destructive behavior? Draw on the example presented by Zimmerman to develop your argument.
4. Some critics of the policy of distributing clean or self-destruct needles to addicts argue that this policy encourages drug use and undermines laws prohibiting heroin and cocaine. Respond to this argument. Write for an audience of students in a political science course.

THE HUMAN DIMENSION OF SCIENCE AND TECHNOLOGY

James Gudaitis

The author is a research associate at the Center for Concern in Washington, D.C.

PREREADING

1. Read the title of the article and the subheadings. Use these as a basis for speculating on Gudaitis's perspective. What aspects of technology do you think he will address? What procedures do you think he will suggest for making technological decisions?
2. The first paragraph of the article mentions the Three Mile Island accident. Consult an encyclopedia or almanac published since 1980 and read a summary of the accident at the Three Mile Island nuclear reactor. Why do you think Gudaitis mentions this event?
3. Read the four points that Gudaitis lists at the conclusion of his article. Freewrite for ten minutes in response to one of these points.

CLOSE READING

1. As you read through the article, enumerate the effects of technology on our society that Gudaitis points out. In the margin, label each effect as either positive or negative. Does Gudaitis imply that the overall impact of technology is good or bad?
2. Enumerate the factors Gudaitis feels should be considered when making technological decisions. Which factors have you encountered in previous readings?
3. Annotate any passages that indicate who should be responsible for making technological decisions.

After recent events at Three Mile Island, attention has turned anew to a basic question facing our society: What promise or threat does technology hold for our global future? In the coming summer months, two major international conferences will explore this question by examining science and technology in their relationship to the development of humanity. The United Nations will hold its last "megaconference" of the decade, the U.N. Conference on Science and Technology for Development (U.N.C.S.T.D.), scheduled to take place in Vienna during August. This meeting will bring to a close the Second U.N. Development Decade and lay the foundation for the

James Gudaitis, "The Human Dimension of Science and Technology," *America, 28* (July 1979), pp. 31-34. Reprinted with permission of American Press, Inc. 106 West 56th Street, New York. N.Y. 10019.

efforts of a Third Development Decade to meet global poverty. One month earlier, at the Massachusetts Institute of Technology in Cambridge, the World Council of Churches will hold its Conference on Faith, Science and the Future. This meeting will explore the ethical and religious questions that arise in today's technological society. These are questions of crucial importance for the future of humanity.

The first encyclical of Pope John Paul II, "The Redeemer of Humanity," clearly revealed the concern of the churches for science and technology. In several paragraphs noteworthy both for realism of approach and idealism of language, John Paul posed sharp questions about technological progress. His basic question: "Does this progress, which has the human person for its author and promoter, make human life on earth 'more human' in every aspect of that life? Does it make it more 'worthy of the human person'. . . ? Is the human person becoming truly better. . . ?"

This issue of technology—whether it is contributing to humanity's well-being or speeding it in the direction of alienation and annihilation—is what I want briefly to point to here, in the light of the two major conferences to be held this summer. An initial look at some of the interrelated characteristics of both modern society and Western technology will be followed by an overview of four specific topics: 1) appropriate technology; 2) reallocation of resources; 3) technology assessment; and 4) basic human needs. These topics, though not principal agenda items for the two conferences, can be identified as issues that should be raised and dealt with if the explicit outcome of the conferences is to be a contribution toward the improvement of human well-being.

In the West, science and technology have become increasingly important factors in every aspect of our lives. They can be singled out as the most significant identifiable cause of social change in the last 30 years. Humanity has been liberated from numerous physical constraints and social insecurities. Medical technology has removed the terror of many diseases and epidemics and offered a longer life to millions of people the world over. Scientific improvements in agriculture have increased global grain yields and opened the way to remove the age-old threat of famine. Breakthroughs in the field of microelectronics have resulted in advances in the communications field that were long thought impossible. Continuous experimentation with, and the application of, computers (artificial intelligence) to industrial control and operations have greatly increased productivity and reduced human drudgery.

No doubt, there have been many technological achievements to list. Yet, in the face of all these accomplishments and potentials, the bright hopes of only a few years ago have somewhat dimmed. Cries that something has gone wrong come from both the general public and the scientific community. Some of the factors that have caused us to take a second look at the direction in which technology is guiding our civilization are: the new and growing awareness of the finiteness of resources; an awareness of the inadequacies of the scientific world and mind-set; and an appreciation of the interdependence among people and of people with their natural environment. Similarly, the scientific community, whose dominant view two or three decades ago was "science triumphant," is beginning to question this attitude, displaying a new humility. Trends indicating this change in attitude include: new ethical concerns arising from certain scientific advances (e.g., genetic engineering and nuclear waste); a growing sense of social responsibility among scientists over the consequences—intended and unintended—of their discoveries; a loss of confidence in science, for though we are able to put a human being on the moon, we have not been able to solve complex social problems confronting the human masses on earth; and the wider recognition of the limitations of science as a way of knowing.

What has the impact of technology meant for our modern Western society? From a technological perspective, there are several aspects that characterize what has been labeled, correctly or incorrectly, our "postindustrial" age. First, and this is particularly obvious to people in the United States, most of us live in a totally human-made environment. Few of us have any direct contact with "nature-in-the-raw" as we go about our daily routine. There is hardly anything that we see, hear, feel, smell or eat that has not been changed by science and technology in the past 50 to 75 years.

A second aspect of modern society is that many major societal problems are either a direct or indirect consequence of technological developments. Some examples are urban congestion, air and water pollution, depletion of raw materials and energy resources, nuclear and/or military arms race, alienation and frustration with an overly complex society. This is not to blame all problems on science and technology, but simply to point out their interrelationships.

Because our lives are so dominated by technology, we then naturally tend to think in terms of technological solutions. This third aspect—solving problems with "technological fixes"—when carried to an extreme can lead to a technological imperative or determinism. Technology can seem to have a force of its own that demands its continual development. Because we can do, we must do!

A fourth aspect is the uniqueness of modern technological development. Though technology has always had an effect on people and their behavior, never has there been a technology of the scope, scale, integration and complexity of Western technology. This has had dramatic consequences. Communication and transportation developments, for example, have reduced the size of the planet to the point where we now see and hear events as they actually take place thousands of miles away, or can physically be on the spot within a matter of hours. This striking diminishment in size has spawned an increase in global awareness and interrelatedness. As a result of the recent breakthrough in microelectronics and other communication technologies, moreover, information has become the dominant commodity in the United States today. Anywhere from an estimated one-third to one-half of the labor force deals directly or indirectly with information in one way or another.

And what occurs when Western technology is transferred to developing countries? (This will be a particular concern of the U.N.C.S.T.D. meeting.) There are, of course, tremendous transformations that have come over societies in the third world, as we have witnessed in numerous African, Asian and Latin American countries, especially since the end of the Second World War. It is important, however, to note the impact on the socioeconomic conditions of these people that have been caused by some of the major features of Western technology. To begin with, this particular style of technology makes extensive use of nonrenewable raw materials and consumes large amounts of energy, which is usually generated from other nonrenewable resources. Due to its capital- and energy-intensive nature, Western technology has reduced the amount of human-power resources involved in the production of goods. In other words, the development of a labor-saving technology—a development necessitated, for instance, in the United States in its early history by a situation of abundant resources and limited human power—has resulted in a decreasing percentage of the total labor force needed to produce all the goods for society. This has contributed to one of the most serious social problems of our day, not only for developing countries but also for the industrialized world, for it has resulted in an increasing rate of unemployment and underemployment, especially among semiskilled and unskilled workers.

Western technology's need for a pool of skilled human power to draw from and for large amounts of energy and capital has led to a centralization of the production process. In turn, this has resulted in the development of a highly organized industrial/urban sector and a concentration of economic power that has had several impacts. It has increased socioeconomic inequalities and promoted large-scale production at the expense of the small producers, whether industrial or agricultural, and benefited economically only the relatively affluent minority.

Two other features of Western technology increasingly seen in the third world are the promotion of unnecessary consumerism (frequently stimulated by advertising) and the increase in social costs (or "externalities") to society. This increase in social costs (e.g., environmental pollution, dehumanization, alienation, unemployment, unplanned urbanization) results from the failure of the production managers and economists to include these variables in their calculations of cost efficiency. Such a failure is due, partially at least, to the fact that the private sector has not, until recently, been held accountable for these externalities. In many developing countries, moreover, it is extremely difficult, for example, to hold accountable huge transnational corporations.

Against this background of Western technological characteristics and their impact on society, we can see the variety of topics that might surface in the two conferences I referred to at the outset of this article: the U.N. meeting that is to focus on the relationship of science and technology to development, and the World Council of Churches meeting that will probe the faith and ethical dimensions of science and technology. Among these many topics, let me choose four and indicate their relevance to the problem of making technology serve mankind, of making "human life on earth 'more human' in every aspect of that life," in the words of John Paul II. The four topics are: 1) appropriate technology; 2) reallocation of resources; 3) technology assessment; and 4) basic human needs.

Appropriate Technology

As many scientists, politicians, development planners and ordinary citizens look at the characteristics and social costs of sophisticated Western technology, they voice a concern about its adequacy for the needs of the day. There is a feeling that much of the technology being developed today neither respects the earth's delicate ecosystem nor is adequately controlled by social institutions, especially at the local level. The growing interest in "appropriate technology" (AT) can be viewed as an attempt by our society to reassess the direction of our development in the view of radically different and increasingly complex socioeconomic circumstances.

"Appropriate" means an approach that takes into account the unique economic, political, ecological, cultural and social conditions within which a specific problem exists. The solution to the problem—at least in terms of the technology chosen—should fit these conditions. For example, improved hoes may make more sense to agricultural production in labor-rich developing countries than expensive tractors; bicycles can provide more efficient transportation than automobiles in congested cities; "barefoot doctors" in developing countries or "paramedics" in developed countries may meet more health needs in both the short and long run than highly sophisticated medical centers; solar/wind/thermal resources may fit the energy situation of both rich and poor countries better than expensive and questionable nuclear projects.

Though associated with the "small is beautiful" philosophy of the late E.F. Schumacher, AT is not necessarily small nor it is by any means second-rate. It might more properly be referred to as technology on a human scale. (Schumacher himself preferred the term "intermediate technology" to describe his encouragement of a low energy-intensive, more people-oriented approach.) AT constitutes an important movement in both developing and developed countries. The push for it is a considerable step in the right direction—toward a world more human. The danger exists, however, that AT could itself become a "technological fix." There is a growing awareness that new or redirected technologies are not sufficient by themselves. Rather, the lack of political will and the ineptness of established sociopolitical structures currently are major barriers to progress. This caution, however, should not dissipate the energies being put toward developing an AT that is more compatible with the needs and goals of society.

Reallocation of Resources

A major stumbling block in the path of the realization of society's technological potential for human development is the limited amount of available resources and the contemporary economic and political mechanisms for resource allocation. Since the 1972 appearance of the Club of Rome's "Limits to Growth," increasing attention has been paid to the issue of the finiteness of our natural resources, especially the energy-generating resources. But other key resources are scarce also. These include capital for investment in research and development (R&D) of new technologies and personnel, the trained professionals able to devote attention to laboratory breakthroughs and skilled manufacture.

The situations of scarcity raise serious ethical issues today about the establishment of priorities in allocating resources. What would the consequences be for the poor, both of this country and of the world? In the United States, for example, a disproportionate amount of raw materials, capital and personnel are allocated for military-defense purposes. Thirty-six percent of our total foreign aid for fiscal 1979, $2.6 billion, went for military and strategic purposes. In the Department of Energy, the fiscal 1979 budget appropriated $4.172 billion for energy research; $2.685 billion was for research with noncivilian applications (i.e., military-strategic). This compares with only $559 million for solar research (all of it for civilian use).

If we explore the issue of military expenditures more closely, we frequently hear the argument that this spending is "good for the economy." This might be true only if 1) in the short run, you cannot think of a better way to invest huge amounts of capital and employ large numbers of people; and 2) you do not think about the long-run effects. Military spending is capital- and energy-intensive. It employs those who are the most employable in the civilian labor market—engineers, managers and skilled laborers. It develops a technology to destroy human life, not to enhance it. And recent studies have shown that $1 billion spent on such national and international needs as improved food production and distribution, environmental control, alternative energy development or mass transportation, would yield a far greater number of jobs than $1 billion spent on military programs.

Technology Assessment

Because of the growing concern over the negative effects of technology, many have called for steps to plan and guide its future direction. Three mutually complementary approaches are mentioned. First, the political system must exert new and more effective control over technology; it cannot be left simply to economic considerations of the market. Second, better means must be found to anticipate the consequences, both intended and unintended, of technology. Third, more reliable information and analysis about technological developments must be available to citizens at large and to public interest groups. All three of these approaches hinge upon the continued development of the relatively new art of "technology assessment" (TA).

Technology assessment is a type of policy analysis that is intended to provide decision makers and the general public with information about the fullest range of consequences of a technological development and of its utilization. With this information, we can be in a better position to make decisions about the possible need for Government action with regard to the technology. What TA does, then, is to provide information to the public about pending technological developments, information that was once available only to the economic or institutional interests that were developing the technology. It looks beyond the intended consequences of the technology, exploring possible side-effects—unintended social consequences (e.g., dislocation of workers), political ill effects on the environment, etc. This kind of analysis is crucial for putting technology at the service of society. It is vitally important, for example, in the whole debate currently raging over nuclear energy.

Basic Human Needs

A fourth issue, and one that is receiving considerable attention these days, is the meeting of basic human needs. This is not, of course, a challenge for technology alone. But the human value of any technological advancement today must be measured by its impact on the effort to address the problem of global poverty. The phrase "basic human needs" refers to sustenance, such as food and shelter; services, such as education and health; and enhancement, such as employment and participation. In many circles, the phrase has become so worn that there is a tendency to disregard it. But it still should be the basis for worthwhile human endeavors. The oft-repeated figure of 1 billion people living in conditions of abject poverty does not therefore lessen their plight. Nor does the claim of some third world spokesmen that the industrialized countries are using the global poverty issue as a ploy to keep them from participating more equally in the international economic order excuse the rich from meeting our major responsibility to try to improve the lot of the poorest of the poor. The fact that many people die each day of hunger and disease while there simultaneously flourishes a "consumer civilization" bent on the production and consumption of luxury goods indicates the inhumanity of the existing socioeconomic structures. This situation brings into serious question the production mechanisms that support and perpetuate the world economy. If the global problems relating to food, health, population, energy, natural resources and the environment cannot be remedied by present mechanisms, then there clearly is a need for institutions and mechanisms that are capable of the job. It is not so much the technologies that have been demonstrated to be inadequate to meet basic human needs as the economic and political structures that control the technologies. In any discussion of the values relating to technology, this issue must be squarely faced.

One major topic that has not been treated in this article is the relationship between technology and culture. As the distinguished development ethician, Denis Goulet, has pointed out, science and technology are major factors in shaping culture. They are by no means value-free instruments. It is the relationship between technology and culture that, in effect, provides the link between this summer's United Nations conference and the World Council of Churches meeting. The latter will explore very explicitly the faith implications of science and technology and will probe the cultural roots of the particular line of development taken by Western technology. If the U.N. conference is genuinely to advance the task of human development, it too must take seriously the value questions raised by the W.C.C. meeting.

It is apparent, both from the world around us and from the headlines we read, that in the development of technology we have too often let individual rights, social improvements and a healthy respect for the ecosystem yield to economic gain and self-interest when considering the cost/benefits of future policies. But today we find that we have moved into a period of transition, exemplified by the "small is beautiful" approach, the women's movement, the antinuclear reaction, technology assessment and the public interest movement, to mention only a few instances. During this period of transition, it will be important that we do not lose sight of certain points:

- ☐ The need is not for less science and technology but rather for the redirection of their strengths.
- ☐ The main barriers to solving global societal problems are not technical but institutional and political; what is lacking is the political will and the social technologies to change the institutions and structures that perpetuate socioeconomic inequalities.
- ☐ There is need for proper balance among private citizens, technical experts, governmental officials and business managers in deciding social, economic and technological policies, in effect bringing about greater participation and more local, decentralized control.
- ☐ Equal amounts of technological development and ethical development are called for today so that ethical considerations will guide the technologies toward a truly human and humane development of mankind.

TAKING NOTES AND ORGANIZING IDEAS

1. Write a one-sentence statement of Gudaitis's thesis. Is this thesis stated succinctly anywhere in the essay?
2. List what Gudaitis thinks should be the most important criteria for making technological decisions.
3. Write four one-paragraph summaries of the ideas Gudaitis presents under the subheadings of "Appropriate Technology," "Reallocation of Resources," "Technology Assessment," and "Basic Human Needs."
4. List the major problems with technological development that Gudaitis mentions. Also list the major elements of the solution he offers and link each one graphically to the problem that it addresses. Does the solution seem adequate for the problem?
5. Diagram the overall plan for Gudaitis's essay. Show graphically how each paragraph fits into this overall plan.
6. How does Gudaitis think that technological development in the West has directly affected Third World countries?
7. Describe Gudaitis's intended audience. What aspects of the essay help you to identify this audience?
8. What is Gudaitis's attitude toward technology in general? How is this attitude expressed in his tone?
9. Paragraph 2 quotes several questions concerning technology that were posed by Pope John Paul II. What are Gudaitis's answers to these questions?

WRITING

1. Summarize the problems of transferring Western technology to non-Western societies. In what ways are Western technological innovations often inappropriate for developing nations? How does Gudaitis propose to solve these problems? Be sure to explain what Gudaitis means by appropriate technology. Finally, evaluate the practicality of Gudaitis's proposed solution.
2. Do Gudaitis's four concluding points provide a firm basis for making technological decisions? Defend your answer by comparing and contrasting each with alternative solutions suggested in other articles in this chapter. Write for an audience of science majors.
3. In paragraph 8, Gudaitis says that we tend to look for "technological fixes" to all our problems. Consequently, Gudaitis feels that technology has gained a momentum of its own that is hard to control. Respond to this idea using examples of your own to support your views. Write for an audience of humanities students.
4. Comment on Gudaitis's statement that science and technology are not "value free." Do technological decisions always involve values? What sorts of values often enter into technological decisions? Are values a nuisance or a useful factor in making technological decisions? What values would you draw on to make a technological decision?

SCIENCE ADVICE: BACK TO THE FUTURE

Colin Norman

Colin Norman is a deputy news editor for Science, *a publication of the American Association for the Advancement of Science.*

PREREADING

1. What sources do you imagine U.S. presidents turn to for advice on science and technology? Do they turn to university scholars and researchers? Private sector industrialists? Military experts? Scientists in civil service positions? Which group do you imagine is the most influential?
2. Few nonscientists can name any of the top U.S. scientists and engineers or even recent Nobel Prize winners in the sciences. However, many Americans can rattle off entire starting lineups of professional sports teams. Why do you think we as a nation pay comparatively little attention to leaders in the fields of science and technology? Freewrite for ten minutes in response to this question.

Colin Norman, "Science Advice: Back to the Future," *Science, 239* (1988): 1082-1083.

CLOSE READING

1. As you read the article, underline the full names of the organizations referred to by the acronyms PSAC and OSTP. Note that AAAS refers to the American Association for the Advancement of Science, which publishes *Science*, the journal in which Norman's article appeared. NASA is an acronym for the National Aeronautics and Space Administration.
2. Where appropriate, label sections of Norman's article according to the presidential administrations to which they refer.

Once again, the presidential election season finds many members of the scientific establishment looking ahead to the next administration with one eye on the late 1950s and early 1960s. Those were the days when science advisers were close confidants of the presidents they served and a powerful President's Science Advisory Committee (PSAC) provided a direct conduit for advice from scientists into the White House.

Arguments in favor of resurrecting a similar arrangement have made their quadrennial appearance in recent weeks, with a congressional hearing, an all-day session at the AAAS annual meeting in Boston, and the publication of a collection of essays devoted to the topic of science advice to the federal government. The discussion this election year is more intense than usual, however, because for the first time in 20 years a change of administration is guaranteed. The next president will have a new chorus of advisers and a free hand to organize The White House power structure—and scientists would evidently like a place in the top echelon.

"There is no question that in this day and age, when science and technology are such an important part of almost everything in front of the President, that there should be a science person at a high-level position in the White House," says Frank Press, president of the National Academy of Sciences and former science adviser to President Carter.

Much of the recent flurry of interest in presidential science advising can be traced to the efforts of William T. Golden, who pulled together the collection of essays, persuading 83 veterans and close observers of past and present science policy regimes to air their thoughts. Golden, who authored a report in 1950 that provided the blueprint for the science advisory apparatus eventually adopted by Presidents Eisenhower and Kennedy, also helped arrange the AAAS session at which some of the authors discussed their papers. Many of the same cast of characters flew to Washington a few days later, in what one participant termed a "traveling road show," to testify before the House subcommittee on research and technology.

One theme that runs through many of the essays and the testimony is the perception that the science advisory apparatus is now so attenuated in scope and influence that scientific matters are not getting their due consideration in national policy-making. In perhaps the most acerbic essay in Golden's book, for example, Jerome Wiesner, science advisor to President Kennedy, claims that "Vital decisions that will not only shape the long-range future of the U.S. but of the world are being deferred or undertaken without adequate debate." He cites lack of action on environmental issues and the Strategic Defense Initiative (SDI) as cases in point. Wiesner also lays the blame for an array of problems, including the Challenger disaster and the decline in American industrial competitiveness, on "the absence of a Presidential [science] advisory group."

The status of the science advisor in fact began to wane in the mid-1960s. It suffered badly during the Vietnam War, when many in the academic community opposed the politics of the Johnson Administration, and reached its nadir in 1973, when President Nixon abolished PSAC and erased the post of science advisor from the Executive Office's organization chart. Nixon was particularly upset because some members of PSAC had gone public with their opposition to the Administration's policies on the development of supersonic aircraft and antiballistic missile defenses.

Three years later, President Ford put a science adviser back on the payroll and Congress that year approved legislation making it a legal requirement for Ford and subsequent presidents to establish an Office of Science and Technology Policy (OSTP) in the Executive Office. But in recent years, the science adviser has not been a senior presidential assistant. Instead, he has functioned more as an advisor to the President's assistants.

George Keyworth, President Reagan's first science adviser, was not appointed until well into the first year of the Administration. He reported to, and derived his influence from, Edwin Meese, who was then Reagan's chief of staff. Keyworth departed at the end of 1985, a year after Meese left the White House for the Justice Department, and it took 5 months for the Administration to name his successor. After several scientists turned the job down, William R. Graham, then the acting director of the National Aeronautics and Space Administration, took the appointment.

Both Keyworth and Graham defend the current arrangement. Keyworth argues, for example, that "the science advisory mechanism is most active—and most important—when it advises whoever the President places most trust in on issues involving science and technology." Graham testified that "the working relationship between OSTP and the Office of Management and Budget, the National Security Adviser and his staff, the Council of Economic Advisers, and the White House office are today excellent."

They received support from Solomon Buchsbaum, an AT&T executive who chairs the White House Science Council, an advisory body established by Keyworth and maintained by Graham. "OSTP has been performing a vital job and doing it with skill," Buchsbaum testified, noting that budgets for basic research have doubled during the Reagan years, a measure he called the "ultimate test" of OSTP's effectiveness.

Few others seem happy with the current status of the science adviser, however. For example, James Beggs, the former head of NASA, testified: "I do not believe that the OSTP has been very effective in carrying out its statutory mandate. . . . The science adviser . . . has in most cases not had the direct ear of the President, so the operating departments and agencies, knowing that his advice will be just one of a number of different inputs to the President, have tended to bypass him." Beggs is said to have been particularly adept at this in winning presidential support for the space station.

Press, drawing on his own experience in the Carter Administration, said "being in the Executive Office but not on the immediate White House staff does not afford sufficient involvement or influence in presidential policy-making." Press's solution is straightforward: "The President's science adviser should be named as an Assistant to the President," a cabinet-level position on a par with the National Security Adviser and with direct access to the President. Failing this, Press suggests that the science adviser be given a position in the cabinet without portfolio. Variations on this theme are repeated by many other authors in the Golden volume, although a few, notably Keyworth and Representative George Brown (D-CA), go one step further by calling for the establishment of a new Department of Science and Technology.

There appears to be broad agreement that the resources available to the science adviser are inadequate. Both Keyworth and Graham have had to cope with a shrinking budget for OSTP. It now stands at $1.89 million, which supports a professional staff of 20, including 12 who are on detail from other federal agencies and four on short-term fellowships from professional organizations. The budget request for next year would trim another $100,000 from OSTP. Donald Hornig testified that he had a full-time staff of about 35 professional people and a budget of over $2 million when he was science adviser to President Johnson in the mid-1960s.

Press argues for a professional staff of 25 to 35 people, who should be "full time, not begged and borrowed from other agencies." He also recommends a budget "of a few million dollars" to cover the cost of special analyses and independent research. "The science adviser should not have to depend on funds from agencies with a vested interest in the outcome of White House decisions," as it is now forced to do, he says.

One other topic on which there is general agreement is that the science adviser must function first and foremost as a member of the President's staff and not a representative of the scientific community. Edward E. David, Jr., President Nixon's science adviser, for example, testified that PSAC lost credibility in the Nixon White House because it was seen as "a special pleader for the academic community."

Press, noting that "the position of science adviser embodies tension between its functions and the expectations of the scientific community," says "the perception that the incumbent regard himself or herself as the resident advocate of particular interest groups . . . will almost certainly be fatal to his or her influence in the long run."

As for resurrecting PSAC, there is a good deal of sentiment for this among veterans of the old system, including Wiesner and Hornig. In its glory days, PSAC served as a high-level source of technical analyses and often provided a counterweight to the studies done by federal agencies. Wiesner grumbles that the Reagan Administration "depends more on the agencies that sponsor individual programs to evaluate them, and on an inchoate collection of informal advisers."

The White House Science Council, a committee of scientists who are generally in political tune with the Administration, has functioned as the chief channel for outside advice to the science adviser in the Reagan Administration. It meets once a month and conducts occasional studies, including an influential report on the health of the universities written by a panel chaired by David Packard, the Packard of Hewlett-Packard.

Those who would like to see PSAC reincarnated generally want a more independent body. Keyworth, however, derides the idea, arguing that "much of the real motivation . . . is the barely-concealed desire of the science community to tell the President what it thinks is important—and if he won't heed their advice, to tell the Congress or the media or anyone else who will listen."

Ashton Carter, a physicist at Harvard's Kennedy School of Government, offers a different objection. "PSAC belongs to a bygone political era," when there were fewer resources of technical analysis of major policy issues, he noted. Now, there is an abundance of independent studies—"the problem is not the strength of the signal, but the signal-to-noise ratio"—and it is far better to rely on the published analyses of organizations with a proven track record than on the opinions of a high-level committee of insiders whose deliberations are not open to public scrutiny.

Press, who used informal panels of scientists convened on an ad hoc basis to study particular issues when he was head of OSTP, notes that the next administration will establish whatever mechanisms for drawing in scientific expertise that best suits its operating style. However, he argues for a system in which outside advisers devote a considerable fraction of their time to the cause. "A pro forma 2 or 3 days a month is barely sufficient to become thoroughly briefed, let alone to formulate and render considered judgments," he says.

One oft-repeated refrain is that the next administration would do well to appoint its science adviser early on, so that he or she could assist in the selection of people to head key scientific agencies. An early appointment would also help the adviser establish a niche in the White House power structure as it coalesces.

However, the early appointees in a new administration tend to be people who have participated in the political process and are already well known to the new president. Scientists and engineers seldom fit the bill. As David points out, the fact that previous administrations have been tardy in appointing a science adviser reflects "the lack of rapport between new presidents and *any* competent scientist or engineer."

John McTague, who filled in as acting science adviser in the long interregnum between Keyworth and Graham, agrees. "The long-term solution," he says, "is for the technical community to become more involved in the political process, in which they are woefully absent—except when they wish to appear as special pleaders, and then it's usually too late."

TAKING NOTES AND ORGANIZING IDEAS

1. Norman is writing in response to particular events. What are these events? How are these events connected to the end of the Reagan administration?
2. Based on the information in Norman's article, chart the status of the presidential science adviser from 1950 up to the present. Divide the time scale by both years and presidential administrations.
3. Why did the influence of presidential science advisers decline in the 1960s?

4. Explain the difference between the PSAC and the OSTP. Why, according to Norman, are many scientists hoping for a return of the PSAC?
5. What examples are given in the article of federal administrative policies that reflect poor understanding of science and technology?
6. Describe the status of the science adviser during the Reagan administration.
7. It can be argued that two distinct organizational plans provide the structure for Norman's article. What are these two plans? Why are they both necessary given Norman's topic?

WRITING

1. Argue for or against creating a cabinet-level position for a presidential adviser.
2. In paragraph 15, Frank Press, president of the National Academy of Sciences, is quoted as saying that "the position of science adviser embodies tension between its functions and the expectations of the scientific community." What conflicts might exist between the views of the scientific community and those of a presidential administration? Does the "tension" that Press refers to mean that the presidential science advisers will never again have the influence they did in the 1950s? Can anything be done to overcome this tension? Write for an audience of political science majors.
3. Based on Norman's article, compare and contrast the arguments for reviving the PSAC with those for relying on outside science consultants. Which viewpoint do you favor and why?
4. Norman's article is confined to the role of government and the scientific community in arriving at scientific and technical decisions. What segments of our society might make an important contribution to scientific and technical decisions but are ignored in Norman's discussion? Present an argument that these other groups should be involved in the decision-making process.

WHAT IS SCIENCE?

George Orwell

One of the most respected essayists in the English language, George Orwell (1904–1950) is also well known as a journalist, novelist, and political commentator.

PREREADING

1. Orwell's title indicates that he intends to write a definition essay. Does he accomplish this? What are Orwell's other purposes for writing? If you have read either or both of these novels, recall what it was about. Using this information, predict what Orwell's attitude toward science might be.
2. Freewrite for ten minutes in response to the question posed by Orwell's essay title. Consider your past knowledge of science.

CLOSE READING

1. Locate and mark Orwell's definition of science that the article's title promises.
2. Preview Orwell's essay. Notice that the introductory and concluding paragraphs discuss science education. As you read the article, look for and mark the passages that explain Orwell's attitude toward science education.

In last week's *Tribune,* there was an interesting letter from Mr. J. Stewart Cook, in which he suggested that the best way of avoiding the danger of a "scientific hierarchy" would be to see to it that every member of the general public was, as far as possible, scientifically educated. At the same time, scientists should be brought out of their isolation and encouraged to take a greater part in politics and administration.

As a general statement, I think most of us would agree with this, but I notice that, as usual, Mr. Cook does not define science, and merely implies in passing that it means certain exact sciences whose experiments can be made under laboratory conditions. Thus, adult education tends "to neglect scientific studies in favour of literary, economic and social subjects," economics and sociology not being regarded as branches of science, apparently. This point is of great importance. For the word science is at present used in at least two meanings, but the whole question of scientific education is obscured by the current tendency to dodge from one meaning to the other.

Science is generally taken as meaning either (a) the exact sciences, such as chemistry, physics, etc, or (b) a method of thought which obtains verifiable results by reasoning logically from observed fact.

If you ask any scientist, or indeed almost any educated person, "What is science?" you are likely to get an answer approximating to (b). In everyday life, however, both in speaking and in writing, when people say "science" they mean (a). Science means something that happens in a laboratory: the very word calls up a picture of graphs, test-tubes, balances, Bunsen burners, microscopes. A biologist, an astronomer, perhaps a psychologist or mathematician, is described as a "man of science": no one would think of applying this term to a statesman, a poet, a journalist or even a philosopher. And those who tell us that the young must be scientifically educated mean, almost invariably, that they should be taught more about radioactivity, or the stars, or the physiology of their own bodies, rather than that they should be taught to think more exactly.

This confusing meaning, which is partly deliberate, has in it a great danger. Implied in the demand for more scientific education is the claim that if one has been scientifically trained one's approach to *all* subjects will be more intelligent than if one had had no such training. A scientist's political opinions, it is assumed, his opinions on sociological questions, on morals, on philosophy, perhaps even on the arts, will be more valuable than those of a layman. The world, in other words, would be a better place if the scientists were in control of it. But a "scientist," as we have just seen, means in practice a specialist in one of the exact sciences. It follows that a chemist or a physicist, as such, is politically more intelligent than a poet or a lawyer, as such. And, in fact, there are already millions of people who do believe this.

But is it really true that a "scientist," in this narrower sense, is any likelier than other people to approach non-scientific problems in an objective way? There is not much reason for thinking so. Take one simple test—the ability to withstand nationalism. It is often loosely said that "Science is international," but in practice the scientific workers of all countries line up behind their own governments with fewer scruples than are felt by the writers and the artists. The German scientific community, as a whole, made no resistance to Hitler. Hitler may have ruined the long-term prospects of German science, but there were still plenty of gifted men to do the necessary research on such things as synthetic oil, jet planes, rocket projectiles and the atomic bomb. Without them the German war machine could never have been built up.

On the other hand, what happened to German literature when the Nazis came to power? I believe no exhaustive lists have been published, but I imagine that the number of German scientists—Jews apart—who voluntarily exiled themselves or were persecuted by the regime was much smaller than the number of writers and journalists. More sinister than this, a number of German scientists swallowed the monstrosity of "racial science." You can find some of the statements to which they set their names in Professor Brady's *The Spirit and Structure of German Fascism.*

But, in slightly different forms, it is the same picture everywhere. In England, a large proportion of our leading scientists accept the structure of capitalist society, as can be seen from the comparative freedom with which they are given knighthoods, baronetcies and even peerages. Since Tennyson, no English writer worth reading—one might, perhaps, make an exception of Sir Max Beerbohm—has been given a title. And those English scientists who do not simply accept the *status quo* are frequently Communists, which means that, however intellectually scrupulous they may be in their own line of work, they are ready to be uncritical and even dishonest on certain subjects. The fact is that a mere training in one or more of the exact sciences, even combined with very high gifts, is no guarantee of a humane or skeptical outlook. The physicists of half a dozen great nations, all feverishly and secretly working away at the atomic bomb, are a demonstration of this.

But does all this mean that the general public should *not* be more scientifically educated? On the contrary! All it means is that scientific education for the masses will do little good, and probably a lot of harm, if it simply boils down to more physics, more chemistry, more biology, etc. to the detriment of literature and history. Its probable effect on the average human being would be to narrow the range of his thoughts and make him more than ever contemptuous of such knowledge as he did not possess: and his political reactions would probably be somewhat less intelligent than those of an illiterate peasant who retained a few historical memories and a fairly sound aesthetic sense.

Clearly, scientific education ought to mean the implanting of a rational, skeptical, experimental habit of mind. It ought to mean acquiring a *method*—a method that can be used on any problem that one meets—and not simply piling up a lot of facts. Put it in those words, and the apologist of scientific education will usually agree. Press him further, ask him to particularize, and somehow it always turns out that scientific education means more attention to the exact sciences, in other words—more *facts.* The idea that science means a way of looking at the world, and not simply a body of knowledge, is in practice strongly resisted. I think sheer professional jealousy is part of the reason for this. For if science is simply a method or an attitude, so that anyone whose thought-processes are sufficiently rational can in some sense be described as a scientist—what then becomes of the enormous prestige now enjoyed by the chemist, the physicist, etc. and his claim to be somehow wiser than the rest of us?

A hundred years ago, Charles Kingsley described science as "making nasty smells in a laboratory." A year or two ago a young industrial chemist informed me, smugly, that he "could not see what was the use of poetry." So the pendulum swings to and fro, but it does not seem to me that one attitude is any better than the other. At the moment, science is on the up-grade, and so we hear, quite rightly, the claim that the masses should be scientifically educated: we do not hear, as we ought, the counter-claim that the scientists themselves would benefit by a little education. Just before writing this, I saw in an American magazine the statement that a number of British and American physicists refused from the start to do research on the atomic bomb, well knowing what use would be made of it. Here you have a group of sane men in the middle of a world of lunatics. And though no names were published, I think it would be a safe guess that all of them were people with some kind of general cultural background, some acquaintance with history or literature or the arts—in short, people whose interests were not, in the current sense of the word, purely scientific.

TAKING NOTES AND ORGANIZING IDEAS

1. Orwell's title indicates that he intends to write a definition essay. Does he accomplish this? What are Orwell's other purposes for writing?
2. Compare/contrast the two definitions of science that Orwell discusses.
3. Does Orwell adequately respond to the argument in favor of strengthening science education that he summarized in the first paragraph?
4. Summarize the major points of Orwell's argument that knowledge of the humanities and arts contributes to making sound decisions about technology. What does Orwell think about the relative importance of the humanities and the sciences?

5. How does Orwell's discussion of nationalism in paragraphs 6 and 7 fit in with the rest of the essay?
6. Annotate passages that show Orwell's attitude toward nationalism and the A-bomb development. Using this information, can you make any guesses about Orwell's political beliefs?
7. What organizational pattern does Orwell use to develop his essay? Mark the sections of the essay that correspond to the components of this pattern.
8. Orwell seemingly favors a traditional liberal arts education as opposed to specialized training in a technical or scientific field. Is his argument still valid given the current growth of high-tech industry?

WRITING

1. Drawing on Orwell's essay, analyze the science education you have obtained in the past. To what extent was science taught to you as a body of knowledge and to what extent was it taught as a way of looking at the world? How might your science education have been improved? Write for an audience of education majors.
2. Argue for or against Orwell's claim that scientific training does not necessarily lead to better judgments about nonscientific matters. Does science promote logical thinking that helps solve everyday problems or is science disconnected from practical concerns? Would a citizenry trained in science make better political and ethical decisions? Use specific examples to illustrate your point.
3. How would Orwell respond to the technological decisions discussed in other articles in this chapter?
4. How might Orwell's ideas impact on technological decision-making processes? How might Orwell's ideas apply to current technological decisions?

SYNTHESIS ASSIGNMENT FOR CHAPTER IVB

1. Use a cause/effect organizational pattern to argue that technological decisions have a major impact on our society. Support your argument with specific examples drawn from the articles in this chapter. Write for an audience of humanities majors.
2. While the greenhouse effect is a potential consequence of advanced technology, the AIDS crisis requires technology-based solutions. Similarly, a range of problems in the Third World can be seen alternatively as either the results of technology or as situations that can be remedied by technology. Is technology a blessing or a curse? Should the world community pursue a course that expands or restricts the use of technology? Back up your argument with specifics.
3. Locate and read several articles that analyze the decision-making process that led to the launch and subsequent explosion of the *Challenger* space shuttle in January of 1986. How might the decision-making pro-

cess be changed to avoid similar disasters in the future? Draw on the readings in this chapter to support your position.

4. In paragraph 5 of Norman's article, Jerome Wiesner, science advisor to President Kennedy, is quoted as follows: "Vital decisions that will not only shape the long-range future of the U.S. but of the world are being deferred or undertaken without adequate debate." Based on readings in this chapter and other information you possess concerning technological decision making, respond to Wiesner's claim.

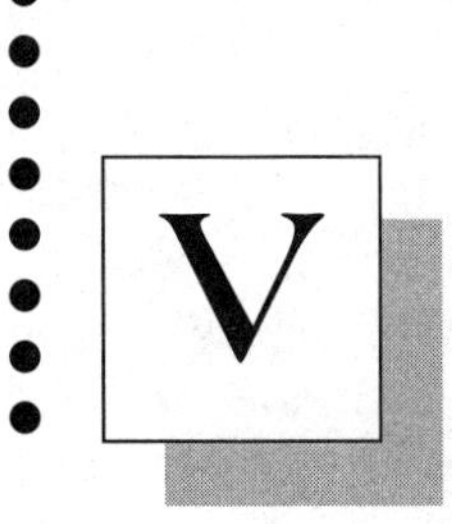

Research

The information age also requires employees who have the ability to conduct effective research. This section provides a process and techniques that can be used in conducting research and in writing a research report.

Research

OBJECTIVES

Research skills are important in your school or work environment. You may want to perform research to better understand a technical term or concept; locate a magazine, journal, or newspaper article for your supervisor; or find data on a subject to prepare an oral or written report. Technology is changing so rapidly that you must know how to do research to stay up to date.

You can research information in computer catalogues, card catalogues, reference books, indexes for technical subjects, and electronic database services. Reference sources vary and are numerous, so this chapter discusses only research techniques.

When you complete this chapter, you will be able to (a) locate information in the library, (b) read and analyze sources of information for your report, (c) form an idea for your research report, (d) write a research report, and (e) document your sources of information.

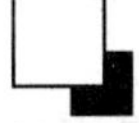

CRITERIA FOR WRITING RESEARCH REPORTS

As with all types of technical writing, writing from research requires that you (a) recognize your audience; (b) use an effective style, appropriate to your reader and purpose; and (c) use effective formatting techniques for reader-friendly ease of access.

☐ Audience

When writing a research report, you first must recognize the level of your audience. Is your reader as technically educated as you are? If you are a student in a technical writing class, your immediate audience is your instructor. Therefore, you would write your research report keeping in mind your instructor's technical knowledge. Unless your instructor is an expert in your technical field of interest, you should probably write your report for a lay audience. When you use technical terms, you'll need to define them either parenthetically in the report or in a glossary (as discussed in Chapter 3C1).

If you are writing to your boss, once again consider his or her level of technical expertise. Your boss probably is at least a low-tech reader, but you must determine this based on your own situation. Doing so will help you determine the amount of technical definition necessary for effective communication.

You must decide next whether your reader will understand the purpose of your research report. This will help you determine the amount of detail needed and the tone to take (persuasive or informative). For instance, if your reader has requested the information, you will not need to provide massive amounts of background data explaining the purpose of your research. Your reader has probably helped you determine the scope and purpose. On the other hand, if your research report is unsolicited, your first several paragraphs must clarify your rationale. You'll need to explain why you are writing and what you hope to achieve.

If your report is solicited, you probably know what your reader plans to do with your research. He or she will use it for a briefing, an article to be written for publication, a technical update, and so forth. Thus, your presentation will be informative. If your research report is unsolicited, however, your goal is to persuade your reader to accept your hypotheses substantiated through your research.

☐ Effective Style

Research reports should be more formal than many other types of technical writing. In a research report, you are compiling information, organizing it, and presenting your findings to your audience using documentation. Because the rules of documentation are structured rigidly (to avoid plagiarism and create uniformity), a research report is also rigidly structured.

The tone need not be stuffy, but you should maintain an objective distance and let the results of your research support your contentions. Again, considering your audience and purpose will help you decide what style is appropriate. For example, if your boss or instructor has requested your opinion, then you are correct in providing it subjectively. However, if your audience has asked for the facts—and nothing but the facts—then your writing style should be more objective.

☐ Formatting

Reading a research report is not always an easy task. As the writer, you must ensure that your readers encounter no difficulties. One way to achieve this is by using effective formatting. Reader-friendly ease of access is accomplished when you use highlighting techniques such as bullets, numbers, headings, subheadings, and graphics (tables and figures).

In addition, effective formatting includes the following:

- ☐ Overall organization (including an introduction, discussion, and conclusion)
- ☐ Internal organization (various organizational patterns, such as problem/solution, comparison/contrast, analysis, and/or cause/effect)
- ☐ Parenthetical source citations
- ☐ Works cited—documentation of sources

Each of these areas is discussed in detail throughout this chapter.

PROCESS

Writing a research report, as with other types of technical correspondence, is easiest when you follow a step-by-step process. Rather than just wandering into a library and hoping that the correct book or periodical will leap off a shelf and into your hands, approach your research systematically: Prewrite (to gather your data and determine your objectives), write a draft, and rewrite to ensure that you meet your goals successfully.

☐ Prewriting Research Techniques

Select a general topic (or the topic you have been asked to study). Your topic may be a technical term, phrase, innovation, or dilemma. If you're in emergency medical technology, for example, you might want to focus on the current problems with emergency medical service. If you're in telecommunications, you might write about satellite communication. If you work in electronics, select a topic such as robotics. If your field is computer science, you could focus on artificial intelligence.

Spot check sources of information. Check a library to determine if sources are available which discuss your subject. A quick review of the *Reader's Guide to Periodical Literature,* the card catalogue, or the computer catalogue should help you locate some of the available information.

Establish a focus. After you have chosen a topic for which you can find available source material, decide what you want to learn about your topic. A focus statement can guide you. In other words, if you are interested in emergency medical technology, you might write a focus statement such as the following:

> I want to research current problems with emergency medical services, including variances in training required, delays in timely response to emergency calls, and limited number of vehicles available.

For telecommunications, you could write,

> I want to research satellite communication maintenance, reliability, and technical innovations.

If you are an electronics technician, you might write,

> I want to discover the uses, impact on employment, and expenses for robotics applications.

Finally, if you are a computer technician, you might write,

> I want to discover the pros and cons regarding artificial intelligence.

With focus statements such as these, you can begin researching your topic, concentrating on articles pertinent to your topic.

Research your topic. You may feel overwhelmed by the prospect of using the library. But there are many research sources that, once you know how to use them, will make the library useful to you and less overwhelming.

Books

All books owned by a library are listed in either the card or computer catalogue. These books are listed under three headings—author, title, and subject.

In addition to using card catalogues or computer catalogues to find information in books, you can refer to numerous periodical indexes for information found in magazines and journals.

AUTHOR

```
                    TJ      Robillard, Mark J. ———————— Author
Call Number ——      211       Microprocessor based robotics / by —— Title
                    .R53    Mark J. Robillard ; [illustrated by ____ Publication
                    1983    R.E. Lund].--1st ed. --Indianapolis,     Information
                            Ind., USA: H.W. Sams, c1983.
Page Count ———————————————    220 p. : ill. ; 28 cm. (Intelligent
                            machine series ; v. 1)

                              Bibliography: p. 215.
                              Includes index.
                              ISBN 0-672-22050-4 (pbk.) : $16.95

Subject
Heading ——————————————————  1.Robotics. 2.Microprocessors. I.Lund,
                            R.E. II.Title. III.Series.
                    TJ211.R53 1983           629.8'92
                                             dc19
                                                         83-60160
                                             AACR2         MARC
```

TITLE

```
              Microprocessor based robotics
TJ        Robillard, Mark J.
211         Microprocessor based robotics / by
.R53      Mark J. Robillard ; [illustrated by
1983      R.E. Lund].--1st ed. --Indianapolis,
          Ind., USA: H.W. Sams, c1983.
            220 p. : ill. ; 28 cm. (Intelligent
          machine series ; v. 1)

            Bibliography: p. 215.
            Includes index.
            ISBN 0-672-22050-4 (pbk.) : $16.95

          1.Robotics. 2.Microprocessors. I.Lund,
          R.E. II.Title. III.Series.
TJ211.R53 1983           629.8'92
                         dc19
                                     83-60160
                         AACR2         MARC
```

SUBJECT

```
                    Robotics.

TJ          Robillard, Mark J.
211           Microprocessor based robotics / by
.R53        Mark J. Robillard ; [illustrated by
1983        R.E. Lund].--1st ed. --Indianapolis,
            Ind., USA: H.W. Sams, c1983.
              220 p. : ill. ; 28 cm. (Intelligent
            machine series ; v. 1)

              Bibliography: p. 215.
              Includes index.
              ISBN 0-672-22050-4 (pbk.) : $16.95

            1.Robotics. 2.Microprocessors. I.Lund,
            R.E. II.Title. III.Series.
TJ211.R53 1983             629.8'92
                           dc19
                                      83-60160
                           AACR2        MARC
```

Periodicals

Use the following periodical indexes to find articles on your topic.

Indexes to General, Popular Periodicals

- ☐ *Reader's Guide to Periodical Literature:* Covers popular, nontechnical literature from a variety of subject fields.

> Bicycle racing
> Wheels of fortune [women's team racing] S. Hollandsworth. il ***Women's Sports Fitness*** 8: 36-39+ Jl '86.

The preceding example tells us that an article on bicycle racing can be found in the July 1986 issue of the magazine *Women's Sports Fitness,* volume 8, pages 36 and following. The article is entitled "Wheels of Fortune," contains illustrations, and is written by S. Hollandsworth. Finally, to clarify the subject matter of the article, "women's team racing" has been added in brackets.

> Schlesinger, Arthur M., 1917–
> The challenge of change, il ***NY Times Mag*** p20-21 Jl 27 '86
>
> ***about***
>
> Report on the republic. P.S. Prescott. il por ***Newsweek*** 108:98 + O 27 '86

In the preceding entry, we are told two things. First, an article by Arthur M. Schlesinger can be found in the July 27, 1986, issue of the *New York Times Magazine* on pages 20 and following. The article contains illustrations and is entitled "The Challenge of Change." Next we are told that we can find an article Schlesinger in the October 27, 1986, issue of *Newsweek* magazine, volume 108, on pages 98 and following. The article is written by Peter S. Prescott and is entitled "Report on the Republic."

- ☐ *Infotrac II/CD-ROM Terminal):* Covers many of the same types of periodicals as the *Reader's Guide.* Figure 5.1 shows a typical Infotrac entry and explains its parts.

Indexes to Scholarly and Technical Journals

- ☐ *Applied Science & Technology Index:* Covers all engineering fields, as well as aeronautics and space sciences, atmospheric sciences, chemistry, computer technology and applications, construction industry, energy resources and research fire prevention, food and the food industry, geology, machinery, mathematics, metallurgy, mineralogy, oceanography, petroleum and gas, physics, plastics, the textile industry and fabrics, transportation, and other industrial and mechanical arts.
- ☐ *Business Periodicals Index:* Covers major U.S. publications in marketing, banking and finance, personnel, communications, computer technology, etc.
- ☐ *General Science Index:* Covers the pure sciences, such as biology and chemistry.
- ☐ *Nursing and Allied Health Index:* Covers topics from a medical viewpoint.

Reference Books

The following are representative examples of reference books available in libraries.

- ☐ Brownstone, David M., and Gorton Carruth. *Where to Find Business Information.* New York: Wiley, 1982.
- ☐ Chen, Ching-Chih. *Scientific and Technical Information Sources.* Cambridge, MA: MIT Press, 1987.
- ☐ *Finding the Source of Medical Information.* Westport, CT: Greenwood Press, 1985.
- ☐ *Handbooks and Tables in Science and Technology.* Phoenix: Oryx Press, 1979.
- ☐ *Statistics Sources: A Subject Guide to Data on Industrial, Business, Social, Educational, Financial, and Other Topics for the United States and Internationally.* Detroit: Gale, 1986.

In addition to these sources, you can consult the following for help: U.S. government publications, databases, and your reference librarian.

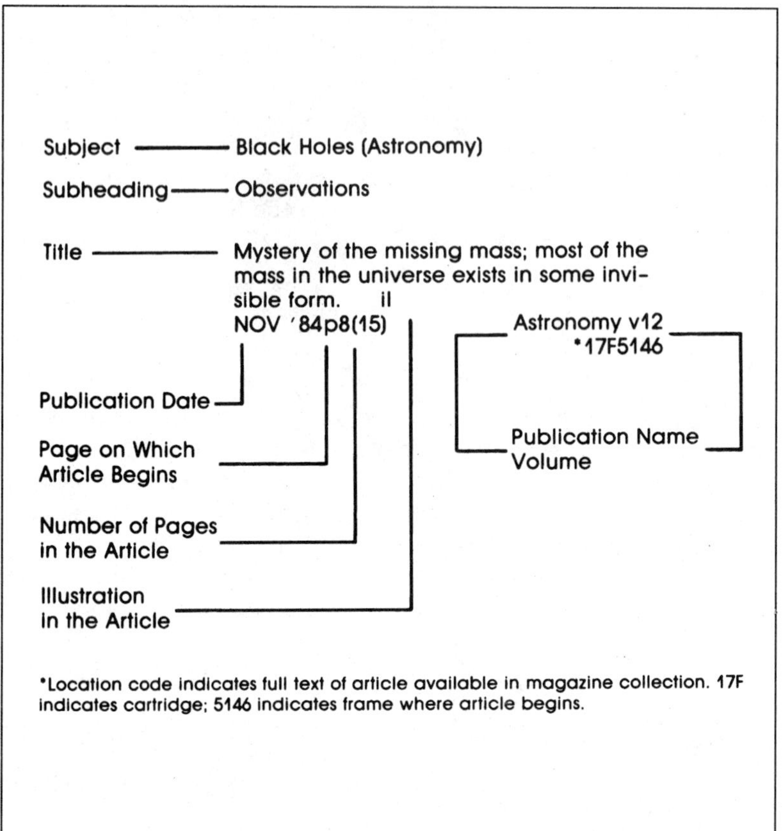

FIGURE 5.1 Infotrac Entry

Read your researched material and take notes. Once you have researched and located a source (whether it is a book, magazine, journal, or newspaper article), study the material. For a book, use the index and the table of contents to locate your topic. When you have found it, refer to the pages indicated and skim, reading selectively. For shorter documents such as magazine or journal articles, you can read closely. Reading and rereading the source material is an essential step in understanding your researched information. After you have studied the document thoroughly, go through it page by page and briefly summarize the content.

For a short magazine article, you can make marginal notes on a photocopy. For instance, read a paragraph and then briefly summarize its main point(s) in several words. Such notations are valuable because they are easy to make and provide a clear and concise overview of the article's focus.

You can also take notes on 3" × 5" cards. If you do this, be sure to write only one fact, quotation, or paraphrase per card, along with the author's name. This will let you organize the information later according to whatever organizational sequence (chronological narrative, analysis by importance, comparison/contrast, problem/solution, cause/effect, etc.) you prefer. Prepare a bibliography of your sources on 3" × 5" cards as well, one source per card.

The following are examples of a bibliography card and a note card with quotation, respectively.

Stephens, Guy M. "To Market, to Market." ***Satellite Communications.*** November 1987: 15-16.

Future need for C-band

"'We believe there is going to be an important need for C-band capacity into the '90s, into the next century, because it's an ideal way to serve many users, particularly video users,' Koehler said."

Stephens, "To Market," p. 15.

On a *summary* note card, you condense original material by presenting the basic idea in your own words. You can include quotations if you place them in quotation marks, but do not alter the organizational pattern of the original. A summary is shorter than the original.

Future need for C-band

C-band is going to be increasingly important in the '90s because of the increasing number of video owners.

Stephens, "To Market," p. 15.

On a *paraphrase* note card, you restate the original material in your own words without condensing. The paraphrase is essentially the complete version rewritten. A paraphrase is the same length as the original.

Future need for C-band

The author asserts the continued relevance of C-band even in the 1990s and beyond. C-band is the top performer, especially for people who use videos.

Stephens, "To Market," p. 15.

Isolate the main points. After you complete the analysis of the document (whether you use note cards and/or marginal comments), isolate the main points discussed in the books or periodicals. You will find that of the major points in an article or book, sometimes only three or four ideas will be relevant for your research. Choose the ones discussed repeatedly and/or those which most effectively develop the ideas you want to pursue.

Write a statement of purpose. Once you have chosen two to four main ideas from your research, write a purpose statement which expresses the direction of your research. For example, one student wrote the following statement of purpose after performing research on superconductivity:

> The purpose of this report is to reveal the future for this exciting product, which depends on further progress of technology, the development of easily accessible and cost-efficient materials, and industry's need for the final product.

Create an outline. After you have written a purpose statement, formulate an outline. An outline will help you organize your paragraphs and ensure that you stay on track as you develop your ideas through quotes and paraphrases. Figures 5.2 and 5.3 are examples of topic and sentence outlines.

☐ Writing

You now are ready to write your research report.

Review your research. Prior to writing your report, look back over your research sources to make sure that you're satisfied with what you've found. Do you have enough information to develop your points thoroughly? Is the information you've found what you want? If not, it's time to do more research. If you're content with what you've discovered in your research, you can start drafting your text.

Organize your report effectively. When you are ready to write, provide an introductory paragraph, discussion (body) paragraphs, a conclusion/recommendation, and your works cited page.

Introduction

Begin with something to arouse your reader's interest. This could include a series of questions, an anecdote, a quote, or data which is pertinent to your topic. Then use this to lead into your statement of purpose.

Discussion

The number of discussion paragraphs will depend on the number of divisions and the amount of detail necessary to develop your ideas. Use quotes and paraphrases to develop your content. Students often ask how much of a

I. Sensors used to help robots move
   A. Light
   B. Sound
   C. Touch
II. Touch sensor technology (microswitches)
   A. For gripping
   B. For maintaining contact with the floor
III. Optical sensors (LED/phototransistors)--Like bowling alley foul-line sensors
   A. Less bulky/connected to computer interface
   B. Not just for gripping, but for locating objects by following this sequence:
      1. Scan gripper to locate object
      2. Move gripper arm left and right to center object
      3. Move gripper forward to grasp
      4. Close gripper
   C. Problem--What force to use for gripping?
IV. Force sensors
   A. Spring and microswitch
   B. Optical encoder discs--Microprocessors determine speed of discs to determine force necessary
   C. Integrated circuits with strain gauge and pressure-sensitive paint
   D. Pressure sensors built with conductive foam
V. Conclusion

FIGURE 5.2 Topic Outline

I. Because robots must move, they need sensors. These sensors could include light sensors, sound sensors, and touch sensors.

II. Touch sensors can have the following technology:
   A. Microswitches can be used for gripping.
   B. Microswitches can also be used for maintaining contact with the floor. This would keep the robot from falling down stairs, for example.

III. Optical sensors might be better than microswitches.
   A. LED/phototransistors are less bulky than switches.
   B. When connected to a computer interface, optical sensors also can help a robot locate an object as well as grip it.
   C. Here's the sequence followed when using optical sensors:
      1. The robot's grippers scan the object to locate it.
      2. The robot moves its gripper arms left and right to center the object.
      3. The robot moves forward to grip the object.
      4. The robot closes the gripper.
   D. The only problem faced is what force should be used when gripping.

IV. Force sensors can solve this problem.
   A. A combination spring and microswitch can be used to determine the amount of force required.
   B. Optical encoder discs can be used also. A microprocessor determines the speed of the disc to determine the required force.
   C. Integrated circuits with strain gauges and pressure-sensitive paint can be used to determine force.
   D. Another pressure sensor can be built from conductive foam.

V. To conclude, all these methods of tactile sensing comprise a field of inquiry important to robotics.

FIGURE 5.3 Sentence Outline

research report should be *their* writing, as opposed to researched information. A general rule is to lead into and out of every quote or paraphrase with your own writing. In other words, (a) make a statement (your sentence), (b) support this generalization with a quote or paraphrase (referenced material from another source), and (c) provide a follow-up explanation of the referenced material's significance (your sentence).

Conclusion Recommendations

In a final paragraph, summarize your findings, draw a conclusion about the significance of these discoveries, and recommend future action.

Works Cited

On a final page, provide an alphabetized list of your research sources. (We discuss this documentation later in this chapter.)

Document your sources correctly. Your readers need to know where you found your information and from which sources you are quoting and/or paraphrasing. Therefore, you must document this information. Correct documentation is essential for several reasons:

- ☐ You must direct your readers to the books, periodical articles, and reference sources which you have used in your research report. If your readers want to find these same sources, they depend only on your documentation. If your documentation is incorrect, readers will be confused. Instead, you want your readers to be able to rely on the correctness and validity of your research.
- ☐ Do *not* plagiarize. Plagiarism is the appropriation (theft!) of some other person's words and ideas without giving proper credit. Writers are often guilty of unintentional plagiarism. This occurs when you incorrectly alter part of a quotation but still give credit to the writer. Your quotation must be *exactly the same* as the original word, sentence, or paragraph. You cannot haphazardly change a word, a punctuation mark, or the ideas conveyed. Even if you have cited your source, an incorrectly altered quotation constitutes plagiarism.
- ☐ On the other hand, if you intentionally use another person's words and claim them as your own, omitting quotation marks and source citations, you have committed theft. This is dishonest and could raise questions about your credibility and/or the credibility of your research. Teachers, bosses, and colleagues will have little, if any, respect for a person who purposely takes another person's words or ideas. It is essential, therefore, for you to cite your sources correctly.

To document your research correctly, you must (a) provide parenthetical source citations and (b) supply a works cited page.

Parenthetical Source Citations

Since 1984, the Modern Language Association (MLA) has used a simplified form for source citations. Prior to 1984, footnotes and endnotes were used in research reports. In certain instances, this form of documentation is still correct. If your boss or instructor requests footnotes or endnotes, you should still use these forms. However, the most modern approach to source citations requires only that we cite the source of our information parenthetically after the quote or paraphrase.

ONE AUTHOR. After the quote or paraphrase, parenthetically cite the author's last name and the page number of the information.

> "Viewing the molecular activity required state-of-the-art electronmicroscopes" (Heinlein 193).

Note that the period follows the parenthesis, not the quote. Also note that no comma separates the name from the page number and that no lower case *p* precedes the number.

TWO AUTHORS. After the quote or paraphrase, parenthetically cite the authors' last names and the page number of the information.

> "Though *Gulliver's Travels* preceded *Moll Flanders*, few scholars consider Swift's work to be the first novel" (Crider and Berry 292).

THREE OR MORE AUTHORS. Writing a series of names can be cumbersome. To avoid this, if you have a source of information written by three or more authors, parenthetically cite one author's name, followed by et al. (Latin for "and others") and the page number.

> "Baseball isn't just a sport; it represents man's ability to meld action with objective—the fusion of physicality and spirituality" (Norwood et al. 93).

MULTIPLE WORKS BY THE SAME AUTHOR. If you are quoting or paraphrasing from an author (Tom Lisk, for example) who has written two or more articles from which you are quoting, you cannot use the author's name only. The reader would not know to which Lisk article you are referring. In this instance, you must parenthetically cite the author's last name, followed by a shortened title to distinguish your source, and then the page number.

> "Maturity is not dependent on chronological age but on acquired wisdom" (Lisk "Age" 16).

ANONYMOUS WORKS. If your source has no author, parenthetically cite the shortened title and page number.

> "Robots are more accurate and less prone to errors caused by long hours of operation than humans" ("Useful Robots" 81).

Works Cited

Parenthetical source citations are an abbreviated form of documentation. In parentheses, you tell your readers only the names of your authors and the page numbers on which the information can be found. Such documentation alone would be insufficient. Your readers would not know the names of the books, the names of the periodicals, the dates, volumes, or publishing companies. This more thorough information is found on the works cited page, a listing of research sources alphabetized either by author's name or title (if anonymous). This is the last page of your research report.

Your works cited entries should follow MLA standards.

A Book With One Author

Naisbitt, John. *Megatrends*. New York: Warner Books, 1982.

A Book With Two Authors

Tibbets, Charlene, and A. M. Tibbets *Strategies: A Rhetoric and Reader*. Glenview, IL: Scott, Foresman and Company, 1988.

A Book With Three Or More Authors

Poole, Lon, et al. *Apple II User's Guide.* Berkeley: Osborne/McGraw Hill, 1983.

A Book With A Corporate Authorship

Corporate Credit Union Network. *A Review of the Credit Union Financial System: History, Structure, Status and Financial Trends.* Kansas City: U.S. Central, 1986.

A Translated Book

Phelps, Robert, ed. *The Collected Stories of Colette.* Trans. Matthew Ward, et al. New York: Farrar, Straus, Giroux, 1983.

A Book With An Author And An Editor

Poe, Edgar Allen. *The Complete Poems and Stories of Edgar Allen Poe: With Selections from his Critical Writings.* 2 vols. Eds. Arthur Hobson Quinn and Edward H. O'Neill. New York: Alfred A. Knopf, 1967.

A Book In Several Volumes

Doyle, Sir Arthur Conan. *The Complete Sherlock Holmes.* 2 vols. Garden City, New York: Doubleday & Company, Inc., 1927.

An Entry From An Edited Book

Irving, Washington. "Rip Van Winkle." *Once Upon a Time: The Fairy Tale World of Arthur Rackham.* Ed. Margery Darrell. New York: The Viking Press, 1972. 13–36.

Periodicals (Journals, Magazines, and/or Newspapers)

A Signed Article In A Journal

Gerson, Steve, and Nancy Roediger. "Ailments and Cures: A Simple Checklist for Improving Your Technical Writing." *Vertiflite* 33 (Sept./Oct. 1987): 60–62.

A Signed Article In A Magazine

Cuadrado, John A. "The Fashion Image: Louise Dahl-Wolfe." *Architectural Digest* September 1988: 66+.

The plus sign (+) following the page number tells us that the article continues on pages not numbered consecutively.

A Signed Article In A Newspaper

Hoffman, Donald. "Bank Consigned to Vault of Gloom." *The Kansas City Star* 24 October 1988: C1.

An Unsigned Article

"Bitter British Memories." *Newsweek* 3 October 1988: 36.

This entry would be alphabetized by the first letter in the title: *B*. If the title had been "The Bitter British Memories," you would still alphabetize by *B*. not by *The*.

Miscellaneous Sources of Research

Encyclopedias And Almanacs

"Rocket." *The World Book Encyclopedia.* 1979 ed.

Television Or Radio Programs

"Campaign: The Choice—a 'Frontline'/Time Special." Host, Gary Wills. Public Broadcasting System. KCPT, Kansas City, 24 October 1988.

Recordings

Hendrix, Jimi. *Are You Experienced?* Reprise, RS-6261.

Computer Software

PFS: Write Sampler. Computer Software. Software Pub. Corp., 1984.

Interviews

Lamb, Bill. Personal interview. 15 November 1988.

Lectures

McGovern, George. Lecture. "Election '88." Johnson County Community College. Overland Park, KS, 3 November 1988.

Alternative Style Sheets

Although MLA is a popular style sheet, other style sheets are favored in certain disciplines. Refer to these if you are interested or required to do so.

- ☐ Social Sciences and Psychology—American Psychological Association (APA)

Publication Manual of the American Psychological Association. 3rd ed. Washington, DC: American Psychological Association, 1983.

☐ Government

U.S. Government Printing Office Style Manual. Washington, DC: Government Printing Office, 1973.

☐ General

The Chicago Manual of Style. Chicago: University of Chicago Press, 1982.

Turabian, Kate L. *A Manual for Writers of Term Papers, Theses, and Dissertations.* Chicago: University of Chicago Press, 1973.

Develop your ideas. You've learned how to organize your report (through an introduction, discussion, and conclusion/recommendation) and how to document your sources of research through parenthetical source citations and a works cited page). Writing your research report also requires that you use your research effectively to develop your ideas. Successful use of research demands that you correctly quote, paraphrase, and/or summarize. Summaries are discussed in Chapter IVA.

☐ Rewriting

As with all types of writing, drafting the text of your research report is only the second stage of the writing process. To ensure that your report is effective, you must revise your draft. Follow our rewriting checklist for your revision.

REWRITING CHECKLIST

1. ☐ *Add new detail for clarity and/or persuasiveness.* Too often, students and employees assume that they have developed their content thoroughly when, in fact, their assertions are general and vague. This is especially evident in research reports. You might provide a quotation to prove a point, but is this documentation sufficient? Have you truly developed your assertions? If an idea within your report seems thinly presented, either add another quote, paraphrase, or summary for additional support or explain the significance of the researched information.
2. ☐ *Delete dead words and phrases and researched information which does not support your ideas effectively.* Good writing in a work environment is economical writing. Thus, as always, your goal is to communicate clearly and concisely. Delete words which serve no purpose, maintaining a low fog index. In addition, review your draft for clarity of focus. The goal of a research report is not to use whatever researched information you've found wherever it seems valid. Instead, you want to use quotes, paraphrases, and summaries only when they help develop your statement of purpose. If your research doesn't support your thesis, it's counterproductive and should be eliminated. In the rewriting stage, delete any documented research which is tangential or irrelevant.

3. ☐ *Simplify your words for easy understanding.* The goal of technical writing is to communicate, not to confuse. Write to be understood. Don't say *grain-consuming animal units* if you mean *chickens.* Don't call the October 1987 stock market crash a *fourth quarter equity retreat.* Don't describe an airplane crash as *uncontrolled contact with the ground.*

4. ☐ *Move information within your report to ensure effective organization.* How have you organized your report? Did you use a problem/solution format? Did you use comparison/contrast or cause/effect? Is your report organized as a chronological narrative or by importance? Whichever method you've used, you want to be consistent. To ensure consistency, rewrite by moving any information which is misplaced.

5. ☐ *Reformat your text for reader-friendly ease of access.* Look at any technical journal. You'll notice that the writers have guided their readers through the text by using headings and subheadings. You'll also notice that many journals use graphics (pie charts, bar graphs, line drawings, flow charts, etc.) to clarify the writer's assertions. You should do the same. To help your readers follow your train of thought, reformat any blocks of wall-to-wall words. Add headings, subheadings, itemized lists, white space, and graphics.

6. ☐ *Correct any errors.* This represents your greatest challenge in writing a research report. You not only must be concerned with grammar and mechanics, as you are when writing a memo, letter, or report, but also with accurate quoting, paraphrasing, summarizing, parenthetical source citations, and works cited.

When revising, pay special attention to these concerns. If you quote, paraphrase, or summarize incorrectly, you run the risk of plagiarizing. If you fail to provide correct parenthetical source citations and/or works cited, you will make it impossible for your readers to find these same sources of information in their research or to check the accuracy of your data. Research demands accuracy and reliability.

Resume

Numerous books and articles are available to provide assistance in writing an effective resume. This brief section highlights some techniques involved in writing an effective resume.

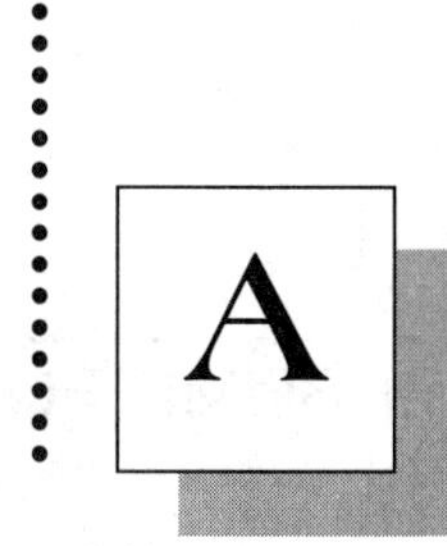

Effective Resumes

It is just like a magic carpet. A well-written resume takes you where you want to go—right into the interviewer's office. It's magic!

I've watched the magic over the years. When I first met Cheryl, she had been unemployed for over a year. She had been fired from her last job. Her self-confidence had long disappeared and she felt defeated.

After reviewing her resume and a sample job application, it was no wonder. Everything spoke of failure. Red flags waved vigorously on both papers. No wonder she couldn't find work.

When Cheryl captured her "best" on paper, her whole outlook changed. She moved from fear to confidence. It was truly magic. Within days of moving to a small community she was back to work. She had received several job offers; then she accepted a full-time and a part-time job.

I often work with men and women who have been fired. They are angry, fearful, and afraid of being hurt again. They are afraid to apply for work knowing full-well they will be rejected one more time. But I have found over and over again, that when they capture their "best" and most relevant skills suited for the career direction, their self-confidence and self-esteem returns.

A well-written resume won't get you a job, but it will give you confidence and it will get you interviews with employers. That is what you're after, the opportunity to present yourself in person. There is no other piece of paper more important to you in the job hunt than a good resume.

How to write an effective resume that opens doors? You write, rewrite, and rewrite until it's right. Read on for more specific information. It's time to weave your own personal magic carpet.

RESUME FUNDAMENTALS

☐ Length

A general rule-of-thumb exists on length:

1. One page for less than 10 years of experience.
2. Two pages for more than 10 years of experience.

If you feel you need more than two pages, reconsider.

☐ Layout

Layout is "eye-appeal." It is the wrappings for your package. Your "Sizzle and Sale." Here are six rules to remember:

1. *Margins:* Top, bottom and sides—1" is best, minimum ¾".
2. Use lots of *white space*. Allow plenty of space between ideas, categories, and margins. Vast, grey expanses of copy are unreadable.
3. Break up the grey with HEADLINES and MARGINAL descriptions. These can be highlighted by using **Bold Lettering**, ALL CAPS, or Underlining. These techniques highlight the areas you want the employer to see first. It makes the reading job easier for the employer.

   Every headline must offer a specific thought, something new.
4. Keep paragraphs and sentences short.
5. Use real-life examples, testimonials, and solutions. Generic images are meaningless. Make your illustrations relevant to your message.
6. Use all the space available. The writing should be well-balanced. The balance should be the same for all pages.

☐ Paper

1. Use 8½" by 11" paper.
2. Use white, off-white, ivory, or grey paper. Avoid other colors.
3. Use a high-quality, 20# bond.
4. Forget about binders and fancy folders.
5. No photos.

☐ Printing

1. Prepare your resume professionally with an attractive business typeface. Word-processing programs provide you with many choices and the capability for quick revision.
2. **Proofread. Proofread. Proofread!** Read your resume word-for-word *backwards*.
3. Photocopies must be clean and unmarked.

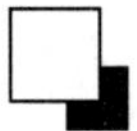

RESUME FORMATS

Choose a format that meets your needs. The four most commonly used resume formats are: *Historical, Functional, Achievement,* and *Combination.* Two other formats include the *Creative* and *Letter* formats.

☐ The Historical Resume Format

Outlines employment in chronological order with the most recent position first.

Advantages

- ☐ Most familiar to employer.
- ☐ Easiest to prepare.
- ☐ Provides excellent format for steady employment and increased responsibilities.

Disadvantages

- ☐ Easily reveals gaps in employment.
- ☐ Duplicates information on job applications.
- ☐ May over-emphasize job skills, narrow industry experience, or numerous job changes.

DAVID KIRK

3987 Silvas Road Bend, Oregon 97701 (503) 389-2385

EMPLOYMENT OBJECTIVE

Restaurant Management . . . Assistant Manager or Trainee

EDUCATION

Associate of Science. Hotel and Restaurant Management.
Central Oregon Community College. Bend, Oregon 97701. 1993.
Personally financed college education by working in field.
Churchill High School, Eugene, OR. Graduated 1989. GPA 3.57.

EMPLOYMENT HISTORY

The Riverhouse Restaurant. Bend, OR. 389-8810. (1989 to Present)
Waiter 6/90 to present. Assistant Waiter 8-12/89.

Management and Supervision . . . Supervised and coordinated activities of dining room. Planned details for banquets, receptions, and other social functions. Hired, trained, and supervised dining room employees and banquet staffs in fine dining service. Directed setting up of tables and decorations.

Tableside and Beverage Service . . . Carved and served dinners on chafing dishes at tableside including Steak Diane, Rack of Lamb, and Chateaubriand. Setup and prepared Caesar and Wilted Spinach salads. Flamed desserts and drinks including Bananas' Foster, Cherries Jubilee, and Coffee Royales. Discussed wines with patrons and assisted in making appropriate selections. Presented and opened wines.

Waiting Service . . . Served meals in formal and informal settings. Presented verbal and printed menus. Recommended dinner courses, appropriate wines, and deserts. Answered questions regarding food preparations.

Albertson's Food Center. Eugene, OR. 342-05261. (1989 to 1989)
Deli Counter Sales and Food Preparer. Boxer and Shelf Stocker.

PERSONAL

Born 1966, U.S. Citizen. Willing to work varied work schedule. Desire relocation to continue education. Punctual. Excellent health. Motivated and budget-minded. Computer literature—use word processing, data base, and spreadsheet programs.

Historical Resume Format

☐ The Functional Resume Format

- ☐ Organizes experience by skills or functions.
- ☐ Leaves out employment history.
- ☐ Usually lists highest skill or most applicable skill first.
- ☐ Eliminates job titles.

Advantages

- ☐ Stresses marketable skills and experiences.
- ☐ Camouflages spotty employment record or demotions.
- ☐ Allows emphasis on professional growth.
- ☐ Positions or experiences not related to current career objective can be played down.

Disadvantages

- ☐ Employers may be suspicious of format.
- ☐ Employers like to see employment history.
- ☐ More difficult to write.
- ☐ May be longer.

CHERYL TURNER

Post Office Box 17 Boise, Idaho 83704 (208) 384-1005

Career Objective

General office employment . . . where a pleasant personality and excellent clerical and secretarial skills are required.

Office and Clerical Skills

Processed payroll, accounts payable, accounts receivables deposits for two checking and two savings accounts. Ordered and maintained a running inventory of all office supplies. Operated IBM computer terminal, 10 key calculator, and various copy machines.

Obtained information for reports and completed prior to deadlines. Assumed the responsibility for typing these reports instead of handwriting them as previously done. Two supervisors remarked that they were done in a professional manner and easy to read. Made adjustments to daily correction of computer print-out edits.

Written Communication Skills

Created and typed letters pertaining to insurance coverage and claims, collection on past due accounts, merchandise claims, and orders and inquiries of stock availability. The letters addressed large companies as well as individual customers. Also, typed loan papers which contained important financial information.

Credit and Collections

Processed loan applications which consisted of calling employers and other creditors for ratings and references. Called and visited customers regarding past due accounts. Often complimented for ability to work with clients on verbal commitments.

Innovative Ideas

Discussed with supervisor the advantages of installing com-lines on the telephones and designating one person to answer the phones for which I volunteered. These two changes reduced the level of noise, added privacy, and created a more workable atmosphere.

Reorganized the files of current policies, freight bills and material orders. Developed a system for dead files. Created and typed my own resume.

Community and School Involvement

1987 Central Oregon Timber Carnival Princess. Appeared in numerous parades. Represented Central Oregon Timber Carnival Association in state-wide timber conventions. Co-captain and assistant advisor for High School Drill Team. High school journalism typist for two years.

Personal

Born October, 1968. Single, no dependents. Excellent health. Willing to travel or relocate. Enjoy meeting people and going to new and different places. Like to be assigned responsibilities requiring creative thinking. Seeking advancement opportunities.

Functional Resume Format

☐ The Achievement Resume Format

- ☐ Highlights outstanding achievements regardless of positions, employers, or dates.
- ☐ Leaves out employment history.
- ☐ Eliminates job titles.
- ☐ Usually lists highest or most applicable achievement first.

Advantages

- ☐ Stresses achievements.
- ☐ Demonstrates ability to get things done.
- ☐ Features accomplishments that support the job objective.
- ☐ Stresses accomplishments that transfer from one job to another and from one industry to another.
- ☐ Excellent format for applicants with minimal or no job experience, career changers, retirees returning to work, military and government personnel entering private industry, and for late-starters.

Disadvantages

- ☐ May be unfamiliar to employers.
- ☐ Employers may be suspicious of format.
- ☐ Employers like to see employment history.
- ☐ More difficult to write.
- ☐ May be longer.

RON JACKSON

1769 Harbor Drive   Portland, Oregon 97201   (503) 243-9845

Employment Goal

summer employment in a lumber mill . . . where excellent physical condition and a good work attitude are required.

Education

Sophomore honors student, Willamette University. Psychology major. 3.957 GPA. Studied in Japan on primarily self-financed exchange program. Pending summer earnings, will study in Tokyo next year. High school GPA 4.00. (1990).

Lumber Mill Experience

Improved working conditions and safety in two major production sheds by meticulously keeping them clear of all scraps debris. By own initiative, improved stockyard efficiency by reorganizing and/or discarding several year's accumulation of unattended stock and debris. Upon leaving for a higher paid position, head sawyer argued for my promotion, but company policy would not allow it. Another sawyer said, "I hate to see you go. This is the cleanest this place has been in a LONG time." (1991)

Bought and Remodeled Old House

As partner with brother, age 18, bought and completely remodeled an old house: 500 square foot addition, replaced all roofing, siding, flooring, wiring, plumbing, sheetrock, and windows. Added new sidewalk and lawn. All financial planning and work, except sheetrocking was done by us. Received many compliments on quality of work. One carpenter said: "When you first got this place I thought it would be a real hole (mess) when you finished, but now I'm really impressed." Sold house for profit. (1988–1990)

School and Community Activities

••Organized two Dance-A-Thons for high school choir. Each raised nearly $4,500. ••Wrote and circulated petition for a stop sign on an unsafe corner. After some debate, City approved installation.

Other College and High School Activities

••Chosen counselor for Japanese exchange students, Willamette University. ••Cross country: 4 letters, team captain, most inspirational. ••High school choir: publicity manager and vice president. Honor Society: president. ••Placed first in local, district, and state Elks' Scholarship Leadership competition.

Personal Data

Born 1972. 6'3". 175 pounds. Weight lifter. Runner. Outdoorsman. Eagle Scout. Appreciate challenges. Willing to work varied shifts, hours, and days.

Achievement Resume Format

☐ The Combination Resume Format

This format provides the employer with your employment history. It emphasizes skills or achievements rather than where and when you worked.

- ☐ Combines the *Functional* or *Achievement* format with the *Historical* format.
- ☐ Employment history is recorded in a separate section, usually listed toward end of resume and on second page.

Advantages

- ☐ Allows emphasize on most relevant skills and abilities.
- ☐ Satisfies employer's desire to know employment history.
- ☐ De-emphasizes employment history, career changes, demotions, narrow industry or government experience.

Disadvantages

- ☐ More difficult to prepare than historical resume.
- ☐ May be longer and more difficult to read.

Although this resume is two pages, combinations can be written on only one page. The main advantage of two pages is the deemphasizing of your employment history. The top page shows only skills and achievements relevant to the job objective. These experiences are prioritized according to the highest and most germane.

Notice the basic parts of this resume and the priority arrangement of the categories.

- ☐ Identification
- ☐ Functional and achievement narratives
- ☐ Education
- ☐ Employment History

The parts and the arrangement you choose is a matter of personal judgment, job criteria, format used, and your background.

FRANCES GNOSE

2161 NE Monterey Avenue   Bend, OR 97701   (503) 389-8808

Career Objective

Real Estate Sales in Central Oregon for a growing, progressive organization.

Sales and Marketing Experience

Supervisor of Marketing Operations
Scheduled and coordinated work flow between marketing, manufacturing, product service, and accounting departments. Supervised 7 contract administrators. Recruited, hired, and trained professional and technical staffs. Conducted employee performance reviews and made salary recommendations. Wrote and implemented standard office procedures.

Redesigned computerized order entry system. Evaluated department requirements for needs assessment. Simplified program to make it "user friendly." Expanded functions to include billing. Wrote training manual. Developed and conducted training program. Trained administrators in 12 districts across the United States. Staff comments included: "Can't believe it was done so quickly," and "These changes should have been made years ago."

Managed department financial reports, budget forecasts, and purchasing. Administered payroll, confidential personnel records, accounts payable, electronic mail, voice-mail, and travel arrangements. Promoted to supervisor within 6 months.

Furniture Sales and Interior Design
Established and managed furniture and interior decorating business. Within 10 years, expanded to 2 locations with annual sales of $500,000. Purchased merchandise in domestic and European markets. Negotiated contractual leases for retail and warehouse operations. Hired, trained, and supervised staff of 10. Created and executed sales promotions and advertising campaigns. Approved customer credit limits. Created open-to-buy budgets. Established merchandise pricing policies. Worked with import and export brokers.

Air Freight Sales Support Representative
Administrative coordinator for the Sales Manager with annual sales volume of $8 million. Liaison between customers and sales staff in fast-paced environment. Prepared business proposals, sales analysis, and statistical reports. Processed payroll. Purchased office supplies and equipment. Created and implemented freight air bill distribution program.

Combination Resume Format, page 1

FRANCE GNOSE

Page 2

Other Experience

College Instructor
Taught credit and non-credit courses for Office Administration, Business, and Community Education Departments. Classes included: Office Management, Beginning and Advanced WordPerfect 5.1, Getting Hired, and Career Change.

Comments from student evaluations include: "Wonderful class! I really learned a lot about communication and management." "She teaches with excitement and enthusiasm," and "Excellent speaking and lecturing. She keeps it interesting and fun to learn the subject."

Vocational Secretary
Assisted the Regional Vocational Coordinator for 3 counties in Central Oregon. Organized meetings, workshops, and in-service activities. Made arrangements for facilities, meals, registration, and transportation. Compiled grant applications for technology vocational programs. Used WordPerfect 5.1, PlanPerfect, Byline, Nutshell, and Twin Programs.

Education

Oregon Real Estate Sales License: Oregon Examination May 23, 1992.
Bachelor of Science. Psychology. Washington State University, Pullman, WA.
Masters Program. Social Work. Smith College, Northampton, MA.
Computer Training: WordPerfect 5.1, Novell Network, Lotus 1-2-3, Wangwriter

Employment History

1990–92 **Instructor.** Central Oregon Community College. Bend, OR.
1991–92 **Sales Representative and Designer.** Interiors International, Bend, OR.
1989–91 **Secretary.** Deschutes County Education Service District, Bend, OR.
1987–89 **Supervisor Marketing Operations.** Anacomp, Inc., San Diego, CA.
1985–87 **Sales Support Representative.** Emery Worldwide, San Diego, CA.
1971–81 **Manager Owner.** Scandinavian Interiors, Eugene, OR.

Combination Resume Format, page 2

☐ The Creative Resume Format

- ☐ May be a sales brochure, a video tape, or other forms less standard than the prior examples.
- ☐ Often provides a pictorial representation of the applicant or of the actual skills and abilities of applicant.
- ☐ Excellent format for consultants, small businesses, and individuals that need to get their foot in the door. Establishing yourself as an independent business contractor provides the employer the opportunity to hire you on a contract without the employer/employee obligations. This can lead to full-time permanent employment.

A Sales Brochure

This example is a tri-fold 8½" brochure. It serves as a handout and a convenient mailer.

Why

Fran Gnose?

QUALIFICATIONS

License and Memberships
- Oregon State Real Estate License
- Multiple Listing Service
- Oregon State Association of Realtors
- National Association of Realtors

Education
- Bachelor of Science
  Psychology and English
  Washington State University
  Pullman, WA
- Masters Program: Social Work
  Smith College, Northampton, MA

Past Experience
- College Instructor
  Central Oregon Community College
- Marketing Operations Supervisor
  Anacomp, Inc., San Diego, CA
- Interior Design and Furniture Sales
  Owner/Manager Scandinavian Interiors
  Eugene and Salem, OR

My Personal Pledge to You

COLDWELL BANKER
Morris Real Estate
209 NE Greenwood
Bend, OR 97701

YOUR REAL ESTATE
PROFESSIONAL

Fran Gnose

Sales Associate

Coldwell Banker Morris Real Estate
209 NE Greenwood Avenue
Bend, OR 97701

(503) 382-4123 Office
(503) 385-3253 FAX
(503) 389-8808 Home

Advantages

- ☐ Provides applicant flexibility in approaching employers.
- ☐ Makes an excellent mailer or handout.
- ☐ Used by
  sales representatives
  advertising/marketing independents,
  graphic artists,
  consultants,
  entrepreneurs,
  part-time applicants,
  handicapped or disabled persons.

Disadvantages

- ☐ Most difficult to prepare.
- ☐ May cost more to prepare.
- ☐ May require hiring a professional.
- ☐ Needs to be professionally printed on quality paper.

Why COLDWELL BANKER Morris Real Estate?

- **America's Premier Real Estate Company Residential—Commercial Ranches—Land—Lots**
- **Member of the Sears Financial Network**
- **Multiple Listing Service**
- **Nationwide Relocation and Referral Service**
- **Large professionally trained staff**
- **#1 Home Sellers in Bend**
- **Easy to find**

Map of Area

For the SELLER

To PRICE your property, I will:

- Provide a Comparative Market Analysis of similar properties in your area that have recently sold and are currently for sale.

To MARKET your property, I will:

- Submit listing to Multiple Listing Service.
- Advertise in appropriate media.
- Provide a Coldwell Banker "For Sale" sign.
- Show property to qualified buyers.
- Counsel buyers with financial alternatives.

To keep you INFORMED, I will:

- Provide notification of property showings.
- Explain the selling process.
- Provide copies of signed documents.
- Present all offers promptly.
- Accompany you to settlement.

For the BUYER

To HELP with your purchase, I will:

- Discuss your needs, style preferences, location, and price.
- Provide listings of suitable properties.
- Provide details on taxes, zoning, and local ordinances.
- Provide community services information.

To provide you COUNSEL, I will:

- Explain mortgage application procedures.
- Accompany you to a lender.
- Provide copies of signed documents.
- Accompany you to the closing.

For RELOCATION

To FIND you a new home, I will:

- Refer you to a Coldwell Banker relocation representative
- Coordinate sale and purchase of properties.

TAILOR YOUR RESUME TO EMPLOYER'S NEEDS

The employer's needs should always be considered when writing your resume. Employers want answers to these questions:

1. Can you do the job?
2. Will you do the job?
3. How will you fit in?
4. How long will you stay?
5. Why are you looking now?
6. How much will you cost?

When you supply satisfactory answers to the first five questions, you are likely to get an interview. The last question is best answered at the interview.

Ask yourself these questions:

1. What are the job requirements and personal qualities needed for this job?
2. What experiences do I have that best match these requirements and qualities?
3. How can I best capture the employer's attention in 30 seconds or less?

Below is a typical advertisement. Read the ad and identify the job requirements and personal qualities the employer wants. Record these requirements, listing the highest priority items first.

HELP WANTED	EMPLOYER'S PRIORITY OF NEEDS and BUZZ WORDS
ELECTRICAL SUPERVISOR Split shift. Opening at modern wood products complex. Must have State journeyman's license. Programmable controller and solid state drive experience desirable. Excellent physical condition required. Must not be afraid of heights. Must enjoy working in cold weather. Excellent opportunity for multi-talented person. Send resume giving work history and salary requirements.	1. ______ 2. ______ 3. ______ 4. ______ 5. ______ 6. ______ 7. ______ 8. ______ 9. ______ 10. ______

☐ Electrical Supervisor

Notice how this resume matches the employer's requirements in the advertisement.

Job Objective. Matches advertisement.

Licenses. Matches and exceeds requirements.

Experience. Fulfills employer requests.

Work History. Provided.

Personal Data. Covers other job requirements.

Salary Requirements. Not covered on resume. Salary history or requirements are stated in the cover letter when requested.

JOHN KENEDAY

311 East Canyon Road | Cleveland, Ohio 44135 | (216) 495-7172

Career Objective

Electrical Supervisor . . . for a modern lumber products complex desiring a multi-talented person.

Licenses/Education

Licensed State Supervisor and Manufacturing Plant Journeyman Electrician. Licensed State Millwright. Former Navy Nuclear Power School Instructor. Completed 4 years Boiler 2nd (E5) rating. Completed training in Gas and Arc Welding. Basic Fire Fighting, Supervisory Training, plus more.

Training and Supervision

Trained and schooled in supervision. Taught state electrical apprenticeship program for local community college. Qualified nuclear reactor mechanic, operator and operator trainer.

Supervised production, maintenance and construction personnel. Full responsibility for mill operations including sawmill, boilers, dry kilns, and planers.

Programmable Controllers

Researched, installed and operated various programmable controllers and solid state drives. Trained operators and maintenance personnel on equipment. Designed electrical power systems for production increases.

Employment History

92 to present — OHIO LUMBER. New London, OH 44851. Phone: (419) 929-5555. Sawmill Superintendent (86 to present). Chief Engineer (82–86).

88–92 — K-P INC. Cleveland, OH, 44982. Phone (216) 445-9876. Electrician helper. Resaw and Retoner Operator

78–88 — U.S. NAVY. Instructor, Mechanic, Operator Nuclear Reactor.

Personal

Seeking long-term career opportunity in Alaska. Excellent physical condition. Unafraid of heights. Winter enthusiast on and off the job. Willing to work flexible hours and schedules. Enjoy traveling. Born 1960.

Electrical Supervisor Resume

☐ Assistant Finance Director

> **HELP WANTED 210** ASSISTANT FINANCE DIRECTOR
>
> Must have strong technical accounting skills in accounts receivable, accounts payable, trial balance, general ledger, cash receipts, cash disbursements, utility billing and LID billing. EDP experience desirable, preferably IBM System 34. Good communications skills required. Minimum education requirements include a degree with minimum of 9 hours of accounting; or any equivalent combination of experience and training that indicates an ability to perform duties.

Notice how the resume matches the employer's needs listed in the advertisement.

- ☐ Is every item in the employer's ad covered by the resume?
- ☐ Strong Accounting skills?
- ☐ Communication skills?
- ☐ Data Processing Experience?
- ☐ Education?

List the employer's hierarchy of needs:

1. ______________________________
2. ______________________________
3. ______________________________
4. ______________________________
5. ______________________________

Are the job requirements in the advertisement ranked according to the employer's priorities?

If not, can you explain why?

JEANNE STAPPLES

Post Office Box 783 Eugene, Oregon 97426 (503) 344-2224

CAREER OBJECTIVE — FINANCIAL MANAGEMENT

. . . working for an organization that needs a team member with a positive attitude and with strong technical accounting, communication, and data processing skills.

ACCOUNTING

Prepared monthly, quarterly and annual operating and capital expenditure budgets. Monitored capital investments and reinvestment programs. Analyzed monthly operating results relative to annual and quarterly budgets. Prepared trial balances, balance sheets, income and operating statements, profit and loss statements. Maintained general ledgers, cost accounts, and prepared journal vouchers. Processed computerized payroll and all related tax reports. Recorded, posted and balanced cash receipts.

Verified credit applications. Authorized credit extensions. Approved and established credit lines. Developed and implemented new credit policies. Personal collection efforts decreased delinquent debts 60% and increased cash flow 63% in two years. Worked with attorneys on legal collection matters. Filed liens and lien notices.

Managed and maintained accounts receivable for over 3700 accounts with average active monthly balances of $400,000. Converted accounts receivable to in-house computerized system which handled all billings. Developed format for aged receivables, identification of COD accounts, account classification listings, and maintenance of current status on active accounts.

Approved, checked and audited cash disbursements for equipment, supplies and services. Monitored contracts and agreements for compliance. Established and maintained internal controls for accounts payable ensuring proper protection of company assets.

COMMUNICATIONS

Published numerous business and organizational newsletters developing logos and format. Wrote many feature articles presenting positive image of organization, emphasizing recognition and accomplishment, and informing readers of changes and upcoming events. Publications created involvement. Wrote news releases. Familiar with printing processes, typography, photography, paper, inks, plus layout of brochures and pamphlets. Wrote employee policies and procedures, legal and financial documents, and data processing parameters.

Extensive speaking experience in business, education and community. Company representative for various civic and educational organizations. Developed and conducted management workshops. Planned special promotions for newspapers, TV and radio broadcasts.

DATA PROCESSING

Diversified data processing background through work experience and formal education (Hewlett/Packard, IBM Integrated Business Computers, Burroughs). Specified computer parameters for accounts receivable, accounts payable, payroll and inventory control. Prepared cost/equipment evaluation for conversion to word processing. Selected and implemented word processing system.

Assistant Finance Director, page 1

JEANNE STAPPLES
Page 2

PENSIONS, EMPLOYEE BENEFITS, TRAINING AND MORE
Wrote and implemented an approved IRS pension plan. Negotiated new employee benefit programs including health, dental, disability and life insurance coverage. Interviewed, selected, and hired employees. Supervised staffs. Conducted orientation and training. Evaluated employee performances. Established cross-training programs. Developed and implemented procedures decreasing work duplications by improving paper-flow of accounting office.
Organized annual conferences with full responsibility for all meeting and social details. Edited board and committee official minutes. Prepared agendas. Established and maintained file systems. Processed and monitored insurance claims. Maintained hourly and salaried personnel records.

COMMUNITY/PROFESSIONAL ASSOCIATIONS
National Association of Credit Management of Oregon.
Oregon Business Education Council, Lane Community College Office Careers Advisory Committee; Lane Community College Vocational Education Advisory Committee.

EMPLOYMENT

82–84 **Credit Manager and Accounting Office Manager.**
City Planning Mill, 1143 Court Street, Eugene, OR 343-5555

76–82 **Office Manager and Executive Administrative Assistant.**
Western Lumber Assn, P.O. Box 16, Eugene, OR 689-5555.

68–76 **Executive Secretary to General Manager and Timber Resources Manager**
Atlantic Pacific Corp, 79 Hill Road, Eugene, OR 342-5555.

75–68 **Administrative Assistant to Professor of Engineering Department.**
University of Michigan, Ann Arbor, MI (313) 888-5555.

63–65 **Secretary, Quality Control Department.**
General Motors Corp., Flint, MI (612) 465-3201.

62–63 **Secretary: Titan Missiles Material Department Manager, Top secret clearance.**
Martin Marietta Corp., Denver, Colorado (303) 721-5601.

EDUCATION
BA Business Education, Colorado State University, Ft. Collins, Colorado. Accounting, Math, History and English Minors. 1962. Updated education at University of Oregon and Portland State College. Courses in upper level math, computer technology with classroom directed programming, word processing and personnel administration procedures. 1968–1979.

PERSONAL
High level of energy and enthusiasm. Willing to travel or relocate. High adaptability to change. Operate well under pressure. Seeking challenging opportunities requiring creative solutions.

Assistance Finance Director, page 2

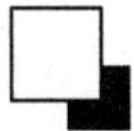

BASIC PARTS OF A RESUME

The information you include on your resume depends upon the picture you desire to create. The order or placement will vary with your format choice, work and life experiences, and personal tastes. Below is a listing the major groups to consider.

☐ **Identification**
—Name
—Address
—Day-time Phone

☐ **Job Objective**

Required:
—Job Title or general functional area

Optional:
—Working hours
—Type of Business
—Location
—Offerings

☐ **Education**

Required:
—Diploma or Credential
—Specialization
—School
—City and State

Optional:
—Zip Code
—School Phone
—Year Graduated
—GPA/Awards
—Scholarships
—Relevant Courses

☐ **Employment History**

Required:
—Employment Dates, generally just the years (89–93)
—Job Title, Company Name, City and State

Optional:
—Mailing Address, Phone Number
—Supervisor's Name with Courtesy and Job Titles
—Other relevant information

☐ **Experience Narratives**
functional and/or achievement descriptions of work and life experience relative to the job objective

Michael D. Woolridge

P. O. Box 311 Bend, OR 97708 (503) 389-5555

Career Objective

CADD operator in mechanical design.

Education

CADD Certification, Central Oregon Community College, Bend, OR
Certification to be completed June, 1993. GPA 3.5
A.S. degree to be completed by 1994.
Burns High School Graduate with 3 years of drafting.

Auto CADD Experience

Operated computer-aided design system and peripheral equipment to design, resize and modify detailed mechanical drawings used in manufacture, assembly, installation and repair.

Examined electronic schematics and supporting documents received from design engineering departments to verify specifications such as dimensions and tolerances.

Computed drafting specifications to determine configuration dimensions using computers, calculators and conversion charts. Prepared final detail drawings of components and equipment.

Located files relating to specified design projection data base library and loaded program into computer. Entered commands for resizing specification. Conferred with engineers to determine design modifications. Produced graphic representation of design for review and approval.

Millwright Assistant

Assisted in building, installing, dismantling, and moving machinery, equipment, and buildings according to layout plans, blueprints, and other drawings. Constructed foundations for machines. Aligned machines and equipment. Read blueprints and schematic drawings to determine work procedures. Used hoists, lift trucks, micrometers, squares, rules, plumb bobs, and power tools.

Basic Parts of a Resume

Michael D. Woolridge

Page 2

Equipment Operation

Operated computerized and manual trimsaws, resaws and bandsaws. Trimmed and sorted lumber to grade. Trained and evaluated new operators on computerized system. Qualified fireman for a 4-boiler powerhouse. Trained new firemen in boiler operations. Supervised crew in repairing boiler inner walls and building scaffolding. Operated heavy equipment: 966 cat, D-8 cat, coal and chip dozer, dumptrucks, forklifts, and lumber carriers.

Auto Body Repair

Repaired, welded, and painted damaged cars, buses and trucks. Examined damage and estimated repair cost. Removed upholstery, accessories, trim electrical and hydraulic equipment, to gain access to body and fenders. Used cutting torches, welders, hoists, jacks, sanders, paint guns. Filed, grinded, sanded, and refinished repaired surfaces.

Operated oxygen/acetylene welder. Welded and repaired broken or cracked metal parts, filled holes, and built up metal parts as specified by layout, welding diagrams, or work orders.

Employment History

1981–1991 **DAW Forest Products Company**, Bend, OR 97701
382-2511
Trimsaw operator. Fireman. Millwright helper.

1973–1980 **Edward Hines Lumber Company**, Burns, OR 97720
(Closed)
Trimsaw operator. Chain Puller. Clean-up. Fireman.

1968–1973 **Burns Ford**, Burns, OR 97720 (Closed)
Apprentice autobody repairman and detailer.

Personal

Seeking part-time employment in CADD operation while completing degree program. Willing to work varied hours and days. Enjoy designing and building decks and awnings. Excellent attendance and safety records.

Basic Parts of a Resume

- ☐ **Other Activities**
  Professional Clubs
  Community Clubs
  CPR, First Aid
  Licenses
  Technical Skills
  Publications
  Hobbies
  Other Relevant Information not listed elsewhere
- ☐ **Personal**
  All Optional:
  Working Hours
  Desired Location
  Travel
  Relocation
  Reason for Change
  Health
  Age, Gender
  Marital Status
  Citizenship
  Personal Characteristics
  Any other relevant information not listed elsewhere.

Identification

Your name, address and a *day-time* phone number appears here. It is advisable to write out your name and not use initials for your first and middle names. For example, A. G. Ames should be written as Alice G. Ames.

Placement of your identification depends upon your personal taste. If your resume is two or more pages, be sure that your name is at the top of each page. In case the pages get separated, it can be easily rejoined.

Job Objective

Because the objective is generally the first thing read on a resume, its importance can not be ignored. If you choose to write an objective, it should relate to your immediate goal. Many applicants decide to eliminate the job objective unless they are applying for a specific position. The experts disagree widely on whether to include it or not. You decide.

Job objective should be short, specific, and clear. They should be general enough to allow consideration of several related jobs at more than one level or department within a company. Read the following examples.

- ☐ **Medical Records** . . . working for a hospital or large medical clinic in Central Oregon offering a full-time career opportunity.
- ☐ **Public Relations and Promotions** . . . working with an organization where a positive public image and excellent media are imperative.

- ☐ **Administrative Management** ... focusing on special projects, program development and community relations.
- ☐ **Sales and Customer Service** ... where personal effort and quality customer service are important.
- ☐ **Summer employment in a lumber mill** ... where excellent physical condition and a good work attitude are required.
- ☐ **General Office Accounting Clerk** ... part-time position with flexible hours and week-ends. Where excellent clerical and secretarial skills and a pleasant personality are required.

Education: Degrees, Licenses, Professional Certifications

This is generally placed immediately after the job objective if it is the next most important qualification you have. List your **highest** and **most relevant** educational credential first.

B.S. Psychology major, English minor.
Portland State University. Portland, OR
Graduated Cum Laude. 1992.

A.S. Health Record Technology.
Central Oregon Community College.
2600 NW College Way. Bend, OR
GPA 3.52. 1989.

Sometimes work experience and skills are more important. For example, a person who has 15 years experience in accounting would probably list education later unless the position required specific educational credentials such as a C.P.A. To be given a top billing, it should be exactly the education required.

High school only sometimes may be placed under personal.

Employment History

The resume format decides the placement of this information. If you have chosen a functional or an achievement resume format it will not be included. Reasons for elimination are explained under resume format information.

Employment Dates, Job Title, Employer, Description of Duties are often included in this section. The amount of detail and arrangement is decided by each applicant's situation and needs. Present your EMPLOYMENT HISTORY in the best light. Consider presenting as much information as space allows and to provide easy access for reference verification. Make the employer's job easy; it's usually beneficial.

Basic format for employment history includes: employment dates (year to year), job title, employer's name and location (city and state). The additional information (telephone number, supervisor's name, and job description summary) presented below is optional.

Following are examples of EMPLOYMENT HISTORY.

```
1982 to 1984  Boxer and Shelf Stocker Albertson's Food
              Center. Eugene, OR. Supervisor: Mr. Lonnie
              R. Hayes, Store Manager at 342-5261. Boxed
              groceries and delivered them to customer
              cars. Checked incoming orders, verifying
              amounts received with invoice. Stocked
              shelves with product.
```

Below is an example of how you can list long-term employment with one employer when you have had numerous promotions and changes in locations.

Following is another example of employment history. This person had been fired from her job and wanted to be sure that potential employers contacted a specific person so she listed the name of a prearranged reference.

```
75-89  GEORGIA-PACIFIC CORPORATION
       Divisional Office Manager and Accountant
       McAdam New Brunswick, Canada
80-86  Timber Department Accounting Supervisor
       Eugene, Oregon
75-86  Plant Accountant, Secretary, Accounting Clerk
       Springfield, Oregon
```

```
Director of Personnel—1987 to present ALCORE LUMBER COMPANY,
    Alcore, WA. Supervisor: Ms. Leona Kenning, V-P: of
    Human Resources. Please feel free to contact em-
    ployer at (206) 773-5555 extension 4569.
    Administered all industrial relations for plant of
    230 hourly employees. Included employment and train-
    ing functions, affirmative action, employee benefits,
    union grievances and contract negotiations, workers'
    compensation, employee benefits, plant and employment
    safety, environmental control, company/employer
    newsletter, payroll. Supervised staff of 3.
```

There are some experiences that should be and can be downplayed on your resume. These include:

- ☐ Large time-gaps between jobs.
- ☐ Numerous jobs with different companies over a short period of time.

- ☐ Being fired or terminated for any reason.
- ☐ Demotions or Salary reductions.
- ☐ Working in positions unrelated below your skill capabilities.

If any of these situations exist for you, they can often be mentioned briefly or not at all. The following are examples of how to handle these difficult situations:

```
86 to 90   Sales positions in real estate, home furnish-
           ings, jewelry, and clothing.
```

```
1979 to 1984   General office positions including
               accounting clerk, secretary, and
               payroll data entry clerk.
```

```
1981 to 1983   Gas Station Attendant, Waiter,
               Sporting Goods Sales Clerk, Ski
               Instructor, Rafting Guide.
```

Experience Narratives

Experience, "What you do," sells. It should take up more space than anything else on your resume. Stress skills, experiences, and accomplishments that relate directly to the job you want.

When you are ready to write your experience narratives, review your data file and exercise #3, THINGS I'M GOOD AT and exercise #4, MY 7 GREATEST ACHIEVEMENTS. Note the experiences and achievements that are relative to your job objective and include them on the resume.

Because of the volume of pertinent experience you have, be very choosey. Select the highest levels of skills and accomplishments to fit the job criteria.

Experience comes from all areas of your life: from paid employment, school, hobbies, volunteer work, club memberships.

You may have many relevant skills from home activities such as carpentry, landscaping, cooking, sewing, and childcare.

If you possess a skill that is relevant to the job, no matter where you learned it, include it on the resume.

Following is a refresher of the writing techniques you want to employ.

- ☐ Think of an activity, job, project or an achievement—one you did well, feel good about, and enjoyed.
- ☐ Begin narrative with an ACTION word.

- ☐ Add the object(s).
- ☐ Fill in the details.
- ☐ Add results, testimonials, comments.
- ☐ Prioritize every verb, date, concept, sentence, word.

When writing experience, begin with **ACTION WORDS** (verbs) like the ones listed below:

Adapted	Filed	Proposed
Adjusted	Followed	Provided
Administered	Founded	Recommended
Analyzed	Generated	Recorded
Applied	Graphed	Reduced
Approved	Increased	Reinforced
Audited	Influenced	Responded to
Charted	Implemented	Retrieved
Coded	Improved	Revamped
Compiled	Interviewed	Reviewed
Computed	Launched	Revised
Coordinated	Lectured	Saved
Conceived	Maintained	Scheduled
Conducted	Managed	Screened
Completed	Monitored	Solved
Controlled	Obtained	Streamlined
Created	Organized	Supervised
Delegated	Originated	Taught
Developed	Performed	Transcribed
Demonstrated	Planned	Validated
Directed	Pinpointed	Volunteered
Eliminated	Prepared	Verified
Established	Processed	Wrote
Evaluated	Produced	X-rayed
Expanded	Programmed	

Write a Skill/Experience Narrative

The examples below were written for the job objective of MEDICAL RECORDS. Now refine a few of your functional narratives in the blocks below.

Skill/Verb	**Object**	**Results/Comments**
Transcribed	physician's written orders	
Compiled and maintained	patient location and status records.	Included admission, transfers, discharge, census.
Charted, graphed and recorded	data in patient medical records.	Included patient identifica tion, vital signs, prescrip- tions, scheduled and canceled appointments.

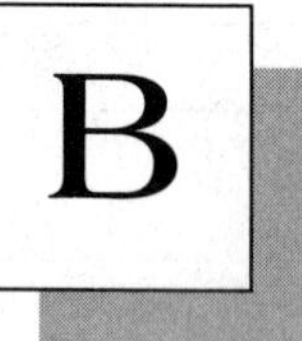

Your Prior Employment Record

For the very few of you who have no previous employment, you truly have a clean slate! That has good points and bad points. To your benefit, you have no black marks to discredit you to potential employers to whom you submit applications—no firings, bad references, or difficult experiences to talk about. On the other hand, you also have no proof of your value as an employee—no recommendations from supervisors, list of duties and accomplishments, awards, or promotions to present. You have only the raw goods—yourself—so concentrate on putting your "package" in the best shape possible.

What kind of experience can you describe to a potential employer if you have had no formal job? You probably have learned skills from various situations in your life that did not involve being employed per se. Those skills can have as much value as skills learned on the job. What kinds of situations can give you marketable qualifications? Here are some examples.

- ☐ Long-term child care—taking care of a child (your niece or little brother, for example) during the day on a fairly regular basis.
- ☐ Helping a friend or family member at their work—similar to an intern position.
- ☐ Taking on special responsibilities at school—heading up a committee, organizing any gathering or group effort, acting as a teacher liaison or aide.

- ☐ Volunteer work.
- ☐ Special duties at home—for example, taking care of the bills each month/budgeting.

What other experiences have helped you develop valuable skills and personal qualities? Brainstorm for a while and you may come up with a few more examples of when your life experience has given you qualifications a potential employer desires.

What qualities would the experiences above show that you have?

- ☐ Child care shows responsibility, flexibility, and a caring nature.
- ☐ Working at a family or friend's business without pay shows dedication and loyalty.
- ☐ Volunteer work shows caring, values, and good time-management skills (Sometimes it's hard to fit volunteering into a busy day!).
- ☐ Performing special duties at school or at home—shows responsibility, dedication, dependability, and energy.

In addition to these general qualifications, the particular jobs that you did and duties that you had show more specific skills that can catch a prospective employer's attention. Here are some valuable specific skills that you might learn in the four areas of work that we have been discussing.

- ☐ *Child care.*

  Did you care for children who have schedules full of school, sports practices, play dates, and other appointments? You have good *time-management* skills.

  Did you care for a baby? You probably have a good working knowledge of basic *first aid and medical care.*

  Did you care for more than one child at a time? You may be especially *efficient.*

- ☐ *Working at a family or friend's business without pay.*

  Did you take phone calls? You *communicate* well and have good *telephone skills.*

  Did you help to resort and clean up files or equipment? You may be skilled at *organization of data and company assets.*

  Did you help to take in money, count it, or keep the books? You might be a whiz at *money management, records, and accounts.*

- ☐ *Performing special duties at school or at home.*

  Were you a representative for your class to any school, administration, or alumni meetings? You show *leadership* qualities and skill in *working with others.*

  Did you help at home with budgeting and financial planning? You may know a lot about *organizing and evaluating information* as well as *budget maintenance.*

  Were you a teacher's aide? You may be good at taking *initiative, cooperating,* and *listening.*

- ☐ *Volunteer work.*

  Did you help out at a center for children who are emotionally disturbed? You may have a talent for *creative thinking* and *decision making*, since you never know what might happen next.

  Did you spend time socializing with residents at a home for the elderly? You may have a solid command of *social systems, communication*, and *listening*.

  Did you help to rebuild and repaint a dilapidated school? You show command of the *equipment and technology* you used as well as a good sense of *cooperation* and *self-management*.

When you have evaluated your non-professional experiences and named the skills that you developed, how can you organize and present this information to a prospective employer? You use a form called a *skill-based résumé*. Unlike a chronological résumé, this form does not list jobs and their respective duties; rather, it focuses on your skills, grouping specific duties and skills under general headings. You can also include skills you have developed in class under your headings.

This form is not just for those who have no job experience—anyone who wants to emphasize skills over specific job experience may use it, although the chronological form is the most universally recognized and accepted. You can even have a résumé in *combination* form, where part lists your skills as in the skill-based form and part lists your jobs as in the chronological form. Here is an example of how Thomas Zetlmeisel might construct a combination résumé.

Thomas M. Zetlmeisel
4757 Cragsmoor Court #9E
Tucson, AZ 85719
602/875-8055

OBJECTIVE: Seeking a position that utilizes my new and updated skills as a computer operator.

SKILLS: **Technology**—WordPerfect 5.1, 6.0; Lotus 1-2-3; dBase III Plus; Data Entry; Windows; Typing, certified 58 wpm.

Managing—Interviewed, hired, and evaluated employees; handled operations on restaurant floor.

Information processing—Entered warehouse locations into database and inventory items into locations; updated database and eliminated out-of-date items; entered student and class data onto school database; maintained and updated class schedules.

Organization—Kept files and made photocopies; organized and distributed materials to teachers; coordinated restaurant employee schedules.

Communication—Handled telephone calls, both incoming and outgoing; reported to teachers as student representative to the school administration.

EXPERIENCE: *Wolfe Industries*, Tucson, AZ. Inventory Control Clerk, February 1994 present.

TGIFriday's Restaurant, Tucson, AZ. Manager, September 1993–January 1994.

TUSD Summer High School. Assistant Secretary, summer 1993.

TUSD Summer High School. Intern, summer 1992.

EDUCATION: *Killingworth Business School*, Tucson, AZ
Microcomputer Software Operations Program, Graduation November 1994.
Dean's List, Perfect Attendance Certificates, Student Representative.

Magruder High School, Tucson, AZ
Diploma May 1993
Honor Roll, FBLA Vice-President, Varsity Letter

REFERENCES AVAILABLE UPON REQUEST

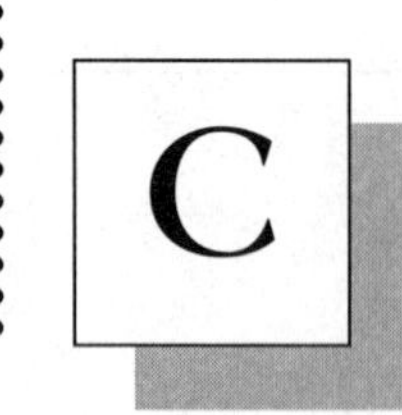

Other Activities

OTHER ACTIVITIES

Other includes publications you've written, awards or special recognitions received, or unusual experiences you wish to mention. It may also include memberships in professional associations and community organizations.

☐ Professional, Community or Social Club Memberships

Dates of Membership:	**Club Name and Location**	**Offices Held**
Accomplishments/Awards Etc.		

☐ Publications

Dates of Publication	Publication	Publisher
Publication Details		

☐ Personal Data

Personal data depicts self-confidence and candidness; traits employers appreciate. Don't permit misrepresentation by omission. Silence often makes the loudest sound and is prone to misinterpretation.

There are no iron-clad rules on what must be included on a resume or a job application. The primary objective is to convincingly sell "what you can do." Do this first, then age, marital status, or sex will not be a major issue. Include information that supports your cause; eliminate data that hurts your case. This may include stating your age, sex, citizenship, or marital status. There are no set rules here. If it sells you, use it.

Refer to your **PERSONAL CHECK LIST** form F22 to ensure that you have covered all items that can benefit you. This form should be filed in the RESUME section of your notebook. Review this form each time you write a resume or complete a job application. Revise answers when necessary. Ensure that all answers reflect the positive. Choose only those items that are relevant to the employer for inclusion on your resume. Let's look at each section individually.

Age

Age becomes a barrier when you believe it is one. Don't convey this to the employer by omission. This only draws attention to it.

State age with only the year. Add supportive comments to build a positive image. Examples include:

- ☐ Born 1986, ambitious and willing to learn.
- ☐ Born 1945. Mature, high energy and excellent track record.

Marital Status

Marital status like age is one of those areas people have difficulty deciding whether to include or not.

Marital Status is a matter of choice. Will it be beneficial or detrimental? It's difficult to tell, but consider the inclusion seriously.

If your marital status is opposite of what you believe is best suited for the job or employer, add descriptive words to establish a more suitable tone.

Rhonda wrote: "Mother of 2 active grade schoolers. Supportive supervision always available while attending evening meetings or traveling." These comments addressed the job requirements and eliminated the employer's objections to hiring a woman with small children.

Suitable descriptions for divorced or separated individuals include:

- ☐ Single, no dependents.
- ☐ Family man
- ☐ Single parent of 2 pre-schoolers. Quality childcare available for extra hours and during school breaks, illnesses.

Gender

Identify Gender only if it provides you with a hiring edge. Since it is advisable not to use initials in place of your name, first names generally inform the employer of sex. Although this isn't always the case. For example, "Terry" could be a male or a female.

Because of stereotypes, other factors affecting gender are job titles. "Electrician" typifies males; while "nurse" identifies females. If stereotyping creates an advantage for you, use it.

Health

Your health doesn't have to be mentioned but when it is left out it could cause questions.

Write: "Health Excellent." This is permissible as long as you are able to perform the job without any health interference.

If you are uncomfortable with "Health Excellent" there are ways of creating a strong healthy image, particularly if you are physically active. Statements such as: "Avid outdoor sports enthusiast—golfer, skier, and swimmer." "Exercise regularly, enjoy hiking and biking." "Physically fit, trim and slim."

Working Hours

Demonstrate your flexibility here and willingness to do whatever the job requires. Possible comments include:

- ☐ Willing to work all shifts and days.
- ☐ Available for night meetings, out-of-town travel, and irregular hours.

Travel

Some organizations are large and may be interested in whether or not you would be willing to travel, even if the job you are applying for may not require it. Employers look for future potential each time they hire a new employee. So consider placing this information in your PERSONAL section on your resume. Here are two examples:

PERSONAL CHECK LIST

ITEM COMMENTS	ITEM COMMENTS
AGE Born in Oregon 1960.	**CITIZENSHIP** U.S. Citizen
MARITAL STATUS Married, 2 children 8 & 10	**SEX** Female
HEALTH Physically fit. Long distance runner.	**TRAVEL** Willing to travel
WORKING HOURS Flexible	**RELOCATION** Will consider Salem, Portland area
SPECIAL SKILLS Computer literate WordPerfect 5.1. Lotus 1-2-3 MS-DOS. Dbase III software	**HOBBIES** Writing children's stories Graphic design and layout
HIRING LIABILITY Little experience in field—all volunteer work in marketing Weight (20 over) Lack of Master's degree	
REASON FOR CHANGE Seeking employment in field of education. Graduating in spring.	
CHARACTER TRAITS Detail Minded. Enthusiastic. Artistic. Fast-learner. Work well with co-workers, employees, and clients. Complimented often on listening skills.	

 Form F22/93

Form F21—Personal Check List

- ☐ Willing to travel.
- ☐ Love to travel. Enjoy exploring different places and meeting new people.

Relocation

Relocation is a factor with large companies. One short statement such as "Willing to relocate" will supply the information.

If you are planning on moving to a new area, you may write: "Relocating to Phoenix area in June." or "Desire relocation to Seattle metropolitan area."

Special Skills and Hobbies

Stop, reread your resume. Are there any skills you have left out? List them here so you won't forget to consider including them on your resume. Some of the important skills may include:

- ☐ First Aid and CPR Certification
- ☐ Public Speaker
- ☐ Calligraphy

Hobbies can also be important. They may provide a common interest with the interviewer. Your hobby may also be a special skill, not part of the formal job, the employer would like to have available on the staff. Some examples are:

- ☐ Photographer
- ☐ Cake Decorating
- ☐ Writing

Hiring Liability

This subject is not included on this form for the employer's information. It is here for your reflection. Often an employer has preconceived ideas or reasons why he won't hire certain people, or your background provides some questionable areas. Here is a place for you to identify your hiring liability as perceived by an employer and develop a plan for removing this obstacle. Hiring liabilities may include:

- ☐ Too many jobs
- ☐ Little or no experience
- ☐ Age (too young, too old)
- ☐ Gender (job usually goes to males)
- ☐ Education (no degree)
- ☐ Personal appearance (weight?)
- ☐ Small children
- ☐ Being married or single
- ☐ Being fired from last job

Reason for Change

Employers are interested in why you want to change jobs, why you're looking now. Consider your reasons and identify a positive reason the employer would enjoy knowing about. Find a reason that makes an employer want to hire you. For example: "Seeking advancement opportunities."

In the chapter on REFERENCES you'll find detailed information on how to handle this question. Remember, there are many reasons why one leaves a job. The first reason that pops into your head often is not the only reason or the right one to provide to an employer. Search your mind for a good, positive answer, one that puts you in a good light.

Character Traits

You're looking for specific traits that fit the job objective. Different jobs require specific personalities and character traits. For instance, being detail-minded and budget conscience is beneficial for an accounting position.

There are general traits and qualities employers want. Meeting and beating deadlines is one good example. Here are some others to consider:

- ☐ Good sense of humor
- ☐ Perfect attendance and safety record
- ☐ High energy level—enthusiastic

Summary Thoughts

As you can see, this form is a catch-all. It forces you to stop and think if there are any messages left to be told the employer.

Put in one-liners that sell expertise, qualities, personal characteristics.

Put in one-liners that provide the employer with answers no one else thinks to include.

Put in one-liners that answer employer's unasked questions.

PERSONAL information helps employers like you and assists them in their hiring decision. Fill this section with "sizzle and sale" instead of "fizzle and fail." It's your last place to shine.

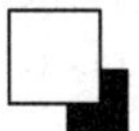

RESUME WRITING TIPS

Here are 12 tips to help you.

1. **Study resume samples.** Some interesting examples can be found in *Getting Hired* by Edward J. Rogers.
2. **Use your data file.** Pull out all relative experiences.
3. **Target a specific audience.** For example: wood products industry.
4. **Include only the necessary and appropriate data** to portray your "best" self.

5. **Use strong active verbs and precise nouns.**
6. **Use testimonials** to build credibility.
7. **Create illustrations relevant to your message.** Generic comments or images are meaningless.
8. **Make it easy to read.** Vast gray expanses of copy are unreadable.
9. **Use lots of white space**. Top, bottom and side margins should be 1" each—minimum margins ¾".
10. **Write short paragraphs and sentences.**
11. **Use Headers or Marginal comments.**
12. **Field-test your resume** on others you can rely on to give you an objective and honest opinion—people who don't know you well.

    Allow them 30–60 seconds reading time. Then ask for a description of your background based on the reading.

    If your resume is fuzzy to these readers, go back and revise it until a clear, sharp image comes across at first glance.

Some more advice:

☐ **MAKE IT READER-FRIENDLY.** It's important to get your readers to like you. So how do you do this? Gary Provost, *Writers' Digest* author, says: "Certainly they will like you if you use strong active verbs and precise nouns. They will like you a whole lot if you say things in a positive way and eliminate unnecessary words. And if you write clearly, colorfully and concisely all the time, they'll be positively crazy about you."

☐ **TELL THE TRUTH.** While it's important not to undersell yourself, it is equally important not to exaggerate or misrepresent your abilities, education, work history, or credentials. Lies have a way of coming back to haunt you at unexpected times.

☐ **WRITE IT YOURSELF.** "I have other reasons, apart from money, for steering you away from the professional resume writing services," writes Robert Half, author of *The Robert Half Way to Get Hired in Today's Job Market*. "For one thing, professionally written resumes often have an assembly-line look. I can usually spot them at a glance, and so can any experienced hiring executive. Some personnel directors as a matter of policy automatically eliminate from consideration resumes that look to have been professionally done.

"But there's an even more important reason for working on your résumé yourself. It helps to give you a sense of just what you have to offer a prospective employer. It prepares you in other words for many of the situations you are going to run into when you go to interviews."

☐ Resume Sample

Using the DICTIONARY OF OCCUPATIONAL TITLES

Below is a page from the *Dictionary of Occupational Titles*. It shows job descriptions for SERVICE OCCUPATIONS.

These descriptions were used in the writing of the resume example on the following page. Notice how the descriptions aid in the writing for the job objective.

3 SERVICE OCCUPATIONS

This category includes occupations concerned with providing domestic services in private households; preparing and serving food and drink in commercial, institutional, or other establishments, providing lodging and related services, providing grooming, cosmetic, and other personal and health care services for children and adults; maintaining and cleaning clothing and other wearing apparel, providing protection for people and property attending to the comfort or requests of patrons of amusement and recreation facilities, and performing cleaning and maintenance services to interiors of buildings.

30 DOMESTIC SERVICE OCCUPATIONS

This division includes occupations concerned with tasks in and around a private household.

301 HOUSEHOLD AND RELATED WORK

This group includes occupations concerned with performing such duties in a private household as cleaning, making beds, caring for children, planning meals, marketing, and cooking. Includes workers managing private household and directing work activities of other workers performing these duties. Occupations concerning primarily with washing and ironing are included in Group 302, and preparation and cooking food in Group 305.

301.137-010 HOUSEKEEPER, HOME (Domestic manager household)

Supervises and coordinates activities of household employees in a private residence. Informs new employees of employer's desires and gives instructions in work methods and routines. Assigns duties such as cooking and serving meals, cleaning, washing, and ironing, adjusting work activities to accommodate family members.Orders foodstuffs and cleaning supplies. Keeps record of expenditures. May hire and discharge employees. Works in residence employing large staff.

301.474-010 HOUSE WORKER, GENERAL (dom. ser.) housekeeper, home

Performs any combination of the following duties in keeping private home clean and orderly, in cooking and serving meals, and in rendering personal services to family members. Plans meals and purchases food stuffs and household supplies. Prepares and cooks vegetables, meats, and other foods according to employer's instructions or following own methods. Serves meals and refreshments. Washes dishes and cleans silverware. Oversees activities of children, assisting them in dressing and bathing. Cleans furnishings, floors and windows, using vacuum cleaner, mops, brooms, clothes and cleaning solutions. Changes linens and makes beds. Washes linen and other garments by hand or machine and mends and irons clothing, linens and other household articles, using hand iron or electric ironer. Performs additional duties such as answering telephone and doorbell and feeding pets. Is usually only worker employed.

301.677-010 CHILD MONITOR (dom. ser.) serves children

Performs any combination of the following duties to attend children in private home. Observes and monitors play activities or amuses children by reading to or playing games with them. Prepares and serves meals or formula. Sterilizes bottles and other equipment used for feeding infants. Dresses or assists children to dress and bathe. Accompanies children on walks or other outings. Washes and irons clothing. Keeps children's quarters clean and tidy. May clean other parts of home. When in charge of infants may be required to NURSE INFANTS (dry nurse). When employed on a daily or hourly basis may be designated as BABY SITTER (dom. ser.).

301.687-010 CARETAKER (dom. ser.) odd job worker

Performs any combination of the following duties in keeping private home clean and in good condition. Cleans and dusts furnishings, hallways and lavatories. Beats and vacuums rugs and scrubs them with cleaning solutions. Washes windows and waxes and polishes floors. Removes and hangs draperies. Cleans and oils furnace. Shovels coal into furnace and removes ashes. Replaces light fixtures and repairs broken screens, latches, or doors. Paints exterior structures, such as fences, garages, and sheds. May drive family car. May now and rake lawn. May groom and exercise pets. When duties are confined to upkeep of house, may be designated as HOUSE WORKER (dom. ser.).

301.687-014 DAY WORKER (com. ser.)

Performs any combination of the following domestic duties in accordance with employer's instructions. Cleans and dusts furnishings hallways, and lavatories. Changes and makes beds. Washes and irons clothing by hand or machine. May watch children to keep them out of mischief. May wash windows and wax and pllish floors.

301.687-018 YARD WORKER (dom. ser.)

Performs any combination of the following duties in accordance with instructions of employer to keep grounds of private residence in neat and orderly condition. Plants transplants, fertilizers, sprays with pesticides, prunes, cultivates, and waters flowers, shrubbery, and trees. Seeds and mows lawns, rakes leaves, and keeps ground free of other debris. Whitewashes or paints patio furniture and garage. Shovels snow from walks. May cultivate flowers, shrubbery, and other plants in greenhouse. May wax floors, tend furnace or groom and exercise pets. May divide time between several homes, working on hourly or daily basis. When duties are confined to upkeep of grounds, may be designated as GARDENER (dom. ser.)

302 LAUNDERERS, PRIVATE FAMILY

This group includes occupations concerned with washing and ironing clothes and household linens for one or several private families.

302.685-010 LAUNDRY WORKER, DOMESTIC (dom. ser.)

Tends automatic washing and drying machines to clean and dry household articles and presses household articles using hand iron. Sorts articles by color and fabric, and loads into automatic washing machine. Adjusts machine settings for temperature, water level, and time duration of wash. Adds measured amounts of detergent, bluing, starches and fabric softener as required. Removes articles from washer and loads into dryer. Sorts, irons and folds dried articles. May iron only (IRONER (dom. ser.)). May perform other housework (HOUSEWORKER, GENERAL (dom. ser.)). May use electric ironing machine.

302.687-010 IRONER (dom. ser.)

Dampens and irons wearing apparel, household linens and other household articles with hand iron. May use electric ironing machine. May be employed on hourly basis.

305 COOKS, DOMESTIC

This group includes occupations concerned with preparing and cooking foods, including special diets for private household.

305.281-010 COOK (dom. ser.)

Plans menus and cooks meals in private home according to recipes or wishes of employer. Peels, washes, trims, and prepares vegetables and meats for cooking. Cooks vegetables and bakes breads and pastries. Boils, broils, fries, and roasts meats. Plans menus and orders foodstuffs. Cleans dishes and cooking utensils. May serve meals. May perform seasonal cooking duties, such as preserving and canning fruits and vegetables and making jellies. May prepare fancy dishes and pastries. May prepare food for special diets. May specialize in preparing and serving dinner for employed, retired, or other persons and be designated FAMILY DINNER SERVICE SPECIALIST (dom. ser.).

Functional

Employers are looking for personal qualities such as:

- ☐ reliability, perseverance, dependability, work ethics, personality, attitudes.

What qualities do you find in this applicant's resume? List them below.

1. ______________________________
2. ______________________________
3. ______________________________
4. ______________________________
5. ______________________________

Lucy Madison

8939 East Main Street Springfield, OR 97754 (503) 746-4333

EMPLOYMENT OBJECTIVE

Commercial or Domestic Housekeeper

HOUSEKEEPING EXPERIENCE

1978-88: Self-employed as a domestic housekeeper. Supported family of five. Worked continuously for six clients over ten years.

Housekeeping: Cleaned furnishings, floors and windows using vacuum cleaners, rug shampooers, mops, brooms, cloths, and cleaning solutions. Changed linens and made beds. Washed, mended and ironed linens and other garments by hand or machine. Washed dishes and cleaned silverware. Answered telephone and doorbell. Fed pets and watered plants.

Cooking: Planned menus and cooked meals according to recipes or tastes of employer observing diet restrictions. Prepared meats and vegetables for cooking. Cooked, boiled, broiled, fried, and roasted meats and vegetables. Baked breads and pastries. Created hors d'oeuvres and salads. Performed seasonal cooking including preserving and canning fruits, vegetables, jams and jellies. Ordered and shopped for household groceries and cleaning supplies. Meal preparation specialties include Mexican, Chinese and Italian.

Child Care: Monitored activities of children. Assisted children in school work. Amused children by reading to or playing games with them. Prepared and served meals and formulas. Sterilized bottles and other equipment used for feeding infants. Dressed and assisted children in dressing and bathing. Accompanied children on walks and other outings.

PERSONAL

U.S. Citizen, born 1953. No dependents. Willing to relocate.
Excellent physical health. Fast, efficient, thorough.
High School graduate. Oregon Driver's License.
Willing to work varied shifts, night or day.
Excellent references available.

Resume Sample / Functional

HELP WANTED PERSONNEL, SAFETY AND PURCHASING DIRECTOR

Responsible for all phases of Industrial Relations and Purchasing. Successful candidate must possess strong administration and communication skills. Salary commensurate with experience. Please submit resume and salary needs. Women and minorities encouraged to apply.

What personal qualities do you find in this resume? List them below.

1. ____
2. ____
3. ____
4. ____
5. ____

List the employer's hierarchy of needs.

1. ____
2. ____
3. ____
4. ____
5. ____

Would you have organized the resume differently?

Notice that there is no Employment History on this resume. Why do you suppose Employment History was omitted? What does "salary commensurate with experience" mean? How should you handle such a statement?

Lonnie Moreland

7712 South Heather Drive
Tempe, Arizona 85285
(602) 831-5502

GOAL

Industrial Relations, seeking long-term career opportunity. Excellent administration and communication skills effective for increasing productivity, safety awareness and job satisfaction. Emphasis on team building and individual employee efforts.

INDUSTRIAL RELATIONS

Wrote and established county personnel policies. Troubleshooter. Intermediary for grievances to avoid formal hearings. Developed employment application to ensure compliance with Federal/State laws on Equal Opportunity, Affirmative Action and Protected Classes. Monitored State Accident Insurance program.

Interacted with current State Accident Insurance Fund staff. Motivated early return of injured workers to sometimes modified positions, thereby reducing employer costs and psychological affects of injury to the worker.

Managed Comprehensive Employment and Training Act participants in coordination with Central Arizona on Intergovernmental Council. Recruited, selected, trained staff members. Urged personnel toward continuing education, goal setting, and teamwork approach.

Researched, evaluated and presented benefit programs to county court, including medical, dental, vision and deferred compensation programs. Maintained department records of sick leave, vacation, disciplinary action, injuries, and unauthorized absences. Evaluated positions throughout county for cost effectiveness and need, allowing cutbacks through attrition rather than lay-offs.

COMMUNICATIONS

Speakers' Bureau presenter for KWAK Radio "Backtalk" program. Speaker for company meetings and community organizations. Designed and presented concise written and oral reports for county and status of lands, roads, laws, benefits and proposed ordinances.

Adult education instructor for community college. Developed ten-week course. Encouraged and aided students to reach out, learn, and participate. Excellent student evaluations.

Experienced in one-on-one interviewing as well as group leadership. Conducted plant and community tours for all ages with historical presentations. Former newspaper correspondent.

Resume Sample / Functional

Lonnie Moreland

Page 2

ADMINISTRATION

Managed State/Federal grants including airport development grant of $500,000. Prepared final audit documentation for Arizona Aeronautics Division and Federal Aviation Administration, Region 10. Received letter of commendation from Seattle Regional Office.

Liaison to state health division. Served as county registrar of vital statistics. Received certificate of appreciation for exceptional dedication. Competent, knowledgeable and experienced in grant writing and management, budgetary processes, and cost controls.

Prepared bid specifications for heavy equipment to office machines. Evaluated proposed purchases. Planned public auction of surplus equipment—sold everything advertised, exceeding anticipated revenue.

Interacted with work crews on daily basis. First woman ever invited to participate in Road Department Christmas party and retirement functions.

Headed report team for Arizona judicial systems analysis of courts takeover. Represented county position in special session of the Arizona legislature.

PROFESSIONAL PARTICIPATION

American Society of Safety Engineers. Past President.
National Personnel Managers Association. Program Chair.
Central Arizona Employers/Medical Co-Op Council. Organizer.
Tempe Toastmasters Club. 1990 State Toastmaster-of-the-Year.

EDUCATION

University of Arizona. BS in Management. Cum laude. 1976.

OTHER DATA

Willing to relocate. Available for travel, night meetings, and public speaking. High energy level. Abundance of enthusiasm. Enjoy music and poetry (dubbed County “Poet Laureate.”)

Resume Sample / Functional

Combination: Functional/Historical

What personal qualities do you find in this resume? List them below.

1. ____________________
2. ____________________
3. ____________________
4. ____________________
5. ____________________

CINDY HUDSON

21445 Back Alley Bend, Oregon 97702
(503) 382-7039 Home (503) 382-6508 Days

EMPLOYMENT OBJECTIVE

Accounting or Data Entry position for a Central Oregon insurance agency working full-time with advancement opportunities.

EDUCATION

A.S. degree with Business major to be completed June, 1992.
Central Oregon Community College, Bend, Oregon.
Education funded by COCC Honor Scholarship.

Bend Senior High School Graduate, June, 1990. GPA 3.96. Ranked 9th out of 234 students. Awards: 1990 Oregon Scholar, Member of National Honor Society 1987–90. Member of Future Business Leaders of America 1989–90.

ACCOUNTING AND SUPERVISORY SKILLS

Trained 5 new employees to cashier. Prepared end-of-night detail transaction reports. Verified and balanced totals transferred from register tape onto daily report sheet against cash and charges-on-hand. Computed dinner tickets from waitresses' brief-hand slips for an average of 200 diners per night. Collected cash and charges, made change and operated electronic data capture Visa machine.

COMPUTER AND OFFICE MACHINES

Operated IBM and Macintosh personal computers using Appleworks, WordPerfect 5.1, Lotus 1-2-3, and data base programs. Accurately type 35–40 words per minute. Operate 10-key calculator by touch averaging 180 digits per minute.

EMPLOYMENT HISTORY

Dinner Cashier Pine Tavern Restaurant. Bend, Oregon.
09/90 to present Phone (503) 382-5581.

Cashier/Server Bachelor View Dairy Queen. Bend, Oregon.
07/90 to 09/90 Phone (503) 385-6880.

PERSONAL

Born 1972, young and enthusiastic. Excellent health. Avid reader and writer.
Enjoy music, math and computers. Dependable and organized.
Detail-oriented. Oregon Driver's license with perfect driving record.

Resume Combination: Functional / Historical

Combination: Achievement/Historical

What personal qualities do you find in this resume? List them below.

1. ______________________________
2. ______________________________
3. ______________________________
4. ______________________________
5. ______________________________

ROBERT CREST

2161 NE Greenwood
Bend, OR 97701
(503) 389-5555

CAREER OBJECTIVE

Video Production and Promotions . . . working for an innovative video production organization.
Seeking challenge, variety and part-time work in Central California.

VIDEO EXPERIENCE

Produced four promotional videos for Mt. Hood Summer Ski Camps. Filmed the first video in 1987 after Mr. Scott suggested making a film of the camp's summer activity program. What started out as just an idea has progressed yearly into a profit-making endeavor. In 1989, 20 videos were sold. In 1990, that number jumped to 110. The 1991 figures are exceeding prior totals despite 35% fewer campers than in 1990.

Produced, edited, and wrote promotional video for Wenatchee Valley College's Ski Area Management and Ski Instruction degree programs. Wrote script, filmed the programs in action, edited the raw footage, and dubbed in music and narration. This video is currently being used by WVC to provide new students information about the programs available and to attract future students.

Produced a creative video on "Coping with Stress" at Central Oregon Community College. Interviewed and filmed students, instructors, employees, and athletes. Edited films, selected sequences and interview portions, dubbed in script and music. Earned an "A" for project and received many compliments from fellow students and participants.

Video-taped local ski race series and produced highlight video at season's end for Sno-Motion Video Services.

WORK EXPERIENCE

Sold skiing equipment and sports gear for Fastgear Sports Outlet. Government Camp, Oregon (1987–91)
Provided ski instruction and coaching for students and faculty at Mission Ridge Ski Area (1987).
Supervised 22 workers in the Competition Services Department. Squaw Valley Ski Corporation (1985–86)

EDUCATION

A.S. Marketing and Management, Central Oregon Community College, Bend, OR.
Will graduate with honors June, 1991. Current GPA 3.56.

A.S. Ski Resort Management, Wenatchee Valley College, Wenatchee, WA.
Graduated with honors 1986. GPA 3.86

PERSONAL

Desire employment in video productions while completing Bachelor's degree in Video Production.
Born 1965. Single. Willing to work varied hours. Available for travel and relocation.
Perfect college attendance. Punctual. Love getting paid to Video!

Resume Combination: Achievement / Historical

Combination: Functional/Historical

What personal qualities do you find in this resume? List them below.

1. ______________________________
2. ______________________________
3. ______________________________
4. ______________________________
5. ______________________________

Michele's Story

When Michele wrote her resume, she took it to a former teacher and asked for his opinion. He said: "I really think you should use a more standard format."

Michele gave serious thought to these comments, but decided to at least test her resume in the real world. So off she went. One interviewer said to her: "You know Michele, usually I fall asleep reading resumes. But yours was different. I felt that I got to really know you as a person." She got the job.

What you choose to put in your resume is really your choice. What do you think of Michele's format and choice of categories?

MICHELE HOPPES

2232 N.W. Everett **Portland, OR 97210** **(503) 223-3512**

Career Objective

Public Relations and Promotions . . . working with an organization where a positive public image and excellent media are imperative.

Education

B.S. Broadcasting and Television Production, University of Wyoming (89).

Visual Communications

In 1988, narrated video recruiting tape for the University of Wyoming women's basketball team. Assisted in script creation and advised on production. Received many compliments from viewers. Typical comments: "Great presence on camera," and "Her voice, the accent and tone are what we in the general public have learned to expect from the electronic media."

Hosted a University of Wyoming television production for the 1989 NCAA ski championships in Jackson Hole, Wyoming. Conducted live interviews of skiers and organizational sponsors. Updated competition results daily on live broadcasts. Guest and impromptu speaker at many community organizations (Kiwanis, Lions, School Career Days). Asked to return several times. Anchored weather and sports sections of student television news broadcasts.

Audio Communications

Interviewed many times by television, radio and newspaper reporters. Diplomatically answered questions on sensitive and controversial issues and successfully maintained integrity of self and organization represented. Recorded radio county campaign advertisement and sports announcements.

Written Communications

Wrote press releases, television and radio announcements, and newspaper feature articles. Revised employee, safety, and general information manuals for Adelaide Brighton Cement Company, Adelaide, South Australia.

Sales and Promotions

Recruited Division 1 players for Australia and Wyoming basketball teams. Sold and promoted memberships for Hyatt Regency Adelaide through international telemarketing. Ranked in top 20% of sales representatives.

Personal Work Ethics and Characteristics (Quotes from reference letters).

Dave Walsh, Dave Walsh Productions wrote "In my 13 years in business, no one has been more professional and pleasant to work with. She is always early to work, late to leave, and as relentless during a show as she was as a player."

Margie McDonald, Executive Director of High Country Athletic Conference, wrote: "You will find Michele very upbeat and excited about what she is doing, and her enthusiasm permeates everyone with whom she comes into contact."

Resumé Sample Combination: Functional/Historical

MICHELE HOPPES

Page 2

Television Equipment Operations

Floor director for the television productions of the "Cowboy Coaches Shows" (the Voice of the Wyoming Cowboys) for two years. Set- up and operated dollies, camera mounting heads, and related equipment for network broadcasting. Covered football and basketball games. Assisted camera operators in acquiring the "perfect" shot.

International Professional Basketball Experience

Played starting forward for the West Adelaide Bearcats, South Australia. Averaged 22 points per game in local competition and 17 points per game in National League. Leading offensive rebounder in South Australia (90–91).

Played starting strong forward and center for Sporting Luxembourg. Voted Player-of-the-Year. Averaged 29 points per game. Team won Luxembourg country championship (87–88).

Special Achievements and Awards

Achieved all-time career leading rebounder and scorer for UW. Nominated for Kodiak All-American Basketball Team. Selected four times for the High Country Athletic All-Conference First Team. Chosen twice for a Converse All-American College Basketball Team. Received a NCAA Sixth Year Grant to complete college education.

Awarded UW Full-Ride Athletic Scholarship for entire collegiate career (83). Voted Most Valuable Player in the Oregon State AAA High School Basketball Championship playoffs (83). Received Oregon State AAA High School Basketball Player of the Year (83).

Employment History

Adelaide, South Australia

90–91 Basketball Player, West Adelaide Bearcats
91 Promotional Sales Representative, Hyatt Regency
90 Special Project, Adelaide Brighton Cement Company
90 Receptionist/Clerical, Kelly Temporary Agency

Laramie, Wyoming

88–89 Floor Director, for all TV sports shows and Assistant Secretary for all non-revenue sports, University of Wyoming
88–89 Operations Assistant, CBS and ESPN Television Networks

Luxembourg, Luxembourg

87–88 Basketball Player, Sporting Luxembourg

Prineville, Oregon (summers)

86–91 Grocery Checker, Scotty's Thriftway
82–86 Lifeguard and Water Safety Instructor, City of Prineville

Personal

Seeking full-time career position in the Pacific Northwest.
Excellent health. Single, no dependents. Available for travel.
Willing to work varied hours and shifts. Always meet or beat deadlines.
Enjoy working with the media and diverse social and economic groups.

Resumé Sample Combination: Functional/Historical

Combination: Functional/Historical

What personal qualities do you find in this resume? List them below.

1. ____________________
2. ____________________
3. ____________________
4. ____________________
5. ____________________

TIMOTHY SMITH
1695 N.E. Purcell Boulevard
Apartment 21, Bend, OR 97701
(503) 389-4336

Job Objective	**Computer Laboratory Supervisor.** Seeking full-time position in a community college that provides a wide range of learning opportunities for the citizens of its region.
Computer Lab Assistant/ Technician	Supervised use of computer hardware and software to ensure compliance with college policies and procedures. Preserved order of computer library. Maintained security of equipment and programs. Organized and inventoried software for check-out by students and faculty. Aided students with computer lab assignments at scheduled times and on a drop-in basis. Advised faculty on classroom related computer projects including selection and use of appropriate software. Instructed students and faculty in use of MS/DOS, Lotus 1-2-3, WordPerfect, Multi-Mate, Perfectcalc, Wordstar, Fastgraph, and other software programs. Performed preventative maintenance on hardware. Recommended necessary on- and off-site repairs and maintenance. Ordered supplies. Refreshed disks to insure bug-free software on quarterly basis.
Assistant Instructor	Taught the wordprocessing credit course using Wordstar software to students for the IBM environment. Instructed students in MS-DOS operating system commands and keyboarding input. Assisted instructor in teaching Multi-Mate integrated software package. Advised faculty in use of word processing programs and other software usage.
Computer and Software Skills	Own and operate Macintosh SE computer with 20MG hard drive with ImageWriter II printer, 2400 baud Hayes compatible modem, and Mac-Charlie Plus which allows operation of IBM/MS-DOS software on Macintosh computer. Set-up and installed equipment and parts. Continually learning new software applications and increasing programming skills.

Resumé Combination: Functional/Historical

TIMOTHY SMITH

Page 2

Security Officer Created data base to monitor, control, and review violations of mail ordinances. Updated report monthly for identification of repeat violators.

Maintained and updated policies and procedures manual for security personnel. Developed current format for the Mall monthly newsletter. Selected and edited articles.

Compiled monthly sales productivity report for top-level management. Interpreted sales information from all stores and assembled according to specified categories.

Salesperson Sold merchandise for automotive, sporting goods, cameras, jewelry, toys, housewares, home improvements, and garden departments. Greeted customers. Ascertained make, type, and quality of merchandise desired. Suggested selections to meet customer's needs. Emphasized selling points of article such as quality and utility. Received payment or obtain credit authorizations. Operated computerized cash registers. Inventoried stock. Displayed merchandise. Built and assembled displays.

Education A.S. Business Technology. Information Systems Management. Central Oregon Community College, Bend, OR. To be completed September 1, 1990.

Employment History

89-present	**Security Officer** CONCORD ASSETS, Mt. View Mall, Bend, OR
89	**Computer Lab Technician** CENTRAL OREGON COMMUNITY COLLEGE, Bend, OR
88 to 89	**Salesperson** K-MART STORES, Mt. View Mall, Bend, OR
85 to 88	**Computer Lab Assistant and Assistant Instructor** WARNER PACIFIC COLLEGE, Portland, OR

Resumé Sample Combination: Functional/Historical

Combination: Functional/Historical

What personal qualities do you find in this resume? List them below.

1. ______________________________
2. ______________________________
3. ______________________________
4. ______________________________
5. ______________________________

Karen L. Simpson

829 SW Deschutes Redmond, OR 97758 (503) 923-5555

Career Objective

Marketing or Office Management Support Services

Education

Associate of Applied Science in Business Technology
Major, Marketing and Management.
Central Oregon Community College. Bend, Oregon. June, 1992.

Management and Supervisory Skills

Prepared and controlled annual expense budgets for up to 18 cost centers. Negotiated equipment and service contracts and monitored for compliance. Reviewed and authorized payment for equipment and supply billings.

Supervised up to 11 hourly employees. Screened, interviewed and hired hourly clerical and production employees. Documented performance and reviewed employees for promotions, pay increases and disciplinary action. Provided new employee orientation training. Documented and participated in termination proceedings.

Computer and Clerical Skills

Used WordPerfect 5.1, Lotus 1-2-3, MS-DOS, and Dbase III software. Used hard drive Fortune system for spreadsheets and word processing. Entered payroll, invoices, credit memos and accounts receivables computer data.

Scheduled conference rooms, auditorium, and company vehicle usage. Typed memos, letters, and employee documentation from dictation. Operated multi-line phone system. Operated 10-key by touch.

Resumé Sample Combination: Functional/Historical

Karen L. Simpson

Page 2

Writing Skills

Wrote manual used for location and definition of functions for groups within Technology Division at Tektronix, Inc. Wrote and revised standard operating procedure manuals for mail clerks, receptionist, and lead positions. Wrote and implemented job description standards for mail clerk, receptionist and stock handler positions.

Community Involvement

Volunteer Marketing Representative for Family Resource Center (RED-CAP) an information and referral service for parents. Created and designed marketing brochures. Wrote public service announcements and news releases. Designed and scheduled public library displays.

School and Employment History

90–92 Student. Business Technology. Marketing and Management.
CENTRAL OREGON COMMUNITY COLLEGE. Bend, OR

90 Clerk. Supervising. Customer Service. Food Preparation.
ERICSON'S SENTRY MARKET. Prineville, OR 447-6291

87–88 Payroll Clerk. Applicant Interviewing. Data Entry.
ACE AIR ELECTRONICS. Prineville, OR 447-1299

87 Clerical. Data entry for payroll and invoicing.
WESTERN TEMPORARY SERVICES. Beaverton, OR 629-9424

86–87 Clerical. General office services. New employee orientation.
NORPAC FOODS. Dayton, OR 627-7895

80–86 General Services Support Coordinator. Supervising. Budgets.
TEKTRONIX, INC. Beaverton, OR 627-7895

Resumé Sample Combination: Functional/Historical

Index